Turned to account

The forms and functions of criminal biography in late
seventeenth- and early eighteenth-century England

Dodd delin.   Whild sculp.

The Body of a **MURDERER** exposed in the Theatre
of the Surgeons Hall, Old Bailey.

from *The Malefactor's Register* [1779]

Turned to account

The forms and functions of criminal biography in late
seventeenth- and early eighteenth-century England

LINCOLN B. FALLER

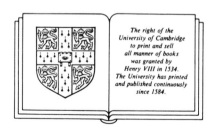

CAMBRIDGE UNIVERSITY PRESS

Cambridge

New York   New Rochelle   Melbourne   Sydney

Published by the Press Syndicate of the University of Cambridge
The Pitt Building, Trumpington Street, Cambridge CB2 1RP
32 East 57th Street, New York, NY 10022, USA
10 Stamford Road, Oakleigh, Melbourne 3166, Australia

First published 1987

Printed in the United States of America

Library of Congress Cataloging-in-Publication Data
Faller, Lincoln B.
Turned to account
Includes bibliographies and index.
1. Crime and criminals – England – Biography.
2. Crime and criminals – England – History – 18th century.
3. Crime and criminals – England – History – 19th century.
I. Title.
HV6945.F35 1987   364.3'092'2 [B]   86–29870

British Library Cataloguing in Publication Data
Faller, Lincoln
Turned to account
The forms and functions of criminal biography in late
seventeenth- and early eighteenth-century England
1. Crime and criminals – England – History
– 18th century 2. Crime and criminals –
England – History – 19th century 3. Crime
and criminals – England – Biography
I. Title
364.1'092'2   HV6945

ISBN 0 521 32672 9

FOR KATHLEEN AND HELEN

the Spider *Spins and Spits*
wholly from himself, and scorns to own
any Obligation or Assistance from without

[Bees] *have rather chose to fill* . . . *Hives*
with Honey *and* Wax, *thus furnishing Mankind*
with the two Noblest of Things, which are
Sweetness *and* Light.
                    Swift, *The Battle of the Books*

Contents

═══════════════

vii

Preface

═══════════════════

The Attention of the Publick is naturally excited towards those, who, by violating the Laws of their Country, are become liable to Punishment. . . . [N]ot only the Crime, but the Connexions and most private History of the unfortunate Delinquents, are eagerly enquired into, and become the Subjects of every Conversation. To be ignorant of, or to have nothing new to offer upon these Topicks, almost excludes us from Society. . . . Hence, too commonly, numberless Falsehoods are invented, every Particular that comes to our Knowledge exaggerated, by the various Hands through which it passes. Hence also arise the different Representations, which are made both of their Offence and Character: Some esteeming them proper Subjects for Raillery, draw, as it were, a pleasing Picture of a Hero in Iniquity . . . others [magnify] each little Error and Frailty.

Memoirs of Darkin (1761), p. [3]

As Necessity compels us, for the Preservation of our Lives, to feed upon Herbs and Roots, for want of Bread, in like manner, when the Knowledge of Truth, which is the proper and natural Food of the Mind, is wanting, we support it with Fiction, which is in Imitation of the Truth.

Pierre Daniel Huet, "Upon the Original of
Romances," in [Samuel Croxall], ed., *A Select
Collection of Novels* (1722), 1:xliii.

More often than not, stylistics . . . ignores the social life of discourse outside the artist's study, discourse in the open spaces of public squares, streets, cities and villages, of social groups, generations and epochs.

M. M. Bakhtin, "Discourse in the Novel," in *The
Dialogic Imagination*, ed. Michael Holquist, tr. Caryl
Emerson and Holquist, p. 259

On the night of 11–12 July 1664, Pepys came awake "into a most mighty sweat," and then, as he wrote in his *Diary*, "knowing what money I have in the house and hearing a noyse, I begun to sweat worse and worse, till I melted almost to water. I rung, and could not in half an houre make either of the wenches hear me, and this mad me fear the more, least they might be gag'd." It was only, after all, a false alarm;

but Pepys's night fears, understood easily enough by anyone who has lived in a large American city, may be taken as a convenient and typical example of a point that should surely need no argument: At the time Pepys wrote, and for at least the next century, one of the prevalent anxieties of the Londoner was fear of criminal assault. "Even at noon-day, and in the most open places in London, persons were stopped and robbed," a fact, it occurs to one writer of criminal biography, that "possibly in future times 'twill be thought an exaggeration of truth."[1] Such a situation naturally produced feelings and attitudes that left their traces, I shall argue, not only in the overt statements of diarists and more public writers but also, more obscurely, in the form and content of the frequent broadsides and pamphlets, the occasional books, news-paper articles, and even multivolumed anthologies that – at prices rang-ing from pennies to as much as ten shillings – described the lives, deeds, and dying words of thieves, murderers, and various other capital scoundrels.

Not all these texts were biographical. Broadside ballads had little room for detail, sessions papers were concerned exclusively with trials, and newspaper accounts were generally brief and fragmentary.[2] Before the growth of newspapers in the first two decades of the eighteenth century, however, and even before the regular publication of sessions papers in the 1670s, pamphlets began to appear that, in anywhere from four to sixty pages or more, tracked the careers of individual criminals from birth to death. It is on these pamphlets that this study will focus, and on the collections of criminal lives that began to be written from them, and other sources, early in the eighteenth century. It aims at providing nothing less (and nothing more) than a "sociopoetics" of criminal biography in England during the hundred years or so in which it first developed. This is no history of crime or criminality in that period, nor even (properly speaking) a history of criminal biography. The work of someone trained in and primarily interested in literary studies, it is, rather, an effort to distill a close reading of well over 2,000 separate narratives into orderly notions of what they were about, how they were shaped, the ends to which they were produced and con-sumed. Within what range of conventions did (or could) seventeenth- and eighteenth-century Englishmen write, read, and so presumably think and feel (or not) about the lives, characters, and actions of crimi-nals? And how were these conventions shaped by social and political constraints? What needs did they satisfy?

Such a sociopoetics may be valuable for more than its intrinsic inter-est. Two of the eighteenth century's most frequently performed plays, for instance, Gay's *The Beggar's Opera* (1728) and Lillo's *The London Merchant* (1731), were each in its way versions (or transformations, or exploitations) of one of the two main forms of criminal biography. Fielding's *Jonathan Wild* (1743) was also a "remaking" of criminal biography.[3] But of course the greatest value of such a sociopoetics – so far as literature is concerned – would be the vantage point it could give on Defoe's odd practice of writing about criminals. Most of his novels pretend to be criminal autobiographies, and, as I started this project, it seemed that one might profitably study them against the conventions of the actual thing. One might yet; the projected book on Defoe was shouldered aside by the sheer fascination of criminal biography itself as a species of fiction. Though far more primitive, and very much more locked into its time than any of his novels, it too shows – and far more clearly than any true novel could – the interplay between actuality and ideality that lies at the heart (or rather "hearts" the lies) of all fiction but most especially that which takes as its realm the "real."

What some literary scholars and critics will miss in this book, then, may hardly be noticed by readers interested in popular (or at least "middling") culture generally and *histoire des mentalités* in particular.[4] As Durkheim points out, criminals are important in all societies because, of course, their transgressions mark the furthest boundaries of the social; this can be useful as well as disturbing. Criminals are always a social embarrassment – societies get the criminals they deserve, says another French sociologist – but, inasmuch as they put themselves so completely at society's dispose, they can also become a kind of social resource.[5] Like chickens come home to roost, they are close to hand. Hauled in carts to the gallows, or even just marched in chains to the docks for transportation, criminals in seventeenth- and eighteenth-century England were made to play the central role in rituals of sacrifice and renewal. Much of what Foucault says about such spectacles in France may be applied, mutatis mutandis, to England as well.[6] England differed from France, however, in the extensive "use" (and "re-use") it made of criminals via the popular literature of crime. Their necks safely wrung, processed and packaged in ways that declared them fit for public consumption, criminals lived their lives over in readers' imaginations, committed their crimes and met their deaths, again and again. Foucault claims that in France the state inscribed its power on the very bodies of criminals, through torture, execution, and display of the physical remains. Torture was rarely practiced in England, and punishments generally were less elaborately brutal. But there the res publica – less "total," more flexible, inventive, and "modern" – had more than the criminal's body on which to figure (and refigure) its particular concerns. It had also the "literary" corpus which, in effect its own creation, it stood in his place: an object to outlast any *thing* it might display on a gibbet to awe the unruly, or anatomize just once.

Criminals at the end had only to thank their own corrupt hearts and the instigations of the Devil; I am somewhat luckier. The primary research for this book was done at the British Library over a period of six years, from 1972 to 1978, with follow-up trips in 1980, 1983, and 1985. For the funds that gave me twenty-two months amidst its rarities, the occasional green thought swimming up out of the North Library's perpetual green shade, I am deeply grateful to the National Endowment for the Humanities, the Rackham School of the University of Michigan, the American Philosophical Society, and my wife, who cheerfully subsidized my last five trips to England. I would like also to thank the staff of the British Library, as also those people who helped me during shorter periods of work at the Bodleian Library, the Bibliothèque nationale, the Houghton Library at Harvard, the Pepys Library at Magdalene College, Cambridge, the Bibliothèque municipale de Troyes, France, the New York Public Library, the Guildhall Library, and the Spencer Library at the University of Kansas. Special mention ought of course to be made of the staff of the libraries of my home institution, the University of Michigan, and particularly of the people who expedited crucial interlibrary loans from the American Antiquarian Society, the Yale Law Library, the University of Illinois Library, and the Northwestern University Library. I must note also my deep personal gratitude to Peter Carter, Geraldine O'Donnell, and Caroline Tisdale, who from the very first and on numerous occasions thereafter made me feel completely at home in London, and to Jean-Claude and Annie Demoulin, and to Michael and Biddy Fein, whose hospitality in Paris and Boston, respectively, was much appreciated.

In writing and revising the manuscript that has become this book, I have had the good fortune to be read carefully and disinterestedly by close friends as well as by people I scarcely if at all know. The whole text in one or another draft was read by Margaret Anne Doody, Russell Fraser, Thomas Green, Cynthia Herrup, Lemuel Johnson, Edward W. Rosenheim, and Thomas Toon, whom I thank for their thoroughness but most of all for their free demurrals. For their comments on very early drafts of parts of this book I thank also Dwight Cathcart, David Erdman, Bertrand Goldgar, Richard Hendrix, Eric Homberger, William Ingram, Ira Konigsberg, and C. J. Rawson. This is, needless to say, a better book for the criticisms of all these readers, even though (such is the inevitable perversity of authors) it might have been better still had I followed all their suggestions for improvement. For lesser but nonetheless important favors, I am obliged as well to Sheridan Baker, Flora Faraci, Steven Fender, Michael Harris, Jay Robinson, Eric Stockdale, and my teacher, the late Arthur Friedman. My chairman, John Knott, and my dean, Peter O. Steiner, found money to prepare the manuscript for publication, and it was ably word-processed by Warren Olin-Amintorp. Finally, I must mention my wife again, and my daughter, who had to live with me as I lived with and to some extent through this project, for perhaps too long. This book is for them, curious gift that it is. I hope, though the one writes and the other contemplates writing very different kinds of books, they nonetheless find it a compensation for my frequent absences of mind and body these many years past.

LBF

PART I

Turning criminals to account: three case histories and two myths of crime

Every man by nature hath a lusting desire to leave God, and live at his own hand; he would stand on his own legs and bottom, and be at his own dispose: Thus it is with every man by Nature. . . . Man would be at liberty from God and his Will, to follow and fulfill his own. . . . He hath a principium laesum, *a devilish principle in his nature; an impulse to range about the earth, as Satan said of himself.*
> Obadiah Grew, *Meditations upon our Saviour's Parable of the Prodigal Son* (1678), pp. 44, 46

All thieves and Murderers . . . may come under the Denomination of Rebels.
> Paul Lorrain, Ordinary Account, 6 June 1707

Myth . . . [has] often been declared to be a mere product of fear. But what is most essential . . . is not the fact of fear, but the metamorphosis of fear. Fear . . . can never be completely overcome or suppressed, but it can change its form. Myth is filled with the most violent emotions and the most frightful visions. But in myth man begins to learn a new and strange art: the art of expressing, and that means organizing, his most deeply rooted instincts, his hopes and fears.
> Ernst Cassirer, *The Myth of the State*, pp. 46–47

Myth functions especially where there is a sociological strain.
> Bronislaw Malinowski, *Myth in Primitive Psychology*, p. 126

After he was hanged and before he was quartered, Captain James Hind was disemboweled for committing high treason against the Commonwealth of England. There is in this the making of a dark conceit, for to his public, to those who followed his exploits for at least the next century and a half, James Hind was without an interior reality. Harmon Strodtman suffered for his sins, which were many and most grievous, including murder, robbery, and irregular church attendance. In this last – as Strodtman, before he was hanged, was himself to explain in several separate publications, for he too had his public – lay the dreadful seeds of the first. Mary Edmondson made no confession and had no public; she died but briefly regarded and little regretted. Were it not for the protestations of her brother-in-law, and the special pleadings of a kind-hearted but credulous "gentleman," all we would know was that, sullen and denying her guilt to the last, she died most recalcitrant for the murder of her aunt.

Hind suffered in 1652, Strodtman in 1701, Edmondson in 1759, and so together their executions span more than a century. Each of them, like so many other criminals condemned in the seventeenth and eighteenth centuries, dropped like stones into the public consciousness. They themselves remain like stones, dense, impervious to our probing, and they themselves sank quickly out of sight. It is what ripples they made, or did not make, that shall concern us here. For their cases show with unusual clarity the ways that popular writers, and presumably their audiences, shaped the facts of actuality into patterns convenient (and useful) to their imaginations. Each was made to conform to a preexisting type, as certain features of their lives were emphasized, played down, or suppressed, and "facts" were often invented. Their individualities, variously compressed and expanded, were ultimately denied; like innumerable others, they were absorbed into either of two myths of crime.

The use of the term "myth" assumes that accounts of criminals' lives served specific cultural functions. These functions may not always have been so dramatic as Cassirer's statement would suggest, with its emphasis on "fear," for the myths of a particular culture can treat all sorts of matters of concern to that culture. A broader and more generally useful definition of myth is offered by Malinowski. "Myth," he wrote, "is not an explanation in satisfaction of a scientific interest" (as others before him had argued, most notably Max Müller) but rather "a narrative resurrection of a primeval reality, told in satisfaction of deep religious wants, moral cravings, social submissions, assertions, even practical requirements. . . . it expresses, enhances, and codifies belief; it safeguards and enforces morality; it vouches for the efficiency of ritual and contains practical rules for the guidance of man." Building on this and other definitions, G. S. Kirk explains that myth has two preeminent functions: it is "speculative and explanatory," as well as "operative, iterative, and validitory." It serves the second inasmuch as it "confirm[s], maintain[s] the memory of, and provide[s] authority for [social] customs, and institutions," and the first by addressing problems that cannot "be resolved by rational means." Instead, myth "offers an apparent way out of the problem, either by simply obfuscating it, or making it appear abstract and unreal, or by stating in affective terms that it is insoluble or inevitable, part of the divine dispensation or natural order of things, or by offering some kind of palliation or apparent solution for it."[1]

Like all terms borrowed by one discipline from another, "myth" is to be treated gingerly. We ought to note Malinowski's warning, for instance, against limiting "the study of myth to the mere examination of texts." Lévi-Strauss has been criticized on just these grounds. Myth is "not merely a story told but a reality lived," Malinowski emphasizes. Like the myths of antiquity, the study of which he himself eschewed in favor of studying those of a living society, the two myths of crime that we are about to analyze "have suffered a very considerable transformation at the hands of scribes, commentators, learned priests, and theologians."[2] What remains to us in print of the attitudes of *any* historical period toward crime and criminals – or indeed toward *anything* – is inevitably only the bare (and very likely misleading) trace of a richer, more complex cultural phenomenon. This need not trouble us quite so much, however, as it should anthropologists or, certainly, the social and legal historians who have recently done so much to recover and interpret the actual facts of crime in early modern England.[3] Our concern is not so much with the real as with the highly selective ways in which the real was represented. This does not mean we are excused from having to consider as much as we can the actual historical facts; without considering at least some of them we have no basis at all for judging the ways in which they were interpreted. But still the question before us is not, primarily, how people thought and felt about crime in the total context of their lives, or what roles it played in the social process, but rather how that fraction of the population with access to the popular press wrote and read about it. In many ways, to be sure, but the most interesting ways it seems to me were two.

Where the one myth was in fact a species of spiritual biography, the other imitated the picaresque novel.[4] Hind's case (the longest of his biographies is called *The English Gusman*) illustrates the influence of the latter. In the writing (and rewriting) of his life there is a tendency to shape the materials at hand into loosely structured and seemingly amoral entertainments. In the course of this process, Hind is depersonalized until finally he is only a name, a faceless emblem of certain specified traits. Succeeding narratives of his life move toward the fantastic, edging away from a "solid" and "realistic" appraisal of his situation. Nor do they make much effort to understand (so far as these could have been understood) his mental processes; there is, finally, no interest in probing the nature of his character. Like so many other highwaymen, Hind is shunted off into the easy world of vulgar romance, his life taken, as it were, twice over. The impulses behind this myth, I shall argue, are more complicated and various than might at first appear. The product not only of fear but of confusion, guilt, even perhaps a sense of embarrassment, its movement loose, disjunct, often hard to follow (and so hardly worth following), it offered readers escape from a variety of real-world concerns, not the least of which was the increasingly troublesome business of hanging men merely for crimes against property.

The other myth is seen most clearly in cases of what I call "familiar murder" (stressing in "familiar" the archaic sense of "familial," and pointing out that "family" would have included one's servants as well as one's spouse and children). Here the tendency of the writing is radically different. Every effort is made to fix such murderers firmly within the context of the "real world," even to the extent of inventing what would otherwise seem to be actual facts. There is a marked concern, as well, with the criminal as a person (however factitious this may actually be), particularly in his consciousness. Though this distinction is only relative – for all their greater "characterization" Edmondson and Strodtman are just as finally made into types – it is nonetheless significant. This interest in consciousness (psychology is perhaps too elaborate a term) tends moreover, along with a parallel concern for presenting the "facts" of the criminal's case, to be turned more toward moral purposes than entertainment. Such narratives are tightly structured, too, in the sense that each event they relate is made to seem part of a causal chain. Here, it seems to me, the aim of the mythologizing process is to reconstruct the real along "happier" or at least more tolerable lines. This myth sought to limit the damage that crime – particularly heinous crime – could do not only to people's sense of themselves and their God but to their sense of what it was that held (or might hold) society together. By focusing on solidities, and arranging them into significant patterns, it aimed at making criminals over into proper objects of concern, which is to say at reconnecting them with their fellow human beings.

In their form and ultimate purpose, then, as well as in their content, narratives concerned with criminals like Strodtman and Edmondson stand opposite those that fed on the historical reality of highwaymen like Hind. In their complementarity, I'll argue, they show the full range of attitudes their society encouraged – or found it expedient to allow – toward criminals, their crimes, and their fates on the gallows. Each in its different ways was an effort at exorcising the "devilish principle" in human nature, a means of coming to grips with the "principium laesum" in one of its more disturbing manifestations, and both worked, too, at soothing ruffled consciences. Both were popular entertainments as well, an achievement all too easily undervalued. Crimes in crime-ridden societies are not automatically of interest; indeed, the opposite may just as well be true. "Several persons, as is usual every Sessions, were Convicted for stealing of silver Tankards, and divers for Shop-lifting," one sessions paper reports with more than usual candor, "the particulars too tedious to relate." These were petty thieves, but the exploits of highwaymen, in and of themselves, were not necessarily more interesting. As the compiler of one collection of criminal lives explains, "there is so little Diversity in the Manner of committing a Robbery on the Highway, that it would be rather tiresome than pleasant to the Reader, if we were to give him the Particulars of every Action." "If this were required," he wryly observes, "a Man who writes the History of Highwaymen, had need have a Fancy as fruitful as the celebrated *Homer,* who discovers his great Genius in nothing more than in the various Manners of giving up the Ghost, which he describes in the Deaths of his Heroes; whereas the Act of Dying is in itself altogether simple, and capable of little Variety."[5] Murder, too, is "capable of little variety" and may – described at length, repeatedly – come to seem as "tiresome." Dressed in the appropriate myth, however, the bludgeonings, stabbings, and poisonings of the popular literature of crime seem not to have palled but rather to have made occasion for special kinds of pleasure – as did, too, in their myth, the depredations of highway robbers. What these pleasures were, and why so regularly indulged, are important aspects of criminal biography considered as myth. But how were these myths fit together, from what kinds of materials, and into what sorts of wholes? The case studies that follow are highly particular. Given the necessarily speculative nature of this book, and the obscurity of the texts it treats, it seems important to begin as solidly as possible, that is, by equipping my reader to disagree with me.

Chapter 1

The highwayman: power, grace, and money at command

=====

He ask'd him, What Friends he had? To which he answer'd, That his Friends were but few, and that he depended upon his Fingers Ends for a Livelihood. . . .then the Prisoner at the Bar said, If he'd venture with him, and do as he did, he should live like a King, and never want Money; and that he'd teach him a better way to get Money, than by going to Service.
Truth of the Case of Palmer (1708), pp. 13–14

Honey, says Plunket *I thought . . . thou hadst Spirit and Resolution, with some Knowledge of the World. A brave Man cannot want; he has a Right to live, and need not want the Conveniences of Life while the dull, plodding, busy Knaves carry Cash in their Pockets . . . ; there is scarce Courage necessary, all we have to deal with are such mere Poltroons.*
John Taylor, Ordinary Account, 3 October 1750

Jack if thou wilt live with me thou shalt have money at comand or any thing thou wantest.
No Jest like a True Jest (1657)

They told me he was the captain of the gang, and that he had committed so many robberies that Hind, or Whitney, or the Golden Farmer were fools to him.
Daniel Defoe, *Moll Flanders* (1722), ed. G. A. Starr,
p. 281

The actualities of Hind's life were mythologized even before his capture. Ultimately, with more than fifty of his confraternity, he would take his place in that compendium of "most Secret and Barbarous Murders, Unparalleled Robberies, Notorious Thefts, and Unheard-of-Cheats," Captain Alexander Smith's *Lives of the Highwaymen*. Here, in the version of Hind's life that persisted through the eighteenth century, one reads in rapid order that he was born the son of a respectable saddler at Chipping Norton in Oxfordshire, that apprenticed to a butcher he ran off to London and there, falling into unwholesome company, took to robbing on the highway. In this he showed remarkable aptitude, having the courage in his first attempt to rob two trav-

elers single-handed, and then the generosity to return them enough
money to continue their journey – which generosity, Smith writes,
made Hind's mentor "very proud, to see his companion rob with good
grace." Hind went on to greater deeds, going even so far as to rob
Peters and Bradshaw, two of the regicides, giving each the merciless
lash of his tongue. And he would have robbed Cromwell too, but "that
infamous usurper" was too heavily guarded and Hind nearly lost his
life. In these adventures he was prompted, we are told, by a "great
respect for the royal family." Eventually betrayed by "an intimate acquaintance" while hiding out in London, Hind was interviewed by the
Council of State and tried at the Old Bailey. When nothing was proved
against him, he was taken to Reading and convicted on "plain" evidence of murder. This sentence being nullified the next day by an act of
general amnesty, Hind was then removed to Worcester, where the
authorities succeeded in getting a conviction and making it stick. And
so he was executed for high treason, but not before declaring his "abhorrence" of the "Republican Party" on the scaffold, and defending the
king's right to the throne. The parts of his dismembered body were
hung over the various gates of the city until they rotted away, "except
his head, which was secretly taken down and buried within a week after
it was set up."[1]

Aside from this last detail, aside from the stories about Cromwell
and the regicides, Smith's version of Hind's life is much on a par with
many others in his book. For more excitement, for a richer look into
the sort of imagination that welcomed Smith's largely fantastic accounts
of crime on the highway, one might look at his lives of Whitney and
the Golden Farmer (to complete Moll's triumvirate), or at his account
of the equally infamous Claude Duval. These exemplify much more
richly the myth of the highwayman, document much more exactly the
points I shall want to make about that myth, than does Smith's life of
Hind. But the case of Hind is notable as those of other highwaymen are
not. For his legend, unlike most others, can be traced nearly back to its
source. Though we cannot see how it was originally formed, we can
watch it resisting transformation, even in rather interesting directions,
once it had already taken shape.[2]

There is one topic in the *Weekly Intelligencer of the Commonwealth* for
Tuesday, 11 November 1651: "It is happy indeed for all that travell
both by Sea and by Land. This day about twelve of the clock Hind that
notorious Robber was brought from the Gate House to Newgate in a
Coach, and committed to the charge of the Master of that Prison." As
the *Intelligencer* goes on disapprovingly to note, the first thing Hind did

once his warders finished shackling him, "although he was sufficiently laden with Irons before, and had money little enough about him, and look't but heavy at his entrance," was to drink to the health of Charles Stuart "with good Ale."[3] For Hind was indeed a staunch Royalist, had in fact (as Smith omits to mention) fought for Charles at Worcester, and, it was rumored, helped him escape to Holland when the battle was lost. Hind himself had come to London to lie low and there indeed had been betrayed, contemporary accounts confirm, by an "intimate acquaintance."[4] Needless to say, it was not for having robbed Peters and Bradshaw or for his attempt on Cromwell that Hind had been arrested on 9 November. Nor was it for any of this that he came to the attention of the Council of State. Smith, who obviously had access to contemporary sources, chose to repeat only part of their story; his life of Hind, like so much else in his book, is at core his own contrivance. Yet the spirit of Smith's account is not inappropriate. Even in his own time, the largest part of Hind's reputation came not so much from what he had done for the Royalists, as from his cavaliering on the highway in his own behalf. Thus it was almost entirely as a highwayman that he figured in a pamphlet published just a little less than two weeks before he was captured.

Hind's Ramble, a collection of anecdotes describing, supposedly, the most notable of his robberies and swindles, epitomizes the first of his myth's three phases.[5] In both substance and appeal it has much in common with earlier jest-biographies and treatises on cony-catching. But it is more important to note that its form and narrative style are typical of the largely fictitious accounts of highwaymen's lives that begin to appear early in the seventeenth century, and which flourish, in cheap chapbooks or in more lavish compilations like Smith's, over most of the eighteenth. There is really no need to give a particular description of its contents – it has Hind doing the usual sorts of things – except possibly to say it possesses an unusual currency, bringing his adventures (remember, he was still at large) right up to the time of Charles's escape from Worcester.[6] Before assisting (supposedly) in that enterprise, Hind ranges over England, Holland, and Ireland, robbing rich travelers, cozening the covetous, and occasionally helping the poor. In none of this, except for Hind's parentage and education, does *Hind's Ramble* confirm the particulars of Smith's account. But then, apart from certain of Smith's details concerning Hind's capture, and where, when, and why he died, neither do any other contemporary accounts. Nowhere else is there any mention of Cromwell or any other regicides; nor, as we shall see, is Smith's account of Hind's last moments – for all its seeming authenticity – confirmed by the one other writer who mentions his death.

On the very day that Hind was committed to Newgate another account of his exploits was published, styling itself *An Excellent Comedy, Called, The Prince of Priggs Revels.*[7] In actual fact, this series of crude dramatic sketches is made of much the same stale stuff as *Hind's Ramble;* both works, quite obviously, are nothing more than timely efforts at cashing in on Hind's notoriety. "Such things as these are less than the least of my *Recreations,*" says the playwright – in this one inclines to believe him – and he ends his work in media res. (In a brief epilogue he pretends to have been called away from his imaginings by the real news of Hind's capture, but the whole work, barely fourteen pages long, could just as likely have been written afterward.)[8] The author of *The Prince of Priggs* is even less interested in Hind as an actual person than the author of *Hind's Ramble.* And the author of *Hind's Ramble,* though mildly critical of Hind – "All that can be said of him that was good, is, That he was Charitable to the poor; and was a man that never murdered any on the Road; and always gave men a jest for their money: Therefore of the Knaves, the honestest of the Pack" – is after all just barely concerned with the question of what his hero is actually like. All that we get from *Hind's Ramble* about the man himself are a few details at the beginning about his origins and then at the end this cursory judgment: "Hind was a man but of mean stature; his Carriage before people was civil; his Countenance smiling, good Language; civilly Cloathed; no great Spender or Ranter in Taverns. But these were onely Cloaks to deceive honest men of their money. Many of his actions savoured of Gallantry: Most of Wit; but least of Honesty."[9] This crabbed and ambivalent comment is all that we hear in either work of Hind's personality and character.

In *Hind's Ramble,* as in *The Prince of Priggs,* the putative adventures of the highwayman are offered up as nothing more than aids to wish fulfillment. Neither means actually to give its readers Hind but rather to give them back a part of their own minds. *Hind's Ramble,* says its author, is "a book full of delight and fit for vacant hours." It shows that "Fantacies may take place as well as Histories." Hind is a man of whom "it may well be said . . . *That the like is not to be seen or ever heard of;* his experience hath made him an absolute Artist in his profession: He may be likened to a place called, *Nonesuch* . . . for all the Histories in the World cannot afford the like president."[10] The very fact of his actual existence is to be taken, it seems, as proof that reality can offer all the dream satisfaction of fiction. Hind's name is used to give to a set of specious stories what otherwise they could not have: the teasing possibility that indeed they are true. In being put to such use Hind of course is not unlike so many other criminals, from the time of Elizabeth right down to the present day, upon whom fictions have been foisted by

popular writers serving, in one way or another, the needs of their
audiences to mythologize reality. Nor was he unlike so many modern
criminals who, for motives of their own, have cooperated in the making of their myths.

Hind lost no time, once he was captured, in doing what he could to
disarm the more dangerous elements of his legend. At the same time,
however, he seems to have been eager to exploit whatever there was in
his public reputation that might make for sympathy. Thus, with the
help of a certain George Horton, he gave impetus to the second phase
of his myth. As the publisher of *The Prince of Priggs*, Horton had
already taken a hand in the shaping of Hind's legend; he was not be-
hindhand in the attempt to remold it. In quick succession two more
pamphlets came from his press: first, *The True and Perfect Relation of the
Taking of Captain James Hind*, and then, a few days later, *The Declaration
of Captain James Hind (Close Prisoner in New-Gate)*.[11] The second of these
pamphlets, mostly a reprint of the first, is prefaced by Horton's an-
nouncement that he has been "desired . . . by . . . Mr. *Hind*, to publish
this ensuing Declaration, for satisfaction, & true information of the
People; together with a Narrative of his Travels" so that "sundry and
various Relations fraught with impertinent stories, and new-invented
fictions" (among them of course Horton's own *Prince of Priggs*) might
then be discredited.[12] Hind himself, in the first of these two pamphlets,
is reported as saying, when confronted by a gentleman who pulled
"two Books out of his pocket; the one entituled, Hinds Ramble[, t]he
other, Hinds Exploits," that yes, he had seen them before, but that
"upon the word of a Christian, they were fictions."[13]

Though willing to admit to "some merry Pranks and Revels," Hind
claimed there was little in these to be reprehended. "[It] is a support-
ment to me," he declared, "that I have taken from the rich; and given
to the poor; for nothing doth more impoverish the Cottage-Keeper,
then the rich Farmer, and full-fed Lawyer. . . . They were the men I
chiefly aimed at." Hind was "confident," or so he said, that "the
wrongs which I have committed doth not cry aloud for vengeance; but
rather the Mercy that I shewed in all my Designs and Actions, may
plead an acquitment of all punishment." Though "every wrong I have
done wrings drops of bloud from my heart," he added, "I never shed
one: Neither did I ever take the worth of a peny from a poor man; but
at what time soever I met with any such person, it was my constant
custom, to ask, *Who was he for?* if he reply'd, *For the King*, I gave him
20 shillings: but if he answer'd, *For the Parliament*, I left him, as I found
him." But "any other Exploits since 1649" Hind most emphatically
denied, wanting rather to emphasize the services he claimed to have
done his king. Though he disavowed helping Charles escape from

Worcester, he proudly described an audience the king had granted him
at Stirling. There he had been received in the king's own chamber and
allowed to kiss the royal hand. Moreover, "because his Life-guard was
full," the king had commended him to the duke of Buckingham "to
ride in his troop." It was not as a highwayman, then, but as a soldier
and a patriot, not as a rogue but as a man of honor, that Hind would
have preferred to present himself. "I shall sorrow not to die; neither
shall I grieve at the manner of my death, though it be never so untimely," he declared in Newgate to those who would listen. "Yet could
I have but that happiness, as to fight for my life, and to encounter an
Enemy in the field," he is reported to have said, "it would be an infinite
comfort, and joy of spirit to me."[14]

Of Hind's actual character, even assuming the accuracy of Horton's
catchpenny pamphlets, we can tell very little. As we have seen, Hind
was not above trying to make himself seem a latter-day Robin Hood,
even though this was a role at least a cut below the more honorable part
of an honest patriot, and even though, actually, it was not as a
highwayman that he had been arrested. Perhaps there were times when
he hoped to seem more amiable – and less dangerously political – as the
"honestest knave of the pack." And yet, it should be said to his credit,
he could, if only when prompted, assume with grace the nobler character. It was thus on that occasion when, claiming to have robbed
landlords and lawyers "chiefly," he went on to cap this dubious defense
with one of his "witty Gingles." One of the gentlemen present, disre-
garding the general laughter this had provoked, reminded Hind just
what precisely was at issue. "[Aye] Captain," he said, "but you are not
brought hither for robbing, but for Treason" – "Treason replyed Hind,
I am not guilty of in the least" – "yes, Sir, but you are, for complying
with Charles Stuart, and engaging against the Common-wealth of England" – "Alas Sir, it seems that is enough then to hang me" – "I am
afraid you will find it so, replyed the Gentleman" – "Well, Gods will be
done (said Hind) I value it not a three pence, to lose my life in so good
a cause; and if it was to do again, I should do the like; [Aye], I protest
would I," he said, "laying his hand upon his breast."[15] Nor did he ever
recant his loyalty to the king.

About Hind himself, then, we cannot suppose any more than this:
To a public he was anxious to impress he played, quite understandably,
both honest patriot and honest rogue. If we are willing to limit ourselves just to the roles that he played, however, we can move beyond
mere supposition. For it is possible to show quite clearly how one of
these roles, and the baser of the two, tended to crowd the other quite
out of the picture. This, the movement from the second to the third
and final phase of his myth, was not an uncomplicated process. Before

finally rejecting all but a single particle of the new material Hind's arrest
had provided, his myth tried first to incorporate this material, to make
it part of an expanding and richer legend.

So far we have mentioned only four of the thirteen separate works
on Hind that survive in the British Library. Of the nine remaining only
an additional four are worth considering. All these are linked by plagia-
ries, all share *Hind's Ramble* as a common ancestor, and all but the last
were published while Hind was still alive. The first two in order of
appearance are interesting for what they added to the popular image of
Hind, the last two for what they subtracted. George Fidge's *The English
Gusman* is the first of the offspring of *Hind's Ramble,* in both intrinsic
interest and in date of publication.[16] Basically it is an enlargement of the
previous work, telling us a little more than *Hind's Ramble* had about the
background of its hero and adding (in keeping with its title) a few more
improbably picaresque adventures. It includes as well the substance of
four pamphlets published soon after Hind's arrest. Two of these – *The
Taking of Hind* and Hind's *Declaration* – have already been mentioned. A
third, also published by George Horton, had given an account of
Hind's petition for better treatment in Newgate.[17] The fourth, which
could also have been put out by Horton (no publisher's name appears
on the title page), adds to a reprint of Hind's *Declaration* an account of
his appearance at the Old Bailey, where, no bill of indictment being
brought in against him, he had been sent back to Newgate.[18] The
contents of these four pamphlets, taken up into *The English Gusman*
pretty much whole, endow the eponymous rambler with something
more like a particular identity, something more like a human face.

Among the new things to be found in *The English Gusman,* however,
the most striking by far is a chapter that claims to give "the discourse
between [Hind's] Father, His Wife, and himself, in *Newgate, the 28. of
November.*" Whether this new episode is Fidge's invention or borrowed
from a source that has not survived, and whether or not it describes
something that did indeed occur, it represents a remarkable departure
from the overall tenor of the piece. It brings to bear on Hind and his
predicament a concern that is, given the rest of the book, unusually
humane. Thus this description of Hind's first encounter with his wife
and his father, so unlike all the previous scenes of emotional distress in
a narrative where, up to now, human suffering has always been played
for laughs: "the good *Old man* with tears in his eyes began to behold his
Son, who was kneeling at his *Fathers* feet; but was scarce able to rise for
the wait of Irons that was on his legs: but being helped by his *Father,*
arose, and went to his *Wife,* who stood wringing her hands, to see her
Husband in that misery: She taking him about the neck, wept to see
him, kissing him a thousand times." Assuring his father that he "is

sorry from the bottom of his heart for his offences," Hind ventures to
hope that "the *State* will have as much mercy on me, as ever the late
King had on *Clavil;* who was far more in danger than I am now." But
his father warns him, "Be not too confident. . . . For friends that
should stir in your business I have none" – here there is a marginal note
in the text: "*Clavil* was a great scoller, and had many friends" – "and
that which should do you most good," the old man continues, "doth
you the most injury: I shall desire you upon my blessing to bridle your
speech" – "meaning," as another note informs us, "his reviling."[19] In
its final paragraph *The English Gusman* gives an account of another visit
to Hind by his father and his wife; here we read of a parting that was,
for all we know, final. Hind's father, "giving him his blessing, bids
him *fare-wel;* wishing him to serve God, who would not cast away a
sinner that doth truly repent." And Hind's wife, we read, "with tears in
her eies gave him a parting Salute; which made the stout Captain
answer the same in the like nature; wishing he were at liberty to have
gone with them; but he still relying on the mercy of the Parliament;
made no doubt, but to visit his friends, before they came to visit him
again; but as yet," the text concludes, "he lies in Newgate in hopes of a
Release."[20] Such cautious optimism, prompted by the fact that no case
had as yet been made against Hind, was wholly ill founded. Parliament
was to have its revenge.

This revenge was to be chronicled by the last two considerable pla-
giaries of *Hind's Ramble,* and the most etiolated. But before turning to
them we might first glance at Horton's final surviving publication on
Hind, for it suggests why Parliament was not about to be merciful. *We
Have Brought Our Hogs to a Fair Market: or, Strange Newes from New-
Gate,* published four days after *The English Gusman,* can hardly have
done much to advance Hind's hopes of a pardon from the government;
indeed, it may have dimmed them. For although Horton claims again
to be concerned with answering "divers impertinancies" that have been
"lately divulged upon the proceedings of Captain *James Hind,*" he
seems to use Hind as a rallying point for Royalist sentiment even more
than he had in his earlier publications. Thus, along with a few new
stories – among them one in which Hind causes a Presbyterian minister
to be taken up as a highwayman, and another in which he escapes
capture by conjuring up a vision of "a Rampant Lyon" (a symbol of the
sovereign?) – it adds to things that had already appeared in *Hind's
Ramble* and elsewhere the text (as the title page indicates) of "his
Orders, Instructions, and a Decree, to all his Royal Gang." In this
"decree" Hind instructs his men "to be in charity with all men, except
the Caterpillars of the Times, viz. *Long-gown men, Committee-men,
Excize-men, Sequestrators,* and other Sacrilegious persons." The title

page promises also to describe "the appearing of a strange Vision on
Munday morning last, with a Crown upon his head; the Speech and
Command that were then given to Cap. *Hind;* and the manner how it
vanished away." This the authorities may have found even more provoking, for as the pamphlet goes on to disclose, the vision was of "the
late King *Charles,*" who said, apparently from heaven, "*Repent, repent,
and the King of Kings will have mercy on a Thief.*" And there in the center
of the page just after this, about two and a half inches high, is a cut of
the Royal Martyr with (as the text points out) "a Crown upon his
head," and (perhaps to the greater annoyance of good Commonwealth
men) his head still attached to his shoulders. If Hind indeed had sanctioned *Strange Newes from New-Gate* – it claims to be "attested under his
own hand" – then clearly he had failed to heed the advice of his father,
or, if his father's visit is a fiction, then of George Fidge or whoever it
was who had counseled him to bridle his speech.[21]

The end did not come quickly. What little we know of it, aside from
Smith's dubious account, comes from two chapbooks, *Wit for Mony*
(1652) and *No Jest like a True Jest* (1657). Each, to what it has taken
from *Hind's Ramble,* adds a brief conclusion. According to them, Hind
spent most of the winter in Newgate, and then on the first of March he
was taken from London to Reading. There he was tried for having
killed a drinking companion, some time before, in a quarrel about a
wager. Found guilty of manslaughter, not murder (which meant the
jury was sympathetic enough to find extenuating circumstances), Hind,
we read in *Wit for Mony,* "was allowed his Clergy, but when he came
to his Booke he could not read, but was much dijected, and spake very
little for himself; so he was condemned, and sentence passed on him to
dye." But Hind's fortune was yet still changeable, for as *Wit for Mony*
notes, "the next morning the Act of Oblivion being sent down to my
Lord [Justice], he was pleased to pardon him for that time, and that
offence." This "left [Hind] a Prisoner in *Reading* Goale upon the account of high Treason against the State, where he yet remains, says the
writer of *Wit for Mony* at the end of his digest of *Hind's Ramble;* and
then, expressing at last his own view of the man and his current situation, he adds: "But it is not probable for any thing he hath yet done, he
will by an untimely death be brought to his *End.*"[22] So lucky indeed
seemed the golden Hind.

Yet Hind had still to face that one last vicissitude. This we find
reported from a distance of five years in a single perfunctory sentence at
the end of *No Jest like a True Jest.* As this pamphlet is a condensation at
something like half the length of *Wit for Mony,* it offers a double distil-
lation of the essential Hind that had appeared in *Hind's Ramble.* It provides, moreover, the version of Hind's life that was to survive the

longest, well into the nineteenth century. Thus it is important to note that, even more utterly than *Wit for Mony,* it purges what little individuality Hind had achieved in print by reason of his capture and sojourn in jail. Not even the curious details of his trial at Reading remain, *No Jest like a True Jest* noting only at the last, after giving the barest details of his arrest and imprisonment, that Hind "was found guilty of Manslaughter [at Reading], and condemned to dye, but on the next morning the act of oblivion being sent, [he was] acquitted all former offences, only the Indictment of High Treason against the State, and for that Fact," it says at the end of its very last sentence, "he was carried to Worcester, and there drawn hang'd and quartered on Friday, Sep. *24. 1652.*"[23] For Hind it must have been a long winter, a longer summer, and a long last Friday. But there is in none of the accounts of him any sense of this, of all the time in prison spent preparing for his end. Long before that fatal Friday the life within him, object as he was of the mythologizing process, had quite been drained away. Smith, to be sure, would provide a few more details about the end of his career, giving, for example, the full name of the man that Hind had killed near Reading, and he would give us all the description we have of Hind's last moments. Yet there is no reason to believe that it was, as Smith claims, a certain George Sympson whom Hind had killed – in fact both *Wit for Mony* and *No Jest like a True Jest* say it was a man named Poole – nor can we be certain that Smith's account of Hind's dying speech is any the less a fabrication than the stories he tells about how and whom Hind robbed.

But it is not Hind himself, finally, that can concern us, however much in our imaginations we see him sweating out his myth, straining, for instance, to live up to his reputation for wit. (When asked during his examination at the Old Bailey where he was born, he delivered this riposte: "At the merry town of Chipping-Norton in Oxfordshire.")[24] Nor do I want to dwell on Hind's emergence from stereotypical roguery for reasons that could have had to do with the political and psychological disposition of certain people in London during the winter of 1651–52, when, after the defeat at Worcester, the Royalist cause seemed hopeless. One well may wonder whether Hind and those who wrote about him were feeding a need to believe in a Cavalier prankster dashing and undaunted, a man not so much a thief as in his own way a leveler, not so much a traitor as a patriot still loyal to a cause apparently lost, a rogue and yet of knaves "the honestest of the pack" – a man whom Parliament, after all, could hardly be so cruel as to kill.[25] Although this very possibly may have been the case, all that one can claim with any certainty is that Hind emerged from his myth only very shortly to subside back into it. Over the long run there seems to have been a tendency to want to see him only one way and not another; this is what I would like to emphasize.

Fidge slips into this other mode when he describes the tearful encounter between Hind and his wife and father, and when he makes Hind a moral object lesson, saying, for instance, that "the Devil when he has a Design upon some frail person, tickles him with the conceit of acting something that may draw a fame upon him; the greediness to purchase which, makes him forget to examine himself, whether it be good or evil; but he runs the hazard, and at the last is taken in it." Many have been drawn in just this way, Fidge warns, "from their honest callings, that might not only have lived contentedly, but died peaceably; and so have lived that death might never have bin feared."[26] Such a point of view is entirely absent from *Wit for Mony* and *No Jest like a True Jest,* just as it was from *Hind's Ramble* and would be from Smith's version of Hind's life. Yet this was a point of view rather generally applied to criminals in the late seventeenth and early eighteenth centuries (we shall see it figuring full in the case of Harmon Strodtman): Why didn't it stick to Hind? For all its suspect piety, such a point of view has at least the advantages of allowing the criminal's character some minimal depth, some bare coherence. All that talk about the Devil and sin, of people drawn from their honest callings, of death and why it should be feared, makes of the criminal's life something more than a convenient locale for the idle imaginings of empty hours, "a place called Nonesuch"; the criminal is honored at least as an emblem of the general human condition. But Hind, his life made into a series of disconnected episodes, most of them jokes, finally is denied even this.

Why was Hind treated as he was, and how representative is his case? Almost all of Part III will be given over to the first of these questions, but we might begin answering the second here, with a brief consideration of Whitney and the Golden Farmer. Their lives, too, were curiously simplified. What hard evidence there is about Whitney's career and eventual end comes from two sources. One of these is a broadside describing his capture on 31 December 1692. The mob, after helping run him down, we are told, huzzahed him as he was carried off in a coach to prison.[27] The other, and by far the more valuable, is a series of entries in Luttrell's *Relation of State Affairs.* A notorious Jacobite, Whitney nonetheless offered "to bring in 80 stout men of his gang to the kings service, if he may have his pardon." Or so Luttrell reported 1 December 1692; three weeks later the number of men involved is scaled down, but we find, astonishingly, that the offer was taken under consideration. "The lords C. and B.," Luttrell writes, "were on a Sattur-

from Capt. Charles Johnson, *Lives and Adventures of the Most Famous Highwaymen, Murderers, Street-Robbers, &c.* [1734]

Capt. Hind Robbing Col. Harrison in Maidenhead-Thicket.

day last to meet Whitney, a great Highwayman, on honour: he offers to bring in 30 horse, with as many stout men, to serve the king, provided he may have his pardon, and will give a summe of money besides: but the issue thereof is not known." Soon after, Whitney was arrested and convicted. Awaiting trial with "40 pound wight of irons on his leggs, he had his taylor make him a rich embroidered suit, with perug and hatt, worth 100*l.*" He also offered to betray his comrades "if he may have his pardon." Still outside, his comrades could afford to be more generous. Robbing three coaches on the Epsom road of two hundred pounds, they told their victims "they borrowed the money to maintain Whitney in prison."[28]

Whitney was convicted on 19 January 1693 and taken to Tyburn on the twenty-seventh in order to be hanged, but then "was brought back, having a reprieve for 10 Days, . . . with a rope about his neck, a vast crowd of people following him." Rumors abounded; some thought he had been reprieved in exchange for revealing "who hired the persons to rob the mailes so often," while others said he had offered to discover "his accomplices, with their houses of reception, and way of living." The truth was actually far more extravagant: on the morning he was to

be hanged Whitney had written a letter to Lord Capell, claiming to
have been involved in a plot to assassinate King William "as he hunted
in Windsor forest, in order to which he and 11 others attended there
when the king was hunting . . . but could not meet with an opportunity to execute the same, and that the design was still carried on."
Capell rushed this letter to Chief Justice Holt, and Whitney got his
reprieve. That night he was taken to Whitehall, where he demanded a
full pardon before saying anything more about the "plot" against the
king. The authorities, by now suspecting "only a contrivance to gain
time," instead took back the reprieve.

Whitney was finally hanged on 1 February, his ruse having length-
ened his life by five days. "He seemed to dye very penitent," wrote
Luttrell, "was an hour and halfe in the cart" – presumably praying –
"before [being] turn'd off."[29] None of this appears in either of the two
pamphlets printed about the time that Whitney was captured and
hanged, except for some versions of the story the broadside tells about
his arrest. *The Jacobite Robber* and *The Life of Captain James Whitney*
(both 1693) differ on the essential details of his "life," even though the
second, published later, absorbs some stories from the first. Neither of
these is much to be relied on, except possibly for entertainment (and
that none too certainly). The more than usually factitious account of
Whitney's life in Smith's *Highwaymen* owes nothing to either of these
earlier narratives, and needless to say it owes little more to actual fact.
Smith does mention that Whitney was reprieved on his way to the
gallows and hanged the next week, but he omits to give the reason
why. Moreover, though he does give the place of Whitney's execution
correctly (he was finally hanged not at Tyburn but at Smithfield), he
dates it wrongly by almost a year and contradicts Luttrell on how it
happened. According to Smith, Whitney was "tumbled out of this
world into another" on 19 December 1694, after having only "some
few minutes . . . allowed him for his . . . private devotion."[30]

Smith's "life" of the Golden Farmer shows the same disregard for
highly interesting actualities. The only surviving printed accounts that
antedate his text – aside from a single ballad – are brief reports of the
Golden Farmer's trial and his dying behavior.[31] Similar accounts of
Whitney presumably were published but lost. It is the latter of these
two reports that is the more interesting. In it, the chaplain to Newgate
Prison reports that

> John Bennet alias Freeman, but more notoriously known by the
> name of the GOLDEN FARMER [was] condemned for the
> Murther of *Charles Taylor,* and several Robberies to the value of
> some thousand Pounds. I was with him several times in his

Chamber, and exhorted him to disburthen his Conscience, by a free Confession of his Evil Courses, yet after much Advice for his Souls Welfare, and many Prayers that God would work his Heart to Repentance, nothing more than what follows could be obtained: That he had been a great Sinner, and was guilty of most sins. That he was not so much grieved for the Shame of this condign Punishment, as for offending God. And that he was not solicitous to lengthen out his Life upon Earth, but to get his Pardon sealed in Heaven. He shed many Tears, yet said That he trusted only in Christ's Righteousness for Pardon and Peace in Conscience.

Though Bennet "gave some Signs of great Remorse," he was not so contrite as the chaplain could have wished him.[32]

Details like these would have had considerable significance for contemporary readers, but in Smith's *Highwaymen* they are absent, as are also the particulars of Bennet's capture. Recognized as he rode through Salisbury Court (Smith does note this) and pursued by the mob after a hue and cry had been raised, Bennet shot Tayler (who was not a butcher, as Smith claims, but a soldier) in his effort to escape. Followed to Southwark, where he mortally wounded another man, Bennet "could not be taken till he was knock'd down by Brick-bats."[33] Smith does not include these latter details either; but, more important, he misidentifies the Golden Farmer, claiming that he was a certain William Davis who was executed "on Friday, the 20th of December, 1689." Smith seems to have gotten Davis's name and the date of his execution from some surviving record, for there was indeed a William Davis hanged on the date he gives (or at least one capitally convicted a few days before), but the account of Davis's trial does not identify him as the Golden Farmer, and he was not charged with murdering a man in Salisbury Court; his offense was burglary.[34] Though it hardly seems likely that Smith had either of the sources I've quoted before him as he wrote the Golden Farmer's life, he very likely knew he was wrong. He just could not have known so much about Davis without knowing Davis was not the Golden Farmer; clearly Smith cared not at all for historical accuracy and sought (when he felt the need of it) only after its appearance. Happening to have a name and a date at hand, he attached it to some appropriate adventures.[35] Nor did Smith's wrongness on the Golden Farmer go unnoticed at the time he wrote; the anonymous "N.B.," in the course of plagiarizing Smith's account of the Golden Farmer's robberies for his own *Compleat Collection of Remarkable Tryals*, silently corrected him on the highwayman's real name and date of execution. Later writers follow Smith's version of the Golden Farmer's

life even more slavishly, repeating the same errors, telling (with occasional embroideries) the same fanciful anecdotes about him, and omitting to mention anything of the last dark nights of his soul.[36]

Historical reality was similarly suppressed in the telling of the lives
of other criminals, not all of them highwaymen. Old Mobb, who
rode with the Golden Farmer's gang and was hanged unknown by any
other name, provides yet another instance where evidence can be
produced.[37] There is the case, too, of the notorious burglar Jack Hall,
who was hanged in 1708 along with several members of his gang.[38]
And even Jack Sheppard, who got a good deal of relatively factual and
sympathetic biographical attention, was made nonetheless – imperson-
ated by an actor in a clown suit – to reenact for the pleasure of theater
audiences his astonishing escapes from Newgate.[39] What all these
criminals have in common with Hind, Whitney, and the Golden
Farmer is that the actual complexities of their lives, as people were
aware of them at the time they died, are not at all to be found in
works that later took them as centers of attention. The transformations of actual criminals into entertaining rogues that we find in Smith
make convenient examples, but, as the popularity alone of his book
would suggest, he was hardly atypical. What we see in him reflects a
tendency in the popular imagination as a whole, and this tendency, I
would argue, can be seen most clearly in the successive narrations of
James Hind's life.

Quite despite their intrinsic interest, the personal – and what is more,
the affecting – details of his capture and incarceration were discarded
and lost. Such details were unnecessary, even inimical to the myth Hind
was made to embody, a myth that required at its center a character for
the most part emptied of individual traits; or so I shall eventually argue.
What, finally, we might note here is that those few of Hind's individual
characteristics that survived in the successive accounts of his life the
longest – and so (one assumes) those most valuable in the minds of the
people who wrote and read about him – were those that had been present from the very first: He was witty, not cruel, a Cavalier of sorts, a
bold man who robbed with a flourish. For all that he endured over the
winter and summer of 1651–52, Hind cut essentially the same figure in
Wit for Mony and *No Jest like a True Jest* as he did in *Hind's Ramble* and
The Prince of Priggs. All that was published between his capture and
execution – at least all that survives in the British Library – served in the
long run only to reinforce an image that, however much it shimmered
and threatened to disappear, never quite gave place to the actual man.
Hind lingered on in the popular imagination like so many other thieves:
eviscerate, scattered into pieces, the chiefest part of him taken down
secretly and buried.

Chapter 2

Familiar murder: sin, death, damnation, repentance, God's grace, and salvation

Home at night, and find that my wife had found out more of the boy's stealing 6s. out of W[illiam] Hewer's closet, and hid it in the house of office, at which my heart was troubled. To bed, and caused the boy's clothes to be brought up to my chamber. But after we were all a-bed, the wench (which lies in our chamber) called us to listen of a sudden, which put my wife into such a fright that she shook every joint of her, and a long time that I could not get her out of it. The noise was the boy, we did believe, got in a desperate mood out of his bed to do himself or William some mischief. But the wench went down and got a candle lighted, and finding the boy in bed, and locking the doors fast, with a candle burning all night, we slept well, but with a great deal of fear.

Samuel Pepys, *Diary*, 29 August 1660

The horrid and unnatural crime of murder has, within a few years past, become more frequent than it was ever known to be; it has been committed by, and on those between whom there were the strictest ties of blood, and the nearest tie of kindred has not been any security against it. What a shudder must human nature receive, when it recollects there is no place where security may be depended on; for at the same time persons are barring their doors without, they are enclosing worse enemies within.

J.G., in a letter sent to Mary Edmondson in prison, printed in Joseph Clarke, *A Refutation of the Narrative of the Trial of Mary Edmundson* (1759), p. 9

The first hint of trouble came when Mary Edmondson ran out into the street crying "Murder!" She had just escaped, she said, from four men who had broken into the house and murdered her aunt. But nothing could be found that night or afterward to confirm her story, and as the evidence mounted Edmondson herself fell under suspicion. The neighbors secured her, she was arrested and eventually tried, and then speedily hanged. All the while she steadfastly denied her guilt. Harmon Strodtman woke no one when he did his mischief. In fact, his crime went undiscovered until the following morning. Discharged on moral grounds from his masters' employ (he served two), he had come back in the night to settle old scores. Bludgeoning his fellow apprentice to death as he slept, he helped himself to some of the dead boy's clothing and a few loose valuables, set the house on fire, and made good his escape. Taken up a few days later as he tried to pass a stolen banknote, he was confronted by one of his former masters and readily confessed. Though he later retracted his confession, he was nonetheless convicted and hanged – but not before reaffirming in print, the confession he originally had given.

Neither of these cases is all that remarkable in the history of eighteenth-century crime, save for what it shows, in combination with the other, about the way a certain kind of crime took shape in the popular imagination. Murder, as the late Randal Lane, Q.C., once pointed out to me, has come to seem the most heinous of crimes only relatively recently. To the Middle Ages, and even during the Renaissance, both heresy and treason were greater crimes. As acts that set one directly against both God and state they seemed far more consequential than the mere killing of an individual.[1] Still, though murder in the eighteenth century had not quite achieved the fascination it would have for later times, a certain species of it did attract an inordinate degree of attention. This kind of murder had (as eventually I'll make clear) overtones not only of treason but of rebellion against God as well. And because it seemed, too, an act of radical rebellion against the discipline of the family, then even more than now the nucleus of social organization, at its starkest it threatened, or seemed to threaten, the very foundation of all social order. Thus it was that the accounts of Mary Edmondson, who committed a form of parricide, and Harmon Strodtman, who commited a form of fratricide, were significant in the first place. And they remain significant to us because, when it came time for these murderers to unburden their hearts to the public (according to the elaborate etiquette of the occasion), the one was so obdurate and uncooperative, the other so penitent and obliging.

Strodtman gave three versions of how Peter Wolter, his fellow apprentice and onetime friend, had come to be murdered. Caught with the stolen goods in his possession and carried before a magistrate, he claimed first that he had entered Wolter's room only to commit a robbery. It was only when the sleeping figure stirred that he hit him on the head to prevent his waking up. Later, at the trial, Strodtman claimed he had no part in the murder at all. Wolter had actually been killed by a man whom Strodtman knew only as "John the Painter." He had met this man in a tavern, and together they got the idea of robbing Strodtman's former masters. But "John the Painter" had said nothing about killing anyone, Strodtman contended, and once at the house had acted too quickly for him to intervene. Still later, convicted and sentenced to die, Strodtman altered his story once more. Now he admitted that "John the Painter" was all a lie, told at the prompting of his fellow prisoners in Newgate. Nor was Strodtman's first story entirely true, either, for now he confessed he had wanted to kill Wolter for a long time. They had been friends in Germany, had come to London to do their apprenticeships together, but had a falling out when Wolter's sister married one of their masters. Wolter became "proud" and "domineering," carried tales, and even sometimes beat him. Conceiving "an implacable Hatred" for his ex-friend, Strodtman first tried poisoning and, when that failed, resolved to stab him. But then, afraid he might lose control and act too openly, and considering also that he ought to wait until Easter so Wolter could take the sacrament, Strodtman ran off to Greenwich for a few days' breathing space. This, and lying about where he had been, caused his masters to dismiss him. Not long after, letting himself into their house after dark with a key he had earlier stolen (so that he might come and go as he pleased, he explained, and pursue his pleasures without check), he took his revenge. The robbery and arson, he confessed, were never more than incidental to his main design.

All this Strodtman freely put down in a remarkable document, which the prison chaplain arranged to have translated from its original German and published along with his more usual accounts of the dying prisoners.[2] In this "ample and ingenuous *Confession*," Paul Lorrain claimed, Strodtman showed himself "a great *Penitent,* and wonderfully restored to a right Mind, by the power of the *Divine Grace*."[3] It is not perhaps an inconsiderable indication of Strodtman's "rightness"' of mind that he can tell us, without rancor, how he was tricked into his first confession – his master had promised to spirit him out of England and so save him from the law, if only he would tell the truth. And probably Strodtman showed his rightness of mind, also, in revealing that his guilt was even more horrid than what he had been willing, in his first confession, to acknowledge. In both these instances we notice, however, not only Strodtman's ingenuousness but also his amplitude. It seems a particular proof of his rightness of mind that he holds nothing back, neither out of shame nor from want of attention to detail. Thus he gives us an account of the conversation he had with his master that led to the first of his confessions, including where it took place – as he and his master were walking away from one of the two lodgings he had taken after being dismissed – and when – just after this lodging had been searched for the stolen goods, and just before they got into a coach to take them to the second (see pp. 210–11). Strodtman is even more circumstantial when, in telling how his resentment mounted against

Wolter, he describes the method he used in his unsuccessful effort to poison him. "To that purpose," he writes, "[I] mixt some Mercury with a certain white Powder, which he had always in a Glass in the Chamber, and of which he us'd to take a Dose very often, for the Scurvy. But it being then Winter-time (I think the latter End of *December,* or beginning of *January*) I found he had left off taking his Powder" (p. 201).

Strodtman goes on to describe what he did when he ran away with just as much attention to detail, with what would seem, indeed, an overscrupulous concern for the facts. All that would seem necessary to the forward movement of his narrative is for him to say he went away without leave, and so was dismissed. It is as if Strodtman would hope to show, if only through the bare accumulation of detail, that he is, after his retractions, finally sincere. Nowhere is he so convincing as when he describes the actual murder itself and its aftermath. "I came to my Masters House on Saturday in Easter-Week, about half an Hour past Eight at Night," he writes,

> and being got in, I first hid my self behind the Entry Door, upon my hearing a Noise of some body's going up Stairs. When this was over, and I supposed the Way was clear, I went up one pair of stairs first; and entring the Room, where I us'd to lie, next to the Compting-house, I went to a Tinder-box (which I knew was there) and having struck Fire, lighted a Candle. Then I took my Masters Dark-lanthorn that was there also, and went up another pair of Stairs higher, and having got into an empty Room adjoining to *Peter Wolter*'s Chamber, I did shut myself in there: Where I was no sooner come but I heard a Noise, as if some body was coming up: Upon which I put out my Candle, and some time after fell asleep. [Pp. 204–5]

Waking at midnight, and concluding from the absolute stillness of everything around him that his victim "and the rest of the Family were a-bed, and fast asleep," Strodtman tells how he crept downstairs to relight his candle, pausing to enter the countinghouse to steal some banknotes and bills, "and some Money too." Then again upstairs, and carrying with him, he tells us now, "a certain piece of Wood, where-with they used to beat Tobacco." (His masters were tobacco merchants.) He found this piece of wood in the chamber where he slept before coming down; it shows something of his narrative skill that he reserves this detail for the appropriate moment:

> When I got up Stairs, I sprung into *Peter Wolter*'s Chamber, and coming to his Bed-side, open'd the Curtains, and with my

Engraved for the Tyburn Chronicle.

Herman Strodtman in the Act of murdering his fellow Prentice Peter Wolter.

from *The Tyburn Chronicle* [1768]

Tobacco-beater knockt him on the Head, giving him four or five Blows on the left side of it, and another on the right. When I had given him the first Blow, then my Heart failed me; yet being afraid to be discover'd by the Noise he made with groaning, I followed close this first Blow with three or four others; and then had not Courage enough to go on with giving him any more. Therefore to stop his Groans, I took his Pillow, and laying it on his Mouth, pressed it hard upon it with my Elbow, as I was sitting on the side of his Bed; and by this means stopp'd his Breath and stifled him. And thus it was, that I most barbarously murder'd this poor Creature; whom I intended (had this fail'd) to have shot to Death, having brought with me two Pistols ready charg'd for that wicked purpose. *The Lord forgive me this Sin!* When I perceived *Peter Wolter* was quite Dead, I proceeded to search his Breeches and Chest-of Drawers, and took a Note of 20*l.* with some Money, out of his Pocket: which (with that I had taken in the Compting-house) amounted to 8 or 9 *l.* Then I pack'd up some of his Linnen and woolen Clothes, and having made a

Bundle of them, went down with it one pair of Stairs, and out of a Window there, threw it into the next House, where no body dwelt. Then I went up Stairs again, and having cut my Candle in two (both pieces being lighted) I set one in the Chest of Drawers, and the other on a Chair, close by the Bed-Curtains: intending to have burnt the House, in order to conceal by this heinous Fact, the other two of Theft and Murther, which through the Instigation of the Devil, I had now most barbarously committed. Then I went through a Window, out of the House, into that where I had flung the Bundle; and staying there till about Five in the Morning, went away with that Bundle (and what else I had took) to my Lodgings in *Queen-street,* where I put on clean Clothes, and then went to the *Sweeds* Church in Trinity-lane. [Pp. 205–7]

At that church the horror of what he had done began to sweep over him. His narrative continues without interruption:

There I heard the Bill of Thanks read which my Masters had put up for their own and Neighbours Preservation; At which my Heart sunk down, and I had great Checks of Conscience, and could not forbear shedding of Tears, which I hid, (all I could) from an Acquaintance of my Masters, who was in the same Pew with me, and told me, that my Masters House was like to have been burnt the last Night, it being set on Fire by an Accident yet unknown; but the mischief which it might have done, was (through God's Mercy) happily prevented, by the *Dutch* Maid, who first smelt the Fire, and saw the Smoak, and thereupon called her Master, and fetch'd up a Pail of Water; by which means it was presently put out. This he told me at large as we were come out of the Church; and at our parting he and I appointed to meet another at two of the Clock upon the Out-Walks of the *Royal Exchange;* in order to go together to the *Dutch* Church in the *Savoy.* I went to the *Exchange* accordingly; and walked thereabouts, waiting for him a while: But he not coming, as he had promised me, I went alone (not to the *Savoy,* as intended) but to *Stepney* Church. And after Sermon walked in the Fields towards *Mile-end,* where I saw at a distance two *Dutch* Men that were hang'd there in Chains. Then I was struck with some Remorse and Fears, and said to my self, *Thou may'st come to be one of them, and be made a like Spectacle to the World.* After this, as I went on, I came to *Blackwall* (as I think) and there saw another Person (a Captain of *French* Pirates) who also hang'd in Chains in that Place. Then the same Thoughts again returned upon me, *viz.* That it may come to my lot to have such a shameful End.

It was "Providence" that had led him "to those dismal and ghastly Objects," but then, not yet "awaken'd to Repentance," still in a "Spiritual Slumber" and "under the Power and Dominion of the Devil," he returned "with heavy Thoughts" to his lodgings. "My Heart," he says, "did not relent at what I had done" (pp. 207–9). Nor did it begin to, until he had been caught. He goes on to describe his capture and trial, his mean and unskillful attempts to evade the death he deserves, and closes by thanking God for giving him "the Time, and Opportunity, and Grace . . . to repent." And he asks God's blessing for "all those who have been the Instruments of my Apprehension and Condemnation" (especially his judges, whom he asks to pardon him for lying) and for the king as well, and for his own family, friends and relations, and also for his masters and their families, and for "all good People of God . . . his Church, these Nations, and the whole World." Strodtman, in the depth of his contrition and the sincerity of his repentance, in his conviction that God is "infinitely good and gracious," had no need to ask God's blessing for himself. He already feels it, not doubting but that "within a few Hours" he will "sing with the blessed Saints above" (pp. 213–14).

All this is indeed both ample and ingenuous. Its spontaneity, that is to say its freedom and originality, is yet another question. For though Strodtman's *Confession,* being published as a first-person narrative, was something of a rarity in its day, it is hardly at all idiosyncratic. With all its apparent ingenuousness, and quite apart from its relation to particular events, it has been assembled from a stock of clichés. The most notable of these are of course religious. Strodtman's pious ejaculations at the close of his confession, and occasionally throughout it, the advice that he gives in a postscript warning "all Men" to heed his "Fall" (p. 216), most of what he says in his last speech, all these, quite understandably enough, are common expressions of religious orthodoxy. "The first Sin I began with," he says, "was Sabbath-breaking: and as soon as I had put my dear God from before my Eyes, the Devil took possession of my Heart; and so I began to hate, and afterwards to Murther this poor innocent Creature; for which I am now come to this shameful end" (p. 217). And thus he explains why all men, however far from doing murder they may feel, should take warning by his fate.

But one is meant to find something heartening as well in his story, for Strodtman, "that once *unfortunate,* but *now,* and *for ever Happy* Young-man," as Paul Lorrain calls him, is more than just a sad example of what the inherent depravity of human nature can come to.[4] The inevitable consequence of sin *is* death – even if breaking the Sabbath only rarely leads to murder – but death need not seem all that fearsome, for as Strodtman's example shows it need *never* lead to damnation. "O

Lord, reveal thy self unto me; Shed abroad thy Love in my Heart. Tell me my Sins are Pardoned; assure me of an interest in Christ, before I go hence and be seen no more, that I may declare to thy People what thou hast done for my Soul" (pp. 219–20). So Strodtman prays with the noose around his neck, his case proving that, however foully men may have sinned, through God's grace they can repent and be saved. And so the devotional papers that Strodtman wrote in prison and left behind were published not only as "a Warning to others against *Sin*" but as "a *Help* to their *Recovery,* who are fallen into it," this being, as Lorrain in his preface to them said, "the pious *Design* of our *Dying Penitent.*"[5]

That Strodtman's confession was put to such pious ends, that his narrative was overlaid, contained, even pointed by conventionally religious concerns, is neither surprising nor unusual. The stories of murderers, though rarely told by the murderers themselves, had been shaped to the same purposes many times before, and would be many times afterward. Strodtman seems only to be writing in the first person what the prison chaplain (or some other solemn chronicler of crime) might otherwise have written about him in the third. Even the most original and striking part of Strodtman's narrative, as it may seem to the untutored reader, conforms also to convention. Strodtman's account of how he bludgeoned Peter Wolter to death, and the nearly Roskolnikovian flight that follows, are similar to other descriptions of cold-blooded murder that were published both before and after his particular confession. Though few of these are written in a style so strikingly lucid as Strodtman's (how much of this is not his but the translator's of course we cannot know), they are essentially the same in their emphasis on the objective details of the act, its impersonality, the insensibility and disorientation of the flight that follows, the gradual return of the murderer to feeling and conscience, his fears, and his inevitable disclosure of guilt. One might mention as rich examples of all or part of these characteristics the appropriate passages in accounts of Nathaniel Butler, who stabbed to death another apprentice (his bedfellow) in 1657, or Catherine Hayes, who with the help of two accomplices murdered her husband and then disposed (unsuccessfully) of the dismembered corpse in 1726, or Elizabeth Jeffryes, who helped her lover to murder her uncle (reputedly also her lover) in 1752.

But rather than cite one instance of murderous mayhem after another, perhaps I can make my point adequately enough by adverting to just one other case, the murder by Thomas Savage of a housemaid, his fellow servant, in 1668. This was probably the most notorious murder in the era with which we are concerned; certainly its fame endured longer and spread more widely than any other murder committed in the latter half of the seventeenth century. One of the pamphlets prompted by the occasion gives us a description of the crime that closely compares to Strodtman's narrative in style as well as in structure. This is worth quoting at length, not only because a paraphrase would vitiate the comparison but because it very likely was in print at the time Strodtman wrote (though I am not arguing he was influenced by its specific example). The pamphlet opens with a directness that is shocking: "*Thomas Savage,* born in the Parish of Giles's in the Feilds, was put out Apprentice to Mr. *Collins* Vintner, at the *Ship-Tavern* in *Ratcliff,* where he lived about the space of one year and three quarters, in which time he manifested himself to all that knew him, to be a meer Monster in Sin."[6] How surprising this last phrase, and then as we hasten to find just what was monstrous, how trivial, seemingly, are his faults. For Savage, we are told as this opening paragraph proceeds, would never sit long enough in church "to hear one whole Sermon, but used to go in at one Dore and out at the other, and accounted them fools that could spare so much time from sin as two or three hours on a Lords-day, to spend in the Lords service." Instead, he preferred to spend the Sabbath "commonly at the Ale-house" in the company of a "vile Strumpet." Savage's story rapidly grows more serious. The woman demands money, urging him to rob his master even though, as he explains to her, he would have first to kill the housemaid. Eventually, of course, he does as she wishes.

"That day that he committed the murder," Savage spent the morning with his whore

> and she made him drunk with burnt Brandy, and he wanted one Groat to pay of his Reckoning; she then again perswaded him to knock the Maid on the head, and she would receive the money; he going home, between twelve and one of the clock, his Master standing at the Street dore, did not dare to go in that way, but climbeth over a back dore, and cometh into the Room where his Fellow-Servants were at Dinner, O saith the Maid to him, Sirrah, you have been now at this Baudy house, you will never leave till you are undone by them; he was much vexed at her, and while he was at Dinner the Devil entred so strong into him, that nothing would satisfie but he must kill her, and no other way but with the hammer; to which end, when his Master was gone with all the rest of the Family to Church, leaving only the maid and this Boy at home, he goeth into the Bar, fetcheth the hammer, and taketh the Bellows in his hand, and sitteth down by the Fire, and there knocketh the Bellows with the hammer. the Maid saith to him, sure the Boy is mad, Sirrah, what do you make this noise for? he said nothing but went from the Chair and lay along in the Kitchen

window, and knocked with the hammer there, and on a sudden threw the hammer with such force at the Maid, that hitting her on the head, she fell down presently, screeching out; then he taketh up the hammer three times, and did not dare to strike her any more, at last the Divel was so great with him, that he taketh the hammer and striketh her many blows with all the force he could, and even rejoyced that he had got the victory over her; which done, he immediately taketh the hammer and with it strikes at the Cupboard dore in his Masters Chamber, which being but slit Deal presently flew open, and thence he taketh out a Bag of Money, and putting it upon his arm under his Cloak, he went out at a back dore strait way. [Pp. 4–6]

Having killed the maid and robbed his master, Savage flees, grows increasingly distracted, and finds no rest until he confesses. To finish his story, he returns immediately after the murder to the alehouse that has proved his undoing (would he have done better to have kept to his master's tavern?) and there

the Slut would fain have seen what he had under his Cloak, and knowing what he had done, would very fain have had the Money; he gave her half a Crown and away he went without any remorse for what he had done; going over a stile, he sat down to rest himself, and then began to think with himself, Lord what have I done! and he would have given ten thousand worlds he could have recalled the blow; after this he was in so much horror that he went not one step but he thought every one he met came to take him, he got that night to *Greenwich* and lay there, telling the people of the house that he was to go down to *Gravesend,* that night he rose and walked about and knew not what to do, Conscience so flew in his face. [P. 6]

Understandably, his behavior began to raise suspicions, and these led to his arrest. Taken up in yet another alehouse, Savage acknowledged his crime and freely agreed to go home. There, "when his Master spake to him of it, he was not much affected at first, but after a little while burst out into many tears" (p. 7).

Like Strodtman, Savage came to a true knowledge of what he had done before he was hanged, and through the grace of God repented. Or so the ministers who comforted him in prison believed, for they had no doubt of his ultimate salvation. Thus the pamphlet they wrote with Savage's help – Mr. "H.B." had the story of the murder and Savage's attempt to flee "from his own mouth" (p. 7) – and from which I have so liberally been quoting, was offered as "a true relation" of his

from Capt. Charles Johnson, *Lives and Adventures of the Most Famous Highwaymen, Murderers, Street-Robbers, &c.* [1734]

THE SAVAGE Returning to HANNAH BLAY'S Lodging

"wicked life, and shameful-happy death."[7] The same phrases could equally well have been applied to Strodtman's own narrative. Even more than Savage, Strodtman managed to die according to the highest hagiographical standards of penitent murderers; and for this the public, according to Paul Lorrain – who called Strodtman's posthumously published papers of devotion "his last Charitable *Bequest*," and his "Last Legacy to the World" – should have felt itself most deeply in his debt. And perhaps the world did, after all, feel a sense of obligation to Strodtman beyond, of course, its duty to hang him as a murderer. We shall investigate this possibility in Part II of this book, after considering the case of Mary Edmondson.

Edmondson did not leave the world in her debt, indeed appears to have left it disappointed of its due. Unlike Strodtman or Savage, she would not conform to type. Even at the gallows she persisted in claiming to be innocent, saying to one of her relatives who had climbed into the cart to be with her, "Cousin, I am not guilty of it, as I must appear before the Almighty God in a few Minutes. . . . I would not trifle at this

Time, when I see Death before my Eyes." She blamed no one for "this shameful End" and asked forgiveness not only for herself but for those, too, who had helped convict her. She seemed confident of salvation and, saying "good People God bless you, pray for me," she told the executioner she was ready when he was. And then "she launched into Eternity," to become forever an enigma. Her body, delivered to the surgeons of St. Thomas's Hospital, was dissected and anatomized according to law; even then, no one appears to have discovered her secret spring.[8]

There are five separate accounts of Edmondson in the British Library, and not all tell the same story. The basic document is a record of her trial, taken in shorthand and published in the sessions papers.[9] It is a spare account of the testimony against her and of her attempt at a defense, told in dialogue that seems more a digest than a straight transcription of what was actually said. As she would not confess, and as there were no eyewitnesses to the crime, the prosecution's case had to be built on circumstantial evidence. But neither was there anything to support her story about the four men; indeed, it just did not seem possible that any four such men could have gotten into the house, using the route she claimed they had taken, and then have made their escape unseen by anyone but her. Moreover, the things they were supposed to have stolen had been found, shortly after the crime, hidden on the premises; as was also a blood-stained apron, by all indications hers. The jury took only five minutes to return its verdict and, within two days of her trial, Edmondson was hanged.

The two questions that lingered afterward were these: Had she done it? And if so, why had she denied it up until the very end? Only a negative answer to the first could provide a neat and convincing answer to the second, and of the four attempts at interpreting Edmondson that will concern us here, only one was so credulous as to come to this conclusion. Even her brother-in-law was unwilling to say out and out that she was innocent, though, to be sure, he was ready enough to contest the construction placed on her life and actions by the two pamphlets that aimed at filling out the bare details of her trial. We shall soon be considering the work of both Joseph Clarke, who was married to Edmondson's twin sister, and of a self-styled "Gentleman of the Law" who argued with unusual simplicity (but great good nature) that she was innocent. But first we ought to look at the two pamphlets that raised Clarke's ire: *A Genuine Narrative of the Trial and Condemnation of Mary Edmondson,* and *The Trial at Large, Behaviour, and Dying Declaration of Mary Edmondson.*

By themselves these two pamphlets would hardly warrant special attention. In them Edmondson seems only another instance of youth gone so far astray, despite the best efforts of parents and friends, as ultimately to commit murder. Though they tell slightly different versions of her story, and are different in manner and point of view, both take very much the same approach to their subject. Both are absolutely convinced of Edmondson's guilt, and both take liberties with the facts of her case to emphasize that guilt. At first glance the *Trial at Large,* which of the two is more concerned with her state of mind while in prison, seems the more sympathetic, complicated, and circumspect. The *Genuine Narrative,* more concerned with spelling out the incriminating details of Edmondson's behavior before the murder, seems the harsher of the two; it is simpler in its rendering of motive and event, and especially moralistic. These differences can easily be illustrated by comparing the two accounts on several of the points where they significantly overlap. Each differs in the description, for instance, that it gives of Edmondson's temperament. Where the *Trial at Large* is content to say that she "was naturally of a morose and of a haughty and stubborn Spirit" (p. 9), the *Genuine Narrative* dilates on her "somewhat passionate, resolute, and . . . masculine Spirit," going on to claim that in her parents' view she was "headstrong, self-willed, uncontroulable and unadviseable" (p. 3). By the time she was seventeen, according to the *Genuine Narrative,* "she could not bear to be rebuked," and "when this happened, once on a Time, from her Mother, on her being guilty of some great Crime, it threw her into such a Passion that she, catching up a Penknife which unluckily lay next her, violently made at her Mother, and stabbed her in the Belly, which Wound proved so deep and dangerous that it had like to have cost her her Life" (p. 4). The *Trial at Large* describes no such incident, though it does report that "it is said that she used her Mother very ill in the Country," going on to add, "but how true this is, we will not pretend to say, for we shall keep up strictly to the Truth in every Particular relating to this unfortunate young Woman" (p. 9).

On Mary's relationship with her aunt, the *Trial at Large* seems equally circumspect. Her aunt asked her up from the country, "intending to make some Provision for her," as Mary was an eligible young lady and "a Favourite of her late Husband." She and her aunt got along quite well until about six weeks before the murder, when Mary began to be disrespectful. One evening Mary wanted to go out but her aunt objected, saying that if she did not care to serve her perhaps she ought to take service in another family. Though Mary stayed home, from this time on she began to be "very careless and indifferent about the Household Affairs" (pp. 9–10). The *Genuine Narrative,* when it describes Mary's coming to live with her aunt, and how they came afterward to quarrel, is a good deal more circumstantial and dramatic. It manages

also, swelling to more than ten times the length of the equivalent section in the *Trial at Large,* to be more significant. That is, it is not only
more sententious but more elaborate in its description of incident and
motivation. Mary's aunt, imagining that her niece "was a towardly
young Woman, and would make her an agreeable Companion," invited
her to come down from Leeds by stagecoach, "and she would pay the
Charges thereof" (p. 5). (This is a much more generous aunt than the
one in the *Trial at Large,* where Edmondson travels by wagon, and
apparently pays her own way.) She would certainly have held her invitation back – and so, too, have saved some money – had she known
what her niece was really like. But such is "the natural Partiality of
Parents to their Offspring" that Mary's parents "concealed the Faults of
their Daughter, and particularly that most egregious one of all, the
attempt at stabbing her own Mother." Her parents had sense enough,
however, to caution Mary against "the inordinate and violent Sallies of
her Passion," and she, not wanting to lose the chance to go to London,
had promised to be better (p. 4). Once there, according to the *Genuine
Narrative,* Mary behaved well enough until her aunt scolded her for
staying out late one night during the Christmas holidays. It was after
this that Mary grew inattentive and only reluctantly obedient, and from
such "Perverseness," we are told, "a continual Quarrel ensued, so that
neither Parties [*sic*] could be easy one or the other." Not only did the
aunt suggest, finally, that her niece might find another service, but she
also told her (fatal error this) that "she had made her Will greatly in
Favour of her." Thus it was that Edmondson – whose soul had been
possessed "to a monstrous Degree" by the "Vice of Ingratitude,"
which "is an Evil, Youth in particular should avoid" – was first put
onto the idea of murdering her aunt (pp. 5–6).

From this pregnant observation the *Genuine Narrative* moves almost
immediately into a close description of the murder itself and the investigation that followed, pausing only to note as evidence of Mary's pre-
meditation that she had gone back behind the house a fortnight before
the murder "and made a Noise by throwing down the Washing Tubs,"
whereupon she "ran in and told her Aunt that four Men had broken
into the Yard" (p. 6). The aunt, in alarming the neighborhood, was
thus made to lay the groundwork for Mary's eventual alibi, or so we
are led to believe. The *Trial at Large* speaks with hardly the same
certainty. Though it notes that Mary, for some time before the murder,
"was frequently alarming her Aunt that Thieves broke in backwards,
and stole the Coals out of the Coal-Hole," as well as a new mop and
several other things, it does not follow her into the backyard to tell us
anything of washtubs being thrown down. In suggesting, however,
that Mary's aim was "purposely to amuse her Aunt with an Opinion of

being robb'd," the *Trial at Large* does purport to give something of her
thoughts: "The old Gentlewoman (thinks the Niece) will of Course tell
our Neighbours that Rogues have broke in Backwards, and robb'd
her; – and if I should murder her, for the Sake of her Money and
Effects, People will naturally conclude that Villains have done it, and I
shall not be suspected. – I'm to be plac'd out to Service, and so put from
her Sight, as I have offended her; – perhaps she may be perswaded to
alter her Will, and cut me off with a Shilling; – then shall I be a Beggar,
and despised by my Relations; so I'll take care of myself, &c." This
collection of clichés, avowedly a fiction, is nonetheless, according to the
Trial at Large, "an Inference that may justly be drawn," given the fact
that "every one of the least Penetration, will pronounce Mary Edmondson *guilty of the Murder of her Aunt*" (p. 10). This seems circumspection
itself, in comparison to the *Genuine Narrative,* which offers as its pièce
de résistance a blow-by-blow description of just how Mary managed to
cut her aunt's throat. It would serve no needful purpose to clutter the
text with yet another account of bloody murder. Suffice it to say that
every detail of Mary's movement before and after the act, up until the
time that the neighbors arrive to investigate, is given in slightly more
than three hundred words.[10] The *Trial at Large,* on the other hand,
merely supposes her guilt from the evidence introduced at the trial.

Even were it not for Clarke's refutation of both these accounts of
Edmondson and her crime, the trial record itself would be enough to
make us aware of the tendencies in each to distort the facts at hand, or
even frankly to invent them. As Clarke felt obliged to remind his
readers, "no confession could possibly be drawn from [Mary], even in
her last moments." Though he himself would not venture an opinion
on her guilt – "whether she was the cruel perpetrator of so horid and
heinous a crime . . . or whether innocent thereof, is a matter which at
present is only known to . . . God" – he felt sure that "every judicious
person" would look with "contempt and abhorrence" on those "who
presume to give as exact an account of the whole transaction of the 23d
of February last in the evening, as if they had been actually present, and
beheld the whole of it."[11] So much for the probity of the *Genuine
Narrative.* In venturing to describe the working of Mary's mind before
the murder, the *Trial at Large* could have seemed only slightly less
censurable to Clarke; but it is not this presumption that brings him to
comment. He finds it especially vexing that the *Trial at Large* gives "a
spurious account" of the testimony in court (p. 79). And indeed, with
all its apparent scrupulousness about keeping "strictly to the Truth," it
is observable that the *Trial at Large* has cooked up an even stronger case
against Mary than that which had actually been heard. To take just one
of the instances Clarke brings forward: The *Trial at Large* has a witness

declaring that Mary was wearing a checked apron just before the murder (the bloody apron found hidden in the washhouse was also checked), but in her testimony this witness could not in fact recall whether the apron in question was checked or not (see Clarke, *Refutation*, p. 7).

By far the most interesting part of Clarke's *Refutation*, however, is that which deals with the *Genuine Narrative* and its version of Mary's life up until her arrest. It is important in this connection to note that Clarke, despite his relation to Mary, seems relatively unbiased. In his discussion of the *Trial at Large,* for instance, he spends a good deal of time showing how deficient it generally is in point of detail, and not all the deficiencies of this kind that he brings to the readers' attention are favorable to Mary's defense. Thus at one point he faults the *Trial at Large* for omitting the testimony of one witness concerning "the two gates about 7 or 8 feet high, which the supposed murderers must have got over, or of the impossibility of their getting out any other way than by a little alley within 24 feet of the door in the same street" (p. 8). Clarke also shows his lack of bias by giving the last half of his pamphlet over (without comment) to several letters written by various clergymen who were sure of Mary's guilt, and concerned that she repent while she still had time. Given his relative lack of tendentiousness, then, Clarke's critique of the biographical details to be found in the *Genuine Narrative* (and, by implication, in the *Trial at Large* as well) seems more than credible. If Clarke is to be believed, a good deal of what the *Genuine Narrative* so confidently asserts about Mary's life, so much of which confirms its opinion of her guilt, and from which it so frequently departs in order to moralize, must rapidly melt away. Clarke denies that Mary ever quarreled with her aunt, or that her aunt ever threatened her with leaving. After coming down from Yorkshire, he says, Mary had stayed at various times with her aunt and with her sister, Clarke's wife. Then, going out to take service "in a very creditable family" but some difference arising (Clarke does not know what this was), Mary returned to her aunt's again, and at her aunt's invitation (pp. 6–7). Nor was Mary of a temper that was likely to quarrel. "From my own observation, and from what her father and mother told me when I was last in the country," Clarke feels he can "with the greatest confidence" assert, "there never was a child born who was more subject to her parents than she was; and," he goes on to add, "as to that (I can call it no other than) malicious paragraph of her catching up a penknife and stabbing her mother in the belly, it is intirely without foundation, and her father did absolutely clear her of that charge when in town" (p. 5).

With the advantage conferred by his privileged position, Clarke can give us far more accurately many more details of Mary's life than either of the pamphlets he attacks. Some of these details seem trivial – for instance, precisely where she was born and whether or not she went to a charity school – but others, it seems, could well have made for a more interesting narrative than those the two pamphlets chose to invent. For instance, there is Clarke's account of how it was that Mary came up to London. Needless to say, this was not "in consequence of her father and mother's discovering any *untoward or wicked dispositions* in her" but rather (and the truth would seem much more interesting than the scandal so meanly insinuated) because Mary was betrothed to a clergyman, a certain Mr. King. The date of their wedding being set ("the 17th day of May, 1759" as Clarke precises) and "her parents thinking her not so well qualified for a clergyman's wife as they could have desired," they suggested to her aunt, who was agreeable, that Mary return to London with her in order to acquire, either at the aunt's house or by the aunt's finding her "a good place elsewhere," what was needful for a clergyman's wife to know (p. 6.) What a superior story all this might have made in the fictionalizing hands of whoever wrote the *Genuine Narrative!* But it was Mary's fate, as it was James Hind's, to be otherwise used by the popular press.

Her guilt assumed despite her protestations of innocence, the public conception of her was molded by the same myth that shaped the cases of both Strodtman and Savage. But where Strodtman and Savage had consented to act the role assigned to them by society (as well as by their consciences – but conscience in their cases was nothing more than the arm of society), Mary would not. Mary, by all appearances, fell far short of what the occasion required. The writers of the *Genuine Narrative* and the *Trial at Large* appear to have been out to meet the unsatisfied needs of their readers' imaginations. Because Mary would not confess, it was up to them to provide her crime with plausible antecedents – thus their accounts of her character and motives – and to confirm with convincing details the supposition of her guilt – thus the blow-by-blow description of the murder, what went through her mind as she planned it, the "cooked" trial transcript. All that either of these two accounts lacks, of course, is Mary's endorsement.

But this, I would suggest, was a gross and troubling deficiency – no happy ending was possible without her confession and repentance – and so a good deal responsible for the distortions and inventions to be found in both the *Genuine Narrative* and the *Trial at Large*. It was only through fictions and quasi-fictions that these pamphlets could make the circumstances of the case add up to a plausible and significant whole. Although neither in the face of Clarke's challenge could have seemed very satisfactory (at least to a critical intelligence), only two alternatives to the conclusions they had reached were, after all, available; she was innocent, or she was inexplicable. And to a public wanting the assurance, for reasons I shall eventually advance, that Mary was guilty, confession or no, and her act comprehensible, neither of these alternatives could have seemed at all preferable.

Neither Clarke nor the Gentleman of the Law was able to explain so much so well as even the *Trial at Large* – to say nothing of the *Genuine Narrative,* which offered those interested in the case of Mary Edmondson not only more fiction but also, particle for particle, more significance. So far as Clarke could tell, only God could ever know whether Mary had done it or not and, if she had, why she had not confessed. The effect of his *Refutation* could only have been to multiply the ways in which she might possibly be understood. After clearing up the misrepresentations of the *Genuine Narrative* and the *Trial at Large* (without suggesting, we should note, that their conclusions are false), he goes on to reprint a letter from Mary in which she declares her absolute innocence, and then, as I've already mentioned, several letters from clergymen urging her to confess her guilt. These letters, both in their rhetoric and in the rhetorical formulas they exhort her to employ, seek to encapsulate Mary in much the same language that was used both on and by Strodtman, Savage, and so many others like them. The reader may accept the clergymen's point of view even though Mary did not, or, going on to the very end of Clarke's *Refutation,* he may find himself encouraged to come to his own conclusions about Mary's version of events. For there Clarke prints a plan of the house where the murder took place and its environs (almost, it seems, in anticipation of Agatha Christie), leaving his reader free to puzzle out for himself whether a person or persons unknown may have had, as well as she, opportunity to commit the crime. For the reader willing to follow him along so far, Clarke's *Refutation* could only have raised unanswerable doubts.

These doubts the "Gentleman of the Law" was more than willing to resolve, though in no way that could contribute to the public's sense of security or self-esteem. Had he been more convincing, his tract may have been more unsettling than Clarke's. For, according to him, the system of justice had gone terribly awry and society had on its hands the blood of a blameless girl. But the Gentleman of the Law is able to make only the most tenuous of cases. The *Trial at Large,* frankly unable to say why Mary has denied her guilt even "at the Gallows," is nonetheless willing to guess that her reticence had come from a sense of shame – she wanted at least "to convince her Father, and her other near Relations, that she was innocent" – and from a reluctance to make even worse (here, it claims, are her very own words) "the Scandal she had brought on her own honest Relations" (p. 11). But the Gentleman of the Law, preferring instead to take Mary more simply at her word, it being his opinion that "every Person ought to be believed when on the Brink of Eternity," chooses rather to argue that she indeed was innocent.[12] He points to her mild character (which she had, he assumes, because she came from Yorkshire), her apparent lack of remorse as well as motive, the inconclusiveness of the testimony against her, and the opportunity that others could have had to do the crime. His argument is surely too ingenuous to have seemed convincing. But, in conjunction with his other main point, it could well have made his readers feel at least some small uneasiness.

For the case against Mary was only a little less suppositious than the Gentleman's argument in her favor, and, as he pointed out to his readers, "it is no new Thing in England to see the Innocent suffer," an assertion "the Judge who tried Poll Edmondson, knows . . . to be true." He recalls the "too recent and affecting . . . Example" of "poor *Dick Coleman,*" who had been hanged some ten years before for an especially brutal rape and murder (pp. 24–25). Of Coleman's case the Gentleman of the Law makes only the merest mention, apparently thinking this to be pointed enough. He expected his readers would remember that Coleman had also been condemned on circumstantial evidence – and in the same court as Mary Edmondson – and that he too had gone to the gallows protesting his innocence and doubting not at all that he would soon see God. No doubt, too, the Gentleman of the Law expected his readers to remember that two years later Coleman had been cleared, sadly vindicating those who all along believed him innocent.[13] In linking Coleman's case with Edmondson's, and in contesting the verdict of a not infallible court, the Gentleman of the Law seems to have thought he was raising some rather troublesome points, for he was wary of legal retaliation. ("As the Author does not reckon himself liable to Punishment for uttering the real Sentiments of his Heart, flowing from cool and mature Deliberation," he writes, "and as he humbly thinks that the present Administration under the mildest and best of Kings will screen him from any Insult, so he shall speak with the greater Freedom and Candour" [pp. 3–4].)

No such retaliation ensued, so far as I can tell, and it is entirely possible that the Gentleman of the Law was overestimating the impact his pamphlet would have on those who had already come to as comfortable a conclusion as they could on the subject of Mary Edmondson's guilt. Yet, if in nothing else, and if only from our point of view, he did succeed along with Joseph Clarke in compounding the "Mystery" (as he called it) of Mary Edmondson (p. 24). For he and Clarke show that unless she could be explained as the *Genuine Narrative* and the *Trial at Large* presented her – a presentation that required at crucial points the support of fiction – then she could not, from an eighteenth-century point of view, be tolerably explained at all. In other words, he and Clarke suggest the terrible necessity of such fictions as those that inform the two pamphlets they attacked.

Even to us, murder of the sort for which Edmondson was hanged can seem, unexplained, the grossest obscenity. And so we too may be tempted to lay its disturbing details to rest, seeing from the superior vantage point of modern psychology, for instance, a case (not all that extraordinary) of psychotic homicide. As we are not limited to finding only rational motives for Mary's behaving as if she were entirely innocent – she may have sincerely believed she was and still have killed her aunt – we need not be troubled by the disparity between her generally mild temper (if indeed she had one) and the particular violence of the crime. That is, we might be tempted to write her off as (say) a schizophrenic, perhaps with paranoid tendencies – especially in view of some evidence that emerges from the trial transcript, not so far mentioned but really quite striking to the modern reader. It seems that in the course of searching the premises for clues the neighbors "took up the seat of the necessary house" and there found "a great quantity of coals, a mop, and a stone bottle," all of which Mary's aunt had reported stolen before she was murdered.[14] Where the *Trial at Large* had taken this piece of evidence to indicate that Edmondson had been planning her story of the four thieves for some time before the actual murder, the Gentleman of the Law saw no real harm in it, even were it to be assumed that she had put the missing objects there. Arguing for her basic honesty (as otherwise her denial of guilt could not seem sincere), the Gentleman of the Law points out that Mary had passed up the chance to steal money and goods of far greater value. That things were found hidden "in that improper Repository the Necessary House," he allows, "may strike at her Honesty, yet it cannot fix on her the Crime of Murder, otherwise more Girls than one two or three, thro' *London,* and *Westminster,* might be charged also" (p. 14); such petty household pilferage was common. So much, we might think with overweening confidence, for an eighteenth-century view of the potential significance of a given bit of human behavior. Surely, given the obvious inference that Edmondson was somehow psychotic, her mad squirreling away of all those apparently valueless objects – considering especially "that improper Repository" – could offer a valuable clue to understanding her case. Perhaps, with a bit more information, the murder could be traced back to psychosexual difficulties beginning about the age of one or two; and perhaps too it is significant that Mary was a twin, a fact seemingly of no importance to contemporary writers (least of all to Joseph Clarke, married as he was to Mary's alter ego).

As the reader has, I hope, already guessed, these last few sentences are meant as a caveat. Such glib psychologizing, objectionable for reasons quite aside from its cheapness and superficiality, can of course provide us with no more adequate a picture of Mary Edmondson than the specious fictions we find in the *Genuine Narrative* and the *Trial at Large*. The fact that Mary hid things in the necessary house, rather than anywhere else, can suggest nothing particular about her at all. Living quarters were cramped for people of her class in eighteenth-century London – the room in which Mary's aunt was found, the best room in the house, measured "not above 10 feet by 12" – and real privacy, it seems, was only to be found in the privy.[15] As anyone caring to get acquainted with the seamier side of eighteenth-century life comes rapidly to see, the necessary house figures extraordinarily often as the site of such secretive, and legally prosecutable, acts as sodomy, rape, abortion, and infanticide (the sessions papers are filled with such detail). And, as the excerpt from Pepys's *Diary* at the head of this chapter will indicate, the "house of office" was not uncommonly used as a hiding place for petty household thefts.

Like Strodtman and Hind, Mary Edmondson remains essentially opaque. All that we can know – and even this only provisionally – is how she appeared to her age, and the uneasiness she caused a brother-in-law, another man, and perhaps some few others who sought to explain her. Perhaps, too, we can guess at another uneasiness, and this is a more interesting one, the uneasiness that lies behind and begets the kind of myth that tried to order and make sense of her case. But such guessing, as I hope to have shown by the clumsiness of my foray into psychohistorical speculation, requires the extremest care. An effort to explain Mary Edmondson in terms, say, of how she may have been toilet-trained (but surely that's too silly) would show not only one's tendency to think in terms of the myths of his own time but also the danger that lies in wait for *any* effort grounded in modern patterns of thought (this included) to re-create the psychic realities of the past.

PART II

Enucleating the truth: the criminal as sinner turned saint

═══════════

Since thou are to die for the evil thou hast committed, endeavour to do good before thy Death. . . . And a principal inducement hereunto would it be, if you would make publick to the world, your carriage from your Cradle to your Death. . . . [B]y your ingenious Confession . . . satisfie the world that are yet unsatisfied.

Blood Washed Away by Tears of Repentance (1657),
pp. [xii–xiv]

Under a sense of that Horrid and Hellish Sin of Murther, which I lately committed, I desire to leave to the World this following Treatise. First, the Cause of my Provocation: Secondly, the manner in brief of the Murther: And thirdly, my hearty and unfeigned sorrow for my Offence, which I hope may stand as a Monument to succeeding Ages.

Mary Hobry [supposedly], A Cabinet of Grief
(1688), p. 1

I have now done with the Introduction to this tragick and dismal story, having unravelled as many of those, almost occult causes, by which being first propagated, it since hath been made horridly publick, as civillity or necessity in enucleating the truth requires.

The Unhappy Marksman (1659), p. 10

New, new, new, and true; is now adayes (to ordinary Readers) an authentication sufficient, for Relations of this or the like nature. But Reader it is the Cry of Blood, of Blood! Therefore more Seriousness becomes our pen: in the perusal of this Relation, thou shalt in a chain of dependencies read the Truth, the whole Truth, and nothing but the Truth.

A Full and the Truest Narrative of the Most Horrid,
Barbarous and Unparalleled Murder (1657), pp. [iii–iv]

Nor do we publish [the perfect Narrative of this deplorable Fact] to gratifie their liquorish Fancies, who delight in hearing strange stories.

The Bloody Murtherer (1672), p. 2

Our analysis of how the popular literature of crime provided appropriate (and useful) versions of criminals and their crimes will start with the myth that shaped and so made sense of familiar murder. Its tightness of form and narrowness of content make it more susceptible to close analysis than the other, looser, less "serious" myth, and against its background we shall see and understand that other myth more easily. Why, to use the terminology of our title epigraph, was it both "necessary" and "civil" (polity as well as politeness figures here) to "enucleate" the truth about criminals like Strodtman and Edmondson? Murderers were not the only criminals pressured to make a clean breast of it, to humble themselves before the public and die on the scaffold as cheerful Christians, nor, as the prison chaplains' accounts make clear, were they the only criminals who offered up appropriate dying behaviors. But only murderers, once made into saved sinners, stayed such. If thieves were remembered at all, they tended to be absorbed over time into the other myth, to be remade, yet again, into rogues of one or another kind.

Murder is of course far more fearsome than theft and in many ways far more problematic. But this can hardly account for the special attention given murderers in seventeenth- and eighteenth-century England, especially as the homicide rate was not particularly high compared to certain current jurisdictions, and apparently declining.[1] From a modern standpoint it might seem enough to say that, as murder is the ultimate act of aggression, familiar murder is that act directed against the ultimate target: if not Father or Mother, then against some real or symbolic sibling. The celebrity of crimes like Strodtman's and Edmondson's, then, might seem to indicate readers wanting to "work out" dark and highly charged fantasies. Certainly the most prominent feature of many murderers' biographies (at least to the modern reader) invites explanation in these terms. Thus their tendency to describe the crime with an almost dreamlike precision, each action broken up into its separate movements, each movement split into its component gestures, the absorption with apparently irrelevant details, the passage of time slowed and made ponderous – all this might easily be seen as a means of enhancing (possibly) the secret delectations of readers nursing (as do we all) private fantasies of revenge.

But there are two main problems with such an explanation. It tells us nothing specific about the period, relying as it does on a timeless psychology, and it overlooks all but a very small part of most murder accounts. For if the kernel of violence in each of these narratives did prompt fantasies of vengeance against one's nearest and least dear, it ought also to be noted these fantasies are given very little room to breathe. The weight of deliberations laid over them, the tight structure of the myth itself, indicate more a need to suppress such fantasies than to express them. The censorship mechanism seems to have been extremely busy here, and ought not to be ignored. How fruitful can it be, in any case, to say that readers of the popular literature of crime harbored urges to do violence against their families (extended or otherwise)? This is merely to confirm that human psychology then and now has, at base, much in common; we have our fantasies and they their "liquorish Fancies." It is far more interesting to investigate the structures of thought that rise variously above that base, insulating and sometimes protecting against it. People in the seventeenth and eighteenth centuries were different from us in the furnishing of (as they might say) their higher faculties, and though this does not mean their processes of reasoning and imagining were necessarily different, it does mean they reasoned and imagined with different materials along different lines. Their urge to do vicarious violence is far less important than the objects on which it was centered and, especially, the ways in which it was shaped and controlled.

These strictures are prompted in part by the only other writer I know to have considered eighteenth-century criminal biography as myth. Though ingenious and plausible, his argument is not, I think, finally very useful. In a criminal like Thomas Savage, whom he styles a "revolted apprentice," John J. Richetti finds an embodiment of "furtive and unnatural longings for disruptive revolt." Along with other criminals whose "sin" is "individualism," the revolted apprentice strikes out "against social and moral restraints, against any sort of control from an external source. His drive is towards self-determination, primarily and overtly economic, but inescapably spiritual and ideological as well. . . . Providence, the concept that invokes the hierarchical orders which support eighteenth-century life from the arrangement of the cosmos to the distribution of wealth among the social classes is being challenged and defied." Thus, along with other criminals – and one may wonder whether the analysis here gets a bit too existential, too modern – the revolted apprentice figures forth "the secular energies of the age which chafe under the traditional system of social and moral limitations and their religious foundations." He is, Richetti insists, "both hero and anti-hero to his eighteenth-century audience." Antihero, and ultimately worse, because in his myth we see mirrored "the ideological tension between the new secular world of action and freedom and the old religious values of passivity and submission," a tension that must finally be resolved in favor of the latter. For, as Richetti puts it, the "latent social aggression" aroused and satisfied in the course of reading about the exploits of the criminal "is, at the same time, a source of guilt and anxiety which must be severely and deservedly punished." When the criminal's revolt achieves proportions that seem "monstrous" (to the ruling classes, one would think, but Richetti does not say), "popular ideology" reacts by "undercutting [its] entire validity." The criminal is not only hanged for his crimes but made to seem a sinner, the elation raised by the vicarious experience of his career borne down by the sobering weight of religious belief. Ultimately then a scapegoat, the criminal is sacrificed so that honest men might have their furtive pleasures and, presumably, be purged of them.[2]

Richetti's model of the reader's experience with criminal biography, to judge from the range of his evidence, seems based for the most part on Smith's *Lives of the Highwaymen*. Even within that context, as we shall see, it is a model that requires extensive modification. As far as the lives of murderers are concerned – and Smith is notably uninterested in murderers per se – it is basically inappropriate. Perhaps because of his great reliance on Smith, Richetti has failed to see that the popular literature of crime included more than one mode of narrative. It is not just that the crimes of Savage and the Golden Farmer are qualitatively different (Richetti quotes from and comments on Smith's lives of each) but that the narratives that present these types are also different, structurally as well as qualitatively. Quite unlike the bold and entertaining exploits of the highwayman, the crime of the familiar murderer – who is not always an apprentice – is made from the first to raise disgust and fear. We have already noted how abruptly and soon we are plunged into the sordid details of Savage's crime in *A Murderer Punished and Pardoned;* such a narrative seems designed to keep the reader from identifying with the criminal until, having committed his crime, the criminal begins to feel guilt. Strodtman's first-person account builds rather more slowly to the description of the murder he commits, but not in any way that might encourage readers to give sway to "furtive longings." Nor do the pamphlets on Mary Edmondson seem very much concerned with titillating the antisocial urges of their readers. The fact is that most accounts of familiar murder give by far the greatest part of their attention not to the murder itself but to the events leading up to it, the murderer's efforts to avoid suspicion, the manner of his being found out, his behavior in prison, and the way in which he meets his death.[3] In all this the mythologizing of the familiar murderer is concerned to bring out the "real facts" of his case and to find appropriate and plausible motives, or at least antecedents, for his crime. Ideally, it would like to record his confession, contrition, repentance, conversion, and, finally, that he made of the gallows a pulpit.[4] These are the most visible elements of the myth, and it is these that require explaining. The treatment of the highwayman in the popular literature of crime is not at all comparable.

Nor does it seem reasonable to suppose that the familiar murderer's rebellion against social and religious authority could have seemed attractive, even at a deep level, to the audience he presumably reached. Guessing what went on in the minds of readers long dead is hazardous, and all the more so when we cannot know just who those readers were. Yet surely the question of who they were, or could have been, should make some difference. In certain, more "sophisticated" circles, it would seem, criminals' confessions could be read for amusement. In 1708 John Mawgridge refused to give the Newgate ordinary "any private Satisfaction, as to his Life and Conversation, tho' often importun'd," because "he had not a Mind to be the Sport and Ridicule of Vain idle Fellows in *Coffee-Houses;* who only laugh at unfortunate dying Men." The idea that Sabbath-breaking was the first treacherous step toward crime, repeated so often in criminal biographies, was especially susceptible to ridicule. It might also be mentioned that George Barnwell's story was thought at first too ludicrously low to serve as the basis of a tragedy.[5]

For apprentices and others who chafed under social discipline the spectacle of former colleagues turned renegade may have had some romantic appeal. But for economic reasons alone it is unlikely that they, or anyone else of limited means, could have provided a large market for criminal lives. Until approximately 1720, the ordinary's *Accounts* generally sold for twopence and apparently could be read for a penny, but the more elaborate instances of criminal biography cost significantly more. Pamphlet lives of individual criminals were priced at sixpence to a shilling, depending on their length, and the larger collections were proportionately more expensive. Volume 3 of Smith's *Highwaymen* cost half a crown, and *Compleat Tryals* ten shillings the set. At a time when two shillings a day was the standard wage for a casual laborer and apprentices got little remuneration if any, none of these publications could be considered cheap. The Johnson's *Highwaymen* of 1734, it is true, was published in parts at twopence the sheet, which would have put it within reach of a broad audience, but the book itself, with its folio format and full-page engravings, bespeaks a clientele of the "middling" sort; it is a book that cries out for the invention of the coffee table. It would seem, then, that tradesmen, artisans, merchants, lower-ranking professionals (to say nothing of people of higher means) made up the largest part of the market for the popular literature of crime. Such an audience would not seem likely to have identified, even unconsciously, with the crimes of "revolted apprentices." Those who were not masters of apprentices themselves would have lived with servants (perhaps no more than one or two) on rather an intimate basis, and the prospect of servants going wrong in the middle of the night would have been as disquieting for them as it was for Pepys.[6]

It might perhaps be argued that "revolted apprentices" offered an opportunity for "identification with the aggressor"; that is, the popular audience might have found pleasure in a vicarious living out of acts they feared, rather a common defense mechanism. But this is not a convincing argument. It hardly seems likely that even an audience with a minimum amount of property and social standing would have relished the vision of murderers overthrowing people like themselves, and all that such people represented – even if only temporarily, furtively, and as a bit of psychic homeopathy. Theirs was not a complacent society, and one does not have to look far into it to see signs of a deep-felt malaise. But in the mythic interpretation of familiar murder, at least, there is no clear suggestion of any ambivalence about the worth of that society, its values, or the legitimacy of its authority. The familiar murderer raised troublesome questions for his society, but he never threatened – as the highwayman often did – to become a social critic.

To judge from the way the murderer's "revolt" was treated in the popular press, then, it was not something to be enjoyed (except possibly for the briefest, most buried moment) but rather something to be repressed, explained, transformed. Perhaps some of this can be explained by the fact that murder had, as it must always have, a political dimension. One of the most popular books in the period called it an act of "War" against "Sovereign *Kings* and *Princes*" on the grounds that it deprived them of subjects. Or, as someone taking a broader view of the polity wrote, "this heinous sin tends not barely (in common with other Offences) to make a *Breach upon,* but even strikes at the very *Dissolution of* Society." Familiar murder was of course especially "hainous and odious," homicide being "so much more vile, by how much . . . nearer bound in any linke or bond" the victim was "to him that doth this wrong; as a brother the brother, a child the father, the wife the husband and such like." Or, as the author of *Remarkable Criminals* pointed out, it was a good deal more "enormous" and "shocking" to kill "him or her to whom we owe a civil or natural obligation" than to murder a stranger or casual acquaintance. The law recognized this distinction by providing special penalties for what it called "petit treason." This was "a Crime where One out of Malice Taketh away the Life of a Subject, To whom He oweth a Special Obedience." In practice, it meant that servants who murdered their masters, or wives their husbands, were drawn to the place of execution on a sledge instead of the usual cart. Once there, if men, they were hanged like all other murderers. Women, however, were burned at the stake.[7]

Just as high treason involved a "violation of the confidence which the king presupposes in his subjects," petit treason was a crime that violated the special trust of "the husband in his wife, and the master in his servants." The basic social unit stood as a microcosm of the whole, or, to speak more in keeping with the fourteenth-century origin of the crime, petit treason was contumacy at the domestic level carried to the extremest act of violence. If this seems too feudal a concept to have operated with much effect in the eighteenth century, consider the fact that at least fourteen women were burned for petit treason in the eighteen years from 1722 to 1739, and that such punishments were inflicted as late as 1750, 1752, 1763, 1767, and 1773.[8] Even in cases where petit treason was not specifically invoked, the courts took special cognizance of murders involving betrayals of trust. In 1741 James Hall, who had murdered his master, was executed two days before all the other criminals sentenced to die that session. He was drawn on a hurdle from Newgate to the end of Katherine Street in the Strand, so that he might be hanged as close to the scene of his crime as conveniently possible. It took about an hour to bring him there from Newgate, but this was brief compared to the time spent bringing John Swan and Elizabeth Jeffryes to their place of execution eleven years later. For murdering her uncle and his master they were dragged by sledge from Chelmsford, where they had been tried, to Epping Forest, so they might also be hanged near the scene of their crime. The journey took from five in the morning until two in the afternoon, and then of course the hanging still had to be done; the authorities, however, seem not to have minded.[9]

Although nothing like the same physical energy was put into the punishment of Savage, Strodtman, and Edmondson, something like the same notion of contumacy would have been implicit in their crimes. In Edmondson's case, the mere existence of a formal contract articling her in service to her aunt might have made all the difference, as far as the law was concerned.[10] Perhaps it was the family's special importance as the basic political unit, as well as the basic unit of production, that made familiar murder so special a crime. Perhaps, like so many of the conduct books of the period, the pamphlets describing such murders were meant to urge "the relative duties," those mutual obligations felt to obtain between parents and children, servants and masters, wives and husbands. It is interesting that Defoe dwelt on the case of a woman increasingly obsessed with the idea of murdering her husband when, in just such a conduct book, he wanted to show an extreme case of wifely rebellion. It is also possible, if Lawrence Stone is correct in seeing this as a period marked by the rise of "affective individualism," that the

Engrav'd for the Tyburn Chronicle.

from *The Tyburn Chronicle* [1768]

James Hall Murdering his Master
Mr. Penny of Clements Inn.

great fascination with familiar murder is an expression of a growing concern with deep familial ties.[11]

But having said so much about the political significance of familiar murder, we are really no closer to understanding the particular features of the myth it evoked. How were the bare, ugly, and anarchic facts of the crime itself transformed by that myth into something less threatening and more manageable? Certainly few murders in the period seemed to have had explicit political significance.[12] This is all the more remarkable, considering the political questions that often, and most provokingly, were made to hover about the exploits of thieves. Highwaymen frequently complain about social inequities, but familiar murderers never claim to have acted from anything more than a personal grudge. The assumption that the "real" foundation, then, of the interest in familiar murder was political (even if true) seems hardly more helpful than the notion that it all can be explained by a taste for vicarious aggression. If we are to understand how this myth worked, down to the specific functions of each of its chief elements, we shall have to explore the superstructure of ideas that – whatever their foundation –

from *The Tyburn Chronicle* [1768]

Catherine Hayes burnt at Tyburn for the
murder of her husband on the First of March 1725-6

strove to contain and transform the thing it addressed. These ideas are
not without political relevance, and they take into account that *principium laesum* later called the id, but they are in the main religious and
moral, and were so of necessity. It was not the crime itself, said a
would-be solacer of one murderer's soul, "the act is not all, though
bloody. . . . The Cause is worse than the Effect."[13] Though the act
itself could not be undone, what was taken to be its source could be
addressed, manipulated, and remade. What the period took to be the
cause and cure of crime, however, were very different from any notions
of our own.

Chapter 3

In the absence of adequate causes: efforts at an etiology of crime

In the politic, as in the natural body, no disorders ever spring up without a cause . . . and such causes must be adequate to the effects which they produce.
Henry Fielding, Providence in Murder (1752), p. 2

It may be now expected that I should give some account what were the Reasons and Motives that instigated me to this Crime. But alas! when I consider the slender Inducements I had thereunto, I must only clap my Hand upon my Breast, and confess it was . . . my own vile and Corrupted Heart.
Edmund Kirk, Dying Advice (1684)

One Sin wilfully committed easily draws on another, and that more; and a Man cannot tell when or where to stop, till it end at last in a sad and shameful Death.
[N.B.], Compleat Tryals (1718, 1721), 3:36

The nature of Malefactors is so amply known, I need not much inlarge upon the subject; for why, they are most of them men of leud Conversations . . . who first most commonly begin with Crimes of a smaller note, and by degrees emboldened in the cursed Trade, they trample upon fear and stifle all remorse; a sympathy so frequently observed in their insolent behaviours, who often have been known, when in their Infancy, to scoff at Admonitions, and make a jest of Piety, but this is only when they are free and unrestrained, roving to and fro. . . . when they are shackled by Justice, and the ends of all their courses come before their Eyes, then they are of other minds.
Execution of 11 Prisoners (1679), pp. 3–4

If once a man indulges himself in murder, very soon he comes to think little of robbing, and from robbing he comes next to drinking and Sabbath-breaking, and from that to incivility and procrastination.
Thomas De Quincey, "On Murder Considered as One of the Fine Arts" (1839), in De Quincey's Collected Writings, ed. David Masson, 13:56

In all cultures, it seems, murder demands a response that extends beyond the workings of mere social and political institutions. Malinowski has written about the Trobriand Islanders' elaborate and ritualized reactions to cases of suspected homicide, but one can cite examples closer to home.[1] In modern Western societies, criminals are caught, tried, and dealt with by the police, the courts, and the prisons (political institutions) under the law (a social institution). But even in cases less exacerbating than murder, this is not the full extent of the cultural response. "Somebody we know gets into trouble," writes a British criminologist, "and at once people remember that his father was once in trouble with the police when he was a boy, or that there was a cousin who went bankrupt, an aunt who was divorced, or a grandfather who got merrily drunk from time to time." Such is the effect of the common belief (in Britain at least) that "crime is 'in the blood.' " Obviously, this writer goes on to point out, such a belief is supported not by the actual evidence but by "our own emotions and needs": "it is our very similarity to the criminal we are trying to deny by portraying him as essentially someone from another world – or at least another family." This very same impulse to differentiate between ourselves and the criminal, he adds, can be expressed in other ways, for instance by blaming crime "all upon the residents of the delinquency areas, 'Them,' the disreputable slum dwellers, or the spendthrift residents of council houses."[2]

Behind both ideas, that criminal tendencies are inherited or that there is a criminal class, is the same denial mechanism, a mechanism that seems all the more obvious because both ideas are now in disfavor. Other, more respectable theories of crime, however, can seem similarly motivated – at least when they come into use on a popular level. Thus the notion that the criminal is "sick," and that this sickness is traceable to his having been "disadvantaged" socially or psychologically, is not without its comforts for the "healthy" majority. It is a notion, quite obviously, that shapes to a large extent the coverage of crime in the American press. The more heinous the criminal's act, the more fascinatingly repugnant his crime, the more doggedly journalists look into his background. Often not even waiting for the courts to find him guilty, they search out the distinctive characteristics of what criminologists call (nowadays wryly) *homo criminalis*. The fifth-grade teacher of the sex murderer or political assassin will recall that he stuttered, seemed withdrawn, had difficulty reading, perhaps even that she recommended he see the school psychologist but somehow nothing came of it. It may be found that his parents were divorced when he was very young or that his mother never married. And while the neighbors will point out that he was such a nice, quiet young man, so kind and considerate to his mother, the suspicions of those of us who live in a post-Freudian world (by now practically everyone who is literate and many who are not) will inevitably be aroused. There may be hints that his mother, a hopeless neurotic, put intolerable pressures on him all his life, that he made the mistake of marrying a woman like her, and that there were even, perhaps, grave inadequacies in the marriage bed. (This last may seem unlikely, but I seem to remember Lee Harvey Oswald's wife saying as much in *Life* magazine – or was it his mother?) And so on: He was a loner, never had a job he was good at, drifted around the country, had peculiar ideas, collected guns. We are all very familiar with the pattern.

It is not a pattern – of course – to be found in the late seventeenth and early eighteenth centuries. No surprise in that: The period was for the most part innocent of abnormal psychology. But what is surprising, at least on first encounter, is that nothing in the popular literature of crime performed an equivalent function. Whenever the question of the criminal's nature and motives arose, it was not his essential difference from the law-abiding majority that tended to be emphasized but his essential similarity. The root cause of crime, one reads again and again, is human depravity. And as all men are equally tainted from birth by original sin, criminals are not different in kind from other people, only in degree. Anyone might become a criminal. The wonder, then, was not that crime was so prevalent but that it was not universal. Given the scope of human depravity, a lot more of it ought to be happening. Only occasionally does the popular literature of crime suggest that a particular person was driven to murder or steal out of madness or necessity, and such suggestions do little to mitigate its insistence on human depravity.

The severity of this point of view might seem disingenuous on more than one account. The idea that we are all depraved makes useful social propaganda; at the very least it is a way of keeping the young and impressionable in line. In regular doses, such propaganda may also have worked prophylactically; perhaps readers of the popular literature of crime could only really feel free to enjoy themselves if, as they took their naughty pleasures, they were provided the protection of some slightly discomfiting edification. But we ought not to be too cynical, too ready to see the writers of criminal lives as serving the repressive (and prurient) interests of a society that, as it was well on its way to being middle class, must have had (shouldn't we think?) all the usual bourgeois hangups. For, whatever else their motives in arguing that the root cause of crime was the inherent depravity of human nature, such writers were trying to place the phenomenon of crime within a context where – given the limits of what they knew of human psychology and were able to see, and admit, about the nature of their society – it could be made into tolerable sense. That this context was religious was largely a matter of necessity; for all its growing obsolescence, there was simply no other scheme of looking at things with so much explanatory power.

In the late seventeenth and early eighteenth centuries the causes of crime were – or at least were made to seem – as obscure and anomalous as (how to find an appropriate analogy?) the causes of cancer now. Nowhere is the popular literature of crime able to offer more than a partial and selective account of why it was that certain men among the rest (for all men potentially were criminals) had actually broken the law and so come to forfeit their lives. This is not to say there was no inclination to search for causes; for every effect, the age was sure, there had to be a cause. The problem was that particular causes could not always be found for particular crimes – causes, that is (and this was a requirement increasingly in vogue), that declared themselves palpably to human observation and reason. It was understood that criminals differed from ordinary people in their want of feeling or understanding, or in the desperation forced on them by necessity. Curiously, however, the popular literature of crime rarely deals with extremes of either case, ignoring madmen almost entirely and regularly discounting the claims of those who said they robbed or murdered only to save their own lives. Economic necessity, or more generally poverty, did not in any case seem in itself a sufficient cause for crime. Though would-be social reformers like Fielding could argue that "an effectual provision for the poor" would "amend their morals" and so reduce crime, it was nonetheless observable that not all criminals were poor. Nor, as Fielding himself pointed out, did most poor people steal.[3] Generally, so far as published opinion was concerned, the fact that a criminal was poor was nothing more than an index to the weakness of his character. "Idleness brings a Man to Poverty," one assize sermon declares, "and Poverty maketh him to disturb the Peace by Murders and Robberies."[4]

The crucial thing about criminals, then, was not that they were driven by need or insanity, but set adrift by a want of feeling and understanding.[5] How else could they have disregarded the fearsome penalty the law so often imposed? As an anonymous writer pointed out at the turn of the century, criminals took no notice of "the great care of Magistrates of this great and Populous City, in putting the Laws in Execution against Fellons," or of "the Terrible Examples of Justice, almost every Month of the Year." Or, as another writer put it a few years later: "Notwithstanding the daily Warnings given by Persons that have come to untimely Ends, for their Cruel Murders, &c, their [sic] still remains most unaccountable Wretches among us, who act worse than the Brute Beasts."[6] Calling criminals "beasts" did not make them any the less "unaccountable," but it could serve to distract attention from the all-important and well-nigh unanswerable question: Why should some men lack the feeling and understanding that in others were sufficient, at least, to keep them from the gallows? To what could the mental and emotional incapacities of criminals be traced?[7]

In some cases, it was possible to point to heredity. Thus William Barton, a highwayman hanged in 1721, "seemed to have inherited a sort of hereditary wildness and inconstancy, his father having been always of a restless temper and addicted to every species of wickedness."[8] Occasionally, too, there is a suggestion along Lockean lines that a criminal's character may have been malformed by an especially brutal childhood or an improper education. "There cannot be a greater misfortune," begins an account of Captain John Stanley, a notorious bully who slashed his mistress to death in 1722, "than to want education, except it be the having of a bad one." Comparing "the minds of young persons" to "paper on which we may write whatever we may think fit," but which, "once blurred and blotted with improper characters" resists the inscription of "proper sentiments," this writer traces the origins of Stanley's crime back to his boyhood when he was initiated into "cruelty and blood." Stanley was only five years old when his father, a soldier, began to train him in the use of a sword, "pricking him himself and encouraging other officers to play with him in the same manner, so that his boy, as old Stanley phrased it might never be afraid of a point." By the time he was old enough to accompany his father on campaign, young Stanley had acquired "so savage a temper" that he "delighted in nothing so much as trampling on the dead carcasses in the fields after an engagement." This "wretched method of bringing up a child," the reader is assured, was "highly likely to produce the sad end he came to."[9]

Similar efforts to ground the etiology of crime on specific material conditions are rather rare. I have come across only a few instances where criminal behavior is linked to inherited characteristics, and only two or three where, in any elaborate way, it is traced to the cumulative effects of an unhappy childhood. Perhaps the most sophisticated of all such efforts is an anonymous writer's pamphlet on the "Suffolk Parricide." This is worth examining in some detail because, insofar as it defines the outer limits of rational investigation into the causes of a specific instance of criminal behavior (and I'm not speaking only of murder), it throws into sharp relief the general inability of the period to produce anything like an adequate etiology of crime.

Late one night in 1740 in a small town in Suffolk, Charles Drew knocked at the door of his father's house and then, when the old man answered, shot him point-blank in front of a witness. Given the family's local prominence, and especially Drew's persistent denials of guilt, the case attracted considerable attention. How could Drew commit so terrible a crime, insist he hadn't, and expect to go unpunished? It

seemed significant that he had been "brought up in a boorish ignorance" entirely unsuitable to his station in life. Though he gave the
appearance of a gentleman – "his Person was fine and his Parts tolerable" – he had none of a gentleman's breeding and, "for want of Culti-
vating," had in fact become "dull and senseless." So far none of this is
extraordinary. What sets it apart, however, is the writer's tendency to
probe for clues to the psychic origins of the crime. Looking further into
the evidence at hand than other writers would (or did), he is, for one
thing, not content to focus only on the criminal himself. "In order to
form a better Idea of the Son," he points out, the reader must know
something of "the Father . . . an Attorney of great Practice . . . but a
Man of an unhappy Temper, and possessed of so much Severity, that it
even amounted to Brutality." This information is given not so much to
explain the immediate motive for the crime as to illuminate the criminal's background, which is certainly peculiar.

When Charles was born, we read, the elder Drew was at first over-
joyed. Charles was the first and only son in a family of five daughters.
But then the elder Drew began to believe that Charles was not really his
son, and separated from his wife. Though he never consented to see her
again he did, however, continue to visit her house to dine with the
children, all five daughters and Charles. But then the elder Drew was
an odd sort anyway, a man who even before the breakup of his marriage would "sit whole Days" and "never converse" with his family,
"nor so much as suffer any of them to speak to him unless to answer
any Question which he should think proper to propose to them."
Given the failure of his parents' marriage, Charles received "no Education: the Father never troubled his Head about him, and his Mother was
as regardless, so that he was bred up in a rough Manner, and among
Persons in the lowest Class of Life." Not only did he not become a
gentleman, but, as he "increased in Years, the wicked Dispositions
which he had acquired increased with him." Finally

> he became of so sordid perverse a Temper that all Men conjec-
> tured Some ill End must be the Consequence of his Proceedings;
> nay, his own Father (whom he hath since so inhumanly mur-
> dered) prognosticated but a few Months ago from some Observa-
> tions which he had made in his Behaviour that his Son *Charles
> would not dye in his Bed:* The old Gentlemans Prognostication
> proved fatal to him tho' at that time he little expected that he
> himself should be the Occasion of it's [*sic*] proving true; yet could
> he have considered rightly, what else could he expect?

Denied an education, and falling in with "a Company of Smugglers
and Poachers, a Herd of mean People of little or no Understanding, but

from *The Suffolk Parricide* [1740]

Charles Drew shooting his Father

of Resolution enough to perpetrate the most daring Villanies," Charles Drew "went on from one Degree to another till he arrived at this last fatal Pitch." The crime itself is attributed to the concurrence of two motives, one longstanding and the other a precipitant. For a long time Charles had resented the fact that his father allowed him only two hundred pounds a year, believing that he needed more to live like a proper gentleman. Rather more recently, or so he claimed, he had begun to suspect that his father was planning to divorce his mother in order to remarry and beget a new heir. As his father's divorce suit would very likely have been based on Charles's presumptive bastardy, he risked winding up with nothing at all. And so, taking heart from his friends' oft-reiterated assurances that shooting his father would be no worse than shooting "a *Cat,* or a *Dog,*" he decided to do him in.[10]

I have not found a more complete account of how a given set of circumstances can combine to make a man a criminal. *The Suffolk Parricide* shows how Drew's character was shaped along special lines by experiences that few people share, and how that character, so shaped, was in more than one way the source of his crime. For as long as Drew lived as badly as he did, his father was not likely to increase his allowance; and, too, given his character, it is possible that his fear of being disinherited had some foundation (if only in a guilt-induced paranoia). But, as I have said, *The Suffolk Parricide* is rare; only one or two other biographies of actual criminals are able to go as far in developing an etiology for the crimes they describe. It is important to specify "actual" here, because a different situation obtains in the literature of the period.[11] Outside the realm of the overtly fictive, however, there seems to have been no small resistance to the idea that criminals are made, not born.

Perhaps part of the reason was that just too many criminals appearing in the popular literature of crime came from decent and respectable families, had been brought up as well as could be expected and given what seemed entirely suitable educations. Thus, though the author of *Remarkable Criminals* was willing to admit that the "want of education hath brought many who might otherwise have done very well in the world to a miserable end," still he felt obliged to point out that "the best education and instruction are often of no effect to stubborn and corrupt minds." Sometimes he tries to explain the existence of such minds, but with no notable success; all he can do is point, with a good deal of pseudoprofundity, to "the various dispositions of men." It is these that cause the "frequent differences in their progress, either in virtue or vice; some being disposed to cultivate this or that branch of their duty with peculiar diligence, and others, again, plunging themselves in some immoralities they have no taste for." More typically, however, he is content to lapse back into a general condemnation of human nature, the task of trying to sort it out apparently beyond him. "Such is the present depravity of human nature," he says in one of his darker moods, "that we have sometimes instances of infant criminals and children meriting death by their crimes before they know or can be expected to know how to do anything to live."[12] This is the writer, we ought to remember, who would like to think of children's minds as blank sheets of paper on which we can write what we will. Perhaps it is the incompatibility of this idea with the notion that human nature is inherently depraved that makes him hedge a bit and speak of its *present* depravity—as if the corruptions of heart and mind that concern him were a special condition produced by circumstances operating now, and not from the beginning of time or necessarily into the future.

The author of *Remarkable Criminals* appears to be caught in the middle of an intellectual revolution, and that can hardly have been comfortable. The forepart of his thinking moves with the new age of Lockean empiricism, but the hinder part, perplexed as it is by the difficulty of establishing a clear and coherent etiology of crime after the new fashion of thinking, continues to drag in the past. To the question of why some people are criminals and others are not, he can finally offer no more adequate an answer than this: "such is the frailty of human nature that neither the best examples nor the most liberal education can warrant an honest life, or secure to the most careful parents the certainty of their children not becoming a disgrace to them, either in their lives or by their deaths."[13] And in this he is entirely typical of his age.

The fact was that some criminals, as some still are today, were simply inexplicable in terms of what was known or could be known of their formative years and previous behavior. But there was more to the problem than this, for despite the efforts of writers like the author of *Remarkable Criminals* the popular literature of crime was not always interested in explaining its criminals away. Christopher Slaughterford, for instance, hanged at Guildford in 1709, had been born to "very Honest and Reputable Parents." His father was "a Farmer of considerable Subsistance [*sic*]," and he, brought up within "the Principles of the Church of England," had been given an "Education suitable to his Birth and Qualification." "Being no way given to Swearing or Drunkeness, Vices too common to Youth in this degenerate Age," he was "look'd upon to be a hopeful and civil Young Man." Yet, pestered by a former sweetheart he'd seduced with promises of marriage and then abandoned, he lured her away and drowned her in a pond.[14] Perhaps Slaughterford's crime, which he steadfastly denied, was not so strange as it seemed. But this cannot be known from the account I've been quoting because the country churchman who wrote it, though on the spot, shows no inclination to explore his subject's background. Such an absence of effort, where the effort might so easily have been made, need not mean the parson was lazy. But it may mean that he valued Slaughterford's incomprehensibility, or was at least content to let it be. If so, he shows a tendency that often operated in the popular literature of crime, a tendency that ran contrary to explanation and often sought to magnify all that was mysterious in criminal motivation. Even *The Suffolk Parricide* shows this tendency, with all its close concern for Drew's peculiar background and its influence on his behavior. "But . . . whatever induced Mr. *Charles Drew* to perpetuate such a Scene of Inhumanity," it at one point confesses, "we cannot justly determine."[15]

This willingness to be perplexed was not unmotivated. More than simple sensationalism was involved here, however. The mysteriousness of crime suited those who held to a religious or even a political conservatism; it could be a rod with which to chastise the ungodly and/or the unruly. By insisting again and again that everyone was capable of crime, it strove to add, to the real fear that people had about being robbed or murdered, another fear: No one could know but that he or she might just come to be hanged. The perilous condition of us all is vividly described by a late seventeenth-century writer. Speaking "sadly" and out of "dayly experience," he comments on the meaning to be found in the case of the Reverend Robert Foulkes, who was hanged in 1679 for the murder of his bastard child. No sooner does God leave us "to the indirect motion of our natural courses," he warns, "but as if we were in Love with our own Ruine, we presently run headlong into the black stream of Vice and Impiety." Which means we are as good as lost: "Our Reason which should be our Pilot, then serves us in no stead; no happy birth, Litterate Education, or sacred Function is able to bribe us to study our own good; but on the contrary, our predominant corruptions overrul[e] them all."[16] Foulkes was a good example of what even the best-seeming among us have to fear from the black and errant tendencies of the human heart. As such he was remembered well into the eighteenth century. Beginning with "hypocrisy" and "uncleanness" he opened himself to the commission of far more grievous sins, says the 1734 Johnson. His "Learning and Abilities," his "sacred Eloquence," made him "exceedingly follow'd and admir'd," and, had he died "in a natural Way," he "might have been belov'd till Death . . . and then universally lamented." But then, as he himself said at the gallows, "You see in me what Sin is."[17]

The conventional wisdom could have brought little comfort even to those whose ends it served. The problems it raised for an increasingly secular, politically liberal England will be considered in the next two chapters; what I want to emphasize now is its emotional and intellectual insufficiency. Criminals supposedly were men who, more than other men, had indulged their propensity to sin. Either this caused God to withdraw His grace, leaving them to fall by the inherent weight of their wickedness – a wickedness, of course, that was not theirs alone but characteristic of every human being – or else indulgence in sin had gradually, sometimes even imperceptibly, hardened them emotionally and morally. The latter view seems to have been preferred in the eighteenth century. Thus the author of *Remarkable Criminals* declares that criminals are people who "abandon themselves to a desire of living after their own wicked inclinations, without considering the injuries they do others while they gratify their own lusts and sensual pleasures." They show how "a long and habitual course of vice so hardens the soul, that no warnings are sufficient, no dangers frightful, nor reflections so strong [to keep them from] those illegal practices which lead to a shameful death." The "common causes" of even the worst crimes, he is sure, are "vices and extravagances." This holds true even when "men of outward gravity

from *The Genuine Trial of Samuel Goodere, Matthew Mahony, and Charles White for the Murder of Sir John Dinely Goodere* [1741]

and serious deportment" break the law, for even they will be found to have been (like Foulkes) "as wicked as those whose open licenciousness renders their . . . crimes . . . the less amazing."[18]

   The limitations of any such explanation of crime are amply revealed by this last locution: At best, one could hope to make it seem "the less amazing." But that at least was something, and so, not surprisingly, the biographies of criminals took up the task of tracing those sins which, in their view, had made their subjects more than usually vulnerable to the wicked inclinations surging in us all. Their efforts, it must be noted, were directed not at developing a psychology (or even a "natural history") of crime but at finding, after the fact, appropriate events to precede it. A clear and more than usually elaborate example of just such an effort is Samuel Foote's account of Samuel Goodere, a captain in the Royal Navy who was hanged in 1740 for ordering the murder of his brother by two seamen under his command. Sir John Dinely Goodere was rich, respected, and known for "the natural Goodness of his Heart." But his brother hated him, apparently for reasons having to do with the family estates, and had him kidnapped. After holding him for a few days aboard his ship, which was anchored at Bristol, he had him killed. Foote was the victim's nephew and so would have had access to privileged information. Certainly he seems (or pretends) to know a great deal about Samuel Goodere. But with all his information he works to a curiously impoverished end. His main theme – one can guess it in advance – is that the murderer's "Inclinations, from the very Dawn of his Life to the Close of it, were very depraved."

Given the evidence he advances, Foote is hardly exaggerating. As a schoolboy, for instance, Samuel and several of his companions robbed his grandfather's house. This was rather more than the usual schoolboy prank, for during the course of the robbery Samuel (here exceeding Mary Edmondson) "clapped a Pistol to his own Mother's Breast." The poor woman's "only Fault," says Foote, was her "great Indulgence to all her children." On another occasion, demanding money from his father, he declared he'd waylay and shoot him if he didn't get it. His relations with his brother were hardly more cordial. That he frequently quarreled with him, that he threatened him with bodily harm several times before he finally had him kidnapped and killed, were all of a piece with his behavior toward the family in general.[19] All this evidence, and a good deal more which I slide over, makes it quite clear that Samuel was a moral monster long before he committed his terrible crime. But it does not do much else, and Goodere seems to have been rather more complicated.

Bad as he was, he was not beyond resenting Foote's attentions. He agreed that his crime was "as shocking as human nature could well be capable of," but thought it "hard" that it should "blacken or sully my whole past life and conversation." "I know that some *Pharisaical* censures will urge that vice is progressive, that no man is suddenly wicked," he says, "and that my crime must have been preceeded by a great many others of the like tendency." But "cruelty and ill nature," he claims, are not his "natural disposition." Appealing to "all those that ever knew me," he asks whether he "was not so well beloved in [his] neighborhood, and distinguished for strict honour as any gentleman in it." Goodere might have mentioned his military career as further evidence that he was no mere monster, but he doesn't. Even in the eighteenth century, when commissions were purchased and promotion gained by influence, one had to be more than simply maniacally wicked to get and hold command of a ship in the Royal Navy. Curiously, however, neither he nor Foote raises the matter; here even the murderer to some extent collaborates in the simplification of himself.[20]

For all his special opportunity to gather psychological detail, Foote's characterization of Goodere holds to type. It is not his motives that interest him, or how these fit into the man's larger psychology, but his moral state before the crime, and for Foote it is enough to show that this was dark "from the very Dawn of his Life." Nor does it much concern him that if indeed this were the case – and Foote, we might note, would gain some reputation as a playwright – the figure he has painted is utterly opaque. For Foote, as for his contemporaries, very little of the "why" of a crime inhered in the criminal's mind. In itself a natural event, the outcome of a long course of delinquency, the questions it prompted had to do with the consequences of that delinquency, not its psychodynamics. What had he done to have merited so hard a fate? Why had God cast him down so terribly? Such questions may seem to reflect a mentality too primitive to have existed in a so-called age of reason, but it was an age that had a taste at all levels for global explanation (but then, as anthropologists like Lévi-Strauss might ask, which age, what culture does not?). Given the notion that criminality was part of a larger pattern of behavior, and the absence of any elaborate psychology to describe that behavior, it was only by asking such questions that sense could be made of phenomena that would otherwise have had to seem senseless.

But few criminals could be made "less amazing" as easily as Foote made Goodere. Some seemed not to have been sinful men at all, even when the most careful inquiries were made. "There is scarce any thing more remarkable," comments the author of *Remarkable Criminals* at the beginning of one felon's history, "than the finding of a man who hath led an honest and reputable life, till he hath attained the summit of life, and then, without abandoning himself to any notorious vices that may be supposed to lead him into rapine and stealth . . . to take himself on a sudden to robbing on the highway, and to finish a painful and industrious life by a violent and shameful death." Here for once the awkward prose is appropriate, for the case the writer is about to discuss upsets his ease of mind. Despite the title of his work, he wants his criminals to seem as unremarkable as possible, and here is one who resists accommodation to his paradigms. The man in question is a certain John Austin, who "being under no necessities, but on the contrary, in a way very likely to do well," committed "so unaccountable an act as the knocking down a poor man and taking away his coat." Austin's description of his crime – "that though he was in a fair way of living, and had a very careful and industrious wife, yet for some time . . . had been disturbed in his mind . . . and from a sudden impulse of mind attacked the man" – could hardly do more to subvert the idea that criminals are men who grow only gradually wicked. "The son of very honest people," as the author of *Remarkable Criminals* is obliged to admit, and educated as he ought to have been, Austin worked hard, had a "fair character" from all his neighbors, displayed "no vicious principles," and "had been guilty of very few enormous crimes, except drinking to excess sometimes, and that but seldom." "The sin which most troubled him was . . . spending the Lord's day mostly in hard work." I have been quoting in sequence, for these last few bits of comment show the writer recovering his lost equilibrium. Beginning to contradict his original view – that the case is inexplicable – he gropes for the received ideas that allow some sense, finally, to be made of the fate of this very likely lunatic man. "He was very penitent," it is in any case consoling to know, "and suffered death with much serenity and resolution."

Death and disgrace can come without warning, we are thus encouraged to infer, even from sins apparently so trivial as failing to observe the Sabbath strictly and "drinking to excess sometimes." One either accepts this inference, which sets a nearly impossible standard for safe human conduct, or else is faced with something far more disturbing: that the criminal impulse can fall more suddenly, and with far less warning, than the sudden dew from heaven. For his part the author of *Remarkable Criminals* would prefer to believe, with all that it entails, that, "generally speaking, the old saying holds true that nobody becomes superlatively wicked at once." Still he occasionally feels the need to warn that even those who never "stumble in the road of virtue" can nonetheless take, "as it were, a leap from the precipice at once."[21] Each time someone mentally deranged was hanged – for such I take Austin to have been, and probably Savage, Strodtman, and Edmondson – it may well have seemed that everybody was indeed footing it along the edge of the abyss and could, at any moment, be seized by the impulse to jump. "You are not secure of your selves, that you shall not commit the Crimes, or worse than those for which she dy'd," warns the writer of an account of a woman hanged for infanticide. "I . . . thought my self too secure and trusted to my own strengths, more than the grace and assistance of the Almighty," explains a soon-to-be-hanged murderer, nor would he have believed it, "had it been formerly told me, I should ever have come to this End." "When you read over this sad Story," declare two different pamphlets on two different murders, "we beseech you lay your hands upon your hearts, and say, 'What a mercy is it, I was neither the *Murderer* nor the *Murdered!*"[22]

Against such pronouncements there was not much defense (which perhaps explains their becoming the central moral of so many criminals' lives; put to use, the idea behind them can seem less fearsome). There was as yet no conception of the criminal as an altogether different kind of human being. The comforts (since blasted) of Lombroso's physiognomy lay far in the future, as also the notion (not quite so far in the future) that crime was the product of a "criminal class," a particular stratum of society that was low, dangerous, and (it goes without say-

ing) certainly not that of the reader.[23] All that writers of criminal lives
could know and think was that crime was a form of indiscipline, an
extreme case of the *principium laesum* unleashed. "There cannot be anything more dangerous," warns *Remarkable Criminals,* "than a too ready
compliance with any [lustful or irascible] inclination of the mind," for
"either transports us on the least check into wicked extravagancies,
which are fatal in their consequences, and suddenly overwhelm us with
both shame and ruin." All the available wisdom on the etiology of
crime was summed up by one criminal who, on his way to the gallows,
hoped "that all by his example would learn to stifle the first motions of
wickedness and sin, since such was the depravity of human nature that
no man knew how soon he might fall." No one knew, or could know,
why certain men became criminals and others did not.[24]

The danger one had to live with, then, was that self-control would
fail, that one would be overcome by a sudden, fatal impulse of mind. In
some cases the onset of malignancy could almost be predicted, but in
others its triggering factor must have seemed as mysterious and as
frightening as – to us, now – a single piece of blue asbestos in the lung.
Seemingly insignificant bits of moral or religious delinquency, insignificant at least on the grand scale of human reprobation, could bring on
whole chains of dooming events. Or, even more sudden and starkly
fatal, God might just abruptly withdraw His supporting grace, and,
given the sinfulness of us all, who could blame Him? Or so the popular
literature of crime encouraged its readers to believe; should we take
what it says at face value? Having made no extensive search of the
diaries and letters of the period, I am in no position to say whether
people actually were afraid of succumbing, either gradually or suddenly, to the tendencies within them that might bring them to be
hanged. The written record in any case is no sure guide; certain central
anxieties may have been unspoken. Dr. Johnson, who held that man's
"chief merit consists in resisting the impulses of his nature," certainly
believed in human depravity. And he shared the views of those who
wrote about crime for popular consumption, at least so far as to assert
that "we are all thieves naturally." Yet he believed, too, that "by good
instruction and good habits this is cured, till a man has not even an
inclination to seize what is another's; has no struggle with himself about
it."[25] Probably most people who bothered to think about these things
agreed with Johnson, or so it seems reasonable to assume, if only on the
grounds of the general human inclination toward psychological self-
defense. I would guess, however, that it was easier to defend against the
possibility that we are all potentially thieves than that we are all potentially murderers.

For murder fit the etiological paradigm in a sense too well; it could be done so suddenly, so unexpectedly, so irrationally, and so often by people who, until then, had not seemed in any way extraordinary. This would have been true especially of familiar murder, and here we have perhaps one of the most important reasons for its special treatment in the popular literature of crime. Thieves, with rare exceptions, could seem comfortably different from the general run of humanity if only for the fact that, however they started, they generally lived for some time as part of the London underworld before they were caught and hanged. The most notorious thieves, almost always professionals, were unlike other people not only in their habits and associations but even in their language.[26] Murderers, however, often showed no such distinctive features. How was a potential Savage, Strodtman, or Edmondson to be told apart from other men and women? Nor were the motives of murderers at all easy to define or comprehend. Robberies could seem at least prompted by some prior calculation, whether in fact they had been or not, and though stupid and short-sighted such calculations could at least seem comprehensible. As one highwayman about to be hanged supposedly sang out, "a merry life and a short one."[27] But rarely was there anything so lucid in the motives of familiar murderers; they killed for obscure or trivial reasons, or perhaps for no discernible reason at all.

More than any other crime, familiar murder thus confirmed not only the darkest suppositions about human nature but the moral precariousness of just about everyone. It could indeed make it seem that all of us were at risk, unless, more scrupulously than most of us would care to, we strove to keep to the strait and narrow. And even then, as the moral propaganda of the popular literature of crime reiterated again and again, we could not be sure of our safety.[28] Such propaganda may have been troubling, as much to those who agreed with its assumptions as to those who rejected it out of hand. So insistent is it, so ugly in its implications, that even those whose views it echoed must have been obliged, if only for their peace of mind, to put it at some tolerable distance. Perhaps this meant that such people reasoned, as we have just seen Dr. Johnson doing in the matter of theft, that the murderous impulse could be cured or controlled. Others, less disposed to dark thoughts on the nature of man, may have joined in with the coffeehouse wits who laughed at murderers' confessions; but laughter, too, is a way of protecting oneself, especially when other means are not available. In any case, if familiar murder were to be put to use, either as an object lesson for the masses or merely as a semiobscene entertainment, means had to be found to modify its starkest implications, to counterbalance and so control all that it so unsettingly suggested of the human condition. Any presentation of the event that lacked such means risked inattention or, worse, mocking disregard.

By now I hope to have shown the inadequacy of reason, given the state of contemporary psychology, to account for a crime so apparently without motive and so generally gruesome as familiar murder. Beyond affirming the general depravity of human nature – an affirmation which, as it happened, was increasingly out of step with a culture coming to take a more optimistic view of human capacities – the myth did not much inquire into the crime's etiology, nor could it. Instead of explaining the crime, it sought to counter its effect (or should I say affect?), making it seem, at minimum, part of a whole. At maximum, it tried to make it seem part of a reassuring whole. The reassurance came with the criminal's readiness to confess and accept responsibility for his crime, to convert and die an enthusiastic Christian, to close out his life in a peculiar mixture of self-abasement and self-glorification. Why and how this should have been reassuring is a question for the next two chapters; here we might pause to consider how far we've come toward understanding one of the central features of the myth that attached to familiar murder, the great stress put on the criminal's confession. There is something more to be said, too, about the tendency of the myth to dwell on the bloody details of the murder itself.[29]

The search for causes or, failing these, precedents adequate to the murderer's crime required information, and often that information could come only from the criminal himself. In its absence, writers dredged up what they could. Anything shady in the murderer's past was likely to be exploited if it could be made to indicate, and practically anything could, that his crime was part and parcel of an enduring and egregious wickedness. But such searches needed confirmation. Thus Catherine Hayes, who murdered her husband in a highly lurid fashion (cutting off his head, dismembering him, scattering his body parts all over London, for which she was burned at the stake) was pressured to confess she committed incest. It seems that one of her accomplices, hardly more than a boy, was not only her lover but also a foundling. This, and evidence suggesting she led a wandering and dissolute life before marrying (a good deal is made of this by itself), prompted the suspicion that her lover was her son, that she knew it and didn't care. Catherine Hayes neither denied nor confirmed this suspicion, but it was not without its logic. For had she in fact violated one of the two great taboos on which human society is built, it could hardly seem surprising that she'd gone on to violate the other, and in so atrocious a fashion. Sabbath-breaking would do when it came to finding appropriate precedents for murder, drinking and whoring were convenient, and a history of violence still better, but sometimes – and the Hayes case was not

from *The Barbarous and Unheard Of Murder of Mr. John Hayes, by Catherine His Wife, Thomas Billings, and Thomas Wood* [1726]

unique – incest was best.[30] But such dark doings were more easily suspected than proved.

Nothing so remarkable is alleged of Mary Edmondson, though she too was inconvenient in her silence. In the absence of a confession that might have supplied precedents appropriate to her crime, writers were encouraged to use their imaginations. Thus Mary was made to quarrel with her aunt, to be disinherited and to resent it, even to stab her mother. All these "facts," like her aunt's variously alleged generosity, made Mary's crime not only the more abominable, and so the more richly illustrative of human depravity, but as well the less amazing. No more than Savage or Strodtman (or Stanley, Drew, Goodere, or Hayes) did she leap from the precipice at once. Without these "facts" her case would be bleak indeed, for Mary would otherwise appear to have committed no previous delinquencies of any real significance – unless, of course, one were willing to attach sinister connotations to the hiding away of some coals and a mop. Significantly, this is just what some people did. Mary's case would have been less embellished, I suspect, had she confessed as fulsomely as Savage or Strodtman, showing how one sin led on to another, even from something so simple as Sabbath-breaking. But as it was, even the Sabbath-breaking had to be supplied (or at least its equivalent), for so I take the claim in one account that she stayed out late at a Christmas party. Did she? And was so seemingly innocuous an excess significant? Mary was the best person to say so, and for other, less crucial information she was certainly the most convenient source.

Mary Edmondson's refusal to confess had one interesting effect in particular. It led one writer to describe the stabbing of her aunt with a fullness of detail that rivals the descriptions of Savage's and Strodtman's crimes, and in a language that closely parallels those descriptions. It is an interesting language, and all the more because it is so conventional, a standard fixture in countless accounts of murder. In "flat," affectless tones, it enumerates with near pedantic precision the blows and thrusts delivered, the blood spilled, and the victim's dying groans; it does not moralize or even comment on what it is describing. It might be argued that this absence of evaluative and judgmental comment served to forward vicarious involvement. But such language is lacking, too, in the sense of excitement one generally finds in prurient writing. There is a tension in it, to be sure; one feels a mounting sense of horror, but this is produced by its peculiar objectivity, its troubling lack of affect compared to the writing around it. And in those instances where writers do interpose themselves to comment evaluatively, it is to pile on all the moral disapproval they can muster. There is never the tiniest suggestion that the victim invited what he got, or deserved it, though such suggestions are rife and loom large in descriptions of violence done by highwaymen and other rogues.

Obscenities are never gratuitous, and the tendency to dwell on the bloody details of murder in the middle of most accounts of the crime ought to seem more than a means of quickening the pulse of readers clogged with moral comment. But, as I have been suggesting, it ought also to seem more than a means of gratifying unconscious hostilities characteristic of the age. Either view assumes that the violence in such accounts is an interpolation, a gratifying departure from boring business that must be done, or the real business of the piece, tolerable only because it is hemmed in by stretches of superego-sanctioned discourse. It seems to me, however, that these descriptions of violence are an integral part of the whole myth. Physically at its center, they are in every sense its starting point, the thing from which it exfoliates (and the thing the text would decently clothe within its leaves). With their strange clarity and frequent lack of emotion these descriptions seem, as much as anything else, efforts at coming to terms with an object of special dread by looking, full-face and unflinchingly, on the thing itself. Or, rather, not the thing itself but a redacted version of it. Written down and broken up into its component parts, the act of murder becomes – in the process of being preserved, in words, as it actually was – something other than what it actually was. And in being made something other, it becomes not only more endurable but more manageable: Surrounded by other sets of words, it becomes one moment among many in the course of a whole life, one event in a set of other events, one sign in a system of other signs.

Once described, the act of murder can begin to lose its dreadful and astonishing singularity; inscribed, it can be written into larger constructs of meaning. It may have been this aim – just as much as any wish to sensationalize the event, to titillate the audience – that caused the murder of Edmondson's aunt to be described as fully and particularly as if she had indeed confessed, had been as helpful and free as Strodtman and Savage in giving all the horrid details. Still, though such cooperation as the murderer could give in the inscribing of his crime was important, there are other reasons for the great value placed on his confession and, more generally, for the great interest shown in his state of consciousness not only before his crime and while he was committing it but afterward, right up to the moment he was hanged. These reasons are more solidly inferable from contemporary concerns, and are about to concern us.

Myths, Malinowski says, seek not to explain but to explain away. Or so it seems from our point of view, for any effort to explain the "peculiar" ideas of another culture asks not only what and how they think but why (at some level or other) they do not or cannot or will not think like us, that is, "correctly." Unable to deal as we would with the human depravity expressed in such crimes, the myth that attached to familiar murder strove to show how that depravity, inevitably, had been checked and overbalanced. At its simplest, as we are about to see, it counterposed God's providence, His justice and mercy, against one of the most vicious – and vividest – expressions of human evil. At a more complicated level, it was concerned to show that even the worst of men could know, want, and achieve goodness. The myth thus had a double aim: to justify the ways of God to man, and to justify man to himself. And as the latter had considerable implications for the justice, health, and prospects of English society, the myth contributed to social solidarity as well. Whatever our prejudice in like matters, then, it was not this myth's efforts at an etiology of crime, psychological or moral, that allowed it finally to achieve coherence, to close its structure over one of the most disturbing things men might do. It would be some time yet before the reading public could seize onto the comfortable conviction that the "criminal intellect" was nothing like "the average intellect of average men" – to quote Dickens – but "a horrible wonder apart."[31]

Chapter 4

Heaven seized by sincerity and zeal: justifying God, vindicating man

=====

It is to be noted, that he had behaved himself alwayes with so much Civility and Regularity, that his Landlord thinking it impossible he should ever be guilty of so heinous a crime as that wherewith he was charged, was ready to offer himself to be his Bail. From all which it may be observed, that neither Birth, Wit, Education, Industry, nor a habit of well-living, can, without the especial Grace of God, free us from the snares of Satan; and therefore a much better use may be made of these fatal Accidents, then the common one of reviling and railing at the lapses of our Brethren.

The Penitent Murderer (1673), p. 7

Our care and suit must be, that the evills which shall not be averted, may be sanctified.

R[obert] Boreman, *Mirrour of Mercy* (1655),
pp. 28–31

I hope thou has some sparks of grace in thee, though deeply buried under a world of rubbish, and I hope all those godly bellows that are used will blow that away, and make thy fire of true repentance and godly sorrow burn clear.

Sir George Sondes, *His Plaine Narrative* (1655),
p. 29

This Morning . . . a Paper was sent me . . . called the genuine Trial of Mary Blandy, Spinster, at Oxford, for poisoning her late Father Francis Blandy, Gent. &c. . . . when I once read the Title of the Pamphlet, I was insensibly led on to read the whole: For indeed, when I was well acquainted with the Reality of the Fact, I had gone too far to recede; nor was Curiosity my only Motive. . . . I read on in Hopes of meeting with some Circumstances that might a little alleviate the dreadful Guilt imputed to the accused, and in some Degree lessen those Horrors which I had conceived at the first Idea of a Child's poisoning her Father.

[Henry Fielding], the *Covent Garden Journal*, No. 20
(10 March 1752)

Great sins must have great Repentance; 'tis not true except it be very deep. . . . tis not true except it bewails original corruption.

The Bloody Murtherer, or, The Unnatural Son (1672),
pp. 15–16

Seize Heaven by the sincerity and zeal of your Contrition.
Samuel Smith, Ordinary Account, 18 September
1691

Murder in seventeenth- and eighteenth-century England was more than what one modern anthropologist calls it, "the most definitive of social relationships."[1] It was a direct attack on God, carrying with it "a sacriligeous guilt" that tainted the murderer's society as well as himself and could threaten both with divine displeasure. For inasmuch as "man is made after the image of God," preached Increase Mather, whosoever "shall kill a man . . . puts a contempt upon the *Divine Majesty;* there is Treason against God contained in the bloody bowels of this Sin." Mather's sermon was published first in Boston in 1686 but reprinted twice thereafter in London, the second time at the end of the first (so far as I know) indigenous collection of criminal lives to appear in England.[2] In the views just quoted, at least, it is free of New England sectarianism. In 1725, for instance, the templars of Lincoln's Inn heard William Lupton preach essentially the same doctrine: Murder was "Defacing and Destroying the Only Image of Himself which [God] hath Impressed upon the Visible World."[3] Nor is Mather's view of murder as "a crying sin" at all peculiar to his particular brand of religion. "The voice of thy Brother's Blood crieth to me from the ground," God says to Cain in Genesis 4:10, and to those who were steeped in their Bibles this was considerably more than a figure of speech. Numbers 35:33 was relevant as well: "for blood it defileth the Land: and the Land cannot be cleansed of the blood that is shed therein, but by the blood of him that shed it."[4] On such authority Mather believed that "one Murder unpunished may bring guilt and a Curse upon the whole Land, that all the Inhabitants of that Land shall suffer for it," but again the view was typical. In 1695 the murder of a man in the street by persons unknown could be called, almost routinely, "a Crime . . . such as brings such Guilt upon the Nation, as cannot be expiated except by Exemplary Punishment." Those who were guilty must "[give] Glory to God, by a publick Confession of their Crime, and [submit] to the utmost Severity of the Justice of the Nation." Their "State and Condition," being "without all question, most desperate," was "not to be otherwise remedied."[5]

Such asseverations no doubt had their role as social propaganda. Those who could feel no compunctions about killing their fellow men might think twice at the prospect of disobliging God. The function of the belief that, if murder were left unpunished, God's wrath would fall upon the nation as a whole, is perhaps less obvious. It may well have been prompted, at least in part, by a wish to have equal justice done before the law. Such a concern would certainly be understandable among the Nonconformists who would have made a market for Mather's writings in England, and the middle classes in general. In the late seventeenth century, especially, London seemed plagued by young swells who often killed each other while drunk, and sometimes the occasional, intervening citizen. If social order were to be maintained, all killers had to be punished with equal severity, however much the authorities might want in certain cases to be lenient.[6] Yet these aspects of the matter, though interesting, are not immediately relevant to our present concern, which is to show how the fear that murder inspired, defined as it was for whatever reasons, prompted a narrative form that was structured and informed by the very terms of those definitions.

It suited Henry Fielding to believe – as doubtless it did many others of his time, and many before him right back to the days of the Old Testament – that "the Almighty hath been pleased to distinguish the atrociousness of the Murderer's guilt, by levelling his thunder directly at his head, in this world." Nor was this all, for citing the "many and unquestionable examples" in "the histories and traditions of all ages, and all countries," Fielding was sure that God "interpose[d] in a more immediate manner in the detection of this crime than any other."[7] It is easy to appreciate the need for such a belief in a society that had no real police force. But just as important was the positive comfort it could bring. The idea that murderers offered, in William Lupton's words, "as much as in them lies, an Outrage to [God's] very Being" brought with it this reassuring correlative: "Vengeance treads always upon the Heels of the Guilty." Or, as one of the best-known books of the period pointed out, "When the justice of man is either too blinde, that it cannot search out the truth, or too blunt, that it cannot strike with severity . . . then the justice of God riseth up, and with his own arme he discovereth and punisheth the murder; yea, rather than [the murderer] shall go unpunished, senceless creatures and his owne heart and tongue rise to give sentence against him."[8]

In the seventeenth century there is no shortage of miraculous stories or (as the text just quoted calls them) "admirable discoveries" to back this claim. Though to my knowledge no reports survive in England of "senceless creatures" suddenly endowed with powers of speech sufficient to convict a murderer, still something close is described in a pamphlet published in 1606. This (the title gives an admirable précis) describes *The horrible Murther of a young Boy of three yeres of age, whos Sister had her tongue cut out: and how it pleased God to reueale the offendors, by giving speech to the tongueless Childe.* Nothing quite so miraculous seems ever to have occurred again, but there are instances enough in the popular literature of crime of comparably functioning anomalies, even on the eve of the eighteenth century. The ghosts of murder victims appear to friends or relatives and so bring on inquiries that otherwise might never have been started; corpses suddenly bleed afresh or give other wondrous signs when the murderer is made to touch them or simply stands near; and murderers themselves undergo startling physical alterations that either betray them or confirm their guilt. Events like these could be taken quite seriously and on occasion were used as evidence in court. Even as late as the mid-eighteenth century it could seem that God worked miracles to uncover murderers. Thus the title of Fielding's pamphlet on "the interposition of providence in the detection and punishment of murder" advertises "above thirty Cases, in which this dreadful Crime has been brought to Light, in the most extraordinary and miraculous manner."[9]

Of course not all God's "interpositions" could seem as miraculous as others. Not all could involve the suspension of natural law, especially as time went on and the population grew less superstitious. Thus in cases of murder, as in other departments, God appears to have found it increasingly necessary to work out of sight.[10] His interventions occur via second causes, and even then He moves conveniently "indoors" from the physical world, into the human psyche. Fielding's pamphlet is a model of this tendency, for though apparently he had no trouble gathering clearly supernatural stories from his older, more credulous sources, when he moved into the area of his own knowledge and experience he discovered (perforce) that God worked almost invisibly.[11] The two most recent of his thirty-three cases illustrate this tendency rather nicely; in both, Fielding argues, providence can be seen as the force that propelled the guilty into self-betrayal. Thus it was no accident that Mary Blandy, having poisoned her father, called attention to herself by an abortive attempt to flee or that, followed by a suspicious crowd, she became confused, lost her resolve, and returned home to be arrested. Elizabeth Jeffryes, who helped murder her uncle, presents just such another case of providence working invisibly, so invisibly as perhaps to pass unnoticed. Some months before her crime, in a wholly unrelated incident, she had vouched for a man who was suspected of being a highwayman (two pistols dropped out of his coat pocket during a fracas in a public house, and he could give no good reason for carrying them). It was the memory of this incident that started people wondering, when her uncle was found murdered in his bed, whether she might be involved. As these two examples show, even when murder was revealed by other than supernatural means, the belief that God was involved in its detection was left unshaken. Apparently Fielding, and presumably his readers, very much needed to believe that murder would (as the proverb promises) indeed "out." It is "the blackest sin," says Fielding, "which can contaminate the hands or pollute the soul of man."[12] How then could God not take special pains to have it punished, and in this world, as a manifest mark of His goodness and justice?

God's providence could be discerned even in something so small as a murderer's inability to conceal his guilt. One of the stories Fielding tells – other versions of the same story stretch back at least to the sixteenth century – concerns a man who robs and kills a friend and then escapes abroad (to Europe in most versions, to America in one). After twelve or twenty years (in Fielding's version the latter), and prosperous now, he returns to London for a brief visit. His crime is long forgotten – by everyone, that is, save himself – and he attends to his business entirely unsuspected. One day, however, as he stands outside a shop cheapening some goods, there is a robbery in the street and people give chase. He hears them crying, "Stop him!" and then, quite without knowing what he is doing, begins to run. The thief gets away, but the murderer, having attracted the attention of the pursuing crowd, is run down and questioned. He blurts out a confession and is hanged for a crime he had almost forgot, and for which, as he had fondly come to think, he would never be punished.[13] "There is a peculiar Vengeance that does pursue this Sin at the heels of it," Mather claims in his sermon on murder: "Hence they that have been guilty of it, seldom live long in quiet. . . . Either they are cut off by the Sword of Civil Justice; or if their murders happen to be undiscovered, a secret Curse of God follows them."[14] As the story just told would show, God's malediction on the murderer could be nothing more than a guilty countenance; and this could be just as effectual as a thunderbolt.

It was the opinion of many in the seventeenth and eighteenth centuries that the mark of Cain was, if not "some visible mark in the face," nothing more than "a horrible shaking over his whole body . . . or an exceeding shame and confusion, in that he ran from place to place to hide himself."[15] It is important to note that this is just how Savage and Strodt-man were perceived, both by themselves and by the public, their guilt plain in their faces and behavior. Both of them succumbed to the damning urge to flee, yet could find no place to hide, and in this did nothing less than they were supposed to do. (Mary Edmondson's failure to observe this piece of decorum must have been one of the things that made her so troubling.) God had no need to point a supernatural finger at either of them, or indeed at most murderers, so easily could He indict them by disordering their minds, spreading them over with confusion and fear. "That the Bloody Murtherer never went to his grave in peace, is Experimentally known," says a mid-seventeenth-century writer, "for either God will give Extraordinary wisdom and Judgement to the Magistrate to finde it, or else infatuate the policy of the Murtherer, and so terrifie his Conscience with the horror and hainousness of the Fact, that he shall not onely oftentimes be his own Accuser, but his own Executioner also." Given the availability of such means, why should God ever have to do that "which is most terrible," which is to say, intervene directly Himself? As Increase Mather preached, "But especially Spiritual Vengeance follows this sin. . . . the murderer's Soul is filled with hellish Horror of Heart." It was here that God worked most powerfully against murderers, a fact Mather took to be confirmed by their confessing "that as soon as ever they had committed the Bloody Fact, they felt the Flames of Hell-fire in their Consciences." It was an article of faith, then, that "the cry of Blood" was "so strong and prevalent . . . the Eye of Providence [so watchful,] that [murderers] seldom go to their Graves in Peace. For, though they may escape the Stroke of publick Justice . . . which is seldom; yet the Almighty has planted such a Witness within them, as will give them no Rest Night nor Day." If nowhere else, the Hound of Heaven lived in man's own heart.[16]

Not all murderers, to be sure, could be shown to have been smitten with terror directly after the fact. But it was enough to confirm God's power (perhaps more than enough, considering Fielding's use of Blandy and Jeffryes) to show them fallen into some irrational and inexplicable state. If the murderer proved unable to take even the simplest precautions to save his skin, if he felt any forebodings after his crime or made any stupid miscalculations, these were seized upon as significant details. Thus in 1635 Thomas Sherwood's "understanding [was] so infatuated by the irefull Judge of *Heaven*" that he went about wearing his victim's clothing the very next morning after murdering him, and as "waite was layd for such fashioned apparrel, which he wore . . . so inconsiderately, suddainly [he] was apprehended." In 1673, after robbing a friend's house and killing a servant, William Ivy prepared to flee England. "But though he had so resolved in his mind, yet it was not in his power to act it; and all the while he was in *Southwark*, he felt the load of Blood and the villainy of his Crime giving him a check." Unaccountably, he returned to his lodging and was arrested. Mathias Brinsden, who murdered his wife in 1722, provides yet another example of a murderer marked by nothing more than a certain anxiety and indecisiveness of mind. Indeed, the details of his case are so intrinsically unremarkable that it is all the more significant that his chronicler saw fit to include them. Brinsden, it is noted, confessed that "when he was escap'd to Mr. *Key's* at *Shadwell Dock*, he felt that Uneasiness in his Mind, that he wish'd he might be taken up; and tho' he was then in Bed, the Apprehensions of his Mind, would not let him sleep, but he fancy'd he heard the *Constable* approaching to Seize him every Moment, even while he was safe on his Pillow." "Such is the weight of blood,"

comments the author of *Remarkable Criminals,* referring to this same
event, "and such the dreadful condition of the wicked."[17]

The widespread propagation of such ideas probably had some deterrent value. Like Cain, who "after he had murdered his Brother . . .
cried and roared out, that his Sin was greater than could be endured,"
the prospective murderer could expect to be marked out by "Hell and
Horror in his Countenance as well as in his Conscience."[18] And such
expectations may even have helped in the detection of the crime.
Murderers may have betrayed themselves all the more readily in their
nervousness that a sudden outbreak of nervousness would betray them;
such culturally programmed behavior would certainly have made the
work of the authorities easier. Perhaps the tendency of murderers to
become more obdurate as time went on, refusing to confess and give
themselves away, can be explained as the result of such indoctrination
losing its hold on the minds of ordinary people. But this is to get off
the point; though myths do serve practical ends, we are not so much
interested in practical reality as in the myth itself. The murderer's inca-
pacity to commit the "perfect" murder, or even just to rest quiet,
would have had no small reassuring effect for those whose peace he
disturbed and who had, perforce, to deal with him. Part of this effect
(and we shall go on immediately to consider another, perhaps more
important part) lay in what the murderer's behavior suggested about
the continuing intervention of God in human affairs. Or came rather
from what could be read into such behavior: God still provided, if only
in the extremest case of human evil, a clear sign to all who would
believe. Even where nothing supernatural had occurred in the detection
of a murder, and in an age of declining credulity such events were
growing exceedingly rare, believers could seize on the murderer's betrayal by his own conscience. For conscience itself was a miracle, God's
law implanted and sustained by Him in the hearts of all men, even the
worst of them.

So far we can claim to have accounted, more or less, for the structure
and content of the narrative form that attached to murder up to the
point where the murderer is caught, confronted, breaks down, and
admits his guilt. The search for his motives, the concern with his personal history, are efforts (never quite sufficient) to find his distinctive
characteristics, to find causes adequate to the effects he has produced.
But the concern with the murderer's consciousness, especially after he
has committed his crime, includes more than this: Where the crime
could not have been understood, still it had to be comprehended. By
this I mean that murder, despite its frequent inexplicability as a series of
causes and effects, had nonetheless to be contained within a framework

of beliefs that could give it an acceptable significance. As we have seen, the popular religious doctrine that God inevitably intervened in the discovery of murder provided a part of this framework, especially as it emphasized the wave of revulsion and terror that overtook murderers and, inexorably, brought them to self-betrayal. Even the flat, affectless account of the crime itself, it seems, could contribute to the making of this point. "For some weeks before the fact was done," confessed a more than usually articulate murderer, "he fell under a darkness and stupour in his mind, which he could compare to nothing but the sense a man has when he is half-asleep." On "the fatal day in which it was done," he said, "though he was not drunk, yet he was like one drunk, for he was almost stupid." It was only after the crime that he felt his faculties revive, and only after being "under great horrour" for nearly a week that he confessed to the magistrates. He was, as the divine who reported his case points out, "wonderfully touched."[19]

By showing murderers sunk to a level of insensate brutality – the very quality of the description of their crimes would have conveyed this – the narratives that dealt with them would have heightened the effect of their sudden restoration to something like humanity.[20] And where, in one who had been so beastly, could this sudden influx of feeling have come from, if not God Himself? Yet the myth moved further, insisting not only on the murderer's complete confession but, beyond this, that he be shown preaching upon the text of his own experience even unto the multitudes come to see him hanged. Why? To no small extent the myth wanted to display the *whole* power of God. Against this the murderer had raised a challenge that could never be completely met. "Good God," asked the elegist of a man murdered by his own brother in 1655, "what can, what shall mans frailty thinke / [when] thy great goodnesse, at this Act did winke?"[21] Such doubly awkward questions are rarely raised in the popular literature of crime, but this is not to say they did not prick the minds of the public. The inspired speakings of the born-again murderer, moreover, showed God's goodness in a double aspect. Even murderers – "the chiefest of sinners" as so many of them ritually called themselves – could hope to be saved. Even someone as bad as Henry Jones, who beat and stabbed his mother to death, could be told "by a worthy divine" that his sin, "though great, is not unpardonable." "You are not yet so far from Heaven," his minister assured him, "but you may by true Faith and Repentance get it." All he or anyone else had to do was "truly believe and heartily repent."[22]

As much as anything could, then, the spectacle of the murderer's conversion completed the encircling assurance that God ruled the world with love as well as justice. The born-again criminal "promote[d]

God's Glory by Proclaiming the Infiniteness of his Love, the Riches of
his grace, and Miraculousness of his power in working good out of
evil, [and] Sanctifying Affliction." "Take this comfort," one murderer's father suggested, "mans sinne cannot be so great, but Gods
mercy is greater. Hell is onely full of impenitent souls." Murderers
who took such advice, wrote a late eighteenth-century student of the
phenomenon, justified " 'the ways of God to man,' in mercy no less
than in judgement," and showed "though clouds and darkness are
round about [H]im, righteousness and judgement are the sure basis of
[H]is throne."[23] Even the penitent murderer's execution could be made
to seem a positive blessing, both for him and for the community. When
Francis Newland was hanged in 1695 some people thought he was
innocent. At least one of them could nonetheless "firmly believe, that
this, which the World may think his greatest Misfortune, was designed,
by the Wisdom of God, for the direct way to his greatest Happiness."
This conviction was based on Newland's behavior at Tyburn, where he
"shewed such a *rare Pleasantness* in his Countenance, as could result
from nothing, in my Opinion, but a supernatural Touch from God."[24]
In everything but his persistent claim that he was innocent, Newland's
demeanor was exactly as desired. Not only did it free God from any
possible imputation of injustice, but (an effect all the more valuable
because, of course, Newland claimed he was being punished wrongly)
it absolved society as well.

This last is quite important, for the strong interest in the consciousness of murderers needs also to be explained in terms less purely
religious. All sorts of catastrophic events could be, and were, treated
as manifestations of God's providence: great storms, outbreaks of disease, freak accidents, conflagrations, assorted anomalies in nature.[25] All
these were like murder inasmuch as they tested the belief that the
universe was ordered and ultimately benign, and all, despite their
outward appearance, could be said to have happened for the best; if
nothing else, they demonstrated the power of God and could be taken
as signs of the price men paid for their wickedness. The one thing that
set murder apart from other such catastrophes was that it tested man's
relation to God in a special way. Because, undeniably, it involved
human agency, murder could be made to seem "a Tragedy, which at
once unfolds the effect of human depravity, and displays the sover-
eignty of divine grace."[26] Indeed, if the comfortable standards of Restoration and eighteenth-century tragedy were to be observed, the un-
folding of the first necessarily required the display of the second. (This
was the age, after all, in which *Lear* was played – *always* – to a happy
conclusion.) For how else could the effects of human depravity be
shown countered but (literally, almost) by a deus ex machina? Where

else could one find a countervailing source of goodness but in a God who left no room for men to think that He could kill them, or allow them to be killed, for His or anyone's sport? Surely not in the hearts of men? And yet – curiously and quite contradictorily – the myth that attached to murder was concerned to look just there, seeking to find in each of the cases that attracted its attention the wherewithal to controvert, if not actually to refute, what in its first, horrified reaction to the crime it had said concerning human depravity. Without going so far as to say that man by himself alone, without God's grace, could know and follow virtue, it nonetheless leaned in that direction.

It is not impossible that people in the seventeenth and eighteenth centuries would have accepted the idea, as gratefully as most of us do now, that the murderer is a very special kind of human being, radically different in class, education, temperament, and psychology from the respectable norm. That this idea was not, however, an available option, that exactly the opposite could so often seem true, explains much, I would argue, of the treatment of the murderer in the popular literature of crime. Surely the feeling that the murderer was, at root, much the same as other men can explain *how* something like a tragedy – a Christian tragedy, to be sure – could be made from the story of his life and especially his death. Translated into neither a mental defective nor a monster of cruelty, as he might in other periods have been, the murderer could stand, plausibly enough, at the center of a narrative form that in its own vulgar but not unimportant way probed the limits of the human condition; he could even be made sympathetic. But *why* was the murderer's story especially (as the highwayman's was not) structured into beginning, middle, and end, and contrived to raise pity as well as terror? Toward what purgings did this "tragedy" aim? And (because tragedy is more than cathartic) toward what consolations of feeling? More than the question of God's justice and mercy hung in the balance. For by his crime the murderer indicted, or at least threatened to indict, all mankind; more than any other criminal he was a libel on the human race.

What was at issue is defined by two similar but contradictory observations; both come from the arsenal of rhetoric that writers of the period customarily directed against murder, and both, as a further means of overawing the sinful multitude, emphasize that murder is a crime against Nature as well as against God. "That this is a grievous Sin is manifest," Increase Mather preached, "*in that it is a most unnatural thing.* Creatures of the same kind are not wont to destroy one another. Naturalists observe concerning Wolves, that although they be cruel Creatures, they will never kill one another; therefore if men do so, they are worse than Wolves and Tygers; so that murder is an unnatural and a monstrous Wickedness." The author of *Remarkable Criminals* also believed that murderers are "bloody and unnatural men," but on significantly different grounds. Murderers, he points out, "beside their losing all respect towards the laws of God, show also a want of that compassion and tenderness which seems incident to the human species." Mather could not have made such a point, because for him murder "is in Man's corrupt Nature. Nothing is more natural than a Spirit of Revenge, as wee see in little Children, which discovers that the Children of Men bring murderous Natures into the World with them."[27] Nearly forty years separates these two sets of comments, but in actual fact the disparate views of human nature they express were, at least in the middle part of our period, contemporaneous. Lockit in *The Beggar's Opera,* for instance, would have agreed with Mather that people behave even worse than beasts toward each other, and more unaccountably. "Of all animals of prey," he says (and with considerably more insouciance than Mather), "man is the only sociable one. Every one of us preys upon his neighbour, and yet we herd together."[28]

This difference of opinion on the question of human nature was not academic. Whether the human race was inherently corrupt, whether compassion and tenderness were indeed, as modern naturalists might say, species-specific (rather than being gifts of God's grace to certain favored individuals), were matters of great social and political importance, as well as of philosophical concern. The clash between Hobbesian materialism on the one hand, and Shaftesburian benevolence on the other, defines this debate at the highest intellectual level. On a much lower level, and with far more confusion, the same basic issues animate the popular literature of crime, especially narratives concerned with murderers. Although here these issues are not as clearly stated as they are by the philosophers – we shall have to look for them behind a fog of ostensibly religious concerns – still, as might be expected, they were felt with far more urgency. Just such a sense of urgency was shown by Gilbert Burnet and Anthony Horneck in 1682, in the wake of a murder that, for a variety of reasons, attracted a great deal of public attention. Burnet's involvement in the case is especially notable, considering his future eminence as a latitudinarian divine.[29]

The murder victim was Thomas Thynne, a prominent Whig and one of the richest men in England. Dryden calls him "Issachar" in *Absalom and Achitophel,* where he rates a brief mention as the duke of Monmouth's "wealthy, western friend." He was shot down in cold blood in Pall Mall, just moments after Monmouth left his carriage. The assassins were three foreigners, Captain Christopher Vratz, a Pomeranian; Lieutenant John Stern, a Swede; and George Borowsky, a Pole. They were suspected of being in the pay of a fourth foreigner, Vratz's friend and

from Capt. Charles Johnson, *Lives and Adventures of the Most Famous Highwaymen, Murderers, Street-Robbers, &c.* [1734]

The Murder of THOMAS THYNN *Esq.* in Pall-Mall

patron, the Swedish Count Königsmark. Königsmark's motives are not important here, but certainly he had ample reason to want Thynne dead. After the murder he tried to flee the country, was arrested, tried with Thynne's killers as an accessory to the crime, and acquitted (some said the jurors were bribed). What is important here are the fates of the three actual killers. All the time they lay under sentence of death, Horneck and Burnet urged them again and again to make "free and ingenuous" confessions. Eventually Stern and Borowsky told all they knew, which was not much: They had been hired to do the job by Vratz. Vratz, for his part, refused to say anything much at all, being persuaded even after the trial that the two clerics wanted him to implicate Königsmark. His suspicions may not have been groundless, for it would have been very like Burnet to want to get to the bottom of the affair. Thynne's murder threatened to take on a political cast. Some Whigs thought the real target of the assassination was Monmouth; after all, the Great Protestant Hope, their very own candidate to succeed to the throne, had quit the spot where Thynne was killed moments before. Perhaps the Catholics were conspiring again; the reverberations of the Popish Plot still hung unsettlingly in the air.[30] But, even without so far-fetched an interpretation, the murder of a prominent Whig politico, especially an outspoken critic of the duke of York, had much potentially in it to embarrass the king. (As Charles II realized, for he personally interrogated the three assassins soon after they were apprehended, and Königsmark as well.) Burnet's typical political role in these years was to work for religious toleration and against factionalism, and he may well have wanted to make it clear that Thynne's murder had nothing to do with the overheated politics of the day, that it was a private matter only. Nonetheless, the pressure he and Horneck put on Vratz and the others to make "free and ingenuous" confessions cannot be explained entirely in terms of specific political motives (p. 1). Much larger issues hung in the air.

During the last of his visits, Horneck reports, Vratz complained "he could not well understand the humour of our *English* Divines; who pressed him to make particular declarations of things they had a mind he should say, though never so false, or contrary to truth; and at this he said he wondered the more, because in our Church we were not for *Auricular Confession.*" "I let him run on," says Horneck, "and then told him that he was much mistaken in the Divines of the Church of England, who neither used to reveal private confessions, nor oblige offenders in such cases to confess things contrary to truth; that this was both against their practice and their principles; The confession I said he was so often exhorted to, was no private but a publick Confession, for as his crime had been publick, so his Repentance and Confession ought to be publick too." Perhaps the fact that Horneck, like Vratz, was a foreigner himself gave him a clearer view of what seemed to the captain, as it must seem to us, a most peculiar, even perverse custom. ("No *English* Gentleman," Vratz protested, "would have been so coarsely used in his Country," and he threatened to set forth in writing "the behaviour and manners of the English clergy, and the strange wayes and methods they take with poor prisoners to extort confessions from them.") As Vratz was unusual in challenging the ordinary custom, so Horneck was forced to state with more than usual clarity the rationale that lay behind it; what he has to say deserves extensive quotation.

"In that he was loth to [confess]," Horneck explained to Vratz,

He gave us too much occasion to suspect, that his pretended repentance was not sincere, and cordial; I told him that in such wrongs and injuries, as he had done, there was either restitution or satisfaction to be made: at which word he replying, how he could make restitution now Mr. *Thynn* was dead? I answered, because he could not make restitution, that therefore he should make some satisfaction, and this he might do by a free and full

Confession of his sin, and of the cause of it, and who they were that put him upon it: I added that where true repentance melts the heart, after such commissions, there the true penitent was readier to accuse himself, than others to charge him with the Crime, and would have that abhorrency of the sin, that he would conceal nothing that served either to aggravate, or expose it to the hatred of all mankind; and that it was an injustice to the publick, not to betray the complices, and assistants, and occasions in such heinous offences. I told him, he seemed to talk too high for a true penitent, for those that were truly so, were exceeding humble, not only to God, but to men too; and one part of their humility to men was, To confess to them, and to their Relations, the wrong they had done them.

To all this Vratz responded that "he was indeed sorry Mr. *Thynn* was dead, but that was all he could do." He believed "it was enough for him to be humble to God," who he trusted would understand and forgive him, "but he knew of no humility, he owed to man." Horneck, however, would not hear of any such distinction; what Vratz owed to God, he owed as well to his fellow men. "I told him," says Horneck, "That Christ's blood was actually applied to none but the true penitent, and that true penitence must discover itself in meekness, humility, tenderheartedness, compassion, righteousness, making ingenuous confessions, and so far as we are able, satisfaction too, else notwithstanding the treasure of Christ's blood men might drop into Hell" (pp. 9–11).

In laying down this program of behavior, Horneck epitomizes the most important goals of serious criminal biography. To judge from the emphasis of his remarks, the "cause" of Vratz's crime is hardly of more than minor significance – even if, along with all the usual preliminary sins, it were to include his being hired to do it. What is most important to Horneck, what occupies the greatest part of what he has to say, is that Vratz – by freely and fully confessing, by accusing himself and sparing no details – will show himself now, as he was not then, "sincere and cordial." The "satisfaction" demanded of him is, essentially, that he show that even a heart as hard and obdurate as his once was can indeed be warmed and melted. Like Horneck, the popular literature of crime wanted to be able to show that now the murderer was all "meekness, humility, tenderheartedness, compassion, righteousness" – in short, all things that he, qua murderer, had not been. By displaying these qualities, the murderer could offer some satisfaction for what he had done; indeed, the only reparation possible. It was important too that all this seem "ingenuous," as Horneck and others called it. It could not seem forced, the result of pressures brought to bear on the condemned man even if in fact (as would seem likely in most cases) it were the result of such pressures. For the murderer's repentance had in a sense to outdo public expectation. As Horneck points out, the murderer could establish his sincerity and cordiality only by being "readier to accuse himself, than others to charge him with the Crime." In other words, he had to offer the public by way of reparation more than it believed (or pretended to believe) it could require; he owed it to the world to overpay his debt to society.[31] Vratz's talk about auricular confession is instructive in this regard. He is right to say that he is being asked to do more than Protestant doctrine could or should require of any believer, but wrong not to offer of his own free will to do it.[32] In effect, then, the murderer was expected to show a great generosity of spirit. Why? Before going on to answer this question, we might briefly reflect on the strength and the implications of this wish to have – after the fact – sincere and cordial murderers.

Burnet and Horneck had more success with Stern and Borowsky. Stern, especially, they found an apt and ready pupil. Confessing to the magistrates within a few days after the murder, he showed himself to be – the phrase has already been quoted – "wonderfully touched." "The morning after he was first taken," he told Burnet, "he awakened full of horror for what he had done. . . . and then began to reflect what a beast he had been, and that it was fit he should be shut up in a prison, and fettered as he then was; and upon that he lookt back with horrour on what he had done, and began to cry earnestly to God for mercy." At first, he disclosed, he was reluctant to confess, but then "he found such inward compunction in his mind, that he wished to die; he grew weary of life, and hated himself so much that he was glad to do every thing that was lawful, which might be a means to bring him to be a publick example." As Burnet emphasized, "he expressed not the least desire of living any longer: He never once asked me if I thought a Pardon might be obtained: on the contrary he said, he deserved to die, and desired it as much as he deserved it." All the favor he asked was that, "if it could be obtained, his head might be cut off," and when Burnet regretted this could not be arranged, "he easily acquiesced" to being hanged (pp. 1, 4). Borowsky, too, was moved to a condign repentance, though less spectacularly.

In both conversions, it could well have seemed, the most important thing was that the turbulence in the murderers' minds had been raised and stilled by God; it was He who worked the change in their hearts. But while Burnet and Horneck deny nothing to the efficacy of God, they seem to have been more concerned with emphasizing something else. Neither of them is especially interested in finding, as per Fielding, the interposition of providence; instead they are on the lookout for "wonderful change" as a thing in and of itself. Now their aims, to be sure, are not incompatible with Fielding's. His wanting to find providence at work in the movement of the murderer's mind and their wanting the murderer to show himself capable of a sudden and unaccountable alteration of heart are almost the same thing. Certainly in an age where few miracles were any longer to be had, both concerns would have had to rely on the same phenomenon, which is that change of heart. Yet there is nonetheless a difference between their two separate aims, and though it is a subtle difference, it is important: Where the one is centered on God, and interprets the murderer's change of heart to His advantage, the other centers on man.

At times Burnet can almost seem indifferent to the operations of providence, as with the meaning he finds (or rather fails to find) in the event that precipitates Borowsky's conversion. Borowsky claimed to have had a vision shortly after being sentenced, a vision "he verily believed . . . sent from God to him, to touch his heart." Considering this "the effect of a disturbed fancy," Burnet dismisses the question of the vision's being "real or only imagined" on the grounds that the main thing is that "it had certainly, a very good effect on him: for from that time he was wonderfully changed" (p. 6). This giving up a clear chance to make a case for supernatural intervention shows where Burnet's true interests lie. What concerns him most is whether or not the murderer's heart can change, and for him that change is equally valid whether produced miraculously by God or by something in the man's own mind. The same concern with mind, or at least that part of it ruled by imagination and sensibility, is characteristic of his concern with all three murderers.[33]

The first thing Burnet says about them is that their crime has "filled all people's minds with a just horror at so vile and inhumane a fact." The operative word here is "inhumane," and, though it does not quite have its modern sense as a term distinct from "inhuman," its use is instructive. Thus when he and Horneck visit the murderers the first thing they look for is something to override their sense of them as creatures other or less than human. They do not find it – "we saw no sense of the crime in any of them," says Horneck – but refuse to be disappointed. They set out immediately to produce such a "sense," aiming to bring the killers' moral consciousness to a level they deem appropriate to human beings (pp. 1, 8).[34] They fail only with Vratz, but this, especially to Burnet, is a most troubling failure. Vratz is not without virtue, especially at the end, but it is of a kind that is totally useless to them.

"It is certain that never man died with more resolution and less signs of fear, or the least disorder," Burnet writes; "his carriage in the cart both as he was led along, and at the place of Execution was astonishing, he was not only undaunted, but looked chearful and smiled often." Even when the rope was placed around his neck "he did not change colour nor tremble, his legs were firm under him, he would not cover his face as the rest did," and there was even "a cheerfulness in his countenance." All this Burnet writes "unwillingly," for as he says there are "some passages" in this dying behavior which "are not such as I can reflect upon with any great satisfaction." Vratz has shown no shame, no humility, no meekness, not the least bit of fear, and a peculiar kind of righteousness. "I had sometimes warned him of the danger of affecting to be a *Counterfeit* bravo," says Burnet, but at the gallows "he said to me before I spake to him, *That I should see it was not a false bravery, but that he was fearless to the last.*" Burnet cannot help admiring this lack of fear, for it is founded, however erroneously, upon the appropriate conviction: "he spake with great assurance of Gods mercy to him" (pp. 6–7). It is not in any case fear that he wants from the dying man, nor is it mere humility or even simply shame, but something more: a bravery and generosity of spirit that he can sanction and (though Burnet himself may not have been consciously aware of this requirement) put to use. It is not only that Vratz's contrition, if there is any, is too private; he has not in any visible way undergone that transformation of heart and mind – that "wonderful change" – that Burnet and Horneck seek and, presumably, feel to be important to the public they are serving.[35]

Now it is certainly possible that the pressure placed on the criminal to repent, and to attest publicly to his repentance, was prompted more by the practical and emotional needs of the public than by any real concern for his spiritual welfare. All the talk about saving his soul may well have been a "cover," witting or not, for what in effect was a variety of police work. It is not insignificant that Vratz is told his confession must include "who they were that put him upon it." Certainly on many other occasions a "full and ingenuous" confession cleared up a lot of loose ends. Prison chaplains threatened even thieves with eternal damnation unless they came clean. Who were their accomplices, where had they stashed their loot, what other, as yet unsolved crimes had they committed? Even in open-and-shut cases, where few if any loose ends were to be tidied up, the murderer's confession could have served to confirm not only the verdict of the court but the public's conception of how and why the crime had occurred.[36] A kind of sadism, too, may likely have been at work in the wish to make criminals bend to the public will – or to the will at least of those clergymen claiming to represent it. There would have been no better time to cut such powerful figures down to size than just before they were dispatched, forever, into the realm of memory and imagination.

But such motives cannot account for all that condemned criminals were required to do. Although the wish to "renovate" them (the term belongs to the bishop of Oxford) no doubt concealed the meanest motives, it was guided as well by an impulse both more humane and, I would argue, more broadly useful than any of the concerns just mentioned.[37] I have dwelt so long on Burnet and Horneck's involvement with Thynne's three murderers because it so fully indicates this impulse. Far more than any evidence for the cause of their crime, or for God's efficiency in detecting it, they wanted them to give proof that they had become new men – and better men than they had ever been before – and not so much despite their crime as because of it. If this was a way of getting to the bottom of things, it seems curiously roundabout. If it was a way of breaking them down, it seems curiously constructive. Nor were Burnet and Horneck at all peculiar, except for their relative eminence, in their response and concerns. Thynne's murderers had committed a crime that, for reasons of the moment, seemed more than usually egregious. But obscurer murderers and even petty criminals brought forth much the same response, provoked much the same curiosity about their states of mind not only before but after their crimes, raised the same concern about their capacity to experience emotional and spiritual change.[38]

Clearly, the pressures brought to bear on murderers to confess and repent had great religious significance. Their behavior spoke not only to the nature of God but to the nature of man and the relationship he could hope to have with God – in short, "to the highest concerns of Mankind in general."[39] Their penitence could be taken as evidence not only that God's justice still worked in this world but that His grace was accessible to all or, as the phrase went, was "free and universal." And more than this, though it began by emphasizing human depravity – as apparently it had to – the myth that attached to familiar murder promoted the idea that criminals were redeemable because conscience was active, at least potentially, in all men. Of course not everyone would have subscribed to this last idea. Though increasingly on its way to becoming one of the orthodoxies of the age, such a view of human nature had still to make its way against the contrary doctrines of Calvin and Hobbes, both of whom argued that man was a creature so inherently and irremediably depraved that only the imposition of a strong outside power – be it God (and the "saints" who represented Him) or a king (divinely sanctioned or not) – could maintain tolerable social order. Like everything else with religious implication in seventeenth- and eighteenth-century England, then, the effort to reshape the murderer – or rather to show him reshaped – was bound up in matters of large social and even (in the broadest sense) political concern. In England, as in France and other parts of early modern Europe, the public display of the confession, repentance, execution, and presumed salvation of notorious criminals was more than merely religious drama. In England, however, they ordered these things differently, using peculiarly English means in the service of peculiarly English ends. Thus the publication of criminals' "lives" could have as its aim not only the justification of God and the vindication of man but the strengthening, too, of an increasingly favored conception of society.

Chapter 5

Love makes all things easy: recementing the social bond

=====

As they could not spend their whole Time in Acts of Devotion, I thought they could not employ some intervals better, than in perfecting the Confessions which they had promis'd, which was a Satisfaction they ow'd their Country.

William Talbot, then bishop of Oxford, *Truth of the Case* (1708), p. 36

That Man who should deprive another of his life . . . has . . . thereby shew'd his Malice and Enmity to the whole human Race.

Trial of Charles Drew (1740), pp. 34–35

Murder is an unnatural sin: A man is a member of the Commonwealth, and so the murderer kills part of himself.

Heaven's Cry against Murder (1657), p. 15

But let us suppose, for once, that Murther reach'd no further than the Man. . . . we should find it to be criminal enough for all considering Men to stand aghast at; because of that Injury which it offers to Humane Society, which is the Band and Cement of the World . . . : it doth . . . by its noxiousness beget a dissidency in Men towards each other. . . . what is it, but to bring in that State of War, which some, though fondly, have imagin'd to be the state of Nature?

Gabriel Towerson, *An Exposition of the Catechism of the Church of England. Part II* (1681), p. 330

He reads by his example, a lecture of consolation.

R[obert Boreman], *Mirrour of Mercy* (1655), p. 30

And yet we can but pity their untimely transmigrations from this lower World . . . considering they are our Fellow-Creatures.

Execution of 11 Prisoners (1679)

The capture, trial, and punishment of criminals can by itself contribute to social solidarity, giving all good people occasion to reaffirm, in a spirit of righteous indignation, the orthodoxies that bind them together. "Crime," says Durkheim, "brings together upright consciences and concentrates them." One of the more peculiar aspects of this phenomenon in seventeenth- and eighteenth-century England was the pressure put on criminals to join in the process, indeed to show consciences more upright, more concentrated, than any that would survive their standing at the gallows. Murderers felt this pressure especially. "Of all other Criminals," said Paul Lorrain, "[they] should be the most concerned to repent." It was not merely that murder was especially offensive to God. The crime opened fissures in the social fabric, and, when murderers died silent and unresponsive, refusing to help in the enucleation of the truths their crimes had clouded, the damage they had done could never quite be undone. Their confessions, however – redacted and broadcast by the popular press – could allow those fissures to be (quite literally) papered over.[1]

Though murder caused theological tremors, there was not really very much in murderers' behavior to imperil religious belief. Whether models of piety or the rankest impenitence, they could be made to serve as examples of one religious truth or another: if not human depravity altered and saved by a wondrously beneficent God, then (and almost as usefully) that same depravity in need of God. The moral implications of their behavior could be far more troublesome, however, for here there was not the same latitude of interpretation. Unrepentant murderers gave human nature a bad press, and this was embarrassing to those who were finding it increasingly attractive to believe in the capacity of men to be good. This tendency was not unconnected with the political movement of the period toward increasing freedom for the (bourgeois, perhaps I should specify) individual. Having shown all too well what could follow from human evil, it was incumbent upon murderers (and especially familiar murderers) to show that human evil could be overcome – and not only with the help of God's free grace but as a result of something operative in themselves. This was the only way they could allay the "shock" they had given to human nature – the phrasing comes from *Remarkable Criminals* – and so repair the hurt they had inflicted on a doctrine of great social and no small political importance.[2]

Of all crimes, familiar murder would have seemed to challenge the very sufficiency of society to sustain itself, at least as it was tending to be constituted in England over the late seventeenth and early eighteenth centuries. The purpose of the political order, ostensibly, was to regulate human conduct according to the laws of God and Nature. If men by themselves were nothing but wicked and cruel – the starting lesson of a good many criminal biographies – the only politics possible would be those of Calvin or Hobbes. Men would have to be kept in check by some superior force – divinely directed or claiming to be – operating from outside themselves. The attractiveness of this prospect to the English polity can be gauged by the fact that, twice, it put an end to Stuart claims for the divine right of kings, nor could it ever really accommodate itself to Cromwell's Presbyterian Commonwealth. Long after the Calvinist threat had been dispersed, Hobbes's view of human nature rankled. "He makes Men a Prey to one another, until they have made themselves Slaves unto some absolute Sovereign," complained Thomas Horne in 1713; "they must inevitably be, according to his Notion, either Brutes by the Law of Nature, or Slaves by the Laws of a Civil State."[3] What Englishmen increasingly wanted, and what eventually they got, was a political order the first aim of which was not repression, a political order that felt it could afford to leave men free (men of the middling sort, at least, and within certain limits to be sure) to follow the dictates of their God-given consciences. But such a political order could only be built on a hopeful view of human nature.

This is of course a simplistic version of the political history of a notoriously complicated period; it deals with only the grossest, most schematic oppositions. Still, it requires no great sophistication to see how Burnet's latitudinarian emphasis on the goodness inherent in Stern and Borowsky, and potentially present even in Vratz – along with his deemphasis of anything possibly supernatural in the "vision" that prompted Borowsky's confession – was entirely congruent with his Whig politics. If even murderers could be shown to have what the third earl of Shaftesbury (Locke's pupil and the grandson of one of the first, most infamous Whigs) liked to call a "moral sense," then no propaganda inimical to the prevailing social order could be made out of their cases. I do not mean to suggest that conscious ideological battles broke out each time an especially shocking murder caught the public attention. Those whom one might call "liberals" (for want of a better term), and those who distrusted the push toward individual liberty, generally fought their battles around far more substantial issues, such as whether or not religious pluralism could or should be tolerated. But in those highly politicized times it seems that even individual cases of murder would have had political implications – however broad, general, and unacknowledged these may have been – and that these implications explain a good deal of the emotional energy invested in efforts to restore the murderer, before he was hanged, to the human community.[4]

Investments look for returns: What was wanted of the murderer was that he return to normalcy and then transcend it. Both Savage and Strodtman fulfilled these expectations by coming at last to a just sense of the crimes they had committed. Both showed a complete willingness not only to accept but even to collaborate in the punishment the law decreed for them. In their ability to stand up under the ordeal of public execution, they must have seemed almost superhuman. Which indeed was just what they were obliged to seem, if they were to compensate for behaving far worse than the "wolves and tygers" that Increase Mather liked (for his own political and theological ends) so unflatteringly to compare with humanity. There could be no more direct means of rescuing the idea of man from such opprobrium than to have the murderer himself show, as once he had sunk below nature, that now he could rise above it. This required that he show no simple disregard for dying. Self-preservation was the first law of nature, and a sullen contempt for death – a "senseless indolencie or blockish stupidity" – could very easily seem just another instance of his gross depravity, of his being more brutal still than the beasts.[5]

To illustrate the social significance of the murderer's conversion, I shall consider one case at length and a few others more briefly. In 1655 Freeman Sondes killed his elder brother, his only sibling and the heir to his father's considerable estate. The murderer, who was eighteen or nineteen years old, repented almost immediately, seemed to welcome imprisonment and death, and trusted that God would relieve him. That he was able to show a "true sight and hearty sorrow" of his "foule sinne" (these are his father's words) was taken to confirm the usual religious doctrines. A clergyman who visited and counseled him saw in Freeman's story that "lecture of consolation" quoted among our epigraphs, "saying, as it were . . . We may not alwaies measure the displeasure of God by his stripes, [for God] is the *Father of mercies* and forgiveness, and never rejected penitent and humble sinners." This same clergyman, inspired by Freeman's pious death on the gallows, concluded that "it is not in the power of man to outsinne mercy" unless by "an open and malicious rejecting of the truth."[6] In these sentiments there may seem nothing unusual – we read them again and again in accounts of criminals' conversions over at least the next century and a half – but in the particular context of 1655 their social (and, by extension, political) implications are especially clear. Perhaps it is important that this is the first full-blown instance I have found of the criminal-as-sinner myth.

Sir George Sondes, father to both the murderer and his victim, was a prominent landowner in the vicinity of Maidstone, Kent. Along with everything else he suffered as a consequence of his younger son's crime (he was a widower and thus lost all his family at a stroke) was no small amount of social embarrassment. Concluding that "certainly these fearful afflictions must be for some notorious sins," certain "Ministers and godly men" presented Sir George with a "Catalogue" of everything they felt he had done "amisse." Sir George was charged with not only personal immoralities, but the following: with failing to observe the charitable bequests included in the wills of his father, grandfather, and father-in-law; with interfering in the happiness of his elder, now-murdered son by blocking his marriage to an undowried (but beautiful) young lady; with being covetous; with rack-renting; with failing to keep up the old traditions of hospitality; with being lax in the observance of his religious duties at home; with having made no adequate financial provision for Freeman; with neglecting certain of his needy relatives; and with being a Royalist.[7] As this bill of particulars shows, a murderer's family could be put in an extremely vulnerable position, becoming fair game for anyone wishing to salvage some kind of meaning from a senseless, brutal crime. (Here the effort to find an etiology for murder extends beyond the behavior of the murderer to that of his family; perhaps one reason Mary Edmondson's brother-in-law wrote his pamphlet was to counter such aspersions.) Sir George was not one to suffer such an attack in silence. He published a reply in which he defended not only himself but his political and religious principles; these, it seems, had encouraged the attack in the first place.

Sondes's politics seem on the whole to have been fairly moderate. He admits to being a Royalist but only out of traditional loyalty to the king. He points out that he never took up arms against Parliament, even though certain estates of his had been sequestered. He pictures himself as a pious and God-fearing country gentleman, with good and sufficient reasons for all his actions, including the squeezing of his tenants for higher rents. "The times be now very bad," Sir George explains, and "Corn is so cheap" that he must have higher rents if his usual level of income is to be maintained. For our purposes, however, the most interesting part of Sir George's lengthy self-justification is the exposition of his religious views. These show him a sound Church of England man, which in the context of 1655 would have made him something of a reactionary. Nonetheless, Sir George is no supporter of priestcraft, believing that clerics (including, presumably, those "godly men" who have taken it upon themselves to upbraid him) ought to keep out of secular affairs. Nor, despite certain of the charges levied against him, is he any great favorer of a formal liturgy. He does not much hold for "praying by roat," believing that he "who cannot or does not upon extraordinary occasions, pour out his soul to God in his own words" can be no more than "a dull Christian." Still, he is no great sympathizer with the religious enthusiasms that gripped England at the time, and which, fragmenting the spiritual life of the country, disrupted its political life as well. He sees nothing wrong, for instance, with using "the set formes of Prayers of the Church, or of some other godly men." More significantly, he believes in the restoration of the episcopacy and the establishment of a truly catholic church. Having "ever loved solidities" he scorns those who would, "to seem more holy and Religious to the world," set "their

Congregations apart, crying stand off to their Brethren." Sir George is referring here to the Nonconformist sects, which excluded all but those who subscribed to their particular vision of the Church Militant; admission to their congregations was by application only, and subject to their approval. The Church of England, by contrast, was open to all Englishmen – indeed, claimed all Englishmen whether they wanted to be included or not. The sectarians may "brag of new Lights," writes Sondes, but these so-called new lights are nothing more than "old Heresies" revived, the product of an ignorance so perverse that it could thrive only in a society where all respect for duly constituted authority was lost. The religious radicals presume not only to alter the "antient Apostolicall, and holy practices of the Church," he complains, and to "have the Sacraments after a new way," but are even "angry if the Scripture be not taken in their sense" – "when God knowes," and here Sondes loses all patience, "they understand not one word of the original to expound it by." But what else is to be expected, when "now our illiterate Mechanicks, who must have seven years to learn their own trade, will at seven days or lesse, undertake to teach . . . Divinity . . . the apex, and chiefe of all the Sciences"?[8]

Sir George must have found it particularly galling that two such "mechanicks" shouldered their way forward at Freeman's execution, wanting to question him. Sir George was all too aware of the role that religious ideology could play in attacks on social prerogative not to feel the affront they offered. Such people, he complains, in being "so very strict in keeping the Sabbath," find license to "break all the other commandments, as if he that said, thou shalt keep holy the Sabbath day, had not likewise said, thou shalt not kill, thou shalt not steale."[9] Here Sondes indicts not only the regicides and the sequestrators but that whole class of people who had nerve enough to fight and win a bloody civil war, and even – some of them – to dream of a redistribution of property. Such people recognized Sir George for what he was, a class enemy – who else would raise rents when the price of corn was depressed and *everyone's* income was going down – and he knew it. Thus their attack, and his defense. What neither he nor they knew in 1655, of course, was that the revolution would be postponed and a large part of it canceled. At the Restoration Sir George remarried, raised a new family, and prospered once more. At the time of his life that interests us, however, he was mainly concerned with preserving his sense of self-respect, restoring something of the family honor, and keeping his religious (and political) principles afloat.

Perhaps it was at his behest – certainly it was to his advantage – that Robert Boreman came down to Kent to minister to Freeman's spiritual needs. Boreman had recently been evicted from a fellowship at Trinity

College, Cambridge. Perhaps his religious views were to blame; Cambridge was very much a place for Puritans during the Interregnum, and Boreman got his fellowship back at the Restoration. But the important thing is that Boreman put as un-Calvinist a face as he could on Freeman Sondes, given the nature of his crime. "When you hear or read his name," Boreman wrote to his fellow Christians, "you will look for a Monster in Nature . . . one *not like other men*." Boreman speaks to this expectation because it is something he wants especially to confront and overturn. "So horrid, so unheard of, so unnatural was the fact," he continues, "that I confesse, when I first made my addresses to him . . . I plainly told him, that *I expected to see the head of a Monster,* (a *Beare* or a *Tigre*) *set upon the shoulders of a man;* So amazed (even to misbeliefe) was I at the first report of the murther." All this near hysteria is prompted by a simple searching question: "For who would think that Brethren, and they but two, nurs'd up in the lap of Religion, and bosomes of the Church should not love each other?"[10] For Boreman this was a large and terrible question.

His naive reaction to the appearance of psychological monstrosity is of course not ours; we know better and can accommodate ourselves rather easily to the idea that people outwardly normal can commit the most horrible acts. We can accept more easily the idea that brothers, even only brothers raised in the bosom of the Church, can hate each other (especially only brothers, perhaps, especially in the bosom of the Church). We enjoy the advantage of having, as Boreman and his contemporaries did not, an etiology of crime that can be made to work – or at least to *seem* to work – to explain (and so explain away) even the most unaccountable crimes. And we have a further advantage, too, for Boreman operated under a double difficulty. Although Freeman's crime was entirely unaccountable to him, others could explain it all too easily. There were those who disliked Sir George and what he stood for, and who (more importantly) had little respect if any for the Church in which his sons were raised. To such people – and especially to the Calvinists among them, who saw nothing but monstrosity in human nature anyway – Freeman's crime would not have been amazing at all, just one more confirmation of a just God's overruling providence, a sign of what awaits the unrighteous. Certainly this was the point of view of those "godly men" who presented Sir George with that "catalogue" of his sins, and it may have been the point of view as well of those two mechanics who showed up (Sir George thought) to insult him at his son's execution.

Boreman seems mainly to be concerned with rebutting the idea that Freeman is a monster in human form (and, as such, a proof of human monstrosity). And he does what he can to make the murder *and* its aftermath seem ultimately God's blessing in disguise. Like a good many of those who reported the dying behavior of criminals after him, Boreman sets out to achieve these ends not only by describing that behavior but (here exercising his clergyman's prerogative) by actually shaping it. And like those who followed him, too, Boreman seems preeminently concerned with keeping the crime on a human level, with making it seem acceptable there, without undue recourse to the supernatural. This may not seem especially evident at first. Thus Boreman explains that Freeman killed his brother under the influence of "a melancholy passion (*he being deeply in love with a fair Gentlewoman*) together with a Diabolicall suggestion (Gods grace for a time deserting him)." This attention to the psychology of his subject, though Boreman neither cares to nor can explain the crime in psychological terms, is important as an intellectual gesture. The "envie" that moved his client to "act so horrid a sin" is inexplicable to him except as "a plant of the Devils setting in the heart of man[, which] choakes the seed of all good Education," but Boreman is too much the humanist to want to leave the matter there. Though men are vulnerable to diabolical suggestion, and consequently have to rely on God's good offices to keep them from evil, this does not necessarily mean they are without a moral character of their own. Thus even as he blames the Devil for the "enmity between *Man* and *Man*" so luridly displayed by Freeman's crime, Boreman chooses not to resolve the problem it presents at a miraculous level.[11] Human evil is not countered by any dramatic intervention of God; rather, Boreman holds out to the public the murderer's heart itself, dispossessed of evil and now given over wholly to good. And though Freeman's conversion has of course to be laid to God's reviving grace, God does not get all the credit.

A "sound" repentance, according to Boreman, is "grounded upon the consideration of God's goodness and mercy." This "consideration" then engenders "that heart-compunction, or griefe of minde" that brings us to understand "that we have offended our good God, our heavenly, and most loving Father." It is this sense of "sorrow," as Boreman calls it, that begins the penitent's process of moral recovery. First there is "a change in the *Mind* or *Judgement,* disproving, or disallowing that evill which we have ungodily committed." This alteration of "mind" then produces in its turn "a change of the *will* which repudiates, or declines that evill, and embraces with a delightfull choice the good which formerly was refused, and enclines to it, as its chief joy and content." It is "this change of the will," finally, that prepares a "true" convert for the ultimate "change of [his] heart or affections": a condition in which, "hating and detesting that sin wherein [he has] offended," the penitent is moved to "a love and prosecution of that good duty which [he] did not, and is to be done."[12] As Boreman describes it, Freeman's conversion followed just this scheme; and it is observable, too, that later murderers followed a similar pattern. It is a pattern that "undoes" the sequence of psychic events that was thought to lead up to such crimes – and indeed to all great sins – the movement of influence that Boreman traces from the penitent's mind or judgment to his will, and from his will to his heart and affections, being the reverse of the psychological (if one may call it that) process that led him away from "good duty" in the first place. Thus the popular literature of crime typically traces murder back to Sabbath-breaking or some other shirking of "good duty"; this is supposed to have led to a hardening or corruption of heart, which (as the criminal goes on to commit even greater enormities) weakens the will and leads eventually to a corrupted judgment, an impaired mind. How else could the murderer have thought to kill? Even had he planned on committing the "perfect" crime and so have hoped to escape being hanged, he would have had to have forseen – had he still been rational – that God would not permit his crime to go unavenged in this world and that conscience itself would torment him.

The social and ultimately political significance of explaining the process of conversion along these lines, as a reversal of the process that leads sinners (and all men are sinners) to ever greater evils, is that such an explanation allows for a compensatory action of the will against the drift to (speaking in modern terms) utter id-ridden anarchy. However insensibly men may move from small sins to even the greatest of crimes, there is always open to them the possibility of reversing the process, of turning themselves again toward the good. "He well knew, when he did amiss," Lorrain reports a burglar saying, "that he ought to have done, and could (if he would) have done otherwise." The implication is obvious: As crime is a failure of the will – "he . . . could (if he would) have done otherwise" – one need only to assert one's will to stay clear of it. Another of Lorrain's charges claimed he had resolved to reform innumerable times but, says Lorrain, "he did not *seriously think* [italics mine] of parting with . . . those wicked Persons who . . . encouraged him in his . . . vicious Course of Life." Had he chosen to think, we are left to infer, neither he nor the commonwealth would have had much to worry about. Such a point of view, and here is the heart of its social and political importance, denies that men are the forlorn creatures a Calvinist or Hobbesian determinism would make them out to be. Not only do they have free will, but they can direct that will – or as the case may be, redirect it – back toward God and "good duty." The "only Use" to be made of the biographical details of one recalcitrant murderer, James Guthrie said, was "to exhibit the Steps by which he gradually declined to this amazing Wickedness, that other young Men who are conscious to themselves of having gone part of the Road, may stop short in Time." Of course this hopeful tendency should not be overemphasized. This same murderer was hanged in Holburn, "as near to the House where the Gentlewoman was murdered as possible, in order to strike a Terror on the Minds of wicked disposed People."[13] Not all hearts and minds were thought to be equally sensible.

Another way of saying all this is that there are grains of goodness even in the worst of men, which, properly tended, may flourish and grow: a dictum Freeman would have disconfirmed had he failed to show what his father called a "true sight and hearty sorrow" of his "foule sinne." It was Sir George's hope, quoted approvingly by Boreman, that there were still "some sparks of grace" in his son and that these "though deeply buried under a world of rubbish," might be brought to "burn clear" with the "fire of true repentance and godly sorrow." Although Sir George believed that such a blazing up could be accomplished only with the help of the clergy's "godly bellowes" (unfortunately this raises an almost Swiftian image), still he emphasized the centrality of Freeman's own efforts to achieve salvation: "It must come from thy own self, thy own heart must beg it, or all will be in vain." The saved sinner cooperates with God and in that cooperation achieves some merit of his own; or, as Sir George says, not even "the strongest blowings" can "kindle fire in a dead coale . . . if no spark of fire lies hidden under the ashes."[14]

Sir George of course was concerned for the personal honor of his son and for that of his family, but broader issues were involved as well. Boreman shows by his own reaction to Freeman's conversion how much was at stake not only for him but for the community at large. Certain "poor mistaken souls," he observes, were "offended" at his giving Freeman "the Holy Communion the night before he was to die." Evidently he means a group of Presbyterians, "envious malicious *Pharisees* of our age," who had seized control of the Church in Maidstone and "debarred" many of their fellow townsmen from the sacraments because (he says) they would not "subscribe to their decrees." From Boreman's point of view, Freeman's dying behavior gives the lie to their exclusionist principles. How can there be grounds for excluding anyone from communion, if even murderers so visibly profit? Who would seem farther from God's grace than a fratricide? "Those who would build a wall of *Discipline* in the Church," Boreman triumphantly declares, with "stones fetch'd out of the Quarries of *Scotland* and *Geneva*," now find those very same stones "are fallen upon their own heads; the wall is beaten down."[15]

Freeman's conversion was a victory for both his father, then, and a certain view of society. It had in it, to use Boreman's phrasing again, a deliverance from "cruelty" and "persecution for conscience" for all "those *Christians,* who live soberly and honestly with repute in their several callings, whose compasse (by which they steere their lives) is *Faith,* not *Faction,* whose profession too, is not to side with parties, but to serve the Lord Jesus." This is not to say that the Calvinists could not have put Freeman to use themselves. Boreman believes they were angry at his success because "they perhaps would have done [it] themselves . . . and so get (which was their aim) a little glory by popular applause to their proud persons."[16] But a Calvinist interpretation of Freeman's dying behavior would have been quite different. Murderers were frequent objects of consideration in New England – both Increase and Cotton Mather used them as examples of the fallen condition of man – but there was none of the emphasis there we find in England, for the next century and more, on the murderer's individual state of consciousness, on the role that he himself plays in achieving salvation. Murderers repented and presumably were saved, or did not and presumably were lost, as the Lord wished and quite irrespective of their individual merits.[17] But this was not the lesson to be derived from or preached to criminals about to die in England. Paul Lorrain, entirely typical, preached an easy and comfortable theology to the inmates of Newgate Prison. "God," he assured them and the public at large, "has made the *Terms* of *Salvation* such, as all Men might receive them and comply with them"; "every one that will not only and barely *Hear,* but also religiously *Keep,* the Word of God, and obey it, shall be *Blessed.*" A key word here – a term that separates Lorrain and English orthodoxy in general from the narrower views of Calvinism – is "everyone." Nor from Lorrain's point of view is religiously keeping the word of God, at least well enough to be saved, an impossible standard to achieve (as it would of course be for a Calvinist). Thus he could assure his audience of condemned prisoners that "if we are kept from Presumptuous Sins" – and by these he meant "such as are both known and wilful; and have . . . a reigning habitual Power in us" – "we shall be safe in and out of Danger: We shall be in a State of Grace, a State of . . . Favour with God."[18]

The comfort of this theology, so reassuring to the individual, was not without political importance. Calvinism, by dividing mankind into a minority predestined to be saved and a majority foredestined to be damned, could be nothing but socially divisive. The latitudinarian orthodoxies espoused by Lorrain, however, served (though only at the religious level) to erase all social distinctions: All men could share in God's grace.[19] And of course it was a more hopeful, more man-centered theology than Calvinism. Calvinism filled the mind "with Horror and Perplexity." Its adherents spoke "rather as if they came to fright [the criminal's] soul into a distracting despair, then to fortifie her with comforts." Lorrain, however, preached that "Men may be renew'd and *born again*," that "*Corruption*, though inveterate and deeply rooted in our *Nature*, yet may be overcome and removed from us." For Lorrain all this was possible because God's grace was "free" not in the Calvinist sense – where it meant that God dished out favor as he pleased regardless of individual merit – but in the sense that it was available to all, almost for the asking. "Do but begin to waken to a Penitent Conviction," Samuel Smith begged the condemned prisoners in Newgate, "Do but begin to arise to Newness of Life . . . and thou shalt find God will Bless such thy good Beginnings, will convince and illuminate thee more and more to see thy past Errors and Miscarriages; will add fresh Supplies to thy renewd Inclinations, and Holy Purposes of Amendment; will make them proceed from Strength to Strength in Advances of Grace, till he has compleated thy Reformation, and fitted thee for Eternal Glory." Neither Smith nor Lorrain nor Boreman nor the many others who preached essentially the same message to criminals – and, through them, to the public as well – could quite be called humanists. They asserted the supremacy of God – it is He who changes hearts – and did not stand so far away from Calvinism as to endow men with the ability to save themselves. Yet they did allow the human will a role in individual salvation, and it is a crucial role, for though men cannot by themselves effect their own repentance and conversion, still it is they who initiate the process. "God's Grace," a late seventeenth-century writer made bold to affirm, "denies not to receive the vilest and most crimson sinners, whenever they wish a sincere and hearty Repentance." This is not quite the humanism that provides the only grounds possible for political liberalism, but it verges near. Lorrain was even capable of saying in one of his giddier moments – he was preaching at the funeral of a man hanged for killing a constable in a Mayfair fracas, and apparently got a healthy fee – that "to *Do well* is . . . an Art which may be easily learn'd by us."[20]

The execution of each criminal, then, was potentially an experiment in human nature. This was especially true in cases of murder, given the debate that went on as to whether indeed it was a crime inherent in us, and most true in those cases where the murderer had violated deeply ingrained beliefs about the natural limits of human cruelty. Each time the murderer, dying in the white heat of religious enthusiasm, could show himself become something better than he had ever been before, better even than an ordinary man, he – who in his crime would have shown himself something worse than a beast – would have given satis-

faction not only to the moral and religious hopes of his society but
(conceiving the term broadly) to its political ideology as well. Indeed,
the importance of his repentance from an exclusively social point of
view would seem to have been its power to raise him – and, if him,
why not other men? – from the meanest, most brutal, and least enlight-
ened self-interest to a death, astonishingly, that could be made to seem
an act of charity to all those remaining behind in this world. Freeman
Sondes did not die an especially demonstrative death; he submitted to
execution "in a calme and sweet temper" as Boreman described it, or,
to use Freeman's own words, "as cheerfully as ever he went to bed."
But other murderers were hardly so diffident. Nathaniel Butler, for
instance, who slit his best friend's throat while the two were lying
abed, offered the world the spectacle of a man who had been "a bloody
and unhuman wretch," but now whose "penitence and . . . reall contrition spake much of a Saint." Expressing "great affection and compassion . . . to the souls of others," he warned all who would listen that
though they might "think themselves in good estate," being "free from
such gross and scandalous crimes," still they had "the same nature."
They too were imperiled at the bar of eternity, as much as he – or even
more, for Butler, playing his role to the hilt, spoke to his audience of
the nature "that I had." He was beyond them now, as before he had
been beneath them. Stern in his own way was even more patronizing,
venturing from his exalted standpoint – "I do already feel the Almighty
God in my Soul" – to give advice not only to the "Governours of the
World" (by whom he meant "Kings, Princes, Vice-Roys") but also to
"ye Officers, Colonels, and great Men," "ye *Gentlemen, Burgomasters,
Aldermen,* and *Grand Bailiffs,*" "ye *Bishops, Abbots, Deans,*" "ye Merchants," "*Seamen* and *Skippers,*" and "*Doctors* of the Civil Law, *Proctors*
and *Advocates.*" Nor did he in the greatness of his heart overlook your
more usual "*Drunkards, Ranters,* and *Blasphemers,* and *Underminers*
of . . . Neighbours," "*Whoremasters,* and *Gamesters,*" "Tradesmen and
Artificers," "Prisoners," and "the common Souldiery." Edmund Kirk
speaks in stark contrast to this manic outburst, saying simply, "I am
now worse than the Brute that Perisheth; and I have nothing of Cleanli-
ness or Humanity about me." But at the same time this is part of his
"Legacy to Surviving Sinners," and as such may seem a form of reverse
snobbery; the statement in any case refutes itself.[21]

Savage, Strodtman, a good many other murderers, and even lesser
criminals died amidst the same preachifying, were similarly transformed. The phrases, postures, sentiments, were all standardized:
"Good People, take warning by my Fall; you see I am a young Man,
who by my Sins have shortened my Days, and brought my Self to this
Shameful but deserved Death. . . . Live not as I have done, lest you

come to the like sad and untimely End. Break not the Sabbath-Day, and keep not Company with wicked Men and Lewd Women, as I have done. . . . Avoid all manner of Sin, even the smallest; for from one little Sin Men easily fall to the Commission of greater ones." These words supposedly were spoken by John Estrick on 10 March 1703, just before he was hanged for robbing a house, but they could just as easily have come from anyone about to be executed, for any crime, some fifty years before or after. When such declarations were not forthcoming, they – and the things they stood for – were missed. Thus Lorrain complains in 1715 that a recently hanged pirate showed he "had no Sense nor Principles . . . that could restrain him from Evil," for though he "should have grown more rational and considerate at the approach of Death, yet he still retain'd his harden'd Temper and Irreligious and Impious Humor." A similar complaint was voiced in 1737, by one of Lorrain's successors, when he reported that certain prisoners just executed "did not appear affected and tender hearted as became such atrocious Sinners in their most miserable Circumstances." In both complaints we can recognize the same disappointment: The expectation was that dying criminals would reveal a resurgent moral sense, would come to seem "free, true, sincere" before they had to die. But even this was not the full extent of what could be expected, especially in cases of murder.[22]

Thus an account of John Marketman's behavior in prison sounds curiously apologetic. Marketman showed a proper regret for killing his wife but was frightened at the prospect of dying. "And though he was . . . jealous and suspicious of the state of his mind," the text hastens to add by way of assurance, "yet he was not found by any to despond, or fall into any unworthy abjectness of Spirit. . . . when Fears and Tremblings through the weakness of the flesh sometimes seiz'd upon him . . . he quickly recovered himself again, and fixed his foot upon the *Rock of Ages*." Marketman is one of the rare penitent murderers to come down to us through the mythology of crime in nervous disarray. He lacks that "happy Disposition, as not only to be well prepared for Death, but to wish it rather than Life itself." He did not "bless God that I ever came to a Prison," as Thomas Savage did, nor did he declare, as another murderer reportedly did, that "it was a happy thing that he ever came to *Newgate,* for by that means he was now brought to a true Sense of his Sins, and of God's Loving-Kindness and Mercy." It was not that Marketman was devoid of such sentiments; he was indeed quite sorry for what he had done, acknowledged his sinfulness, accepted the religious counselings of the clergy who visited him, and finally managed even to make the requisite speeches. It was that he singularly lacked the kind of sustained enthusiasm for death that, for instance, Stern could show. Protesting to Horneck that "it was not . . . the punishment that was like to attend him in this world that moved him to repentance, but the blackness of the Crime, and his offending a Gracious God," Stern "broke forth into holy Ejaculations fit for a Christian and a true Penitent." Horneck was convinced that he was "content" to die, and impressed by how "chearfully" he could speak of it. The trouble with Marketman's dying behavior was that it failed to live up to this high standard. His "jealousy" and "suspicion" as to "the state of his mind," his "doubts" and "tremblings" – the particular phrasing is highly significant – did not "make him meet to be a partaker of the Inheritance amongst the Saints in life."

The reference to "saints" suggests the Calvinist notion of "election," but the writer here is clearly not much of a Calvinist. Were he, Marketman's damnation would seem plain to him, and he would not be arguing that the man was nonetheless "acted [upon] by a more than ordinary Spirit, and that the Spirit of the Lord." What we have here is a peculiar and rather promiscuous adaptation of the Calvinist notion of sainthood: the idea, indeed the wish, that murderers show themselves "saints in life" before, perforce, their lives are ended. Butler's "reall contrition," we have noted, "spake much of a Saint," and though the term seems to have fallen out of use as time went on (very likely because of its Calvinist connotations), murderers and even lesser felons continued to show something peculiarly exalted in their dying behaviors, something that was certainly noted and appreciated in the popular literature of crime, and that was sufficient to gain them the grateful esteem of all who came forward to help them out of this world. Thus, for example, though Francis Newland's friends were disturbed to see him die for a murder they felt he had not committed, they were pleased to see him show "a well satisfied Acquiescence in his Disposal, whatever it might seem to Flesh and Blood." William Boteler's friends were similarly pleased that "his Affections were wholly set on things above, so as to be little solicitous for, or about his Temporal concerns." Perhaps what impressed them most was that, when his execution date was set, he received the news "with an unmoved Christian-courage, as tidings he had long expected, serving only to waft him out of the raging straits of a sinful world into an Ocean of Beatitude." Even lesser criminals could assume this style, could sail round the same cape of good hope into the same pacific ocean. "Tho my sensual Pleasures had lull'd me into a perfect Neglect of my Future State," declared a burglar in a written statement given to the Newgate ordinary, "the sweet Refreshments which I constantly received by the elaborate Performances of the Reverend Mr. *Lorrain,* encourage me to esteem this" – his execution – "as the happiest Minute of my Life, tho attended with all these outward Marks of Infamy." "Oh! the Transcendent Joys," cried an arsonist about to be hanged, "I am not able to express the Joys I have since I have been condemned." Less ecstatic but no less "happy" was a convicted forger, who said "his Fears of Death were removed, and that he found true Consolation. . . . Accordingly, when he first appeared under the Tree, he was smiling."[23] Only "saints" could rise so joyfully above the shame and terror of a public execution, or so those who subscribed to the myth apparently wanted to believe. Thus they could be sorely perplexed when the likes of Mary Edmondson coolly braved the gallows, claiming to be innocent; she did not fit their paradigm.

The lifting of the murderer out of the normal world of ordinary men had several socially useful functions. For one thing, like so many other elements in the myth we are considering, it served to validate religious belief. Few things could testify more to the power of religious consolation than the enthusiasm with which criminals greeted death, "nothing being more frightful than Death; especially when attended with . . . the Pomp of a publick Execution, and the Scorns of a gazing Multitude; which are additional Terrors, that unassisted Nature knows not well how to bear."[24] But why was it expected that murderers especially should greet death enthusiastically? Part of the reason, I suppose, was merely the magnitude of their offense. The worse the sinner and the greater his repentance, the greater the glory that would have accrued to those who saved his soul; all professions must advertise, and the priesthood is no exception.[25] But not all those who encouraged or cajoled great criminals into something akin to sainthood were clergymen; other motives were at work. One of these would seem preeminently practical: It was easier to hang "saints" than ordinary men, as "saints" minded less. Consider the problems inherent in restoring a criminal to the human community when, ultimately, he was to be hanged. Suppose that, now made as good and as whole as anyone else, he (and others) should begin to wonder if indeed he should die. The problems such feelings could open up would be especially acute if the criminal's offense was nothing so bloody as murder (a subject considered at length in Chapter 7). But no such problems could arise, really, if the criminal were to seem indifferent to his fate in this world – or, better yet, to welcome the prospect of leaving it for a happier, more glorious one. There was of course no question but that murderers had to die. God specifically commanded this, on pain of collective guilt. But hanging even an ordinary murderer can be distasteful, and hanging a "born-again" murderer who does not want to die might well risk another kind of collective guilt. The extraordinary unconcern that murderers like Butler, Savage, Boteler, even the possibly innocent Newland could show in the face of their imminent and necessary demise had, among other things, this great value: It allowed their friends and supporters the luxury of wondering whether they indeed deserved to die. Or, to make my point more explicitly, it freed them to love the beautiful thing they had helped to create (all the more beautiful because of the ugliness it replaced) and which had to be destroyed. And, as we are about to see, the friends and well-wishers of penitent murderers could be numerous indeed.

"God suffer'd him thus to be thrown down," Stern told Horneck, "that through that toss he might rebound the higher." By reversing the process of his "fall," by returning to the "zero-point" of normalcy and then surpassing it, by reaching a level of transcendence that arced him as high above the norms of "nature" as previously he had sunk beneath them, the murderer made his death a gift to the community. Even if "there was no profite at all in his life to his Countrie," said one writer of a penitent murderer, "his Discoverie and Death" could be of "some use, and good service." The notion could extend to other criminals as well. "Oh take warning by my sad Example," said a servant girl hanged for firing her master's house, "pray get some good to your selves by my Sin, and shameful Death."[26] And, in making his gift to the community, the murderer did more than merely flatter its values and aspirations. He provided a deterrent example, to be sure, and – more importantly – supported its religious and moral orthodoxies, testifying to the existence of a beneficent order not only in the universe but in man's own heart. Beyond this he also provided a certain kind of social occasion, the effect of which was twofold. It restored the connection he so viciously had broken between himself and other men and served to bind those other men (at least some of them) more firmly together among themselves. I am speaking of the creation of a feeling of mutuality that is both vertical, the murderer joining himself together with all right-thinking men by coming to espouse and embody certain key doctrines they hold dear, and horizontal, the joining together of all right-thinking men in the experience of the same, now charitable emotions toward the same, now worthy object. By showing himself a "saint in life," the murderer stimulated both kinds of mutuality. By becoming an object of admiration (the original sense "to wonder at" is apposite) he made himself something that people could afford to love as well as destroy. "Love," as we shall see, is not too extravagant a term.

In a few cases Durkheim's "upright consciences" could come together dramatically. In 1635 Thomas Sherwood was hanged for a series of murderous muggings. Confessing that "all the while he lived, his life was a kinde of Hell unto him," he "joyfully embraced" death and "sent his soule out of his Body flying, calling on the name of the Lord Jesus to receive him." This prompted "all the people" watching his execution to speak "likewise with their [loud] voyces, and strong acclamations, *Lord Jesu* take mercy on him, sweete Jesu forgive his sinnes, and save his *Soule.*" Post-Restoration England was hardly the place for such public displays of religious enthusiasm, at least on official occasions. Generally it was only the chaplain who prayed at the place of execution, singing a few psalms with or without the accompaniment of the condemned. Still, if only at a distance and more decorously, the spectacle of a criminal's execution – provided he was properly penitent and especially if he were guilty of a more than usually heinous murder – could bring great portions of the public together in compassionate concern. A case in point is that of Robert Foulkes, mentioned earlier as the minister hanged in 1679 for the murder of his bastard child. Provided with "an excellent Prayer fitted for his occasion," Foulkes "transcribed [it] with his own hand, and caused [it] to be sent to most Churches in *London.*" As a result, he "was earnestly pray'd for, through the whole City."

A similar focus for compassionate concern was provided by Samuel Goodere, whose murder of his brother (as we've already noted) seemed only the last and wickedest of a whole series of bad deeds. His friends, once he was imprisoned, had "several Sermons preached to him" in hope of bringing him to "a sense of religion." One such sermon was delivered "by an intimate Friend" shortly before he was hanged. The preacher spoke "in such a pathetick and moving Manner, that it drew Tears from his Eyes and most of his Audience." The pronomial ambiguity here keeps us from knowing whether it was the preacher himself or Goodere who wept, but not long after this Goodere finally came to "a true Repentance and Abhorrence of [his] Atrocious Crime." Some of the credit for his turnaround goes, conventionally enough, to "the Blessing of God." But perhaps even more important, judging from the attention they get, were "the Power and Grace" of "those pious holy good Men" who "mollified his Heart by . . . their Speeches and Admonitions." Goodere's heart had to be softened so that it might answer to a certain softness they wanted to find in their own; this need could make them adamant. Thus, when all other measures seemed to have failed, they had a coffin delivered to his cell, with this inscription on its lid:

SAMUEL GOODERE, *Aged 53 Years,*
who departed this life April 15, 1741.

The date, a week in the future, was that fixed for his execution. This reminder of his *terminus ad quem* seems to have concentrated Goodere's mind wonderfully, for, handsomely repaying his friends for their "charitable Assistance," he finally submitted to his fate with "a becoming Decency" before "the greatest Crowd as ever was known in Bristol."[27]

Admittedly, this is not a typical case. As in the Sondes affair a special effort was being made to minimize the scandal murder brought down on an otherwise reputable family. Still, as we have seen, the same sort of "well-wishers" gathered around Savage and Strodtman, and no doubt would have swarmed as eagerly around Edmondson, had she given them the slightest encouragement. The public response to Wood and Billings, who helped Catherine Hayes murder and dismember her husband in 1726, was entirely typical. As they "desired the Prayers of all the Persons that came to see them in *Newgate*" so (we are led to infer) they got them. Many of their visitors, moreover, "generously relieved their Necessities by giving them Money, and pious Books suitable to their Circumstances." Such attentions may seem nothing more than gratitude for services rendered, and may even be dismissed as bribery. Certainly there was an element of quid pro quo; the public was not willing to be sympathetic if it got nothing in return. When in 1722 Arundel Coke asked the spectators at his execution to pray for him, they called him "Rogue" and "Villain," said "Hanging's too good for him; he should have been torn in Pieces with wild Horses; he should have been boil'd in oyl; he should have been burnt at a slow Fire; and the like." "This Rage of the People, uncommon in the generous English Temper," was prompted by the nature of his crime, a "hellish and abominable" attempt on his brother-in-law's life, and by the rumor that he had earlier poisoned one of his victim's children. But it owed a great deal, too, to Coke's "behaviour," which "was to an extream mean dejected, and attended with a seeming Despair, or, like, a Man, stupid and not present to himself." "Had he given such Testimonies of Repentance as [his] Villainy call'd for," says an eyewitness to the event, and shown himself "as a Man, touch'd with a true Remorse . . . the People, touch'd with his Misery would at least have sent one Lord have Mercy upon his Soul along with him to the Gallows."[28] Coke's audience was repulsed, it would seem, because he didn't try to meet them halfway; far worse criminals had gained the sympathy of the public.

But there was more to this phenomenon than the mere exchanging of compliments. A compassionate attachment to the murderer had in it the power to make people feel good in the wake of something that, quite understandably, had made them feel especially bad. Though his crime set him apart from the mass of men, his repentance could bring him back into their midst; moreover, in rejoining the family of man, he could bring that heterogeneous grouping into a closer relationship. A description of the crowd that gathered at William Boteler's execution in the late seventeenth century will show what I mean: "There were present a great many persons of Quality; and a vast number of common people" – the semicolon where a comma would do seems almost to emphasize the separateness of the two classes – "but so affecting was his language and behaviour, extorting tears from his very Enemies . . . that scarce any there but wept, and bewail'd his untimely end, as if he had been one of their own Relations." And of course to the extent they all felt related to him, the more they would have felt related to each other. Gentry, common people, Boteler's friends and enemies: all wept together with the same heart's sorrow.[29]

This feeling of kinship with murderers (and others who clearly deserved to die for their crimes) would seem to have been valued for reasons both individual and social. "E.S.," one of the several people who came forward to solace and defend Francis Newland, justified his involvement with the convicted murderer on the grounds that he had "a special Sense and Feeling" that what he was doing was right; and this "sense and feeling," he added, was confirmed by the "Satisfaction that I then had in my own Soul of [Newland's] Approbation and Ratification of what I then did." The feeling of a bond with a repentant criminal about to die, then, had no need of any justification beyond itself: It was a good feeling, and not the less so because it testified to one's own goodness. "One must want humanity and be totally void of that tenderness which demonstrated both a man and a Christian," opined the author of *Remarkable Criminals*, "if we feel not some pity for those who are brought to a violent and shameful death from a sudden and rash act." Or, as the author of a letter offering spiritual advice to a capitally convicted felon wrote, "a Concern for Mankind is no more than a Piece of Humanity." This was all the explanation he felt he needed to give for writing such a letter to someone he did not know and had never met. The writer of a similar letter, to a man who had drunkenly beaten his wife to death in the street, was even more direct in expressing his motives. He wrote, he said, "from that Principle of Love I bear to your soul," and hoped to visit him soon in prison. His use of the word "love" is hardly extraordinary. Paul Lorrain, for instance, could find no other way of explaining the perseverance of "a Gentleman of Piety and good parts" (himself a prisoner for debt) in helping to bring a condemned man to a condign repentance. This "gentleman," notes Lorrain, spent "two whole Nights in reading and praying with him in the Condemn'd Hold; a place of no pleasant Abode" – "but," Lorrain adds, "Love makes all things easy."[30]

The ability of men to express such "love" was important, for it like the criminal's repentance (and even ultimate sanctity) was evidence for the human capacity to be good. Rising above anything that smacked of a spirit of revenge, those who felt compassion for the (to be sure, appropriate kind of) criminal could congratulate themselves – and each other – on their Christian "tenderness." And this was no small thing socially, for as Lorrain preached to his charges, "the Want of . . . Christian Love in Men, is the Cause of most, if not all, the Murthers, Robberies, Injuries, and other Mischiefs committed in the World." On such occasions as William Boteler's execution, when even "the most marble-hearted Spectators . . . melt[ed] at their Eyes, and compassion seize[d] the most obdurate breasts," the world Lorrain describes – a world too filled with crime and "other Mischiefs" – may have seemed a better, or at least an ameliorable, place. The consolation that "E.S." could take after Francis Newland was hanged (unjustly, he and others thought) is instructive. Remarking that "it pleased God to raise him up divers *Friends,* who were Strangers to him before, and yet were so affected with a Sense of his Circumstances," he declares that he had "never known the like in any such Case," and takes heart from the joining of so many people together in a common effort "upon the meer Principles of Charity and Christianity."[31]

At best, then, the hurt the murderer had done society was healed over by reciprocal acts of generosity. "The Cement that unites Mankind, the Bond that holds Communities together," preached Richard Newcome in 1728, was "mutual Love and Kindness." Even a less than perfect murderer, then, could help restore a sense of community; all that compassionate people needed was an opportunity to share their generous emotions with others similarly affected by his fate. When Mary Blandy was hanged at Oxford in 1752 for poisoning her father, many of the five thousand spectators, "and particularly several gentlemen of the university," were sufficiently overcome to "shed tears." Though she refused to take complete responsibility for the crime, blaming it all on her lover who had escaped prosecution by fleeing abroad, her willingness to forgive the jury that convicted her may have been one of the things that disposed the crowd in her favor, along with her readiness to be offered up as a warning "against the sallies of any irregular passions" (her own words). There were, to be sure, peculiar circumstances that made her guilt seem less than absolute. But the tears of all those spectators may well have been prompted, too, by nothing more than the simple and powerful attraction of experiencing, in the aftermath of a peculiarly horrid and senseless crime, something like the purgative pathos of tragedy – and, perhaps most important, of experiencing it together.[32]

Something like this is clearly at work in Thomas Purney's description of a scene between the wife-murderer Mathias Brinsden and his eldest daughter, a scene that seems described for no other purpose but to heighten the "drama" of the case by stirring the reader's emotional interest. Brinsden's daughter had been the chief witness against her father and, it was rumored, had replaced her mother in his bed. After the trial she went down on her knees in the prison chapel to beg her father's forgiveness. Some twenty people were present, some of whom knelt as well. After resisting her entreaties for half an hour, Brinsden finally forgave her but could not be induced to kiss her (as Purney makes sure to tell us) until the next day. Tableaux of a similar kind are frequently to be found in the papers put out by Purney's successor, James Guthrie. In 1736 a condemned murderer and his wife "embraced each other very tenderly, and with so feeling a Sympathy, that all the By-standers were sensibly affected at such a melancholy Sight." During a similar event a year later, "the Grief was communicated to the Specta-tors, and every Eye flow'd with Tears."[33] The value of such scenes for the contemporary reader was that he could know, so long as he was "sensibly affected" by them, that he had nothing to worry about as far as his own morality was concerned. And, too, so long as other men responded similarly, he could trust in their morality as well.

I suppose I need hardly point out that the reflexiveness of such a response to the criminal's situation – it leads to what one writer of the period called "self-approving joy" – would have tended to diminish the importance of the criminal as an object of consideration in his own right.[34] He becomes a litmus paper important only for the coloring he gives to the eye. We are not particularly concerned here with tracing the changes undergone by the mythology of crime over the late seven-teenth and early eighteenth centuries, but it ought to be noted that this vicarious, self-congratulatory feeding off the miseries of the criminal is a development peculiar to the eighteenth century, and that it occurs only gradually. It probably owes a great deal to the influence of senti-mental drama, seeming to share with it the belief that one can be washed as clean by disinterested tears, perhaps, as by the blood of the lamb. We see, in another of Guthrie's papers, a similar reaching for the reader's heart. A mother is nearly overcome by the sight of her con-demned son in Newgate, and the text zooms in to dwell on the situa-tion: "upon Sight of her Son in that miserable Condition, [she] with Difficulty was prevented from swooning; while the Son stood, a mournful Spectator of his Mother's Distress. When she had recover'd herself a little, she fell on his Neck – He dropt down on his knees and threw his Arms round his aged Mother's Neck, imploring her Blessing, and Forgiveness of his Folly, in bringing himself and her to Disgrace." Were this passage to stop here, it might be read as yet a further illustra-tion of the painful consequences of crime. But Guthrie continues, first to make clear what is for him the paramount meaning of this "moving

Scene," namely, that it "drew Tears from the Eyes of those who were accustom'd to Scenes of Black [sic], Distress and Death." The criminal's suffering here becomes secondary to the response of those who witness that suffering and sympathize; their capacity to respond assures them and us that there is still something live and quick beneath their calloused sensibilities. Guthrie rounds out his account of mother and son with this last sentence: "The Evening before his Execution she took her last Leave of him, under all the Distress that a tender Parent must feel, for a beloved and only Child under such direful Circumstances."[35] Now the reader is invited to imagine yet another "moving scene" – what *must* "a tender parent" feel? – and, having been cued to the appropriate mode of responding, to participate in it emotionally. What we have here, in the space of a paragraph, is a neat little device designed to certify that one's moral sense (and the stress should be on *sense*) is still in proper working order.

Sentimentalist aesthetics, of course, were hardly different from sentimentalist ethics. One *does* good, as Shaftesbury and Hutcheson explained, because it makes one *feel* good (and, conversely, the capacity to feel properly leads one to act properly). Feeling good about a criminal's execution, however, could not be managed without some minimal assistance from the criminal himself. He (or she) had both to seem a worthy object of pity and yet, at the same time, no longer quite like a living, breathing human being. That is, the spectator had to be able both to form an emotional attachment to the criminal and to hold him (or her) at a safe aesthetic distance. Perhaps the outstanding example of the "aestheticization" of a murder in the eighteenth century is provided by the Blandy case, where a tender, loving father was poisoned by a daughter who, seduced and abandoned by a character more appropriately the villain in a bad stage play, may not even have known exactly what she was doing. (In fact, a bad play *was* written about the Blandy case but never performed.) Miss Blandy generated a great deal of sympathy among those who prided themselves on their "charitable and compassionate Disposition." "Your amiable Character," wrote an admirer who had never met her, "those fine Qualities and Accomplishments which made you an Ornament to your Sex, and the Dignity and Good-breeding of your Behaviour, make me consider [your] Misfortune . . . the most deplorable Event that has happened in my Time." Not to feel such "tender" sentiments, declared the editor of the pamphlet in which this letter appears, was to have a mind "not susceptible of even the least Degree of Compassion." And to have so unsusceptible a mind, according to yet a third writer, was to rank among "the vile Vulgar."[36]

For all its fervor, however, the compassion extended to Miss Blandy seems rather narrowly defined. No one suggested, for instance, that

from *The Malefactor's Register* [1779]

MISS BLANDY *at the place of Execution near Oxford, attended by the Rev*. *M.*' *Swinton*

perhaps she ought not to be hanged, until it was (safely?) too late. The writer of the admiring letter just quoted, the possessor of "a noble and generous Disposition," was about as sympathetic as anyone could have been, yet his sympathy was curiously constrained. "I dare say you have often wept at Distress in a Tragedy or Novel, where, perhaps, every thing was fictitious," he wrote to Miss Blandy, "much more may I, at your too real Tragedy." But "real Tragedy" is an oxymoron. And insofar as her distress could seem part of a tragedy – "where, perhaps, every thing was fictitious" – how could it (and she) have seemed quite real? To see Miss Blandy as a tragic heroine is to deprive her of her very real, soon to be terminated existence as an actual human being. But, from the viewpoint of an interested bystander, this perhaps was not so bad a thing. This writer, at least, seems to have found some solace by ascribing to Miss Blandy a state of mind entirely worthy of a tragic heroine. "I cannot bewail your untimely leaving this World," he assures her, "if it was more engaging than it is" – the word "engaging" is a dead giveaway – "for alas! Madam, after what has happened, I think it is impossible you should ever have much relish of Life."[37]

Miss Blandy tried bravely to cooperate in sustaining such a view of herself, going even so far as to close her dying testament with something very like the closing lines of *Oedipus the King* (she was well educated for a woman of her time, and closely attended by at least one Oxford don). But she seems to have been unable to suppress her "relish of life" entirely, and this was held against her. Thus one unsympathetic writer held up her behavior in prison – "from the very Day of her Commitment she was alert and gay" – as evidence of her unrepentant nature. He especially emphasized her behavior after the trial, when she was returned to the prison under sentence of death. She "stepped into the Coach with as little Concern," he says, "as if she had been going to a Ball." But worse was to come, for at her arrival, "finding the [Gaoler's] Family in some Disorder, the Children being all in Tears," she didn't sit down and have a good cry with them but "said very cheerfully, *Don't mind it: – What does it signify: – I am very hungry: pray, let me have something for Supper, as speedily as possible.* – Accordingly Mutton Chops were dressed, of which, and of an Apple-Pye, She eat very heartily."[38] The passage is redolent with distaste and disbelief; with each successive bite Mary Blandy damns herself the more. She ought to have shown herself heavier in spirit or else already risen above things of the flesh. Parricide and apple pie, this writer seems to be saying, don't mix. Mary Blandy is behaving too naturally for someone in her situation, and in seeming too natural, I would suggest, she can seem too "real." Perhaps one last reason for the criminal to become a "saint in life," then, was that it freed his audience to experience his demise as drama – or, more exactly, as *sentimental* drama, where dark beginnings and distressful middles work toward reassuring, self-approving, and complaisant ends.

The penitent criminal strengthened social solidarity in a number of ways: by showing that all men were alike in their accessibility to God, in their possession of a moral sense, and in their capacity for altruistic self-sacrifice. But not the least of his contributions to social solidarity was the occasion he gave all good men to congratulate themselves – and each other – on the warmth of their hearts. They may have had no choice but to believe that they too were potentially criminals, that their nature was, in theory, as depraved as his had been; they were constrained by the etiology of crime their culture supplied them. But as they stood compassionating with the about-to-be-hanged criminal (and if not with him, at him) they could know that in actual fact they were different from the cruel and desperate men who insensibly committed crimes. The proof – at least for that moment – was in their capacity for feeling, in their sense of their own kindness and generosity of heart.

Thus those who tendered a liberal and charitable view of man, who liked to think well of themselves, and who for these reasons would have been especially vulnerable psychically, socially, even politically, to the implications of crime, could close ranks with each other – could even, into those ranks, recruit the chiefest of sinners and criminals, the murderer himself.

Or so at least in theory: In practical terms the myth did not always work satisfactorily. Though applied in varying degrees to almost all criminals whose executions attracted public notice, it stuck with relatively few. Thieves and other offenders against public order and private property tended to elude its grasp, and real life often had a way of poking through its best efforts to drape or screen it into decency. Even at its most successful, it left tensions it could not resolve, threatened to raise questions it could not answer. Still, it survived a remarkably long time, well into the nineteenth century. Only then, and for reasons imperfectly understood, do popular writers and their audiences stop wanting to see the "Monster *not like other men*" remade into their own image, and so redeemed, before the unpleasantness of doing away with him. Once more the murderer becomes what he had been at the beginning of the seventeenth century, a "fiend in human form."[39]

PART III

Palliating his crimes: the thief as various rogues

What hatred the effect of his Feates purchased, the quaintness of them palliated.

> G[eorge] F[idge], *The English Gusman* (1652), p. [v]

They will rather joke upon this want of security on their roads, if you reproach them with it, than own it is a scandalous thing. . . . There are some Englishmen not less vain in boasting of the address of their highwaymen, than of the bravery of their troops. . . . a noted thief is a kind of hero, in high repute among the populace.

> [Jean Bernard] Le Blanc, *Letters on the English and French Nations* (1747), 2:293

What we are still more to wonder at, is, that . . . People should delight to hear the Actions of these Men rehearsed, and be even pleased with a Highwayman, who robs like a Gentleman.

> Charles Johnson, *Highwaymen* (1734), p. 150

When such a gallant Man as our Captain robs only for Necessity, and then makes Choice only of such Persons to collect from, as he of whom we have been last speaking, the Reader is not much displeased with him. There appears something so agreeable in the Manner and Circumstances of such a Story, as takes away a great Deal of the Resentment, which would otherwise arise against the Felony.

> Johnson, *Highwaymen* (1734), p. 82

What think you of a Newgate Pastoral, among the whores and thieves there?

> Jonathan Swift to Alexander Pope, 30 August 1716, in *Correspondence of Swift*, ed. F. Elrington Ball, 2:330

We must . . . use some illusion to render a Pastoral delightful; and this consists in exposing the best side only of a shepherd's life, and in concealing its miseries.

> Pope, "A Discourse on Pastoral Poetry" (1717) in *Poetry and Prose*, ed. Aubrey Williams, p. 5

In Pepys's library there are four small volumes in matching bindings, part of what he called his "Vulgar Ware." One is labeled "Penny Godlinesses," and the rest "Penny Merriments." The ratio is what we'd expect of Pepys but, still more interesting, is that the first of these volumes contains a copy of *A Murder Punished and Pardoned*, and that *No Jest like a True Jest* is bound into one of the other three. Pepys read many more books than he kept, and so the presence in his library of the "standard" works on Savage and Hind, respectively, attests to their hold on his imagination. His labels capture with nice concision, moreover, not only an important similarity between the two kinds of criminal biography (both were cheap, and so widely available and presumably highly popular) but also an essential difference. Where the one addressed matters of the highest seriousness, the other (and by far the more popular, judging from Pepys's ratio of interest) seems to have been read only for amusement. We have just finished considering the whys and hows of making criminals "godly": What could have made for a contrary impulse? Why were so many criminals, only the most heinous murderers excepted, turned into objects of entertainment? And what sort of entertainment did they offer?

The fascination of the period with highwaymen, and the form it took, is almost too easy to understand. "The highwayman in a sense was, of course, bound to be a hero," writes Christopher Hibbert with enviable assurance, "for he was a rebel, a free man in a society in which those who were not free were exploited and oppressed. A sort of emblematic figure of liberty and pleasure, he was in revolt against the law and against morality."[1] Such a view of the highwayman suggests that – scraped clean of moral and social significance, as well as most of his individuality – he was something of a tabula rasa on which readers were free to figure their own emotions, their own motives, their own drives. And what were these? There would seem nothing surprising here: As Hind supposedly said to one young recruit, "Jack, if thou wilt live with me thou shalt have money at comand or any thing thou wantest." For if indeed, as another, later highwayman reportedly said, "any brisk young Fellow might easily make his Fortune, and live like a Gentleman, by going upon the Highway," then many fellows (not all young) may have found in such a life something at least to dream on.[2] Riding out in their imaginations with highwaymen like Hind, robbing with them in ways that honored, however crudely, their sense of justice and social propriety, they would have been free to gratify – vicariously, to be sure – the usual variety of aggressive impulses. Eventually, of course, the hangman's rope would have snapped them back to reality; their ids released, the superego would have resumed control.

All this fits comfortably enough into our usual notions of the motives behind the popular literature of crime, whatever the historical period. It is, moreover, nicely congruent with the "atomic" or "possessive" individualism supposedly characteristic of the late seventeenth and early eighteenth centuries.[3] In his own stylish way, the highwayman is doing no more than other men would do, were they similarly able to free themselves from social constraint. As Hobbes, that great discerner of the dangerousness of individualism pointed out, "Amongst men, till there were instituted great Common-wealths, it was thought no dishonour to be a Pyrate, or a High-way Theefe; but rather a lawful Trade."[4] The last term is not insignificant, for the highwayman (with all his stylishness) is nonetheless *homo economicus,* saluting the values of an increasingly money-oriented culture even as he breaks its laws. To the usual wish to rise in the world and prosper, he adds the spice of his easier, more dangerous means. Duval was supposed to have thought that the highwayman's "way" was "the best that ever he could have fallen into; yea better than an Estate in Land. . . . For now, if he wants Money, 'tis but taking his Horse and riding out."[5] And it is a fact that many London tradesmen with appetites for living above their means did just that.[6] Others, staying at home and minding their shops, may have felt a certain envious sympathy. As Brecht says with his usual trenchant tendentiousness, "the predilection of the bourgeois for gangsters is explained by a fallacy: that a gangster is not a bourgeois." The only real difference, actually, is that "a gangster is often no coward." In the late seventeenth and early eighteenth centuries this would have seemed no slap in the face of middle-class morality but a plain truth. As an epitaph proposed for a hanged burglar reads (he was, incidentally, also a solicitor, a "colonel," and a onetime Cavalier): "He did what all that saw him fear'd to do."[7]

But the idea that thieves' biographies aimed at not much more than giving their readers a chance to dream darkly of being their own men, of amassing money and exercising power, cannot take us very far. Doubtless many highwaymen were, for many readers, id-driven alter egos. Why else would they have gone off with them so gladly to Nonesuch? Still the explanatory power of this notion remains quite weak, for however much we posit readers with certain kinds of minds, all we can legitimately speak of is the texts they presumably read. And the problem with speaking of these texts as though they were vehicles for vicarious gratification is that it leaves certain of their central features unexplained, or else tends to explain them in terms that are, finally, farfetched and unconvincing. The problem emerges all the more clearly once we begin to range beyond Hind, our main example of the criminal

from Capt. Charles Johnson, *Lives and Adventures of the Most Famous Highwaymen, Murderers, Street-Robbers, &c.* [1734]

Du Vall *Robbing Squire* Roper. *Master of ye Buck Hounds to King Charle in* Windsor Forest.

cum rogue so far. For though Smith's version of his life is entirely typical of the genre in certain essential respects – in its lightness of tone, its apparent lack of structure, its unconcern with the human qualities of its protagonist – there are certain considerable elements of rogue biography it does not represent.

Chief among these is the violence, or threatened violence, that animates much of the purported doings of thieves of all sorts, including highwaymen. Such violence ranges from the coarsest obscenity – e.g., "*William Coe* . . . eminently noted for killing his first Wife, by farting in her Mouth" – to acts of inhuman cruelty.[8] If we assume such stuff was vicariously enjoyed, then are we to assume as well a cruel and thoroughly perverted audience? Or ought we rather to modify our view of the ways in which such episodes were likely read? Further problems arise when we consider the highwayman's taste in victims. Hind is not unique in his loyalty to a usurped king or in his hatred of those who have displaced him. Later highwaymen are generally not so explicit in their political avowals, but a good number of them – in popular opinion at least – were true-blue to the Jacobite cause or at minimum staunch Tories. A solid body of evidence ranging from the 1690s to the early 1720s can be cited to prove this point, and Smith's two collections of highwaymen's lives illustrate it further. Thus his thieves not only show a definite tendency to prey on eminent Whigs and Republicans but, with few exceptions, they leave Tories, Jacobites, and Interregnum Royalists alone.[9] How is this to be explained in terms of vicarious identification? Are we to posit an audience with a taste for Whig (or Republican) bashing? And, if so, how is such an audience to be explained?

According to Eric Hobsbawm, certain criminals acquire a political dimension and become "social bandits." "Insofar as [they] have a programme," social bandits are concerned with defending or restoring "the traditional order of things 'as it should be.' " One of their distinctive features in this regard is that they see "the king or emperor" as "the fount of justice." Their quarrel is actually not with him but with those of his underlings who abuse his authority or with interlopers who rule unjustly. Robin Hood is a good example of the social bandit, not only because he robs the rich and gives to the poor but because he adheres to the rightful king and scorns the usurping Prince John. Outlaw though he is, Robin stands as a symbol for what justice there is in an unjust world. Something of this quality would seem to hover about the popularized highwayman. Though not especially generous to the poor, he often speaks against the corruption of things as they are, or rather as they have come to be. "I follow the general way of the world, sir," says one of Smith's highwaymen, and it is a world, he need hardly add, "which now prefers money before friends or honesty."[10]

The animus such highwaymen show against Whigs and their Republican surrogates may perhaps be explained by the fact that, in many minds, the Whigs seemed to embody the essential values of this newly corrupted world. For in the ordinary way of thinking they were the party not only of "placemen, projectors, and financiers" but of financial scandals, fixed and bought elections, unpopular foreign wars, and the prolix expenditure of public funds for private purposes. Like the Republicans before them, the Whigs could easily seem "the Caterpillars of the times." Hind scorned *Long-gown men, Committee-men, Excize-men, Sequestrators,* and other *Sacrilegious Persons* for taking more than their fair share of the social pie, but the Whigs were similarly chargeable. They also claimed to be defending liberty against the dangers of kingly encroachment but, as their leading modern historian (and sometime apologist) admits, their unsavory dealings "festooned the body politic like shingles." Some of their critics went so far as to liken the forced abdication of James II to the martyrdom of Charles I. Corrupt, unprincipled, interested only in power, the Whig oligarchy seemed little better than crooks themselves; at least this is how many saw them.[11] The irony of their going free while more conventional criminals were hanged did not escape contemporary notice. As one Tory poet wrote, "little villains must submit to Fate, / That great ones may enjoy the World in State." He was quoted often, and many writers paraphrased him, speaking of "great rogues" instead of "villains" or merely, with ominous irony, of "great men." It says much about the spirit of the times that this last phrase could almost never appear in print without sarcastic connotations.[12]

In seeing Whigs and Republicans robbed for a change, there must have been much malicious pleasure. "Why, surely friend, thou knows't not who I am, do you?" says Lord Wharton to a highwayman who stops him, "for if you did, you would not presume to be so bold." As indifferent to this bluster as a desk sergeant booking a state senator for drunken driving (remember, we are speaking at the level of myth), the highwayman ventures a guess. Looking at Lady Wharton, he makes an obscure (to us) and insulting joke, the upshot of which (state senators being as yet uninvented) is that Wharton must be "some great brewer." But mainly he tells him to "be quick" in handing over the usual money, rings, and watches.[13] At the time of this purported robbery Wharton was a prominent member of the ruling Whig junto, and other prominent Whigs are similarly served. Marlborough, his wife, one of her servants, and several of his principal lieutenants are all made victims of Smith's insouciant and often insolent thieves, as are a significant number of Dutchmen brought over by King William, with their newly minted English titles and fortunes. But Republicans get shortest shrift, as of course they deserve, being worse versions of the Whigs, and Smith makes the regicides particularly frequent targets. Conceiving of the highwayman as a social bandit, however, makes more problems than it solves. For even if we can suppose that readers, themselves eager to seize the main chance, would have enjoyed seeing other, greater, and more successful opportunists humiliated (such, we must sigh, is the natural human tendency to envy and spite), a difficult question would still remain. Why, assuming a taste for Whig and Republican bashing, would writers and readers have settled on the thief cum rogue as their instrument? As an arbiter of justice he seems all too easily and quickly compromised. The highwayman who does Lord Wharton's business, for instance, goes on immediately thereafter to rob and rape a farmer's wife, for which he is hanged (the details are *not* given luridly; it is a simple, nasty fact). Why attack self-interested greed with a figure embodying just that trait, and even worse traits?

The highwayman's attack on social corruption raises further problems, because it extends beyond mere party politics. "Who is there now-adays does not rob?" asks one highwayman provocatively, "there is cheating and cozening in all trades but mine." He shows what he means by cataloguing at length the dishonesties and sharp practices of tailors, weavers, surgeons, apothecaries, merchants, scriveners, grocers, vintners, butchers, victualers, cooks, bakers, and shoemakers.[14] With equal explicitness or tacitly, by the force of their example, other highwaymen invite comparisons between their forthright way of getting money and the skulking rapacities of lawyers, physicians, courtiers, and clergymen, as well of course as politicians. What is to be made of such comparisons? With them highwaymen attack not only the political tendencies of their time but the very nature of its economic relations. Such attacks were widespread in the period – thus one journalist speaks of "the mercenary low-priz'd Humour of the Times," and another declares that "Dishonesty and Knavery, Cunning and Circumventing [are] become the general Usage of Trade" – but how seriously ought they to be taken when highwaymen make them?[15]

None of these questions admits easy answers. Neither the idea of vicarious gratification nor the notion of the social bandit, taken separately or together, can adequately explain the specific content and form of criminal rogue biography. Why, to go back to our original question, should highwaymen – as well as housebreakers, pickpockets, thieves of all sorts – have been made so often into "merry" rogues, full of jests and pranks? Why were the personal details of their lives and deaths discarded and lost when – as we have seen so clearly in the case of Hind – they had so much intrinsic interest, and might easily have served the same moral and social purposes served by the biographies of criminals like Savage and Strodtman? Why should the narratives that passed for their lives be (or at least seem) so randomly organized, so unstructured and plotless? And why should these narratives oscillate so obviously between fact and fictitiousness? And, finally, why should all these storied thieves, considered individually or in bulk, seem ultimately so trivial? Answering these questions requires first a look at criminal rogue biography in general, with a view to sorting out certain of its conventions and formulas, and then a consideration of what, for lack of a better term, may be called the psychosocial realities of crime. The insouciant gallantry of a highwayman like Hind needs its original context, both mythic and real, to be fully understood and appreciated. Like all those robbers who, in the literature at least, engage those they rob in dialogues, he himself has to be considered dialectically.

from Richard Head, *The English Rogue [Part I]* [1655]

The English Padder or Hiway Robber. Portrayd.

Criminals like Hind were rare, both in real life (which is to be expected) and in the popular fictions that came to stand in its place (which is perhaps a more curious phenomenon). His appeal – and he was not in any case quite the Macheath-like figure he can so easily seem to be, but then neither was anyone else – is not so easy to explain as at first it might appear. In their redacted versions at least, Hind and the few highwaymen like him are simple enough, to be sure. But their simplicity can only be gauged and properly understood once we have come to appreciate the moral and emotional complexities that (as they were made over) they were made to eschew. The fictions that so lightly informed their lives – fictions nowhere so completely present as in the utterly fictional, utterly idealized Macheath – were entertaining largely because the actualities these fictions displaced were hardly to be entertained. Or so, opening up my conundrum, I shall argue in the next several chapters. The immediate object of our attention must be the ambivalence and confusion which, though not directly apparent in the telling of Hind's life, plays over and through the purported biographies of most other memorable thieves.

Chapter 6

Smiles, serious thoughts, and things beyond imagining: a provisional typology of thieves in action

=====

The Reader may depend upon having the most authentic Accounts of every Highwayman, &ct. that can be any where procured, and of having those Accounts in a more agreeable Manner than they have ever yet appeared in. Our Reflections, when we make any, shall be just, and naturally arising from the Story, whether they are calculated to raise a Smile or a serious Thought.

Charles Johnson, *Highwaymen* (1734), p. [2]

But though his life was strange and most unaccountable, yet his death was not less admirable. For having done things beyond imagination, the fame, or rather infamy of Dun increasing every day, the country resolved no longer to endure his insolencies.

Alexander Smith, *Highwaymen* (1719a), p. 17

Her . . . Pranks and Feats will be good diversion to the honest and ingenious, and to him they are commended, desiring him to Excuse the Abruptness and Discontinuance of the Matter, and the severall independencies thereof; for that it was impossible to make one piece of so various a Subject, as she was both to herself and others.

Life and Death of Mary Frith (1662), sig. A6r

In short, his whole Life . . . was as confused as the Account which we now give of it. He was one Day a Saint, the next a Lover, the next a Satirist, and the next a Highwayman, or Imposter, according as the occasion offered.

Johnson, *Highwaymen* (1734), p. [2]

In their several characters the reader will find the most unaccountable relations of irregular actions as ever were heard.

Smith, *Highwaymen* (1719a), p. 1

The mythic Hind is a creature of absences, a figure defined by subtractions and displacements as much as by the stuff that goes into him. He is not the real man, whoever that was, nor is he any of the several other mythic figures he might have been (another rubric for this and the next two chapters: "Newgate Pastoral and Its Discontents"). As we have already seen, the very different version of Hind produceable by the criminal-as-sinner myth (had it operated) was apparently no more in demand than the actual man himself. But it is important also to realize that the Hind who appears in *No Jest like a True Jest,* or in Smith's *Highwaymen,* is only one of several possible kinds of thief. Even within the limits of the criminal-cum-rogue myth, Hind's life need not have taken the particular shape it did. The positive qualities of the mythic Hind, then, are shaded by certain crucial negatives: He is not real, not a penitent and mealy-mouthed moralist, nor certain other kinds of thief. But what other kinds of thief could he have been? Answering this question will lead not only to a better understanding of the loss of his actual historical self, and his exclusion from the other, more meaningful myth, but to the seeing of him as something more (or less) than a vehicle for vicarious gratification.

The central figure of the criminal-as-sinner myth takes a graduated sequence of steps downward, away from the social norm toward ever greater sin, and then an equivalent sequence of steps back up toward social reintegration and grace. At the end, hanging from his rope, he is lifted higher than he had ever been before, far above the ordinary level of men. The process is so highly ordered, so coordinated in its opposing gradations, that it could easily be graphed. The structure of criminal rogue biography is a good deal looser, and so much more difficult to analyze and explain. Far from following any overall "curve," the typical "life" of a highwayman or other notorious thief presents only a string of episodes, bracketed by an introduction and a conclusion, all of which can vary in length and specificity of detail. The introduction is typically concerned with the criminal's origins and how he began his life of crime, and the conclusion – which may sometimes appear before the end of the narrative (see Smith's account of Whitney) – with how he was captured and hanged.[1] Thus the material that in the criminal-as-sinner myth would form the main body of the narrative becomes, in this other myth, little more than front and back matter.

The main matter of a typical thief's life is a series of discrete and independent actions, which proceed without apparent logic and resist normal efforts to organize them coherently. Rarely, for instance, are these actions related causally to each other, nor do they follow other obvious lines of development. They do not tend to rise in the intensity of their violence or humor, say, nor do they move from the relatively less to the relatively more bizarre; some of them may not even be criminal.[2] The one possible exception to this disjunctiveness – a matter to concern us at the end of this chapter – is that the very last episode in a thief's life may show him doing something more than usually violent or stupid, and this may (though not always) have something to do with his being caught. Slightly more than half the biographies in Smith's

Highwaymen are marked by such a feature, but again it hardly seems possible to establish a general rule.[3] Why should thieves' lives have been so disorderly and disjunctive while murderers' were not?[4] Because questions of function inevitably come down to questions of form (and vice versa), we shall try to discover some kind of order in the seemingly random confusions of this second species of criminal biography.

We may begin by positing three categories of thief: hero, brute, buffoon. Though very few redacted thieves are wholly one kind or another (a point to be taken up later), practically all of them from Gamaliel Ratsey (1605) – the first highwayman to get full biographical attention – to Sixteen-String Jack Rann (1774) – arguably the last "classic" figure of his kind – may be described within the range of these three terms. To keep within manageable limits, however, we shall restrict our discussion here primarily to examples taken from Smith's two compendious collections of criminal lives. These texts, much pirated and paraphrased from the time of their appearance until at least the end of the eighteenth century, are frequently based on plagiarisms themselves; thus they are entirely representative of their type. Their availability in modern reprints, moreover, allows my conclusions and interpretations to be checked rather easily against the raw data.

We have already seen the hero at his best in Hind. Gallant, witty, judicious in his selection of victims, he uses the minimum force necessary to achieve his ends. In a better world, his would have been a happier fate. As things stand, it is not he so much as the times that are out of joint: a point he himself will sometimes raise in his own defense, for though an outlaw he maintains a sense of social justice. Thus Hind strikes against the oppressors on behalf of those whom they oppress – "I have taken from the rich; and given to the poor, for nothing doth more impoverish the Cottage-keeper, then the rich Farmer and full-fed Lawyer," he says – and eventually comes to fight for that symbol of absent authority and justice, the king unrightfully denied his throne. At the end, at least according to Smith, he dies a martyr to a cause beyond his own. Few highwaymen live up to this standard, or even come close to it – not even Robin Hood, whom Smith called a "bold robber . . . of a very licentious and wicked inclination."[5] Hind is one of Smith's most heroic highwaymen, though not necessarily his most interesting.

At the opposite end of the spectrum, and in his purest form as rare as Hind, is the brute. His bizarre and disgusting qualities are developed to a mind-boggling extreme in the figure of Sawney Beane. Beane and his large family live in a cave by the sea in James VI's Scotland. For twenty-five years they maintain no commerce with the outside world, except to rob and murder unwary travelers: "neither did they ever

from Capt. Charles Johnson, *Lives and Adventures of the Most Famous Highwaymen, Murderers, Street-Robbers, &c.* [1734]

SAWNEY BEANE at the Entrance of his Cave.

frequent any Market, for any Sort of Provision; but as soon as they had Robb'd, and Murder'd, any Man, Woman, or Child, they left not any Carcase behind 'em, but carried it to their Den, where cutting it into Quarters, would Pickle them, and Live upon human Flesh, 'till they got another Prey of the same Kind." "But," adds Smith, having killed "above 1,000 Men, Women, and Children, they had generally Superfluity." Eventually one of their victims escapes, alarms the countryside (which long had been curious about the disappearance of so many people), and a party of four hundred men is gathered to hunt them down.

The expedition, led by the king himself, finds the Beanes' cave only by the merest chance, for it is extremely well concealed. At high tide "the Water went for nearly 200 Yards into their subterraneous habitation," which "reach'd almost a Mile under Ground." Making their way through the "intricate Turnings and Windings" of this "private Recess from Mankind," the searchers probe the very heart of darkness. At last they come to Sawney Beane's "Apartments" (the curious domesticity of the term gives edge to the horrors to come) and find, "to their great Surprize . . . the Legs, Arms, Thighs, Hands, and Feet, of Men, Women, and Children, hung up like dry'd Beef, and some Limbs lying in Pickle, a great Mass of Money, both Gold and Silver, Watches, Swords, Pistols, and a great Quantity of Cloaths, both Linnen and Woolen, and infinite other Things, which they had taken from them they had Murder'd." The fate of Beane "and his murdering Family" – "which besides him consisted of his Wife, 8 Sons, 6 Daughters, 18 Grand-Sons, and 14 Grand-Daughters, begotten in Incest" – is as terrible as their crimes:

> the Men, without Process, or any Manner of Tryal, had their privy Members cut off, and flung into the Fire before their Faces, then their Hands, and Legs, were cut off, by which Amputation they Bled in some Hours to Death: All this Torture being justly inflicted upon them in Sight of the Wife, Daughters, and Grand-Children; they were then all Burnt in 3 several Fires, all Dying like the Men too, without Repentance, but Cursing, and Venting, dire Imprecations, to the last Gasp of Life.[6]

The buffoon is not so powerful a figure as the hero or brute, and most of Smith's buffoons are in fact not highwaymen but commoner sorts of criminals. As the term indicates, the buffoon either plays tricks or has tricks played on him, but to say this is hardly to do him justice: He is the source and butt of the most incredible grotesqueries. Patrick Flemming, an Irish highwayman hanged at Dublin in 1650, illustrates the type more fully than most highwaymen (though not so fully as certain housebreakers and sneak thieves). Not a complete buffoon, he is successful at robbing the archbishops of Armagh and Tuam, the bishop of Raphoe, and the Lord and Lady Baltimore. Nor is he without a certain style. Such is his "insolence" that he claims to be "better born and bred" than the people he robs, telling them they must "support his grandeur," for he is "chief lord" of the highway, and they owe him "tribute" for "trespassing on his ground."[7] Flemming cuts rather a different figure, however, in the two most notable episodes of his life.

His first robbery, according to Smith, was the indirect result of an elaborate practical joke. For reasons that will soon be clear, the joke is omitted from the twentieth-century reprint of the *Highwaymen,* but it deserves retelling. A scapegrace lad, Patrick has had the luck to become a household servant of the marquis of Antrim. The marquis, who is Catholic, keeps a Franciscan priest as his confessor, and one afternoon Patrick finds him snoring "like a Rattle-Snake" in a darkened room. "Whatever pleasant Dream of the Confession of some pretty Wench had come into his Head, *Patrick* knew not; but his Label of Mortality [i.e., the priest's penis], he decumbing on his Back, had broke Prison, and Maypole like, disdain'd its Loftiness should be hid." Happening at this moment to hear a hungry calf bleating for his mother, Patrick leads him into the room where the priest lies sleeping, "and guided him so near, that he soon espy'd what he directed to; which he taking for his Mammy's Teat, greedily seiz'd it, and fell to tugging." The priest is pulled to the floor, but sleeps happily on.

Binding him hand and foot, Patrick puts the final touches to the scene by erecting a placard on which he has written, in phosphorus so it will shine in the dark and seem "more dreadful," "Woe be to you Whoremongers." Then he finds a safe place to watch the outcome:

> Now this Babe of a Cow, as *Patrick* suppos'd, finding no Milk to come, sucked and nibbled so hard, that he waked the drowzy Priest; who seeing himself thus surprized, and the dreadful Hand-writing on the Wall, betwixt Pain and Fear, made him roar out. . . . Which alarming the Maids in the Pantry, they came running to see what the Matter was; but seeing their Ghostly father so entangled, and seiz'd on by a cloven-footed Beast, and the harmless Flame still burning . . . they ran out screaming; whilst he, in a lamentable Tone, cry'd after them to bring his pot of Holy-Water, to douce the suppos'd *Daemon,* and send him packing to the Red-Sea. The Noise these Wenches made, brought several young Ladies, and the rest of the Servants; who, under-standing the cause of the Outcry and Disturbance, peep'd in at the Door, but durst adventure no farther; till, with much struggling, the good Father got loose, and came running out among them, crossing himself, the calf still following at his Breech, pushing him forward, and nuzzling him in search of the mistaken Teat; which, now depriv'd of its Vigor, hung dangling out, which caus'd the Females to scamper and squeek.

As the onlookers come to understand what has happened, "Pannick Fear" gives way to "Loud Laughter":

> The Priest, upon this, bit his Thumbs, rag'd, stamp'd, and fret-ted, drawing his Knife, to take bloody Revenge upon his Af-fronter [i.e., the calf, for Patrick's role in this goes unsuspected]; but was hinder'd and the matter excused, as happening by Acci-dent, thro' the Innocency and Mistake of the Beast: But how the strange flaming Hand-writing came, they were at a Loss to define; some of them concluding this happen'd as a Judgment to discover the secret Sins of the confessor. However, it made a great Noise

in the Family; so that the Priest thro' Shame and Anger, shut himself up in his Chamber and appear'd no more that Day in publick, though he was often sent for to prayers.[8]

Patrick's part in this scandal is soon discovered, and he is "turn'd out . . . at a Minute's Warning." This leaves time enough, however, for him to steal "above 200 Pounds in Money, and as much of the Marquis of Antrim's Plate."

Turning housebreaker, then highwayman, eventually he is captured and imprisoned. Though he manages to escape, it is not without suffering certain inconveniences. The narrative describes these in greater detail than any of his robberies, again pausing to delectate upon circumstances. Crawling into the chimney leading from his cell, Flemming begins to look for a way to climb out the top. As he ponders his predicament a group of prisoners below, lodged in a cell that shares his chimney, throw some extra wood on their fire. "This . . . sent up a terrible smoke which in a manner," Smith observes, "turned him into a bacon." Flemming finds this "troublesome," but the heat is worse than the smoke. "Sometimes he thought to descend and put off his being there with a pretence he only did it in a frolic," but realizing his jailers would hardly be so gullible – "merciless, unbelieving dogs," Smith calls them – "upon second thoughts he resolved to stand it, though he suffered martyrdom." But then Flemming thinks again:

> He bethought himself that in such a conflagration an engine was necessary, and therefore pulled the spout he had out of his breeches and, as he saw opportunity, played it as long as the water in the cistern would supply it, which somewhat lowered the proud curls of the aspiring flame. He knew not whether his fellow prisoners perceived it or not, but imagined they did, for says one of them, *It rains, I vow, very terribly abroad.*

Unfortunately, Flemming's "cistern" goes "dry," the fire blazes up again, and he is "put . . . into new perplexities." Desperate, he begins "to beat and blow down the smoke with his hands and breath," and the prisoners below, seeing that the chimney refuses to draw, give up the fire as a bad idea. His "fiery ordeal" over, Flemming succeeds in climbing up the chimney to freedom, "all sooty and smoke-dried." This episode is not as funny as the one involving the priest, but it's worth noting if only because Flemming becomes the butt of its humor.[9]

Each of these three types of thief – hero, brute, buffoon – is a very different piece of work. In one way or another all beggar credulity, but beyond this it is difficult to speak intelligibly and succinctly about all three together. And it is important to speak about all three together, because, in sum, they represent all that popular writers and their readers could conveniently imagine of thieves. Looking at them together is the only way we can appreciate the partiality of that imagining, its limitations and its bent. None of these three kinds of thief is normal, to be sure, and all take stands against society (these are hardly illuminating things to say about criminals), but each is abnormal in different ways, and they differ in the ways they relate (or rather fail to relate) to social values. Hind rises above the normal, and the social values he attacks are in themselves pernicious and unjust. He is an enemy of *wrong* social values, and his preferred targets are those hypocrites who, in the name of justice, have usurped the rightful political order (at least this is how Smith, and the pamphleteers before him, chose to see the regicides). Beane, on the other hand, is subnormal, and not so much antisocial as simply (and horribly) *un*social. A cannibal, a committer of incest, he neither lives in a proper dwelling nor (never going to market) is he part of any economic system. He is more beast than man, living where a beast might live and eating as a beast might eat (except for the pickle). Twice Smith calls his cave a "Den," and he describes its usefulness to the Beanes in these terms: " 'twas [not] in the least Suppos'd that any Thing Human, would reside in such a dismal Place of perpetual Horrour, and Darkness." The cave entrance is discovered, it might be added, only because bloodhounds sniff it out: The Beanes quite literally lurk beyond the range of human cognition. That they are put to death "without Process, or any Manner of Tryal" is no violation of human rights.[10]

As mythic figures, both Hind and Beane are richly potent, and in curiously opposite ways. Where Hind, who does a minimum of damage and some good, can in a sense be said to celebrate human capacities, Beane, dwelling as he does in his "private recess from mankind," bespeaks subterranean horrors at the periphery of consciousness. Indeed, the two invite schematic comparison. Both come to the direct attention of the king, but where Hind is accepted as the sovereign's ally, Beane comes to earn his special disfavor; an indication, I would think, that where the one is agreeably subversive of the existing social and political order, the other is frighteningly subversive of all order. Both, too, are at the last dismembered – a tribute it would seem to their potency – but again in opposite ways. Where Hind, once dead, is quartered and decapitated, Beane is left to bleed to death, having lost not his head but (Freudians please note) first his "privy Members" and then his hands and legs (this seems a reduced and almost parodic version of decapitation and quartering).

Flemming is not so richly considerable a figure as either of these two, and it is not at first easy to see him in terms that allow us to compare him to both at once. What he does, or what is done to him, is more interesting than what he is (or may stand for). Like Beane, he is an agent of chaos, but it is a comic chaos. Obscene, even disgusting, he is not frightening. Like Hind, he is something of a "justicer" in his rebellion against society, but again this effort is not to be taken quite seriously. The priest is a ripe target for Flemming's prank not only because he represents a despised and mistrusted minority but also, and more simply, because he is caught in a situation singularly inappropriate to his function (with his pants down, as it happens). The story may rely on an animus against Catholics (and more generally against the clergy), but its main concern is to be outrageous. More than anything else, Flemming's own function is to exceed the bounds of decorum, not the bounds of morality (as do Hind and Beane in their very different ways). Bouleversement is his specialty – he is the cause, or at least the occasion, of outrageous happenings – and the narration of his life is more concerned with the upset he creates, or experiences, than it is with him as a symbolic figure in his own right. In fact, it is rather difficult to get a clear view of him apart from his actions; unlike Beane or Hind, he fails to register as an individual presence.

To say more than this about all three highwaymen at once, and to make some better sense of what has been said so far, I shall rely on a series of diagrams. These are based on the idea that each episode in a thief's biography may be analyzed in the terms of a simple "grammar" (as in sentence = subject + verb + object).[11] The criminal, whom we can term *actor*, performs an *action* (usually but not always a theft) upon another person, who thereby becomes the *object* of his action (and usually but not always his victim). Each of the three kinds of thief, as we shall see, performs characteristic actions upon characteristic objects. In diagram 1 the differing qualities of hero, brute, and buffoon, as *actors*, are set out along two axes of comparison.[12]

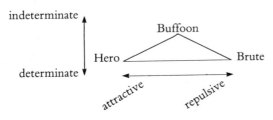

Neither simply attractive nor simply repulsive, the buffoon is some third thing which yet has affinities to both. Flemming is thus remarkable for his quick wit *and* his scurvy sense of humor (as in the story of the priest), both for his initiative *and* where it leads him (as in the story of his escape from prison). In making him more difficult to grasp, this particular combination of qualities prevents him from seeming quite so considerable a figure as either Hind or Beane, but it is this also that can make him seem so outrageous. The buffoon, qua actor, confounds affective categories in a way that sets him apart from both brute and hero.

Still, the buffoon in action can be quite memorable, as the following anecdote will indicate; it is taken from Smith's "life" of Richard Sheppard, a footpad hanged in 1720. Traipsing through Europe, Sheppard gains so much fame as a "Merry-Andrew" that Louis XIV invites him to Versailles to compete with his own fool. At stake is "a new Suit of Cloaths, and 20 Pistoles," the latter being equivalent to some eighteen or nineteen English pounds:

> Accordingly the 2 Fools (if we may reckon *Dick* one, who could be as much a fool as any one, when he pleas'd) . . . play'd over a thousand ridiculous Fooleries; the King, and the whole Court laugh'd heartily, and 'twas hard to judge who would have the better. At last, *Dick* bethought himself of a Project, which he believ'd would not fail, for he had a strong Itching for the Money and the Cloaths; he therefore all of a sudden, before the King, and the whole Court, whips down his Breeches, and dropt a small Pancake in the Middle of the Hall, and pulling a Knife out of his Pocket, divides it into equal Parts, and slips one into his own Mouth, offering the other Half to the King's Fool, saying, *Here, do as I do, Sh——t you in the Middle of the Hall, and eat half my Pancake, and I'll eat half yours. The Devil confound you for a nasty Dog,* says the *French* Fool, *were I sure to go naked all my Life, I would neither eat yours, nor mine.* You may easily judge who got the Reward, the King laugh'd heartily, and was as good as his Word; and *Dick* remain'd always in his good Graces, as long as he stay'd at *Versailles,* which was about 6 weeks.[13]

What can one say or feel about a character like this? Dick certainly is a "nasty dog," but in outfacing the French (if dropping his trousers can be called that) he scores points for English honor and pluck. "*Dick Sheppard* Sh——ts before the King of France" is how the feat is described in Smith's table of contents, and that sentence, splendid in its way, captures both the folly and the incredible nerve of the act. Louis may *not* have been amused, may have seen what an English audience very likely saw in Dick's breach of court etiquette: a rather more buccal equivalent to thumbing one's nose, an earthy gesture of scorn and contempt for the *roi soleil*. Still, for all his obvious pleasure in Dick's cheekiness, the writer's ambivalence reasserts itself at the end of the episode. In eating his *own* shit, Dick has shown an originality of mind

and independence of spirit rare among courtiers, but what is his reward? The wavering construction of that last trailing sentence would
seem to make a subtle comment of its own. Thus Dick enjoys the
king's "good graces" not "always," as the text appears at first to indicate, but only so long as he remains at Versailles, "which was about 6
Weeks." By that time, one imagines, the twenty pistoles are spent and,
considering Dick's standard of personal hygiene, the new suit is showing signs of wear.

Diagram 2 situates the three kinds of thief with respect to the qualities of their *actions*.

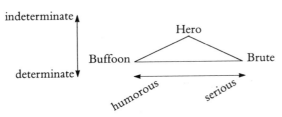

Here the hero is in the ambiguous and multivalent position. His robberies are neither simply humorous nor simply serious, but a peculiarly
indeterminate mixture of both. Pausing to bandy words with his victims, as heroic highwaymen customarily do, he can seem to have something of the air of a satirist. A rich farmer relieved of forty pounds by
Jack Withrington protests, "Is this not a downright robbery?" "So let it
be," replies Jack, "who is there now-a-days does not rob?" Going on to
catalogue the dishonest practices of a wide variety of businessmen and
professionals, Jack concludes that, "as there is cheating and cozening in
all trades but mine, you cannot blame me for borrowing this small trifle;
which I shall honestly pay you when we meet again." Of course such
talk can have none of the actual force of satire, as it is too reflexive. Jack is
in no position to deplore the viciousness of others, nor can we in any case
be sure of the intent of his remarks. (I am speaking of him inasmuch as he
has a character; the intent of the author is another thing, mysterious in its
own right.) Is Jack speaking humorously to make a serious point, as
satirists do, or, like a deadpan comedian, is he only seeming to be serious
in order actually to be funny? (His promise to repay his victim is "honest" only because he has no intention of risking a second encounter.)
There is a lot of truth in all Jack says about crooked business practices,
but it is just as hard to take him seriously as it is to laugh him off. Later he
will rob a tailor, a member of one of those trades he accuses of dishonesty, and find that the man has lied in claiming to have handed over
all his money. "Well, I vow and protest," Jack will say, "this is a sad
world we live in, when one Christian cannot believe another."[14]

This peculiar mixture of humor and seriousness – which melds into neither satire nor dark comedy, the two leading emulsifications of humor and seriousness – presents itself rather differently in Smith's life of Hind. Here something of the same indeterminate effect is achieved not at once, as in Withrington's paradoxical speeches, but as the reader moves from episode to episode over the course of the whole life. It is something of a second-order phenomenon, preventing us from classifying Hind's behavior as a whole, even when certain parts of it seem rather clear. After the introductory paragraph, Hind's life divides into six separate episodes. Five of these are various highway exploits, and the sixth describes his capture and heroic death. The two most detailed of Hind's exploits, where he robs the regicides Peters and Bradshaw, come second and fifth in the series. Here humor and seriousness do mesh rather easily into satire, unlike the examples taken from Withrington's life. Hind's encounter with Peters will illustrate what I mean.

When Peters starts to "cudgel" him with "some parcels of scripture" to the effect that robbery is wrong, Hind turns the Presbyterian parson's "weapon" against him. "Friend," he says, "if you had obeyed God's precepts as you ought, you would not have presumed to have wrested His Holy Word to a wrong sense, when you took this text, Bind their kings with chains, and their nobles with fetters of iron." Peters continues protesting, and Hind finally shuts him up with a well-chosen phrase from Solomon – "Do not despise a thief" – and by threatening to shoot him on the spot. The story does not end here. Having taken Peters' money and let him go, Hind rides after him and stops him again. Two more phrases from the Bible have come to mind, one permitting him to explain why Peters has been robbed – "Provide neither gold, nor silver, nor brass, in your purses for your journey" (Matt. 10:9–10) – and the other giving him an excuse to take Peters' coat, too: "And him that taketh away thy cloak, forbid him not to take away thy coat also" (Matt. 5:40). The episode concludes with Peters in his pulpit the next Sunday, preaching a sermon against theft. But even here Hind prevents him from having the last word. His text, curiously enough, is 5:3 of the Song of Solomon: "I have put off my coat, how shall I put it on?" Hearing this read, a "cavalier" calls out, "Upon my word, Sir, I can't tell, unless Captain Hind was here."[15] Peters breaks off his sermon and retires in confusion.

In telling this story Smith uses Hind to mock the bibliolatry of the Dissenters, who justified their political agitations (in Smith's view, quite a common one) by crazily inappropriate misinterpretations of the Scriptures. By having Hind beat Peters at his own game, Smith shows how easy it is to play, and how absurd in the first place. But in rebuking blasphemy, Smith comes dangerously close to blasphemy himself, which brings a certain tension to the story.[16] This builds as Hind plays fast and loose with God's Holy Word, but then is released when the story ends on a different note, shifting instead to the idea that Hind has now become the regicide's nemesis. Even on his own ground, and by proxy, Peters must suffer the highwayman's daunting, deflating presence. But Hind's misuse of the Bible does more than merely satirize Dissenters. The verses he cites are not entirely inappropriate to Peters' situation. Both passages from Matthew come from contexts in which Christ is beseeching His followers to leave behind all worldly things. How is it that someone professing to be His minister, then, has conspired to seize power from the king? And how is it that this same minister is wealthy enough to be robbed of "thirty broad-pieces of gold"? (The number itself is evocative; Judas only got silver.)

Hind's encounter with Sergeant Bradshaw can be seen similarly. The target now is not the Puritan rebels' false learning and hypocrisy but their cowardice and greed. Here again humor and seriousness combine unequivocally for clear satirical purposes. It is only when we look at Hind's actions in total that their indeterminacy becomes apparent, for sandwiched between these two coherent bits of action are two more problematic events. After laughing at Peters, the narrative moves to telling briefly, and without much detail, how Hind robbed a certain unnamed gentlewoman of her marriage portion: "the money being lost before she performed the rites of matrimony, the sport was all spoiled; for her sweetheart's love was not so hot but this news quickly cooled it, which evidently shows that money in those days was the chiefest drug to get a young woman a husband." Clearly Smith is being ironic here, but it is difficult to pin the irony down. The last clause is both a joke and a piece of satire; satire because money is still a great attraction in a woman, and a joke because Smith pretends to be saying the opposite. But what of the rest? Is it good or bad that the couple's "sport" was spoiled, funny or not so funny? Was Hind's victim really hurt by losing her money-hungry suitor, or did he actually do her a favor? The episode is all the more curious in that it is the only cruel thing, potentially, in all of Hind's career.[17] (Smith just barely mentions the killing Hind is eventually tried for, giving the reader little or no occasion to think about it.) With the exception of his first victim, whom he treats so handsomely, everyone else Hinds robs or attempts to rob is a regicide – outlaws far worse than he because they strike at the very source of law, and so fair game.

The episode following that of the gentlewoman is even more curious. Hind and his mentor attack Cromwell and a party of his soldiers but, being outnumbered, are forced to flee. Hind's friend is captured, and Hind is "obliged" to abandon him, ultimately to be hanged. Hind's role in this fiasco seems a tribute as much to his foolhardiness and hubris as to his bravery and Royalist feeling. It leaves him in rather an ambiguous position, especially considering the fact that Smith allows other, lesser rogues the privilege of embarrassing Cromwell freely. Why not give such largesse to Hind? One wonders whether the episode of the gentlewoman has anything to do with Hind's awkward posture in this, his subsequent adventure. It is as if the highwayman has gotten "off form" and doesn't recover until he meets up with Bradshaw, where he can recapitulate his robbery of Peters. Hind's effort against Cromwell has something of the quality of an aborted prank – on every other occasion Cromwell appears, Smith makes him a farcical butt – and it is, too, in a sense a truncated tragedy. Hind loses the man who taught him to rob with "good grace," but the text leaves the dramatic potential of this undeveloped as well. This bungled robbery makes an interesting comparison with Hind's first, where he acted with so much finesse. His allowing his victims enough money to meet their immediate travel expenses may be neither humorous nor serious, but it is admirable. Hind's attempt on Cromwell, being none of these, seems in fact the antithesis (or at least the opposite) of his first, most hopeful action.[18]

In the third and last of my diagrams the hero, brute, and buffoon are situated according to the effect they have on the objects of their actions.

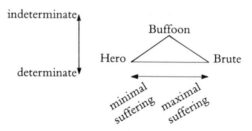

What I mean by "maximal" and "minimal" suffering may need some elaboration. The former is illustrated by Smith's one description of a Beane family crime. Their victims are a married couple, ambushed while returning from a fair. Despite the man's fighting "bravely," his wife is "Murder'd before [his] Face; for the Female *Cannibals* . . . cut her throat, sucking her blood with as great a Gust as if it had been Wine, ript up her Belly, and pulled out all her Intrails."[19] At the sight of this the husband fights all the harder, gets away, and alerts the authorities. The wife's suffering is extreme enough, but Smith compounds its horror by having her killed before her husband's eyes, and he survives. "Minimal suffering" is what we see in the objects of Hind's attentions. No real harm is done, even to those who ought to be made to suffer badly. Only Hind's robbing the gentlewoman is problematic in these terms, and in this case the suffering is minimalized by the simple expedient of making her as anonymous as possible; all that we know is she loses a suitor more interested in her money than her, which may be a blessing in disguise. Where a great deal of pain is inflicted on the victims of the brute, then, the hero's experience little or none. Of course this is a comparison made only within the context of the genre; by other standards the anguish the Beanes inflict on the husband and wife might seem relatively unrealized, the disappointment of Hind's gentlewoman excruciating.

The buffoon's victims, too, typically suffer in some physical way, but – and it is this that makes such violence indeterminate in effect – without emotional consequence. The violence done them is like that seen in animated cartoons: total, painless, temporary, inconsequential, and often just plain physically impossible. The buffoon's victims are made the butts of grotesque (and impracticable) practical jokes, but they never seem pained or even long embarrassed (thus Flemming's priest, who retires to his room for the rest of the day). They suffer calamities but do not themselves seem to suffer, and the calamities in any case beggar belief. My point cannot be illustrated better or more simply than by the story Smith tells about a country yokel's encounter with Simon Fletcher, a cutpurse. The countryman is so entirely absorbed by some London street singers that he loses all sense of himself. "In the meantime his balls hanging out of his codpiece, as wide as King Henry's, and Simon supposing it to be his purse . . ." – well, Simon does what cutpurses do, and slips away "without any discovery." Eventually the "poor fellow" comes to miss his "fishing tackle" and begins "a jumping and capering about like a madman." "I am ruined, I am ruined," he calls out to the people gathering around him, "I have lost a good pair of b——ks, for which I shall have more noise with my wife, than if I had lost a hundred pounds."[20]

Another story of a husband and wife makes the same point more elaborately. One night while a notorious sodomite tailor is out "a-raking," John Wheeler breaks into his house. Wheeler gets a warm welcome from the tailor's wife, who feels neglected. Afterward, there being nothing else worth stealing, he begins packing up her husband's tools. "Oh! sir," the wife calls out, "you will ruin my husband if you carry away his tools," but Wheeler shows no sympathy. He calls her "b——ch," says he's sure her husband never used his tools "about" her, and as a final insult decides to "leave the yard [i.e., yardstick] in the right place, that it may be ready to hand when [her husband] has occasion to make use of it." Tying the woman to the bed, he puts "about Nine Inches of the Yard in her Vessel of Generation," and leaves. The next morning the tailor returns feeling "pretty mellow," until he spies the "yard" in his wife's "Aye-forsooth." "In a stammering manner (for he horribly stuttered)," he asks "who it was had been yarding her so prettily." When she refuses to answer, he is so enraged that he takes the "yard" and breaks it "all to pieces, in the presence of the neighbours, who jeer about it to this day."[21]

This richly obscene joke plays not only on the differing sexualities of the tailor and his wife but on the double meaning of his unused "tools." The tailor's "yard" – put where it supposedly belongs and then withdrawn and broken to pieces – may strike us as an especially apt metaphor for his misplaced sexuality. But for once the eighteenth-century reader would have been ahead of us in sexual matters. "Yard" was no mere metaphor but common slang for "penis," and with so loud a double entendre ringing in his ears (reread my synopsis of the story to get the effect) the eighteenth-century reader could not have felt much for or against the discomfited tailor and his wife, even had he wanted to. Like all farce, theirs is a story "light" on morality and emotion (taking pains to exclude such considerations), and what justice it provides is simple, active, and mechanical. What they suffer is no more consequential, in the end, than the fact that one is an adulteress and the other a sodomite. The reader's ability to ignore the "real-life" aspect of the last, especially, makes no small contribution to the story's humorous effect; sodomy was a crime punishable by death.

This tendency to trivialize serious matters, to show horrendous things happening without much effect – or affect – can go to quite shocking lengths. Or rather, I should say, to lengths that would seem shocking if one were able to see such events in a "correct" frame of mind. An anecdote from Smith's life of Arthur Chambers, another housebreaker, will provide a last example of the curious state of the buffoon's victims. Chambers breaks into a house in a fashionable district of London where, covered with a white cloth, a dead child is laid out upon a table. "Supposing that which appeared white on the table was a parcel of linen," he bundles it up with everything else he has stolen and tosses it out the window to his confederates. When they discover the child's corpse among their booty, one of them suggests "throwing it into a privy," another is for "cutting it up into pieces and throwing it into the Thames," but Arthur claims it for his very own. "As I stole the child," he says, "I'll dispose of it as I please." Nailing the corpse up into a deal box, he hires a porter to deliver it back to the house. It is necessary to quote all the next paragraph to show how peculiarly this gruesome episode is concluded:

> The people were at first somewhat scrupulous of opening it, as not knowing from whom it came; but the porter being positive it must be delivered there, and pressing them to open the box, they then broke it up, and found therein their dead child, which put

them into a great consternation. And going at once up stairs, they found chests of drawers, scrutoires, and cabinets broken open, and several things of value stolen, so they apprehended the porter, who insisted on his innocency, and declared where he received the box. The people went in all haste with a constable to the house where he was employed to carry this box, but the birds were flown, and the poor porter was sent to the Gatehouse at Westminster, where it put him to great charges for following his occupation.[22]

And thus ends the story; how is one to respond to it? At least in the two cases cited previously we could see how or why the buffoon's victims were appropriate targets for his pranks, but this seems an utterly pointless joke, a wholly gratuitous obscenity. Still, and this is important, it fails to register as a gross victimization. For one thing, nothing one might reasonably expect to happen actually does happen. For another, the story is vague in many of its details. What relation do these unspecified "people" have to that dead child? And what is the nature of their consternation? The robbery seems to upset them more than the grotesque indecency of the child's corpse being handled about like a piece of none too valuable goods (and why was it left on a table?). And of course the anecdote prevents any knowledge of Chambers's victims after the event, shifting its attention to the plight of the porter, which, it might be added, is described with anticlimactic phrasing.

The story, in effect, comes to no conclusion. It is, however, succeeded by another, lengthier, and more digestible anecdote on essentially the same theme; this has a bearing on the first because in a sense it inverts it. Here Chambers gains entry to a house he wants to rob through an elaborate hoax, pretending to be a corpse in a coffin. Once everyone is asleep, Chambers rises from his "mansion of death" and begins to prowl about in his winding sheet. The inhabitants of the house wake up, are frightened half to death, and, as they cower in their beds, Chambers and his accomplices strip the place bare. Here again we have a corpse in a box, and moving about, and in the meanwhile the robbery of a house. But this time the sequence of events is reversed (in the first it was robbery + corpse moving about + corpse in a box/ hoax), and it is a case not of Chambers manipulating the corpse but of *being* the corpse (which is to say the corpse is active, not passive, is in fact no longer a corpse), and thus no indecency is committed. I emphasize the structural parallels because, it seems to me, the second story with all its easy humor works to undo, and so to counter and conclude, whatever uneasiness may have been produced by the first; its structure is antidotal as well as anecdotal. As with Hind's various actions, so here; not only are the episodes themselves important but so, too, the relations between them. It is these relations that shall concern us next.

Two points, however, remain to be made about my analysis so far. The first is somewhat particular, concerning only the buffoon; nonetheless, it relates to larger matters. As we have seen with Flemming, the buffoon can often become the object of an action, shifting from actor to acted upon. (In such a case we might speak of the "grammar" of the episode undergoing a basic transformation, as when a sentence is rewritten from the active into the passive voice.) This characteristic, yet another that sets him apart from both brute and hero, does little for his standing as a criminal but a great deal toward making him seem a clown. And not at all a clever-seeming clown: Tom Taylor makes the mistake of trying to pick the same man's pocket twice, and the second time his victim has taken the precaution of having his pockets lined with fishhooks. Tom is able to extricate himself only after he has paid back twice the amount he had stolen the first time, and even then gets beaten and dunked in a horse pond. Sawney Douglas attempts to make off with a pearl necklace by swallowing it but falls immediately under suspicion. His interrogators force him to strip, put him in a sack, and hang him out a second-story window until he confesses; when he does they make him swallow a huge dose of emetic. Moll Raby, interrupted while trying to rob a house, hides under a bed and is nearly detected by a dog who crawls there after her. She is so frightened she fouls herself, but luckily the odor is blamed on the dog, and, the people in the room leaving in disgust, she makes an escape (but no clean getaway).[23]

Such incidents play havoc with the tidy categorizations I've tried to set up so far. Although such buffoons are humorous in their actions, as per my second diagram, they fail to fit quite as they should into the first (how can they seem at all attractive?), and of course the third diagram is simply inapplicable, because of the shift in the "grammatical voice." But sic transeunt even the most glorious of diagrams; mine were never meant to be more than heuristic devices. The important point to be made is that figures like Taylor, Douglas, Raby, or Flemming are poor prospects for the vicarious identification so easily assumed by some writers to be the big lure of criminal rogue biography. That Flemming is a highwayman who robs with something like the usual style makes him no different, ultimately, from the Taylors, Douglases, and Rabys. He is no more an "emblematic figure of liberty and pleasure" than they, this "bacon" so memorably imaged in the throes of pissing down a chimney to keep from being roasted alive (certainly no way even for a bacon's goose to be cooked). Readers may well have identified with a criminal like Hind, but it hardly seems reasonable to suppose they would have identified with the likes of Flemming, or could have wanted to. Certainly a reader gains nothing by fancying himself in Flemming's place as the joke is played on the priest. The event is funniest, and naughtiest, when peeped at, when seen with the disinterested passion of a voyeur; putting oneself into it only complicates matters. And why should anyone want to have fantasized about being stuck in a smoking chimney? (Freudian metaphors, and they come easily, make no sense here.) Much the same point can be made about "yarding" the wives of sodomite tailors, castrating rustics while they gaze at city sights, or playing fast and loose with coffins and corpses. To argue that a popular audience would have wanted to participate in such events, even vicariously, is simply to endow them with tastes too recherchés. Nor would anyone but a madman, an incipient Jack the Ripper or (considering the family aspect) another Charlie Manson, want to identify with Sawney Beane. Quite apart from his being a Scotsman (no small matter for an English audience, even today), he represents horrors that can only be ruthlessly suppressed – root and branch, as the final mutilations quite literally suggest.

Even the hero, and this is the second point I would like to make before going on, would seem to invite less than maximal identification. It is the indeterminacy of his actions that is crucial here, ambiguities being more difficult to "grasp" than clear and simple qualities. Either the ambiguity of the hero's actions would have proved somewhat more engrossing to the reader than his relatively clearer, simpler features, because such ambiguity would have allowed the reader's imagination greater "play," or just the opposite: Looking for easier work, the reader's mind would have drifted away from the ponderable and have tended to fix on the definite and easily comprehensible. It seems to me the latter would have been the more likely response. Only a writer with considerable skill can bring his reader to engage with "difficult" characters – thus Lovelace, Heathcliff, Raskolnikov, Kurtz, all of whom are the work of subtle imaginations and embedded in complex narrative structures – and writers of Smith's sort are obviously without such skill. In books like his, where easy writing and reading go hand in hand, there is little to prompt consideration of the ambiguous and multivalent; incongruities seemingly abound for their own sake, not so that we can recuperate them at higher or deeper levels. But in either case the determinacy of the hero's actions would have tended to encourage a certain detachment. Ambiguity breeds ambivalence, and though ambivalence may accompany identification, it is no strong encourager of it. It is possible, of course, to imagine a figure as simply and definitely positive as the brute is simply and definitely negative, but the heroic highwayman is no such figure. Even Hind is not quite Robin Hood; indeed, so far as Smith is concerned not even Robin Hood (requiscat in pace, Errol Flynn) is quite Robin Hood. That even so powerfully attractive a highwayman as Hind retains something ambiguous – is in a sense haunted by the possibility of a truer, clearer heroism – strikes me as especially significant.

The idea that narratives like Smith's were read simply and mostly to blow off steam, I hope by now to have made clear, just does not make sense in terms of the narratives themselves; they are ill designed for such a purpose. Some of Smith's stories may have been read, and written, in the interests of vicarious gratification, but obviously some more capricious theory is needed to explain the phenomenon as a whole. And this need grows all the more obvious once we turn our attention from the heuristic examples of Hind, Beane, and Flemming to consider the "average" case. As I pointed out at the beginning of this chapter, few of Smith's criminals are so consistent as to be all of one type; they shift from one to another quite freely, and often in the middle of a gesture. (It would have been more appropriate, though more confusing, to have spoken from the start of three "modes" or even "registers" of thief, rather than of three categories.) In theory, the thief's polymorphism could well have made conditions all the more favorable for readers to indulge in free-floating fantasies. By seeming to dispense with any controlling logic, and by having their rogues play out several roles, writers like Smith might possibly have provided their readers with wider-ranging, more variegated vicarious experiences. We need only look at a few examples of thieves shifting from one character-type to another, however, to see that this – at least in Smith – was very likely not the case.

The protean features of Smith's thieves do more than merely make them difficult to "grasp"; often they provide for distinctly uncomfortable reading. Consider the difficulties raised, for example, by the story of how one Henry Sandal, a hop merchant, is robbed by William Blewet and his gang. Sandal is pulled from his horse and hands over seventeen pounds. Finding this "a trifling Matter," Blewet decides to make Sandal "Sweat." What ensues, described in one rather long and more than usually ill written sentence, is not without a certain nervous comedy – at least at first:

> So the said *Blewet* pissing in his Hat, and forcing *Sandal* to drink it off upon Pain of Death, at the same Time holding a Pistol to his Breast, they then forc'd him to strip himself stark naked; then drawing their Swords, as the Hop-Merchant danc'd, according to their direction, they now and then, gave him a Prick to move brisker, and to shew Capers, 'till at last he was so much out of breath, that he fell down upon the Ground, as if expiring his last,

which he did the next Day, through this Fatigue, and the Wounds they gave him, which prov'd a little too deep.[24]

Up to this point I've been talking of conditions being unpropitious for vicarious identification, the object in question being either too repulsive to engage the reader's sympathetic attention, or too ambiguous, or simply insufficiently disambiguous. Here, however, something quite different is at work. The reader may well go along with the joke, at least in its earlier stages; the sadism there (they certainly do make the merchant hop!) is not without a bizarre charm. But then, like Sandal's injuries, the fun goes suddenly just a bit too far and the reader is pulled up short, with a jolt directly proportional to the extent he has been vicariously involved. Blewet's treatment of Sandal is ultimately called a "tragical Villainy," but the comment comes too late for the reader who has let himself go. Had it come earlier, it would have helped to cue his response, but, coming where it does, it can only increase his sense of complicity.

A second example shows even more forcefully how Smith sometimes traps his reader into an embarrassing vicarious involvement. His description of Patrick O'Bryan's last robbery is not far advanced when it begins to offer the reader some classically cheap thrills:

> *O'Bryan* being captivated by her extraordinary Beauty, quoth he, *Before we tye and gagg this pretty Creature, I must make bold to rob her of her Maidenhead.* So whilst this Villain was eagerly coming to the Bedside, protesting that he loved her as he did his Soul, and design'd her no more harm than he did himself, the modest Virgin had wrap'd her self up in the Bed-Cloathes as well as the time would permit; as he took her in one Arm, and endeavour'd to get his other Hand between her self and the Sheet, she made a very vigorous Defence to save her Honour: For tho' she could not hinder him from often kissing not only her Face but several other Parts of her Body, as by struggling they came to be bare . . .

The "modest Virgin" in question is the daughter of a country squire. O'Bryan and his gang have already tied and gagged the rest of the household, so there is no one to come to her rescue. The description of the rape continues, only to turn without warning into something quite nasty indeed:

> yet by her Nimbleness in shifting her Posture, and employing his Hands so well with her own, they could never attain to the Liberty they chiefly strove for: She neither made great noise, bit or scratch'd, but appear'd so resolute, and her Resistance was made with so much Eagerness, and in such good Earnest, that the las-

civious Villain, seeing there was nothing to be done without more Violence, his Lust incited him to downright brutish Force; and no sooner had he obtain'd his Will, by ravishing the young Gentle-woman, but such was his Barbarity, that he most Inhumanly stabb'd her; then he and his companions murder'd her Father and Mother.

O'Bryan and his friends net 2,500 pounds from the robbery, burn the house to the ground, "and . . . the Flames also destroy'd all the poor Servants." As with the Sandal affair, Smith closes out his account of these mass murders with a somewhat tardy moral comment, calling them "an unparalleled piece of villainy." But again the comment comes too late to warn the reader against vicarious involvement.[25]

Such shifts in the affect of the text make for unsettling reading. They illustrate yet another way in which criminals in narratives like Smith's tend to stand beyond easy categorization. Very likely the unpredictable movement of Smith's text made his narratives more interesting, no small matter considering their relative "plotlessness," their reiteration ad nauseum (or so it seems to a modern reader) of the same impover-ished themes. A sense of risk can heighten pleasure, especially when the pleasure has something furtive about it in the first place. Smith's readers could never be sure but that their fun might suddenly come to redound against them. Even the most heroic thieves are capable of dirty or, at the least, diminishing actions. The Golden Farmer caps off a long and distinguished career by robbing an impoverished tinker of all the wealth he has, a pittance.[26] Duval steals a baby's silver bottle straight out of its mouth and is finally caught, drunk, in a tavern. Whitney's first, abor-tive attempt at theft concludes with him locked in the embrace of a dancing bear, and he sails out of life on the mocking words of a hang-ing judge.[27] Even Hind, in the 1734 Johnson's version of his life, is made to sink into a final bit of nastiness. Hind, who supposedly has robbed yet another regicide, is in full flight and his horse beginning to tire when he hears another rider coming up fast behind him. Turning in his saddle, he kills the man with a single, well-placed shot. The heroism of this gesture is wasted, however, for the dead man is merely a gentle-man's servant eager to catch up with his master, who is riding some distance ahead. It was for the killing of this "unfortunate Countryman" that Hind was tried and eventually pardoned at Reading, according to the 1734 Johnson, and not the death of a man in a quarrel.[28]

The process I've been describing is not reciprocal; a thief's stock never suddenly rises. Buffoons and brutes never surprise by suddenly showing heroic traits, for if buffoons slip at all, it is into brutality, and brutes remain brutes. The slippage of thieves from one character-type

from Capt. Charles Johnson, *Lives and Adventures of the Most Famous Highwaymen, Murderers, Street-Robbers, &c.* [1734]

The Golden FARMER *and the* TINKER

to another is not so random, then, as at first it might seem. It may come at any time, but it moves unidirectionally. A certain configuration can also be found in the synchronic relations obtaining among the three types of thief, and this, combined with what has just been said about the slippage from one type to another, will finally allow us to say something about the overall shape or "curvature" of criminal rogue biography, at least as we find it in writers like Smith.

As my three diagrams show, only the consistently off-putting brute stands clear of ambiguities. Repulsive, unfunny, and cruel, he is a relatively simple figure, being the most determinate of the three. Perhaps this explains his great power to disturb; he invites the easiest all-around comprehension, and is utterly nasty. As admirable and generous as the hero may be, he can pose no equal and opposite attraction, given the indeterminate and problematic nature of his behavior. Still more problematic is the buffoon, simple only in that his actions are humorous, for it is this only that the mind can actually latch onto. If we put this configuration of types into motion, so to speak, we might venture to suggest an overall forward movement or "curve" to Smith's biographies, that is, insofar as they move toward anything more than the gallows. As they fall away from the (albeit limited) attractiveness of the hero toward either the weak (because so indefinite) attraction of the not-to-be-taken-seriously buffoon and from there to the highly definite ugliness of the brute, or else directly toward the brute, Smith's "lives" indicate, finally, that thieves are ugly and if not quite ugly, then foolish and difficult to comprehend. Not all Smith's biographies follow such a curve; many, to be sure, follow no curve at all. Still, very few of Smith's "heroes" preserve their original qualities.

So much for the structuring, such as it exists, of criminal rogue biography. Plotless and impoverished as it generally is, what purposes could it have served? Why make thieves into clowns, into monsters, into – at best – not entirely unambiguous heroes? Why package them in these forms and not others? And, insofar as redacted thieves tend to ends other than the rope's, why should they have sloped so pervasively down toward buffoonery and brutishness? Why do they move toward the vague and frivolous on the one hand, the distinctly repulsive on the other? We have yet to account for the elusiveness of the thief, for that instability of presentation which prevents any fixed or settled point of view. Writers like Smith not only robbed thieves of most of their humanity, they made what little character they left them exceedingly difficult to grasp. Their goal, as the 1734 Johnson says, was to make them appear "in a more agreeable Manner than they have ever yet appeared in." But more agreeable than what?

Chapter 7

Barbarous levities: fear, guilt, and the value of confusion

It is not the smallest among those Sufferings which Men under Sentence of the Law endure, that a censorious World are continually propagating evil Reports, and spreading from one to another Rumors without Foundation. The Miseries which real Breaches of the Laws draw on unhappy Criminals are heavy enough in themselves to excite Compassion, and it is either Cruelty of Disposition, or a Barbarous Levity of Mind from whence Men are led to scatter such Detractions . . . turning their Conjectures into formal Stories, merely to blacken one already overthrown.

William Gordon, a condemned highwayman
hanged in 1733, quoted in *Select Trials* (1742),
4:61–62

And, indeed, if Shepherd had been as wretched, and as silly a Rogue in the World as upon the Stage, the lower Gentry, who attended him to Tyburn, wou'd never have pittied him when he was hang'd.

From a review of *Harlequin Shepherd* in Mist's
Weekly Journal, 5 December 1724

What a lamentable case it is to see so many Christian men and women strangled on that cursed tree of the gallows, insomuch as if in a large field a man might see together all the Christians, that but in one year, throughout England, come to the untimely and ignominious death, if there were any spark of grace, or charity in him, it would make his heart to bleed for pity and compassion.

Sir Edward Coke, Epilogue to *The Third Part of the Institutes* (1644)

How shocking soever this Consideration may be, it must be owed, that these Terrors and these Punishments are . . . absolutely necessary for the Preservation of Order and Government.

Herbert Randolph, Assize Sermon, 12 March 1729,
p. 2

As they were riding to the place of execution, Ogden flung a handful of money out of the cart to the people saying, Gentlemen, here is a Poor Will's farewell. And when he was turning off, he gave two such extraordinary jerks with his legs as was much admired by all the spectators.

Alexander Smith, *Highwaymen* (1719a), p. 353

149

Behind the tendency to debase or debunk the thief it is possible to see a moral purpose. Certainly this is the standard justification for criminal biographies of the type Smith and others wrote, that they were warning the impressionable against "the tinsel splendour of sensual pleasure, and the dreadful price men pay for it."[1] Buffoons and brutes show the criminal impulse at its least sympathetic, and even the cynosure of criminal longings can do repulsive things. "*Hind* has been often celebrated for his Generosity to all Sorts of People," writes the 1734 Johnson. "Never was Highwayman more careful than [he] to avoid Blood-shed, yet" – this is the lead-in to his story of Hind's shooting the gentleman's servant – "we have one Instance in his Life that proves how hard it is for a man to engage in such an Occupation, without being exposed to a Sort of wretched Necessity some Time or other, to take away the Life of another Man."[2] The fact that this one "Instance" is placed at the end of Hind's adventures – and that so many like instances are similarly placed in other highwaymen's lives – strikes me as significant. Even the best of thieves tends ultimately to commit inexcusable acts, passes beyond the reader's capacity to identify easily with him. Hind's killing that man, in this revision at least, seems meant to wean the reader away from his criminal frolics by having them suddenly go sour. The technique is not unlike that used by certain behavioral therapists in the treatment of sexual deviates: Shown photographs or movies that cater to his perversion, the subject finds that arousal brings a painful shock. Modern technology allows this to be electrical rather than merely emotional (a powerful advantage), and the jolts continue until the objectionable behavior stops.

Lest the standard claims for the moral importance of Smith's type of writing begin to be taken too seriously, however, let me hasten to add that another kind of conditioning process is more pervasively at work in criminal rogue biography: desensitization. Writers like Smith were far more interested in anesthetizing their readers to certain of the implications of crime, it seems to me, than in inoculating them against any impulse to commit it. Their aim was not so much to rouse the emotional and intellectual apparatus of the reader (my analogy is to the immunological response) as to bemuse it.

Certain main features of late seventeenth- and early eighteenth-century crime tend to be obscured by the idea of the heroic highwayman, and distorted practically beyond recognition by the doings of brutes and buffoons. Along with fires, falling houses, epidemics, mobs running wild, crime was one of the great nuisances of the age. Writing in 1635, Henry Goodcole warns there are "lewd tempting persons lurking in the Streets and High-wayes." Friendly-seeming men may "intice you to play at Cards or Dice for a Pot of Beere," and equally friendly women may offer "to meet you in the Fields, or some other private remote places." So far this sounds like the cony-catching pamphlets of some forty years earlier, but to emphasize his point Goodcole cites the cases of two men who recently accepted such invitations, and were lured out into the dangerous suburbs and killed.[3] The fear that prompted such advice persisted far into the eighteenth century. In 1752, returning to the City from Holloway, Thomas Tipping witnessed a rape. "The Woman was down on her Back," he later testified in court, "her Cloaths up, her Legs open, and the Man upon her. She said, *For God's Sake Master, Help; Murder, Murder!* The Man said, *Hold your Tongue, you Bitch.*" Reluctant to intervene, Tipping continued on his way. Later, however, "reading in the Papers that a Man was taken up, and hearing the Woman had a good character," he offered to come forward and testify. He had been "afraid," he explained, that "there was more in it than there should be, there being many Traps to draw People in, such as Strategems of Women crying out, and the like."[4]

Tipping's cowardice, if we can call it that, is not entirely to be condemned. Historians of the period have recently concluded that crime rates in England declined over the seventeenth and eighteenth centuries, but contemporary observers believed quite the opposite.[5] The lawlessness of the period was such, an attorney claimed in 1740, "that a Gentleman cannot venture a few Miles out of Town without Danger of being robbed." Nor could gentlemen (or any other people for that matter) be at all certain of their safety even in town. Writing in 1755 but expressing views that obtained over most of the century, Jonas Hanway described the dilemma exactly: "I sup with my friend; I cannot return to my home, not even in my chariot, without danger of a pistol being clapt to by breast. I build an elegant villa, ten or twenty miles distant from the capital; I am obliged to provide an armed force to convey me thither; lest I should be attacked on the road with fire and ball."[6] Goodcole's advice would be echoed as late as 1790, when visitors to London were advised to be always alert and to keep on the move: "never . . . stop in a crowd or look at the windows of a print-shop, if you would not have your pocket picked."[7] The thrust of this last suggests that violent crime seemed less of a threat in the latter part of the eighteenth century; pickpockets, after all, are not nearly so threatening as other kinds of criminals. But in the early part of the century, the period of most concern to us, everything indicated (however incorrectly) that crime was on the rise in both frequency and violence. To Alexander Smith writing (or plagiarizing) in one of his soberer moods, crime apparently kept pace with moral progress, "the Devil being as industrious to improve his followers in the schools of vice, as our best instructors are in those of virtue."[8] "It is amazing," thought the *London Journal* in 1721, "that People will Travel with any Charge about them, when there are daily, nay almost hourly Accounts of Robberies committed in every Road about the Town." Understandably, the newspaper writers sometimes felt hard-pressed to keep up. "The Street-Robbers seem to increase upon our Hands and grow more Numerous than formerly," observed Applebee's *Original Weekly Journal* in 1728, "so that we shall be oblig'd to Crowd [their] Actions . . . into one corner of our Paper, without affording a single Paragraph to each of them."[9]

Pepys had reason, then, to shiver in his bed at strange sounds in the night, or to worry all the way when, on one occasion, he had to transport a large sum of money by road. The prospect of being robbed was part of everyone's life, and many who never had been, and never would be, nonetheless gave the matter thought. They were careful, for instance, not to overstay the daylight hours in Hampstead or Richmond if they had to return to town for the night. Footpads were "often abroad" on both roads, which were "very unsafe."[10] Dr. Johnson's single recorded opinion on the subject of highwaymen, it is interesting to note, was evoked one night as he got ready to travel down to Streatham to visit the Thrales.[11] The lives of other notables were more directly invaded by crime. Swift woke up one night in London to find thieves trying to get in at his window, and later suspected his manservant was involved. As John Evelyn rode toward Bromley he was set upon by two "cut-throats" who took all that he had of value, including his boots, and tied him to a tree. Until he managed to free himself two hours later, he was "grievously . . . tormented with flies, ants, and the sun." Horace Walpole had a number of encounters with thieves, including one in which he was nearly killed. A highwayman in Hyde Park was robbing him when the gun accidentally discharged, missing Walpole's head but singeing his cheek. On a later occasion, when it seemed he might come face to face with a gang of burglars, he prudently put himself at the proper end of a gun. "Col. Seabright with his sword drawn went first," he wrote George Montagu, "and then I, exactly the figure of Robinson Crusoe, with a candle and lanthorn in my hand, a carbine upon my shoulder, my hair wet and about my ears, and in a linen night-gown and slippers."[12] Finally, and this shows the insolent ubiquity of the breed, thieves had broken into Walpole's parents' house in London when he was a child. Walpole's father was of course the most powerful man in England, but English thieves respected no one.[13]

Much was made earlier of the threat posed by psychopathic or psychotic murderers, but this threat was more metaphysical than personal. In the practical terms of everyday life common thieves were probably more threatening. They may not have been so vastly disturbing as familiar murderers, but then neither were they so rare.[14] To anyone who owned anything they might steal (and that certainly would have included all the readers of the popular literature of crime) thieves must have been a constant source of uneasiness. Nor, and here is a second, more curious point, would this uneasiness have been prompted entirely by fear. Thieves were a grave social embarrassment, and not the least of that embarrassment came from the question of what ought to be done with them.

The official response to theft was really, on the face of it, quite simple. From 1688 to 1820, according to the standard estimate, the number of capital statutes increased from something like 50 to more than 200.[15] Then as now the main argument for capital punishment was deterrence; it was "the most powerful Restraint that could be thought of, to put a Stop to the Violence of unreasonable and wicked Men." By hanging some such men (and women too) the authorities hoped to keep the vast bulk of similarly "unreasonable and wicked" people in check.[16] And upon this hope they had to rely a great deal, for the means at hand of suppressing crime more directly were ridiculously inadequate. To a large extent, the catching and prosecuting of criminals was a do-it-yourself affair. A person who was robbed would raise a hue and cry, providing of course he had not been killed or seriously injured, and then, with the help of whoever gathered, would run the criminal down, collar him, and bring him before the nearest magistrate. The magistrate, often upon payment of a fee for the necessary paperwork, would then bind the accused over to the next sessions or assize, on which occasion it would be his responsibility to defend himself and the victim's to prosecute. Such a system may have worked well enough in the country as a whole, but in London, where the population had grown to more than half a million, it was grossly outmoded. Not until the early nineteenth century would there be a real metropolitan police force.[17]

The reliance on maximum deterrence was not merely a practical necessity, however, or even simply a symptom of social backwardness. It was part of a clearly defined political logic, and it had its positive uses. "In a commercial country like this," William Frankland argued in 1810 during a parliamentary debate on abolishing the death penalty for stealing from shops, "such laws are necesary for property could not be safe without them."[18] In 1810, and long before, the obvious alternative to protecting property via the death penalty was to institute a prison system and the kind of police force that would speedily and efficiently put criminals into it. The problem, however, was that prisons and police could be used for other purposes as well; this was all too obviously the case in France. As William Paley observed, "The liberties of a free people, and still more the jealousy with which these liberties are watched, and by which they are maintained, permit not those precautions and restraints, that inspection, scrutiny, and control, which are exercised with control in arbitrary governments."[19] Or, to quote Frankland again: "In a country where personal and political freedom is so much enjoyed as amongst us our criminal statutes must, of course, be numerous and severe. The multiplied punishments are part of the price we pay for our liberty."[20] It is in the absence of any better or more acceptable means of controlling criminals, then, that we are to understand the proliferation of the capital statutes.

Their primary function, as both contemporary and modern commentators remark, was to enforce "the division of property by terror." The phrase quoted belongs to Douglas Hay, apparently a Marxist, but William Paley would have accepted it without demur. Sheep stealing and horse theft, according to him, merited the death penalty "not [because] these crimes are in their nature more heinous, than many simple felonies which are punished by imprisonment or transportation, but because the property being more exposed, requires the terror of capital punishment to protect it."[21] Terror can of course be a useful political tool, especially when exercised with tact. Hay makes some interesting points in this regard. Although not all thieves were hanged, he observes, the threat of capital punishment was always present, ready to be invoked or not as the authorities chose. Pointing out that "roughly half of those condemned to death during the eighteenth century did not go to the gallows, but were transported . . . or imprisoned," Hay finds that "here was the peculiar genius of the law." To put the meanest face on the whole affair, the proliferation of the capital statutes gave the ruling class a means of maintaining hegemony over the lower classes by a sort of carrot-and-stick approach. The stick was the statute book and the carrot (poor carrot that it was) that stick held in abeyance. By granting pardons, by changing death sentences to transportation, by throwing out indictments on technical grounds, by occasionally refusing to prosecute, the powers-that-were presented a gracious face not only to those they ruled but to themselves as well. Or, in Hay's words, by not hanging everyone the law allowed them to hang, "the class that passed one of the bloodiest penal codes in Europe [was able] to congratulate itself on its humanity."[22]

Hay's argument brings a new perspective to an old idea. The notion of a bloodthirsty body politic defending property with an iron hand, and all the while feasting its soul on its own hypocrisies, has long attached to the eighteenth century. I do not want to overturn this point of view, only to set it aside. It is all too easy to dismiss contemporary comment on capital punishment as the sheerest self-serving poppycock. But so long as we do we shall not be hearing all that it was saying. The hanging of people for theft was not so simple a matter as Hay – who asserts that "the rulers of eighteenth-century England cherished the death sentence" – would make it.[23] Far from cherishing it, they employed it faute de mieux. Indeed, though political considerations were not irrelevant, there seems to have been a certain squeamishness about hanging men for theft. As admittedly there is little direct evidence to support this point, it will take some arguing.

Hay may well be right about the intentions of Parliament in framing the laws, for its viewpoint was chiefly that of the landed interests. The remission of punishment in rural communities may well have worked as he describes it, strengthening the hold of the squirearchy on closely knit communities. But things were more fluid in London.[24] Most Londoners were not native to the place and, this being a great encouragement to crime, it was largely a city of strangers. Given this situation, what political advantage could have been gained by not hanging thieves? And by not hanging so many? In Hay's view the remission of punishment produced "bonds of obligation on one side and condescension on the other," allowing those in authority "to terrorize the petty thief and then command his gratitude, or at least the approval of [the] neighborhood."[25] But when London judges threw indictments out on highly technical grounds, when juries there found thieves guilty to less than a capital value even when they had stolen more than that in cash, when gentlemen robbed in its environs chose not to prosecute highwaymen (this was a sign of "class"), and when its citizens (more businesslike) merely turned pickpockets over to the mob to be "pumped" or beaten, what political ends could they have been aiming at? Given the relative impersonality of London, such "generosity" could hardly have been known outside their immediate circles. Thieves, too, would have had fewer local connections in London than in the country, and so less of a claim on the "condescension" of those empowered to dispose of them.[26]

If less, not more, political hay were to be made out of the remission of punishment in London, why then did it occur there so often? It is possible that London judges and juries were more easily corrupted than their country counterparts and that prosecutors, feeling freer from social pressure, were more easily placated or even bought off. But as yet no evidence suggests this was the case, and the fact remains that in London there was a notable reluctance to hang merely for offenses against property; and this where, according to Hay's analysis, we should least expect it. What this reluctance could mean in concrete terms is illustrated by the cases of two petty, thoroughly unprepossessing thieves.[27] Neither would seem an apt source for bribery, or even especially likely to arouse public sympathies. John Crudleigh was

Engraved for The Malefactor's Register.

View of HOUNSLOW HEATH, with the GIBETS and Men hanging in Chains

from *The Malefactor's Register* [1779]

hanged in 1710, aged thirty-two, and Elizabeth Price, aged thirty-seven, in 1712. Both were confirmed criminals, with strings of prior convictions that stretched back years. Crudleigh had been convicted in 1704 for stealing two hundred pounds of lead from the roof of St. Paul's, but because the jury chose to value the lead at no more than ten pence, the crime was considered noncapital, and he was let go after being whipped around the cathedral by the common hangman. In 1705 he was up on charges again, this time for stealing a sizable quantity of iron and brass. Acquitted of felony because of a flaw in the indictment, he was retried on a misdemeanor charge, found guilty, and fined twenty pounds. Unable to pay, he spent the next five years in Newgate and was finally executed, barely six months after his release, for two counts of housebreaking. It is perhaps worth noting that in his last robberies he took, among other things, a goose and (robber of base mettle that he was) two pots. Price's career, from our point of view, is even more impressive. Five times convicted of theft, she was burnt on the cheek in 1701, whipped in 1702 and 1703, sentenced to death but

from *The Malefactor's Register* [1779]

Engraved for The Malefactors Register?

JOHN SMITH *cut down at* TYBURN, *in consequence of a reprieve which came five Minutes after he had been turned off.*

pardoned in 1704, and burnt in the hand and committed to the work-house in 1708. It was only after she had escaped from the workhouse, and upon her sixth conviction, that she was finally hanged. It is diffi-cult, in terms of Hay's thesis, to know why the courts were so patient. It should have been clear that Price was a thoroughly bad sort by her fifth conviction, after she resumed stealing despite her pardon. Crud-leigh may have had friends to intervene on his behalf (there is no evidence he did, though he had done his apprenticeship in London and worked there as a journeyman), but Elizabeth Price had never been anything more, at her most honest and respectable, than a ragpicker and street peddler. Considered in political terms only, she ought to have been more speedily hanged.[28]

I am not by any means arguing that hearts bled at the prospect of hanging thieves, or even – despite Coke's reflections at the end of his *Third Institute* – that there were major palpitations. But there was, I would argue, a certain squeamishness, an occasional and vaguely felt nausea, which had to be kept from developing into anything more.

That relatively few writers argued against the hanging of thieves is not as inconvenient to my argument as it may seem, for it is just as interesting, and probably more significant, that so many writers felt a need to argue *for* the practice, as if it needed to be defended. Thus most of the sermons preached before the assizes and nearly every treatise and pamphlet on the law are concerned to make the strongest possible case for the execution of thieves. Even books like Smith's *Highwaymen* pause to take up the subject, and every ordinary's *Account* addressed it. The need to execute murderers was not at all so prevalent a topic. Nor was the task these writers set themselves an especially easy one. They could advance several bad reasons for hanging thieves and only one good one, and even the good one was vulnerable to criticism. Well aware that neither natural nor Mosaic law prescribed death for crimes against property, the best argument contemporary writers could make was that hanging thieves was politically necessary.

To argue on political grounds only, however, was very nearly too crude. Though he believed there was "no way left to civilize the World, and stop the Torrent of Vice and Immorality, but to bring wicked Men to speedy Justice," a divine preaching in 1721 felt constrained to add, "Let it not be thought an Act of Cruelty, but of Discretion."[29] For what was in fact a political act, then, something more was wanted than mere political justification (but then something always is). There was no lack of writers ready to give a higher tone to the hanging of men for theft. Two such apologists were John Haslewood and John Conybeare, both typical Church of England clergymen (Conybeare later became bishop of Bristol). Haslewood preached at the Kingston assizes in 1707, and Conybeare at the Oxford assizes in 1727. Both argued that political order is built on the power to "take away . . . Lives" (Haslewood), that given the "Heedlessness of Temper [and] Depravity of Will in the Generality of Mankind" (Conybeare), nothing else could serve as a "Fence and Guard against Mens wild Desires and injurious Passions" (Haslewood). Yet neither was willing to leave the matter at that. Wanting some higher sanction for the death penalty, and well aware that natural law could give none, both argue that God Himself must sanction the practice. But on what grounds, given the fact that the Bible prescribes nothing more than restitution for theft? Conybeare baldly asserts that the authority to impose penal sanctions "must be *ultimately* resolved into The Will of God Himself," for otherwise it can have no justification at all. He takes comfort in the fact that "all sober men agree" on the civil authorities' "Right to this Power," and argues, dizzyingly, that as "God wills the *Happiness* of Mankind," and as that cannot be achieved except in society, and as society depends on government, and government upon laws, and laws on enforcement, so God "cannot but *approve* of those Methods which are necessary to the Attainment of it."[30] Haslewood is more clear-minded and direct. The magistrate "either . . . must have this Power from on High," he argues, "or else he can never lawfully Exercise it, but every Execution will be downright Murder."[31] Intending a reductio ad absurdum, Haslewood means to present this terrible possibility as unthinkable. But the phrase leaps to mind with a speed that suggests it is all too thinkable, and certainly something very near to it was present in the minds of many of his contemporaries. "There are many," wrote Zachary Babington in 1680, "that are full of S[i]r *Thomas Moore*'s Kindness, and think it too much that a man should lose his life for Crimes under Murther." "The People are affected, it is true, with the Sufferings of [executed] criminals," wrote the author of *A Complete History of James Maclean* in 1750, "but they are affected with Compassion, Sympathy, and Pity. They rather condemn the Severity of the Laws, than express their Horror at the Crime."[32]

As the weak efforts of men like Conybeare and Haslewood show, there could be no good argument for hanging thieves except the political. Though cruel, it made good sense; social grounds alone could seem to justify the practice. "The execution of Offenders would be of little service to Society, consider'd barely as removing so many Malefactors," explained one of the Newgate ordinaries, "the Benefit expected from it arises from the Example, or rather the Effects of the Example." Thieves were not hanged for what they *had done* so much as for what others *might do*. Thus one judge smugly told a thief who complained it was "very hard" to be hanged for stealing a horse that he was wrong, for the point of his being hanged was rather "that horses may not be stolen." And "the benefit of the example" could seem far-ranging indeed. Given the belief that all crime started with vice, Tyburn could serve "as a beacon to warn . . . men from indulging themselves in sensual pleasures." Quite apart from its immediate deterrent effect, then, hanging criminals was a way of promoting social discipline in general. Or, as Edward Tuke slyly points out, "To tame a lion, they use to beat a little Dog before him."[33]

So much in theory, at least, for the social value of killing thieves. Bigger things hung in the balance, however, than little dogs who'd gotten bad names. In actual fact capital punishment was delivering none of the benefits promised by its apologists. "It is well observed by the lo[rd] *Coke*," a legal commentator writes late in the seventeenth century, "that . . . Those offences are often committed, that are often punished; and he gives his Reason for it, That the frequency of the punishment makes it so familiar, as it is not feared." Agreeing with

Coke on the basis of his own experience, he concludes that hardened
criminals are reformable by neither "favour, terror, example."[34] Other
writers saw the same phenomenon and came to less complacent conclusions. If executions were not having their desired effect, and obviously
they were not, then in one way or another it was necessary to make
them more impressive. In 1701 the author of *Hanging Not Punishment
Enough* urged that torture be introduced into public executions. The
spectacle of felons being whipped to death or broken on the wheel, he
thought, might have a sobering effect on others similarly inclined. "To
Men so far corrupted in their Principles and Practices, no Argument
will be so cogent," he wrote, "as Pain in an intense degree." George
Olyffe made essentially the same recommendation in 1731, describing
in lurid and possibly self-revealing detail just which tortures might be
employed. Others arguing for severer executions (and it ought to be
said with rather more human sympathy than Olyffe and his predeces-
sor) included Defoe, Mandeville, Fielding, Paley, and Boswell.[35]

Mandeville and Fielding are especially interesting, both for what they
say and for what, not quite managing to say, they nonetheless show to
have been much on their minds. Of the two, as we would expect,
Fielding takes the broader view. The "late Increase of Robbers" according to him is basically attributable to the failure of the upper classes
either to provide properly for the poor or to set them a proper example.
"When . . . Vice descends downward from [the nobility and the gen-
try] to the Tradesman, the Mechanic, and the Labourer, it is certain to
engender many political Mischiefs, and among the rest . . . Theft and
Robbery." Elsewhere he approvingly quotes Sir Matthew Hale: " 'The
Want of a due Provision . . . for Education and Relief of the poor in a
Way of Industry, is that which fills the Goals with malefactors.' " But
as Fielding is "not too sanguine" that the upper classes will either
reform themselves or take steps to improve the condition of the poor,
he proposes "some Methods . . . which, if less efficacious, are perhaps
easier than those already proposed." Thus he advocates stricter controls
on vagabonds, sterner measures against receivers of stolen goods, and
various legal and procedural reforms that would make it easier for
thieves to be arrested and convicted, and more difficult for them to be
pardoned. But the most striking of his proposals is that public executions be made into true spectacles of terror and shame, admitting little if
any pity for the condemned. These ends would be achieved not by
torture, "which I am an Enemy to the very Thought of admitting," but
by "Celerity, Privacy, and Solemnity."[36]

In making this last point, Fielding very much wants to convince "the
good-natured and tender-hearted Man" that he ought "to be watchful
over his own Temper": "Here . . . is the life of a Man concerned; but of

what Man? Why, of one who being too lazy to get his Bread by Labour, declares War against the Properties, and often against the Persons of his Fellow-Subjects." Readily allowing that "no Man indeed of common Humanity or common Sense can think the Life of a Man and a few Shillings to be of an equal Consideration," Fielding denies "that the Law in punishing theft with Death proceeds . . . with any View to Vengeance. The terror of the Example is the only Thing proposed, and one Man is sacrificed to the Preservation of Thousands." Then Fielding goes on to clinch his argument in a curiously self-revealing way. "If therefore the Terror of this Example is removed (as it certainly is by frequent Pardons)," he writes, "the Design of the Law is rendered totally ineffectual; The Lives of the Persons executed are thrown away, and sacrificed rather to the vengeance than to the Good of the Public, which receives no other Advantage than by getting rid of a Thief, whose Place will immediately be supplied by another." Fielding's "if" makes it sound as though he were speaking hypothetically, but it seems to me that here we are very close to his view of things as they actually, terribly are: "As the matter now stands, common Humanity . . . exacts our Concern," he says in the last sentence of his treatise, "for that many Cart-loads of our Fellow-creatures are once in six Weeks carried to slaughter, is a dreadful Consideration."[37]

Mandeville, too, writes out of an acute sense of distress. "The Multitude of unhappy Wretches, that every Year are put to Death for Trifles in our great Metropolis," his essay begins, "has long been afflicting to Men of Pity and Humanity, and continues to give great Uneasiness to every Person, who has a Value for his Kind." Mandeville's specific recommendations, which need not especially concern us, are very much like Fielding's (and indeed Boswell confused the two works in No. 68 of the *Hypochondriack*). Mandeville wants to persuade his readers that "whoever justly prosecutes, and convicts a Person of a capital Crime, has nothing to answer for to his Conscience," and he wants also to make public executions more solemn and so more persuasive occasions. Essentially he would like condemned prisoners to behave in actual fact as the criminal-cum-sinner myth so often portrays them: "Some of them [might] prove stupendous Orators, that would not only spread Amazement all around them, but likewise find uncommon Ways to reach the Heart with Violence, and force Repentance on their Hearers."[38]

Mandeville is not so sensitive as Fielding to the ways in which society itself is partly responsible for crime. There is nonetheless – again as we would expect – something more piquant in his language as he expresses just what is bothering him; and here, significantly, is none of the irony that informs his most famous work. Realizing that "the Punishment [for theft] is greater than the Laws, framed by God himself for the *Jewish* Commonwealth, inflicted; or what natural Justice, proportioning the Punishment to the Crime, seems to require," Mandeville sees perhaps too clearly that the practice can only be "vindicated" on the grounds of its deterrent effect. And it *must* have such an effect (thus his recommendations), for the alternative is beyond abiding even for the author of *The Fable of the Bees*. "If those valuable Sacrifices we are obliged to make to the publick Safety are render'd insignificant," he thinks, if all that is accomplished by the hanging of thieves is "the Death of those poor Souls," then what the law prescribes is "little better than Barbarity, and sporting away the Lives of the indigent Vulgar."[39] Or so he nearly thinks. I tease this insight out of a larger, more tangled mass of prose; it has something fugitive and buried about it, being apparently too radical a thought even for Mandeville. And so he leaves it behind him, as Fielding does his larger views on the causes and potential cures of crime, bending his mind instead to the task of making a cruel and – what perhaps is worse for him – hopelessly inefficacious social institution work. If Mandeville pursued that fugitive thought, he might have had to change his whole way of thinking about the treatment of criminals in his society.

Both Mandeville and Fielding saw, but were reluctant to admit, that the logic of capital punishment involved their society in an ever more vicious circle. For if in fact the hanging of thieves had no apparent effect, except that thieves grew less and less impressed by the event – "there is nothing in being hang'd," Mandeville imagined them saying to each other, "but a wry Neck, and a wet pair of Breeches" – then it was necessary to hang still more of them, and to be always enlarging the range of the capital statutes.[40] Mandeville and Fielding were not alone in their sensitivity to the problem, and the moral and emotional tensions they exhibit permeate the popular literature of crime. In the ordinary's *Accounts* especially, with their obsessive efforts to make thieves as well as murderers conform to the criminal-as-sinner myth, one sees the pertinacity of the issue with special clarity. That "so many Christian men and women" had to be "strangled on that cursed tree of the gallows" wrenched Coke's heart. But what if the victims of the law were truly Christians, at least by the time they died, accepting death as due punishment for their sins and pleased to be of use as an example to others? Surely then there would be nothing upsetting in their fate, nothing to cloud the consciences of those who felt in one way or another a party to their death, nor any reason to doubt the justice and utility of their sentence. It was not thieves' crimes, then, as it was with murderers, but their punishment that had to be framed within an appropriate myth.

Given all that has been already said of the social and personal usefulness of the criminal-cum-sinner myth, the point need not be elaborated. It ought to be observed, however, that this myth was rather less successful in accommodating thieves than murderers. As we have noted before, thieves tended over the long run to slip out of the structure and meaning it attempted to impose on their lives, becoming only one or another kind of rogue. But even from the first, thieves appear to have been recalcitrant subjects, frequently prompting the ordinaries and their like to show a Procrustean strain in dealing with them. Battered with the idea that hanging is the best and indeed the only thing to do with them, thieves are hacked at, pressured, and stretched in ways that are neither so apparent in the cases of murderers nor, I would argue, so needful. Thus, for example, Guthrie "admonished" his doomed charges – his language uninspired but relentless – "how unjust, how dishonourable, and how irreligious it is to rob Mankind of their Right and Property, how directly contrary and destructive it is to all Society in general, turning everything into Disorder and Confusion, which makes it absolutely necessary that . . . all who are guilty of Rapine and Plunder should die."[41] Complaints, when recorded at all, are overborne with a mass of self-serving verbiage. When in 1656 Richard Hannam presumed to protest that "by the Scripture Thieves were not to be put to death," Edward Tuke responded at considerable length, declaring finally, as if to close the matter once and for all, that Christ was crucified between two thieves, and "if they ought not to have suffered at all, or if they had suffered unjustly, then questionlesse Christ would have declared as much." Besides, "one of the Thieves confessed . . . they suffered righteously," he pointed out in a shrewd switching of the topic, "where mark," he adjured Hannam, "the antiquity and usefulness of a malefactors confession at the place of execution."[42] For Tuke the usefulness of such a confession may in no small part have been that it mooted the troublesome question Hannam had raised, and far more effectively, of course, than Christ's silence ever could. For "questionlesse" there were far more urgent matters on His mind as He hung on His cross than the moral correctness of the Roman penal code.

One of the priest's primary duties, all these accounts make clear, was to bring the criminal around to a point of view society could live with as he got ready to die. "One Thing above all, stuck for sometime terribly in his Stomach, namely, that he should suffer death for only breaking into a House, when he did not carry any Thing off." But, given the ordinary's good offices, this thief came "at last" to see his situation in a better light, "seem'd better reconciled to it, owned the Justice of his Sentence, and declared he heartily repented, and forgave every one, dying in Peace with all Men, and hoping for Salvation."

"We hope," adds Guthrie, "he was sincere, and are inclined . . . to believe . . . so, since he did not seem desirous of living longer." Rarely are such consoling disclosures absent from Guthrie's *Accounts* or those of his predecessors.[43] And such consolations would seem to have been all the more important as the criminal's crime moved down the scale of heinousness. Thus when two ignorant countrymen were condemned for pulling down turnpikes and thought it hard they should die for such an offense, Guthrie took special pains to show them their crime "was most atrocious," being quite as bad in fact as "Murder, Robbery, House-Breaking, &c." Though the more recalcitrant of the two finally acknowledged "that his Punishment was equitable and just," Guthrie was left unsatisfied. For the man "still was not so sensible, or at least so early sensible as could have been wished of the Nature of his Crime."[44] Perhaps his coming to a right spirit of self-criticism so slowly still seemed to impugn the justice of what was about to be done to him. These two turnpike breakers were executed under the Black Act of 1723, an infamous statute that at one sweep greatly enlarged the range of capital offenses. This law was just because it was necessary, according to the author of *Remarkable Criminals,* no matter if its "severity" (among other things, it hanged men for going on the highways in disguise) could make it appear "cruel and inhuman."[45]

The ordinaries' edginess, and that of the audience they wrote to, can be seen in one of the more curious arguments they directed against thieves. When a burglar "thank'd God he never committed Murther," Paul Lorrain got him to admit "that he would have done it, and had actually prepared himself for it, in case he had been oppos'd in the Execution of his wicked Designs." Persuaded, therefore, that he was "guilty of Murther before God, and . . . ought to repent of it, as if he had actually committed it," the burglar concluded he was "still more criminal than he thought he was."[46] Obviously, had mere theft always seemed unquestionably to merit the death penalty, there would have been no reason to make it the moral equivalent of murder.[47] Nor should it surprise us that theft at times was made to seem a kind of treason. Lorrain said as much, the author of *Remarkable Criminals* called thieves "enemies of mankind," and Guthrie pronounced them "destructive of all human Society and Conversation."[48]

Not infrequently the popular literature of crime declares that the laws of England are "tender" of human life. In such declarations, I hope by now to have shown, there was a nervous need for reassurance.[49] Conscience was in fact tenderer than the law, but, barring total reform of the penal system (which would not happen until the nineteenth century), conscience had no choice but to tough it out. Mandeville, Fielding, the preachers at the assizes, the ordinaries and other writers of

criminal lives, presumably many of the public at large, had to deal as
best they could with the simple, unpalatable, and even "horrible and
grievous" fact that in their society certain human lives actually could be
worth less than "a few shillings."[50] Striving in various ways to cope
with this fact, some people proposed ways of reimbuing the ritual of
public execution with meaning or rehearsed yet again the arguments
that only seemed to justify it. Others adopted an attitude of resignation,
like the author of *Remarkable Criminals* in speaking of several poachers
hanged under the Black Act: "They said deer were wild beasts, and
they did not see why the poor had not as good a right to them as the
rich. However, as the Law condemned them to suffer, they were bound
to submit." Yet others, no less resigned to the exigencies of the law,
apparently found some relief by opening their hearts to those it
doomed. Thus Thomas Gent describes his response to the hanging of
two men at York around 1716 for stealing one and a half pence on the
highway. They claimed that in fact there was no robbery; they had only
asked two passing travelers for the price of a pint of ale and had been
misunderstood. Gent thought their lives may have been sworn away
for the reward (it would have amounted to eighty pounds), "but at that
time, as the determinations of law were above my tender capacity, I
could say nothing but heartily wish the deplorable sinners a happy
immortality." And yet still others, for all their affectations of sympathy, could be utterly callous. On one of the occasions Guthrie
preached so fulsomely on the moral equivalence of theft and murder,
twenty people were crowded into two carts and hanged. Four of them
were women, and it had taken seven carts and (for one moneyed individual) a mourning coach to haul them all to Tyburn. Finally, there
would have been those as well who, more than a little confused by the
punishment of thieves, would have felt themselves torn in several directions at once. A mid-eighteenth-century clergyman, just finished minis-
tering to four hanged men, provides a case in point. In his halting and
awkward language (truly tortured syntax, one might say) we see not
only his confusion but also an attempt to win through, at the last, to at
least some partial coherence. "The Sight of our Fellow Creatures, Men
like wild and destructive beasts, with Shackles and Fetters; those
Badges of Slavery in a *free Country*," he writes, his prose widening in
ungainly and discordinate gyres, "tho' they have the just Reward of
their Deeds, and much Severity is absolutely necessary for the Safety of
the Community, yet to the tender sentiments of Humanity, they are far
from pleasing Objects; and to convince and bring such Wretches to a
Sense of their Crimes . . . is an Office of great Labour and Fatigue; but
it has its comfortable and joyous Reflections!"[51]

It was the aim of the criminal-as-sinner myth to produce such "comfortable and joyous reflections," but with thieves, by all indications, it often failed. The work of the ordinaries, who were the myth's only consistent practitioners much interested in thieves, was not very highly respected. It was not only that their clients frequently disappointed report. "The generality of Paul Lorrain's Saints," wrote a correspondent to the *Tatler,* "seem to place a peculiar vanity on dying hard." Nor was it merely that the ordinaries were commonly judged to be, in their petty ways, greedy, self-serving men.[52] The credibility of their accounts was not unimportant, but the central problem for the myth they purveyed was that it recognized no essential difference between thieves and murderers; it assumed they ought to be dealt with in the same way. But whatever the capital statutes indicated, theft just could not seem the moral equivalent of murder. As the author of *Remarkable Criminals* observed (and he was no bleeding heart), "petty thieveries and crimes of a like nature seem to fall very short in comparison to the atrocious guilt of murder."[53] And though the law by itself might well seem inadequate before the awful facts of murder, necessitating the invocation of an elaborate mythic apparatus, as a cultural mechanism it was more than enough for dealing with theft. "In every other crime [but murder]," wrote Fielding, "the offender who hath paid the price of his life may flatter himself that he hath fully expiated his offence."[54] Why then should thieves be made to jump through the ordinary's hoops?

Not surprisingly, many thieves refused to conform to the proffered protocols. As they well knew, accepting the prison chaplain's terms meant giving up whatever moral leverage they had to pry loose a pardon or reprieve; it was as much as consenting to be hanged. "He was so far from designing Murther at any time," one highwayman made a point of telling Lorrain, "that he always resolv'd rather to be killed than kill." Such declarations get recorded at least as frequently as the ordinaries' insistence (with its unspoken correlative, that there is nothing wrong with killing men for stealing) that stealing and killing are essentially the same.[55] Perhaps such statements were published because they showed that even thieves had some sense of morality. But if the hanging of decent-minded murderers could make, as we have seen, for difficult emotions, what then of the sympathetic thief? One of the main reasons thieves' lives were cast into an alternative form, it seems to me, was that the criminal-as-sinner myth was simply unable to control the implications not of what he had done but of what had been done to him. It was not the thief's crimes that were so scandalous but the way he was punished.

James Maclean, arguably the last of the highwayman heroes, was hanged nearly a hundred years after Hind. Among his well-wishers was Horace Walpole. It was Maclean who had nearly killed him, and Mac-

lean had publicly apologized. Walpole followed this highwayman's fortunes with no little interest up to the point it became certain he would
hang. Then he tried to put him out of mind: "As I conclude he will
suffer and wish him no ill," he wrote Horace Mann, "I don't care to
have his idea."[56] Walpole added that he was "almost single" in not
having gone to visit Maclean in his cell at Newgate, an exaggeration
meant to lighten the tone of his remarks, but his essential meaning is
clear. "Idea" in contemporary usage was synonymous with "image,"
and, given Maclean's fate, Walpole wanted no solid notion of the man,
no sense of him in the flesh. Essentially the same disposition, I would
suggest, lay behind the progressive etiolation of Hind's life history and,
of course, the life histories of so many other thieves. It was also in large
part responsible for the confusions and ambiguities that make narratives
like Smith's, and most especially their protagonists, so difficult to
grasp. As it is not possible to have *no* idea of something once it has
impinged on one's consciousness, the popular literature of criminal
roguery offered an acceptably diminished and weakened idea of the
thief. And as inchoate as this idea was, it was clear enough to justify or
render irrelevant the fact he had suffered. It ought to seem highly
significant that thieves who had not been hanged – those still on the
loose, for instance, or who had been transported – almost never attracted biographical attention.[57]

If thieves – at least as they were imaged in the popular literature of
crime – were not much like other men, then how or why should other
men's sympathies be engaged? If the thief turned out a brute, as so
many did, then all well and good. "Many Things, which I have done
amiss, have been aggravated; many that I have not done, invented, and
laid to my Charge," complained William Gordon before he was
hanged, "in order to impede the Course of Mercy, and represent me
worse than I am." If, alternatively, he showed himself a buffoon, then
there would be no reason for pity here either. One writer describes
how, trying to squeeze a few more minutes out of life, a burglar stood
at the gallows and spun out "a long speech full of tedious tautologies."
He then goes on to tell a "Collection" of the hanged man's "Pranks and
Exploits," so as to "give the Reader some divertissement after this sad
story." And if the thief remained heroic to the last, as some few rare
ones did, then he could seem something of a demigod, confronting his
tragic fate in a realm beyond mere mortal pain; this is how Smith has
Hind die. "Any man who had excelled in his Way," as the 1734 Johnson says about Hind, "will always be loaded with so much Praise as to
make his whole History seem a Fable."[58] There were those many
thieves, too, who never quite came to cohere into any one of the three

"pure" types I've described, who never project – even within these highly reductive terms – any particular image. They remain vague and ambiguous, even as stereotypes, but this too would have served to put off guilt. For as such smudged objects make for correspondingly vague and ambiguous emotions, readers would have found it even easier to overlook the fact that they, too, had once been living, fellow human beings.

Once got into the context of criminal rogue biography, the thief could no longer seem an object of real concern. Richard Hannam's bravado led to his being rebuked for "desperately" acting a kind of "Theatre."⁵⁹ He was not sufficiently serious for a Man facing imminent death. And yet this same writer takes obvious pleasure in Hannam's insouciance, illustrating it no doubt so that his audience might relish the man's depravity but also for its entertainment value. For so long as a thief's behavior could be seen as a kind of theater, his life – and most especially his exit – could be judged on aesthetic, not ethical grounds. This explains not only *Harlequin Shepherd* but also, in its smaller way, Will Ogden's parting gesture (for both, see this chapter's epigraphs), which "was much admired by all the spectators."⁶⁰ Thus, too, the snappy talk given various members of a gang hanged en masse in 1726. One of them, a Hollander, explains he had come to do his thieving in England "because his own Country was so miserable a Place, that it would not afford him Provision to subsist on, Wood to hang him on, nor Earth to bury him in." Another "was only sorry, that he could not have a Game of Shuffle-Board before he dy'd." A third declared "that if he was Hang'd, he should never be his own Man again," and so on. Such bad men – and such bad actors! – to be making such bad jokes at a time like that.⁶¹ "Hanging is now become a Pastime and Sport," observed an anonymous writer in 1750, "the Number of Criminals which are executed, tend to familiarize the Terrors of Death, and make the Minds of the Multitude, who crowd to see the fatal Tragedy, less affected with the Scene, as if it was Fiction and not Reality."⁶² Much the same effect could well be ascribed to criminal rogue biography. As a late eighteenth-century anthology claimed, its lives of highwaymen and "other daring adventurers" had been "collected and comprised, so as to render the Whole . . . as much a Object of Wonder as of Pity!"⁶³

Fear, too, could be mitigated by turning reality into fiction. Fidge spoke of "palliating" Hind's crimes, which he did mainly by "none-suchifying" him. Hind was translated (as saints are translated) into a world bearing only the most adventitious relation to the real world of the reader's experience. There was no "precedent," Fidge insisted, for anything Hind had done, and this was a common claim in criminal rogue biography. Smith was never so explicit in outlining his own program, but, tickling the fancies of his audience with figures bizarrely beyond anything the normal world could offer, he followed a simpler method. The thief's deeds, themselves strange and unfamiliar, have the effect of making not only him but the whole "theater" of his actions into something strange and unfamiliar. For all that he has a real name, travels through real localities, and is said to rob real victims, none of it can ever seem quite real. Even the viciousness of the brute, that most scarifying of all thieves, tends to be exaggerated, and so situated as to parody real occasions for fear. How could anyone have actually believed in the likes of Sawney Beane? And even if such a monster had once actually existed, this was at a distance of more than a hundred years and (at least for a London audience) some hundreds of miles. To use what is (I hope) an entirely lucid modern analogy, the experience of reading about Sawney Beane must have been rather like watching one of those horror movies which, with its over-vivid colors and palpably implausible special effects, typically takes place in settings as distant from ordinary life as nineteenth-century Transylvania, or Los Angeles.

Smith's protagonists, to be sure, are capable of terrible deeds, but for all their intrinsic violence these inevitably are either so blanched by their manner of representation that they register with little affect, or else embedded in contexts that interfere with their normal meaning. The first strategy can be illustrated by comparing Smith to the ordinary of Newgate when both describe the same atrocity. Here first is Paul Lorrain:

> *Alexander Dalzi[e]l* [was] condemn'd for Piracy by him committed on the 20*th* of November, 1714; in company with a French Sea-Captain, and four other Mariners, who all coming on board a certain French Vessel, then at Anchor about a League off *Havre de Grace* in *France,* assaulted, and ty'd both Hand and Foot, the Master (one captain *Maurice*) and his Crew, being in all but six Persons; and one of them, thus ty'd, either fell, or (which is most probable) was thrown into the Sea, wherein not being able to help himself, nor receive any Assistance from his Companions, to whom he cry'd, *Dear Friends save me,* he then perish'd.[64]

Smith's version of the same event is briefer, and nominally worse: "he turned Pirate, and set upon a French ship near Havre de Grace, tying all the crew neck with heels, and throwing them overboard, so that they perished in the sea."[65] Smith inflates the act by increasing the arithmetic of its cruelty, but compresses it at the same time into a few easily forgotten phrases. And though here Dalziel's monstrosity is clearly more than enough to justify his being hanged – in Lorrain there is some question whether the killing was intentional – it lacks pathos. An unknown number of anonymous men, however large the number, perishing silently in the sea can have none of the emotional effect of a single man crying out, helpless, to his equally helpless friends, and whose drowning may have been an accident. Smith arouses disapproval but not disgust. His Dalziel is so casually and vapidly monstrous as hardly to seem real. Of course Smith writes more vividly of violence elsewhere, and can be more shocking. But even then, the context in which such events appear invariably keeps them from seeming as disturbing as they ought to be. Thus, to recur to the terrible fates of young Miss Wilmot and Sandal the hop merchant – the one ravished and murdered in her own bed, the other forced to drink piss and then pinked to death – even such cruelties as these lose something of their ordinary emotional effect by following so closely on the arousal, respectively, of prurient and scatological interest.

This dissevering of the object from its "proper" emotion, or, alternatively, the introduction of an "improper" emotion to vitiate what would otherwise be a normal response, is of course the very essence of the desensitization mentioned at the beginning of this chapter. Smith's readers, once they put down his book, may have been just as anxious as before about walking the streets, traveling the highways, or snuffing out the candles in their bedrooms at night. Perhaps for a while they were even more anxious. But for as long as they were immersed in Smith's version of crime they were engaged with something far different from, and yet at the same time imaginatively substitutable for, the kind of crime they were all too likely to encounter in actual life.[66] I would not make this point so confidently – it sounds all too pat and "modern" (gangster movies often work the same way) – were it not that the text itself so persistently advertises its own facticity. No less than Fidge, Smith wants his readers to *know* "that the like is not to be seen or ever heard of." Thus, having admitted at one point that he has been making up most of his narrative as he goes along, he promises that he will stick to the facts "for once." Or, as he grandly declares, "I will . . . renounce the pleasure which I generally take in my own imagination." He then goes on to tell a series of stories at least as improbable as any he has told before.[67] This is hardly the best way to get your audience to believe you; quite the contrary, it works to heighten the reader's sense that here is nothing but persiflage.

But then Smith's business is to debase the truth, to make all the features by which it is usually recognized seem spurious or unreliable. Even his giving so many precise details – the inn near which a robbery occurred, for instance, or the name and various affiliations of the victim, or an exact inventory of all the goods stolen – conduces to no sense of authenticity but rather to the opposite. The modern reader rapidly

becomes suspicious of such details and finds that many are utterly specious. Thus Zachary Howard, for example, is said to have ravished
Lady Fairfax, the wife of the Republican general, and their daughter
Elizabeth as well. Given his anti-republican bias, Smith may have
thought these women proper objects for a bit of salacious imagining, but
that is beside the point: The Fairfaxes never had a daughter named Elizabeth, at least none who lived to a ravishable age.[68] Or, to cite another
example, Tom Wilmot supposedly encounters the wife of Thomas
Blood while robbing the London coach. She offers him half a crown,
which he disdains, saying "no less than a crown would serve your husband, when he robbed the king," and rifles the lady's pockets of "about
fifteen guineas . . . and a silver thimble." All this is circumstantial
enough, especially the silver thimble, but as it happens the whole story is
a blatant historical impossibility. Blood stole the crown jewels 9 May
1671, more than a year, on Smith's own information, after Wilmot had
been hanged.[69]

Would Smith's contemporaries have noticed these facticities? The
author of *Compleat Tryals* observed, and silently corrected, Smith's errant version of the Golden Farmer's demise (see Chapter 1, n. 36), but
few other readers would have been as scrupulous as he – or as certain
modern, necessarily humorless scholars must be – in checking out
Smith's "facts." But then why should they have bothered? They must
have been aware that "most of his Stories," as Smith's most diligent
plagiarizer himself pointed out, were "barefac'd Inventions."[70] Even the
most credulous reader could not have believed that Cromwell was actually robbed on four separate occasions (not counting Hind's attempt),
that Mull Sack got at him twice, that in the course of one misadventure
he broke his leg and was ridiculously set astride an ass, and that during
another he was crowned with an upturned chamberpot "pretty well
fill'd with the nauseous Excrements of this much more nauseous
Rebel."[71] Smith's tendency to crib material from previously published
sources might also have alerted his readers to the essential facticity of
his narratives. Whether they recognized his specific sources or not, the
fact that so many of his stories had been published elsewhere suggests
their presence in the public domain, as part, perhaps, of the general
folklore.[72] Smith's apportioning of fictional adventures to actual historical personages, then, especially when so many of these stories had
appeared in avowedly fictive contexts, ought to be seen as yet another
of his techniques for "palliating" both thieves and their crimes.

Smith even shows a tendency to crib from himself. Thus Arthur
Chambers and William Throgmorton both practice exactly the same
trick on unsuspecting country bumpkins, and a certain Mr. Thurston,
variously the mayor or merely an alderman of Thornbury in Glouces-

tershire, is robbed twice at an interval of some sixty years.[73] Our old friend Henry Sandal also makes more than one appearance. Thus, some forty years and 150 pages before he is so brutally done in, he and his wife are robbed by a certain William Cady. Not content with shooting their horse and taking their money, Cady demands Mrs. Sandal's wedding ring. She begs him to let her keep it; he swears, says some ungallant things about womanhood, and threatens to cut off her finger if need be. When she thinks to outsmart him by swallowing the ring, he swears and rages all the more, and then,

> Shooting her thro' the Head, he ript her open, and took the Ring out of her Body, saying at the same Time to her Husband, whose Heart to be sure relented to see such a tragical, nay more barbarous than inhuman Action, *Your Wife's a Bite I see, but I think now I have Bit the Biter.*

The reader's heart, too, may feel an impulse to "relent," but only for a moment and (along the lines discussed earlier) rather less than it would in a "properer" context. For up to this point Cady's life story has proceeded in the usual way, beginning with a benignly funny anecdote and going on to tell tales of his cleverness, pluck, and outrageous imagination. And "leaving the sorrowful Widower to attend the bloody Corpse," he rides off to still more lively adventures.[74]

My main reason for referring to this episode, however, has to do with its effect on Sandal's fatal reappearance some 150 pages later. The reader who remembers Sandal's earlier misadventure (and they are not large pages) will find it hard to be moved by his second: *Two* such events, however terrible taken individually, simply beggar the imagination when considered together. And such a recurrence of horrors must of course influence one's attitude toward the violence in the book as a whole. In addition to all else that gets attached to and so encumbers Smith's deracinated violence, there is the recurrent suspicion that, somehow, he may be settling old scores by making this person or that the putative victim of this or that thief. I very much doubt that Sandal and his wife actually met the fates Smith says they did, but it would not surprise me to find there actually was a Henry Sandal and that Smith, in using his name, was trying to embarrass him or someone close to him.

"So many . . . Robberies happen daily," Applebee's *Journal* observed in 1722, "that 'tis almost incredible."[75] Smith's business is to abolish that "almost." He aims to plunge his audience into a world where crime, staggering credulity, beggars response. As he blurs the line between fiction and reality, the real world of places, actions, objects, and, perhaps most important, of both kinds of victims, begins to melt away: the robbery, the person who is robbed, seem at last no more real than the robber himself. And yet not all reality is left behind; that would defeat Smith's purpose. Just enough accurate history is salted among his confections to keep alive his reader's sense of piquancy. Smith's reader cannot simply succumb to the conclusion that here there is nothing but lies. The criminals' names, the dates and places of their executions are usually right, insofar as these can be checked against other sources. And sometimes Smith can be remarkably accurate. When he says that James Turner's last burglary, for instance, netted him "Diamonds, Jewels, Saphires, Rubies, Emeralds, Ophirs, Pearls, and other precious Stones to the Value of 4007 Pounds, several Pieces of Gold, to the Value of 16 Pounds, 4 Shillings, and 3 Pence, and 1023 Pounds in Silver Money," and "numberd in all 5946 Pounds, 4 Shillings, and 3 Pence," his information tallies exactly with the bill of dindictment. This is more than can be said of the two lives of Turner that were published on the spot.[76]

Ultimately, then, Smith seems to have wanted his readers to be so utterly mixed up that any deep feelings in the face of crime and punishment would seem otiose, uncalled for. All the time playing with his readers' emotions, he scrambles and confuses the ontological status of the events he narrates, inverting (but not consistently) the signals by which the truth would normally tend to be known. His aim, it seems, is to short-circuit the mechanism by which his audience might truth-test, and to so outrage and abuse their sensibilities that these also go dead. And yet for all that Smith debases the truth, he never quite leaves it behind. He wants to maintain a profitable confusion of realms. Thus his inversion of fact and fiction is never so consistent as finally to become intelligible in its own terms, nor does he ever leave his readers completely and permanently numb to the moral implications of the events he describes. Such a confusion of realms was profitable, I would argue, not only because the actualities of crime got lost or at least obscured in a haze of patent unreality, but also because Smith's narrative never quite leaves behind the reality it would vitiate: It keeps its despoiling hooks firmly in it. Smith's criminal biographies – and all those others in the genre they so fulsomely represent – are not then *gratuitously* chaotic, factitious, or frivolous. Rather, in their proximate and ultimate triviality, they are more appropriate than at first they may seem to the phenomenon that – for good reasons – they only purport to describe.

Chapter 8

Everyone left to his own reflections: the oddity of the highwayman as hero and social critic

What to think concerning him, *is left to every one's own Reflections.*
Rev. Dr. Allen, *Account of Maclaine* (1750), p. 27

Doubtless it must make some of our Readers merry, when they observe how often the Heros of these Sheets are introduced as talking of Conscience, Virtue, Honour, Generosity, & c.
Charles Johnson, *Highwaymen* (1734), p. 165

Every Sessions-Paper shows you with what Contempt and Detestation those poor Dogs are treated for stealing three Silver Spoons, . . . a pair of Breeches and two Shirts, . . . [or] four Sheep, . . . not to mention the Heroes of this Class, the Horse-stealers, who are tuck'd up every Assizes without Mercy or Pity. But this can by no means be thought to extend to the numberless Arts and Branches of Industry and Policy, by which People of Rank and Distinction increase their Fortunes. . . . this would be an effectual way of cutting all the Nerves of Industry at one stroke, a fatal check to all the Mysteries of Trade and Commerce, and an absolute Discouragement to all sorts of Jobbers, Gamesters, Fortune-Hunters, and Jockeys, who are the Directors and Managers of all our Parties of Business and Diversion, and would be an insufferable Reflection upon . . . the glorious Titles of . . . able Ministers, cunning Statesmen, and consummate Politicians.
A Letter to a Member of Parliament, Containing a
Proposal to Revise, Amend or Repeal the Ten
Commandments (1738), pp. 17–18

This is it which indeed makes her remarkable . . . and of so different a mixture[:] she was like no body, nor could not be Sorted *by any* Comparison.
Life and Death of Mary Frith (1662), sigs. A3ᵛ–A4r

What odd Sentiments these unfortunate Persons entertain of Honour?
James Guthrie, Ordinary Account, 25 April 1733

The attitudes of the period toward thieves are a tangled knot of ambivalences, difficult to tease out. Unlike the biographies of murderers, which do all they can to "contextualize" (as certain anthropologists might say) the criminal within an appropriate and complete frame of cultural values, thieves' biographies try to keep their subjects from seeming part of any meaningful whole. Haphazardly assembled, mostly of discrete and apparently interchangeable parts, thieves' lives – to the extent they cohere as anything – seem little more than fragments broken off from the larger phenomenon of crime, and bent and warped fragments at that. Needless to say, they convey little of the real concerns that crime could raise. Thus, where the murderer is made to stand for all criminals and indeed all sinners, the thief becomes a special case: When he is in top form (which generally means laid properly low) there is no one else quite like him.

The confusions and incongruities of criminal rogue biography, I have been arguing, were not accidental. It was convenient that complex and important questions, difficult and disturbing questions, be lost in a welter of stuff and nonsense. Too frivolous to be taken seriously, too inchoate to be grasped except at the simplest level, the typical thief's life sought not to enucleate the truth or even to suppress it, but rather to avoid it. Such lives, it seems to me, were designed to please an audience that found the various social, political, and moral implications of crime against property too often at the margins of consciousness, and too ready to intrude. The typical thief's life kept such matters comfortably at bay. To a certain extent, however, the heroic highwayman would seem to escape this scheme. More than most other thieves, he resists reduction to absurdity and confusion; there is something about him that remains positive and coherent, that invites consideration.

The problem facing us now is how to define that "something." How lucid, how attractive, how sympathetic, finally, is this, the most sympathetic of all thieves to be found in the popular literature of crime? If he is not merely a figure offering vicarious gratification to the darker and wilder impulses of economic individualism, then what ought he to seem? And more particularly, to resume a question raised two chapters ago, if he is not one of Hobsbawm's social bandits, what are we to make of his attacks on social corruption? My argument here will be that, for all his relative coherence, the heroic highwayman is still something of a shifting and indeterminate figure. We can define his range and limits but can assign him no fixed meaning. Now taking on this value and coloring, now taking on another, he swims in and out of focus as he moves through his texts, and it is finally this shifting significance that determines his usefulness as a cultural symbol. Strange fish that he is – "feared, admired, envied" – he is not quite what animals are to Lévi-Strauss's totemism: for though *bon à penser* to some extent, he is even better for not quite thinking with.[1]

But what thoughts – or kinds of thoughts – would the heroic highwayman have prompted or blocked? This may seem a futile question, for as the first of this chapter's epigraphs points out, he was "left to everyone's own reflections." We cannot assume that he – or any other kind of my-thologized criminal – would always have meant essentially the same thing to all readers of criminal biography. This is one of the main reasons that speaking of reader response in the rather impoverished terms of – it must be said – vulgarized versions of Marx or Freud is so unsatisfactory: it lumps all readers together. Still, neither does it make any sense to suppose that readers would have been utterly (and so indescribably) free to think as they liked. The specific qualities and structures of the texts they read, and the specific social and cultural context in which they were reading them, would have made certain reflections – or at least certain kinds of reflections – more likely than others. Though we cannot know what readers actually thought, it should nonetheless be possible to sketch out the space within which, variously, they were free to think. The more obvious boundaries and contours of Nonesuch might at least be mapped, if not the movements of those who rambled there.

The heroic highwayman's potential range of meaning, I'd suggest, may be defined along the axes of three comparison-contrasts. (Like all good cognitive space, his was at least three-dimensional.) Two of these comparison-contrasts define James Guthrie's ambivalent comments on William Gordon, a highwayman hanged in 1733. To get their full fla-vor and, most important, to follow the movement of Guthrie's mind, he needs to be quoted at length. Commenting on a robbery in which Gordon was notably generous to one of his victims, Guthrie reflects on his "odd Sentiments" of honor. Such sentiments are "yet strong enough" in people like him

> to prevent their doing many Mischiefs and to engage them in doing some Acts, which if done by others would merit Applause. Certainly, next to Honour and Virtue, Civility has the greatest Charm. How many by using those they robbed well, have avoided Death? And how sure and unpitied does an untimely End befall those, who, to the Crime of Rapine, add also the Folly of treating those ill who fall into their Hands. One would imagine that the Reflection of this should be sufficient to extinguish Cru-elty among Thieves; but we see in all Cases such Considerations are not minded; the Villains, who t'other Day shot a Gentleman on the *Hampstead* Road, are pregnant Instances of Cowardice, and a Blood-thirsty Spirit, which doing him Justice, could never be ascribed to the Deceased Mr. *Gordon*.[2]

It is odd in itself that the Newgate ordinary should call a highway-man "odd," given the ready availability of so many other, harsher terms, and odder still that he should want to do him "justice." But the most curious thing in this passage is the way Guthrie's mind plays over Gordon, shifting from sarcastic dismissal to a limited sympathy, from disapproval to some kind though grudging words. This shift occurs as he moves from thinking of Gordon in terms of one comparison to thinking in terms of another. Set against true "honour" and "virtue," the mere "civility" of the highwayman cannot look too good – but then it doesn't look so bad, either, compared to the brutality of commoner thieves, out there robbing still. It is interesting also that Guthrie's thoughts go no further, for within the categories of legitimacy and honor that define his thinking there is room for yet a third comparison, and a fourth quality (as indicated by my simple grid).

	HONORABLE	DISHONORABLE
LAWFUL	honest men	?
UNLAWFUL	Gordon	common thieves

Prime candidates for this fourth class of dishonorable but lawful men, I should think, are not only the Whigs and Republicans Smith so delights in humiliating but everyone else who, quite legally, "followed the general way of the world." Guthrie leaves this third possible comparison alone, but other writers are hardly so discreet.

A highwayman's "civility," then, can turn out to be rather a curious and complicated thing: something to be defined and measured not only against the honor and virtue of true gentlemen on the one hand and the practices of thieves in general on the other, but too – there is a third hand as well! – against the bad citizenship (literally the *in*civility) of all those who value "money before friends or honesty." Inasmuch as this last comparison raises powerful social and political issues, it ought to make us wonder about the motives of writers and readers alike. Why should the most popular and attractive criminal in the popular literature of crime have challenged (in all but a few years from 1688 on) the dominant political party? Why should writers, through him, have attacked the ethos of so large a share of their potential market: tradesmen, merchants, professionals, courtiers and other politicians? We could of course assume that writers like Smith were concerned with reaching only a very narrow audience – Tory country squires, perhaps – but this, though highly simplifying, is also highly unlikely. Given the mass character of the popular literature of crime, we have no choice but to face this question directly: How and why could the highwayman's attack on the political and economic relations inhering in his society have seemed tolerable, even entertaining and possibly useful, to an audience that, in its variousness, would have included readers in a position to resent such attacks, or at least to find them embarrassing? The question is complicated, but so is the heroic highwayman. Ultimately no more a social bandit than a fantasy-fulfilling, finally scapegoated alter ego, he was far more interesting and versatile than either role would have allowed him to be, and for this he had to thank his peculiarly inviting indeterminacy.

A good deal of the heroic highwayman's attractiveness – and this is what makes it so fragile, so tenuous, and so easily compromised – comes from his being compared to thieves of an uglier kind. As one writer remarked of Macheath, that quintessentially heroic highwayman, "Set up . . . in a Point of Light . . . all the Horrors of his Trade . . . the dark Lanthorn, the Pistol, the Dagger, and the Ruin and Spoil of the Poor are concealed; he appears . . . surrounded with Pleasures and Glory."[3] Such a criminal can seem attractive, this writer suggests, only because the actualities of crime are momentarily forgotten or suppressed: It is the surrounding darkness that makes him look bright. A good deal has already been said on this theme in the last two chapters, my argument there being that all three kinds of mythologized thief were defined not only in terms of their mutual contrasts (Chapter 6) but by their differences from actual thieves as these were perceived by the real world (Chapter 7). In their separate ways the buffoon and brute are debasements of real-life thieves, and the heroic highwayman an exaltation. It is this last point that I would like, briefly, to carry forward here.

The heroic highwayman's peculiar status as a robber can best be gauged against two facts. First, most real-life highwaymen were not the mounted horsemen the popular literature of crime makes them out to be, but footpads. Second, whether mounted or not, they generally robbed in gangs. These facts had implications for individuals, fearing for their safety, and for society as a whole, concerned as it had to be with the maintenance of order, but they play no great role in criminal biography. Though Hind, Whitney, Old Mobb, and the Golden Farmer (to name just four of the most fabulous highwaymen) were all members of large gangs, and though this was well known, at least in their own lifetimes, their biographies typically show them robbing alone.[4] The reason, I suspect, was that organized crime was too disturbing a notion to find much of a place in popular entertainment. The case of Burnworth and his gang is illustrative. Burnworth was little more than a thug (he was hanged in 1726 for shooting down a thief catcher in cold blood) and his gang nothing but a loose collection of housebreakers and street thieves. *Remarkable Criminals,* however, calls him "extraordinary." He "brought rapine into method," it says, "and bound[ed] even the practice of licentiousness with some kind of order." As one more proof that society of some kind is natural to men, even to unnatural men, this might seem to have its comforts, but Burnworth is excoriated as an "egregious" villain even as he escapes the root sense of the word. "An attempt of this sort was scarce ever heard of in Britain," huffs Remarkable Criminals, "even in the most early times," and it notes with pleasure that the gang's arrest was greeted with "loud huzzas . . . for they, like Jonathan Wild, were so wicked as to lose the compassion of the mob."[5]

The references to Wild and the mob are important, for what they say and do not say. The fact that Burnworth and his gang were rejected even by that larger, more diffuse and powerful threat to good social order is meant to be telling, and Wild was perhaps the most despised criminal of his time. But the mention of Wild also points to a curious absence of mind on this writer's part. For Wild, who was still very much in the public memory, had headed a larger, more efficiently organized, and far more powerful gang; it was utterly notorious, and Wild had been hanged only a year before Burnworth.[6] This oversight, if we may call it that, though not identical with the tendency to forget that practically all notable highwaymen were members of gangs, may well have stemmed from the same cause. Organized crime appears to have been offensive to the popular imagination, or at least to the imaginations of those who wrote and read about crime. The idea of outlaws organized into societies of their own (or rather antisocieties) was not so attractive to the eighteenth century as it had been, and would be, to other eras. Robin Hood, as we've already noted, produced conflicting responses in Smith, but to the author of Remarkable Criminals he and his so-called merry men were nothing more than "banditti," an earlier version of Burnworth and his gang.[7] Gangs of any sort were unsavory, and nothing to be countenanced. Thus the passage of the Black Act and, not very much later, the ruthless suppression of the "New Minters"; the mob, of course, was the great bête noire of the age.[8] Highwaymen typically were shown acting as lone gunmen, it would seem, because they were at their most attractive and most entertaining when they stood outside all bodies politic.[9]

Most real-life highwaymen were even more unsavory because they were footpads. Pedestrian indeed, their methods were brutal and utterly without elegance. Because they worked without guns, they generally surprised their victims with a sudden, disabling blow. Then, trussing them up, they would throw them in a ditch or other convenient place where their outcries, if heard, were likely to be ignored by passersby. The lumpen proletariat of thieves, footpads had no other means of

Colonel Jack Robbing Mrs Smith going to Kentish Town

from Capt. Charles Johnson, *Lives and Adventures of the Most Famous Highwaymen, Murderers, Street-Robbers, &c.* [1734]

gaining or keeping the upper hand, or of making successful getaways. Well-armed horsemen, of course, did.[10] And inasmuch as they exercised this ability, robbing alone and even with courtesy and grace, they notably refrained from imposing (as much as they might have) on public sensibilities. Indeed, their motives and manner of robbing may even have seemed to flatter those sensibilities. Relatively gentle (relative, that is, to other thieves) and aspiring to be genteel, they could seem to want nothing more than the unearned income, the status and accoutrements (as they saw them) of gentlemen. They could seem to show, in other words, an essential respect for the best values of their society; if not credits to their race, they were at least no scandal on it. The popular literature of crime was quick to take such highwaymen up. It especially liked to show them doing their work at a tolerable distance, on the heath usually, that waste ground beyond the city and its suburbs which, for all its nearness, is a world apart from the usual realms of human activity. Here their robbing could acquire an extra dimension of diffidence. Unlike real-life footpads, who tended to infest the city and its immediate environs, they kept from striking home.

A good part of the appeal of such thieves, then, was negative. They carried their audience away from the perils of housebreakers, the nuisances of pickpockets, the thuggeries of streetrobbers – away, in short, from all the hazards and gros ennuis of ordinary urban crime. "He never practised pilfering, stealing, Shop-lifting, Street-robbing," claimed one convicted highwayman in an obvious bid for sympathy, "nor any of those little Ways used by petty Thieves."[11] But the attraction of such thieves was more notional than real; the man just quoted was hanged just the same. That thieves like him could be appealing at all, moreover, required a clear distinction between them and lesser, cruder, more banal thieves. But such a distinction could not always be maintained. The fact that well-armed, well-mounted highwaymen could afford to be courteous was no guarantee they would be, and often they could be quite nasty indeed. In 1695, for instance, two "eminent" highwaymen about to be hanged "boasted . . . they killed a woman great with child." In 1722 three horsemen were robbing the Bury coach, when a peddler woman called out that she knew them. "One of them put a Pistol to her Head asking if she would choose to die on the spot, or suffer her Tongue to be cut out of her Head." After "many Tears and Entreaties," she made the only choice she could, and they "threw the Woman's tongue into the Road." In 1730, to cite one last example, five highwaymen robbed "a poor Man" as he returned from marketing his turnips. The twenty shillings they took, he told them, was "all the Money, he had in the World." As they rode away he made the mistake of calling them "Yorkshire Rogues, for robbing a poor Man," at which they wheeled about and "said to one another, Damn him, the Dog knows us, go and shoot him," which they did. He died a few days later.[12] Nor was such dirty work always done at a decent interval from town, for mounted highwaymen sometimes even robbed in London parks and streets. It was in one such incident that Walpole was nearly killed; that his assailant was well-mannered, that he fired the gun by accident and later apologized profusely, offered some consolation.[13]

Such events, and they are common enough, indicate that images of heroic highwaymen were preferred and presumably held against the weight of everyday experience. Perhaps this explains something of their tendency, usually toward the end of their careers, to sink into an unworthy or reprehensible act. Romance can only strain so far; even a fictionalized, wish-fulfilling highwayman must make some concession to observable reality, or risk being wholly unrecognizable. In any case, such "civility" as highwaymen showed could only have seemed impressive in contrast to the brutality or simple boorishness of commoner thieves – and this impression, it is important to keep in mind, would always have been dogged by the deeper, inescapable comparison between them. For however much he embodied qualities valued by law-abiding men, even the most heroic of highwaymen would have, finally, to be seen as the criminal he was. The mere fact that he had been hanged would have required as much.

His social pretensions, which encourage comparisons to men of genuine honor and gentility, would have been similarly susceptible to a double view. Much is said of his "aspiring Mind" and "Greatness of Soul," of his scorn for "mechanical Drudgery" and his desire to "live like Gentlemen," or at least "on a Level with Gentlemen." It is not uncommon to hear that, with his talents and energies, he "might have done good Service" to king and country.[14] But at the same time it is clear that in leaving his proper station he has erred egregiously, and not merely for moral reasons or because he eventually is hanged. The aspiring thief pursues a will o' the wisp, and is burned. As one thief's biographer says, "high Chymeras" prompted him "to throw his Chance in Fortune's Lottery."[15] But even as he thinks he's riding high (to shift the metaphor slightly) he's only crapping out. Those in the know never do take him at his own, dearly bought valuation. His sense of himself is shoddy goods and easily shown up. "Those discontented, designing profligate Wretches, the Robbers upon the High-way," fumes one late seventeenth-century writer, "by their own Heraldry intitl[e] themselves Gentlemen of the Road, and glory in . . . the most *Gentile* Trade of Ruining Mankind." But you need only "look into their *Pedigree*," he adds, to "find them . . . far from men of Honour or Vertue . . . the best of them but *Cadets,* [and the rest] most commonly the spawn of broken Tradesmen and worst of Debauchees."[16] In their more equable way, mid-eighteenth-century writers can be far more devastating. "Though he has been called the Gentleman Highway-man," the Newgate ordinary wrote of James Maclean, "and in his Dress and Equipage very much affected the fine Gentleman, yet to a Man acquainted with good Breeding, that can distinguish it from Impudence and Affectation, there was very little in his Address or Behaviour, that could entitle him to that Character." As a consequence, according to another writer, Maclean "was always slighted by People of Sense and Discerning; who can always discover in the most dazzling Dress, Assurance and Insolence from good Breeding."[17] Or, as another highwayman's biographer says more plainly, he was "the Gentleman in nothing more than the outward Appearance."[18] From such judgments there can be no appeal; the highwayman's snobbery is turned against him.[19]

Highwaymen who want to be gentlemen become objects of pity and fun, as well perhaps of envy. In a long last letter to his wife (or in at least what purports to be) William Page commends their children to her care, asking particularly that she "banish from their tender Minds all Notions of Gentility and the Affectation of appearing in a Rank of Life to which they have no Pretensions." For this, he ruefully adds, was "the fatal Rock on which their unhappy Father unfortunately split." Other highwaymen are treated more dismissively. A certain Wager is quoted, complaining that Horsenail "us'd him ill, in turning Evidence against him, he ought to have consider'd, that he was the Person that put him into a more Gentleman-like Way of subsisting himself than meanly on Foot . . . that he provided them with Horses, and equipp'd them for Highwaymen." It is hard to see how the social pretensions of thieves like Wager and the curiously named Horsenail could have appealed to readers who were socially ambitious themselves, at least in any positive and direct way. Their efforts to rise and their inevitable fall would seem less an outlet for readers' hopes and envies than a convenient sticking point. If any vicarious gratification is on offer here, it would have to come from the dreams of these two "fellows" (in the sense of the term that was an insult) going bust. Such highwaymen must have been useful for the opportunity they gave to sneer at the lower orders, just as others offered a chance to reflect on one's betters. Thus in Smith we hear of a highwayman named Tom Jones (no relation) who takes a brief fling at going straight. Feeling rich with all that he has saved from his robberies, "he form[s] very fine designs to himself of growing honest." This involves "keeping right quality's hours, which he much imitated by dining when others sup, supping when others breakfast, going to bed when others get up, and getting up when others go to bed." By such "profuse living," however, he is "soon left moneyless." There is nothing for him to do but resume his "natural disposition," become "as great a robber as ever," and eventually get hanged. "Those good designs," says Smith, "were only the flourishes of his imagination."[20] And, we might add, of an impoverished imagination at that.

But Jones is not Smith's primary object in telling this anecdote. Where did he get his impoverished notion of "right quality," if not from the bad example of those for whom life at the top is scarcely less empty, less self-indulgent? Those "others" Smith so coyly speaks of, people whose habits are necessarily defined by their involvement in the workaday world, are all of us who are neither high-living highwaymen nor members of the idle rich. By lumping these two categories together Smith encourages a comparison, challenging us to see what differences there are between them. And the comparison is not particularly to the advantage of the latter, for they are superior to the highwayman only in having more money. Jones at least recovers a "natural disposition," resynchronizing himself with the social world, and at the end is made

to pay for what he does amiss. Such satire probes the mettle of the
upper classes, but practically all "genteel" highwaymen would have
done as much.[21] If gentility is something so easily aped, what can it
mean to *be* a gentleman, or to want to *seem* a gentleman? "All the poor
Rogues that make such lamentable Speeches . . . at Tyburn," writes
Steele, "were in their Way, Men of Wit and Pleasure."[22] So much then
for "wit" and "pleasure," and so much for such men – but then Steele's
mind is not really on criminals. He is speaking tropically, using them to
say other, larger things.

The closer the examination, the more the highwayman demands to be
seen as something more – or less – than a vehicle for vicarious gratification. For all that he may indeed have been a secret sharer of the id and a
scapegoat for the superego, he was other things at the same time,
capable of functioning, even at his simplest, on more than one level and
in a variety of ways. Unless this point is taken, no real sense can be
made of his social and political function. Consider, for instance, even a
gesture so simple as this, a highwayman's quite typical dying declaration: "I might have lived happily enough, if I could but have apply'd
my self to Trade, and been contented with a moderate Station of Life;
but I was impatient to make a gay Figure in the World, and that
hastened my Destruction."[23] Such a speech may seem nothing more
than a device for bringing readers back to reality, a way of concluding
their identification with the highwayman and so their fantasy trip to
Nonesuch. But it is something else as well: the moral message of this
man's life, and, as such, expected from the beginning. To imagine
readers who daydreamed and then came awake, or, more simply, had
fun and then got the moral, assumes too facile and coherent an experience of the text. Long before the highwayman's story ends, it takes
measures to heighten its reader's consciousness, encouraging him to
have his doubts, to be critical, to reflect on what he is reading. Thus
there is always the possibility that even the most heroic and least problematic highwayman will suddenly take a downward turn and that,
dislodged from his Macheathian "point of light," he will have to be
seen in darker, more complicating circumstances. Experienced readers
would always have been aware of this possibility, and for them the
heroic highwayman's status would have seemed peculiarly unstable.
This would have been truer of him than of any other mythologized
criminal (murderers included) because, given the "narrative curve" of
criminal rogue biography, heroes can drop into buffoonery or brutishness at any moment, but the process is not reversible. Buffoons can
only fall into brutishness, and brutes can only come to be hanged.
   This instability, and especially the reader's consciousness of it, has

several important implications. Not the least of these is the light it casts on the highwayman's role as a political and social critic. First, however, I'd like to point out its consequence for his wish to seem genteel, for it can bring an especially powerful moral to bear on this, and even infuse it with a special poignance. In deciding that the status of gentleman thief is "far more desirable than," say, that of "reputable Tradesman," the highwayman starts his career by robbing himself of a solid and determinate if modest social identity.[24] That which he takes on in exchange is bright and flashy but bound to fall to pieces. The more "heroic" his character, the more this will seem the case, and the more powerful will be the effect when, finally, his counterfeit identity proves non-negotiable. Thus, Gordon's "odd sentiments of honor" not only get him hanged but, what is worse from his point of view, make him the butt of "barbarous levities." He may complain about such treatment all he wants, but the public is not obliged to credit him. As Gordon apparently found in the end, much to his despair, for he took the sacrament the morning of the day he was to be hanged, returned to his cell, and cut his throat. Only the intervention of two surgeons, luckily nearby, saved his life. One of them "sow'd up his Throat" and Gordon was hanged according to schedule. But before he died, he denied trying to kill himself. His neckcloth had been tied too tight, he said (think of it, as he waits for the rope), and he tried to cut it free but the knife slipped. "A trifling Excuse," says the author of Select Trials (1742), "I leave it to every Man to judge upon the Penitence of one guilty of such a horrid Crime."[25]

It is the highwayman's peculiar fate, then, in his efforts to enhance his status as a person, to call that status utterly into question. Having left his proper place in society, he finds there are no other places for him; he has in effect decategorized himself. If he is ultimately left to everyone's own reflections – "I leave it to every Man to judge" – it is because it is difficult to know, collectively, just what to make of him. A disgraced younger son, a ruined tradesman, or a dismissed servant who would live like a gentleman, he can seem a gentleman and yet be no gentleman.[26] Curiously, too, as an honorable and decent robber (no small part of his claim to being a gentleman) he is a thief and yet not like other thieves, a robber who can paradoxically yet not inappropriately claim to have "never practised . . . stealing . . . nor any of those little Ways used by petty Thieves." These comparisons to lesser, coarser thieves on the one hand, and to better, truer gentlemen on the other, set up a field within which he (or rather the reader) enjoys a shifting, unsteady, multivalent character.

He need not be taken seriously, though he may be taken seriously. It is this that determines his usefulness in the comparison often drawn between him and all the others who, less illegitimately, also pursue the main chance. Because he is a gentleman yet no gentleman, a thief and yet no thief, his declamations against public corruption can be honored or scorned, heeded or ignored, just as any individual reader likes. No doubt he was useful to those who enjoyed seeing Whigs embarrassed (though only, to be sure, in a marginal way, for there were far more powerful ways of embarrassing Whigs). But he would also have been useful, given his highly impeachable status, to the Whigs themselves. "All the *Rogues, Whores, Pimps, Thieves, Fools,* and *Scoundrels* in the Kingdom," one Whig newspaper could claim with an air of plausibility, were Tories.[27] The theme recurs from William's reign through at least George I's, and its burden is obvious: You can tell the Tories and their friends, the Jacobites, by the company they keep.[28] But if the highwayman's politics could be used in opposite ways and have contradictory meanings, then in effect – which is to say in terms of his affect as a mythic figure – he had no determinate politics at all. The most that can be said of his political tendencies is that they indicate and embody the chief political divisions of his time. His putative anti-Whiggery could be taken and interpreted by individual readers in any of several ways: against or for the Whigs or, and this perhaps most frequently, with bemused indifference to the claims of either party.

The highwayman's attack on economic individualism invites much the same interpretation. Here, too, though more generally and diffusely, his value is determined by the fact that he is a highly impeachable source. Readers can agree with him, or find what he says agreeably easy to impugn. His claim that he, though a thief, is more honest and noble than most tradesmen, merchants, and professionals could be appreciated by those who resented the pretensions of the middling classes, or just as easily dismissed. In a play by Christopher Bullock there is a character named Vizard, a "notorious cheat" and "ambi-dextrous Knave," who speaks at length on "the Corruption of the Age." "The greatest Part of Mankind," he claims, "[are] Rogues within, or without the Law. . . . greater Rogues ride in their own Coaches, than any that walk on Foot. . . . he that has the most Money is now the worthiest Man: Every Thing is to be sold; both ends of the Town are become Markets, and Consciences rise and fall, at *Westminster,* as Stocks do in *Change Alley.*" This is "very Satirical," as a character named Freeman says, but then "the greatest Knaves are the most severe Judges," for "they view all Mankind in the false mirror of their own Actions."[29] Such prompt and explicit comment is rare in the popular literature of crime, perhaps because it is hardly necessary. With few exceptions a thief's "life" is his obituary. Knowing that he'll finally dance to their

from Capt. Charles Johnson, *Lives and Adventures of the Most Famous Highwaymen, Murderers, Street-Robbers, &c.* [1734]

Whitney Robbing an old Userer tyeing his hands behind him with his fac: to th horses tail.

tune, that he'll never get the last word or laugh, his targets are free to smirk even when, at their expense, he's being his most "satirical."

But what we have here is actually not satire so much as the shadow of satire. When Hind lectures on the corrupting influence of money in English society, claiming that among other things it "makes Justice deaf as well as blind," the 1734 Johnson observes that what he says "contains . . . much Truth, and might have been . . . pleasing, had it come from another Mouth." The "conscientious" thief seems so ludicrous a paradox that none of his shots land squarely, if they land at all. He is a failed satirist, but then, from the point of view of his targets, who could be a better satirist? The more readers doubted their honesty and honor, the more they felt vulnerable to *real* social criticism, the more they may have welcomed his. Thus, taking a less flattering but probably more accurate view of his audience, the 1734 Johnson was sure that some of them "doubtless" would be made quite "merry" by "the Heroes of these Sheets . . . talking of Conscience, Virtue, Honour, Generosity, &c." And to the extent they secretly feared that they themselves were mean, grasping, or just plain crooked, they would have laughed the more. For words like conscience, virtue, honor, and generosity lose their value in the mouths of thieves and, for the moment at least, their power to criticize; "much Truth" may be pleasing, too, when it is made to seem impotent or irrelevant.[30]

In his very eagerness to criticize the corrupt values of his society, the highwayman did those who felt inextricably enmeshed in them a favor. The sure mark of a rogue, according to Smith, is that "he'll tell you every man robs his own way; and will not believe you (though you be ever so honest) an honester man than himself."[31] Such a fellow is no small gift to a guilty conscience, for he provides a golden opportunity (though you be ever so *dis*honest) to rise, laughing, to your own defense. Even the sootiest kettle can be glad a pot had called it black, for thereby attention is called to their difference. What the highwayman says may give pause, but it is a pause that ultimately refreshes. Talk that elsewhere might be deeply disturbing is easily dealt with here: The dog has been hanged and so has a bad name; out with the baby goes all such bathwater. To a self-doubting bourgeoisie – and which isn't? it is one of their few enduring charms – enemies like him are convenient indeed.

Expressive of the contradictions inherent in a world uneasily aware that it "now prefers money before friends or honesty" – a newly and therefore uncomfortably capitalist world – the highwayman's value comes not so much from his mediating these contradictions (pace Lévi-Strauss) but rather as, roaming vivid in the mind, he muddles and moots them. His social criticism is a red herring. Finally not so much something to think with as something to *not* think with, he spoils doubts by spoiling thoughts. He can do this, resonating as he does within the fields of the three comparison-contrasts just sketched out, because he makes so rich and interesting a figure. "In shape, in being, place and name," as one writer put it, he changes "with every day, like the mutable chameleon, but never into white Innocence."[32] His having no single, fixed, and comprehensive meaning must often have vexed, or at the least embarrassed him – witness Gordon's terminal complaint – but also it must often have pleased his readers. Whatever he was as an object for thinking or not thinking with, he gave his readers occasion to use their imaginations. And he did this more than any other mythologized criminal not only by virtue of his variousness but because, as I've already said, of all criminals he was potentially the most sympathetic. One last look at one last highwayman will illustrate what I mean.

William Page, whose pathetic farewell to his wife has already been quoted, was hanged in 1758. He was one of those highwaymen whose considerable talents, it was regretted, had not been put to better use, and so popular that many refused to believe the news he was hanged. They even bet money, at odds, that he was still alive. His chief biographer is generally sympathetic, being especially impressed by his dying behavior, which was "decent and becoming the Solemnity of the Occasion." Page, he says approvingly, showed "great Resolution and Firmness." But then, with no apparent sense of incongruity, this same writer moves on to quote the following "humorous Paragraph," which he has taken from a newspaper:

> *Page,* the Gentleman Highwayman . . . being a smart Fellow and of an aspiring Genius . . . was so infatuated with the Notion of being a Gentleman, that he carried the Quixotism of Gentility to the Gallows. Having fee'd the Executioner to grant him all the Marks of Honour the Gallows can afford, he therefore was indulged with giving a Signal, the dropping of a Cambrick handkerchief; and has established a Precedent for treating gentlemen with Decency; for instead of being cut down as your common Horse and Sheep-stealers are, *Jack* [i.e., Jack Ketch, the hangman] was at as much pains in loosing the Knot that deprived the World of this great Man, as if he had been his own Brother.[33]

For all that the larger text commends Page's dying, this is all we get of the actual event itself.

This sudden deviation into humor is nothing uncommon and, for all the reasons advanced in the last two chapters, should hardly surprise us. It is a way of dealing with fear, guilt, and what might be called a kind of embarrassment at the ill regulation of society, to say nothing of individual envy. Its presence in an otherwise sympathetic biography testifies to the ambivalence of the biographer, but it is itself ambivalent. The tensions it sets up are thus peculiarly rich and complex. The use of the term "Quixotism" is key. Quixote, after all, is no contemptible character. Whatever the large, unfeeling world may think of *his* odd sentiments of honor, they give him a claim to the sympathy and compassion of all discerning readers and finally make him heroic. Even an eighteenth-century newspaper writer would have known something of this, and more than a few of his readers.[34] The comparison to Quixote, then, like all the others is double-edged. To speak of "the Quixotism of Gentility" is to mock at Page but also, almost despite oneself, to pay him tribute. Considered coldly and from a distance, he may look an utter fool. But closer up his folly can seem sad, even to have a tincture of nobility.[35]

The allusion to Cervantes' novel is just one of the things that make this paragraph more than a mere report of a hanging. The linkage to the world of literature, however tenuous, is important. Made (for a moment at least) the English Quixote as Hind was the English Guzman, Page is detached from real-world contexts and real-life values. His death can almost become an aesthetic event (a tragicomic morality play, to be specific). Much along this line has already been said of other thieves, and of the ways such "aestheticization" served social exigencies. The paragraph before us, however, has a certain special quality. It sticks in the mind, and I am not speaking of my mind only, for there is the mind of Page's biographer, who quotes it approvingly despite its variance with the rest of his text. It can do this because it gives readers a chance to interpret its object, this now aestheticized Page, rather than merely to passively apprehend him. Its own ambivalence, and its ambivalent relation to the larger text, open up a "space" around Page, a "space" that readers are free to fill in for themselves.

One may dwell, for instance, on such details as the cambric handkerchief and the carefully loosened knot. As Page's biographer tells us, he had "a lively and active Spirit, which made him aspire to Things above the Sphere of his condition," and "he always acted with great Bravery and Generosity, considering him as a Highwayman."[36] All his yearnings and posturings and where these led him – considering him as a highwayman – might seem in the end brought down to that handkerchief and that knot, to the images they evoke and the contrast between them: the fine linen of the one flourished as though he were some state prisoner signaling the axe, and the coarse hemp of the other uniting him, as if indeed they had been brothers, to the obsequious, even servile, certainly most common hangman. Not all readers would have seen as much, and none may have seen just this, but then I've only meant to show what could have happened in the cognitive and affective space that opened up around certain redacted highwaymen. Within that space, details like the handkerchief and the knot provide ample materials for constructing a variety of metaphors to a variety of ends – each reader being left, within the limits of that material, to his own reflections.

Variable in form and coloring, then, a mutable chameleon indeed, the heroic highwayman is both more and less than protean. Firmly grasped he would go suddenly dull, and what truths he would utter would be equally dull (but, considering his lack of subtlety as a social critic, perhaps "dull" only in the way blunt instruments are). He cannot, however, be firmly grasped. He remains too various and contradictory. Murderers may stand as metaphors, but he is simultaneously part of several similes. "Like no body" because he is like so many bodies, he cannot be "sorted" by any one comparison because, in a number of pregnant comparisons, he functions as a floating term. How fine, how foolish, how sad, how sordid, he stimulates readers to think, how entertaining, how monitory, how like these times, how like so many people, how like – or unlike – me!

Such heady pleasures, however, eventually lose their charm. Biographies of thieves grow more sober as the eighteenth century continues, and rarer. The earliest casualties are the petty criminals whom Smith so delights in making rogues and buffoons. By the 1740s, they no longer get much attention except where their trials, reported in expanded sessions papers, offer colorful but realistically detailed accounts of life among the low or louche.[37] And by the 1770s, though they still stalk the roads, highwaymen of the classic type no longer make their way into collections of criminal biography. The last enduring example of the breed is Sixteen-String Jack Rann, hanged in 1774. Rann, who got his nickname from an affectation of dress – he wore breeches with eight silver-tipped laces at each knee – comes across as no threatening or charismatic figure but rather as a vaguely pitiable casualty of bogus values. He gets considerable sympathy from a surprising source, the Newgate ordinary, and – still more remarkable – it is the ordinary's version of his life that survives. A sort of eighteenth-century zoot suiter or superfly, but without the menace, he becomes, finally, an object of patronizing contempt. "This fellow" was one of "the impudent and arrogant self-created gentlemen who levied arbitrary contributions on the highway," say later writers, and tended to dress "in a manner above his style of life and his circumstances." Rann, they note, appeared before Justice John Fielding with "a bundle of flowers in the breast of his coat almost as large as a broom; and his irons were tied up with a number of blue ribbons."[38]

The highwayman's decline is doubtless the product of many factors, among them simple fatigue. After a while, he stopped being amusing, or even particularly interesting. The slow sale of the 1734 Johnson may be the first clear sign that tastes were changing, as would, too, its comparatively severer tone.[39] If by the 1730s the public was getting saturated with stories of highwaymen and other roguish thieves, the growing newspaper coverage of crime may be partly to blame. Criminals could "usefully" be trivialized only so long as the absurd and often comic brutalities attached to their "lives" impressed readers as fantastic, beyond the bounds of real experience, or at the least highly implausible. Writers like Smith would have done much themselves to wear out the distinction between the real and the fantastic on which (as I've argued) much of the value of their writing was based. The tendency of newspapers to imitate their rhetoric in reporting actual crimes, however, may have accelerated this effect.[40] How was that rhetoric to keep its archness, by which I mean its ability to arc readers away from the actual thing, if it was regularly attached to the actual thing? Crimes in any case grew more frequent, with no proportionable growth in diverting stories to tell about them. When a highwayman attempted a robbery "within fifty yards" of Horace Walpole's "own dining-room," nearly killing a watchman as he rode off through Picadilly, Walpole voiced an opinion likely held by many other midcentury Londoners: "His profession grows no joke."[41]

Highwaymen grew less interesting, too, because their value as symbols declined. Writing early in the nineteenth century, Andrew Knapp and William Baldwin lament the loss of the "spirit of the middle part of the last century," when the "abuse of . . . power" by "great men" was "boldly attacked" by comparing them to criminals like Macheath.[42] They blame fear of prosecution – "Who would now, in the face of a modern Attorney General . . . dare to write like Gay?" – but it's far more likely that such comparisons lost their appeal with the fading of Jacobites and Tories as politically significant forces, and as confidence increased in the morality of trade. The great crooks of the latter part of the eighteenth century, in any case, are forgers. These are a very different kind of economic individualist from the freebooting highwayman and, toward the end of the century, more likely to have come from respectable circles.[43] As fiduciary instruments became increasingly important to the economy, the laws against forgery were steadily stiffened, and more forgers hanged. Such occasions prompted much more special pleading about the law than the hanging of even the most sympathetic thieves, and seemed greater social embarrassments; witness the case of Dr. Dodd, or that of the Perreau brothers and the (for many) happily acquitted Mrs. Rudd.[44] If once it had seemed that anyone might take to the highway, so much more it seemed that anyone, in a pinch, might alter a note or bond.

Anyone, that is, of a certain station in life. Class consciousness increasingly infiltrates the popular literature of crime as the eighteenth century advances.[45] In 1724 the author of *The History of John Sheppard* notes the fascination his subject has for "the common People" and "the vulgar," i.e., "Porter[s]," "Butchers," "Shoemakers," "Barbers," and "the Rabble." Their interest is not quite his, and he speaks patronizingly of their appetite for "Ballads and Letters." Still, Sheppard's own class origins (his father and grandfather were carpenters) are described quite neutrally, and nothing much is made of the gulf between him and the "Citizens" and "People of tolerable Fashion" who came in great numbers to visit him in prison. He is an object of interest to the higher and middle orders quite as properly as to the low, "his Case being so very singular and new," and he himself "a Creature something more than Man, a Proteous, Supernatural, Words cannot describe him."[46]

"Man" is a concept that cuts across social divisions; in transcending it, Sheppard rises above a humanity which, however variously, all social orders hold in common. It is this sense of a common humanity that allows writers of the late seventeenth and early eighteenth century to use highwaymen and other thieves to embarrass the pretensions of the rich and privileged. By midcentury, however, it is the pretensions of the highwayman himself that come under fire. It is foolish of him, really, to try to set himself on a level with gentlemen; so says a voice superior to his, which may itself be only marginally genteel. A highwayman like Rann has nothing of the exemplary force of the Perreau brothers, solid middle-class types who may stand a "solemn warning" – as no "sixteen-string jack" can – to "all thriving and reputable tradesmen and men of business [not to quit] their certain lawful gain, with a view to rise into the wide regions of uncertainty, disappointment, and despair."[47] Where anyone might have been a highwayman, from high to low, and where highwaymen might have commented on all sorts of economic and social behavior, now highwaymen shrink down to pathetic parvenus. The crime that comes to interest instead is eminently middle-class; committed in a weak and private moment, it risks all to preserve or enhance a precarious respectability.

Postscript

Criminal biography and the novel

===============

> *I make no doubt but the Reader will think the remaining Part of this Story very odd, and perhaps a little improbable. However, if he considers the Characters of the Persons concern'd in the Adventure, he will find nothing related but what may be supposed to have been really acted. Boccace, La Fontaine, and other celebrated Writers have met with universal Applause for Histories less reconcileable to Truth than this. But, be that as it will . . . [t]he Writers of the Lives of Highwaymen who have gone before, are a sufficient Apology for this and many other unaccountable Relations, which must of necessity be interspersed in this Work. A Reader that cannot relish these Passages, will find enough for his Diversion without them, and those who have a pretty deal of Faith may easily stretch it to our Standard. At least what will not pass for real Truth, may please by the same Rules as many of our modern Novels, which are so much admired.*
>
> Charles Johnson, *Highwaymen* (1734), p. 114

Two myths, then, define between them the sociopoetics of criminal biography in late seventeenth- and early eighteenth-century England. The one, highly structured and univocal, seeks to reintegrate the criminal into the social and moral order, to smooth over the disruptive effects of his behavior, to digest whatever cruelties he may have committed; the other, disjunctive and ambivalent, heightens his disruptiveness, invents and amplifies cruelties, presenting a fractured, etiolated, absurd, and often frankly fictitious version of his life and character. Like all poetics, this is meant more as a model than an empirical description of practice, for, to be sure, much writing about criminals escaped these neat schemes, or fulfilled them only partially. Nor is it – nor can it be, as a *socio*poetics – a timeless construct. The two kinds of criminal biography this book describes, analyzes, and attempts to explain have each their definite dates. Both come to prominence fairly suddenly, displacing earlier modes of writing about criminals, and each gives way to other forms. Rather than rehearsing what has already been said, however, I'd prefer to close this study by considering, briefly, where it might lead. One direction certainly (the deferred book on Defoe remains much in mind) is toward the novel.

The myth that preeminently supplies stories for murderers makes meaning by selecting and arranging actual and created events into plotted sequences, in this way resembling narratives we more properly call fiction. But fiction does more. Among other things, it creates a "space" inside our minds, a "field" in which we are more or less free to disport us as we may. (One meaning of "play" is free movements within limits; familiar murderers, overdetermined images that they are, provide little opportunity for such movement.) The idea is not so modern as we might think. Just a few years after the spate of biographies on Hind had flourished and deliquesced, a new translation of Aleman's *Guzman* was recommended to English readers as a "delightful Grove . . . a Meadow of Mirth, wherein ingenious Head-pieces may recreate themselves" as they follow its "ingenious Paths."[1] The best of Hind's biographies was written with *Guzman* in mind, and perhaps it, and all the texts that followed in *its* paths, hoped to give their readers something of the same opportunity. Certainly highwaymen like Hind or Page (to name the alpha and omega of our series) were too like literary characters not to have given readers similar pleasures.

The comparison was plain enough in the period; thus the 1734 Johnson's hope that his work be judged no more harshly than "many of our modern Novels." Still, this is a comparison that ought not to be carried too far. Fiction worthy the name involves more than excursions to Nonesuch, just as it involves more than the imposition of plots and meaning on recalcitrant materials. Nor does it put much stock in comfortably intelligible (or unintelligible; the emphasis is on *comfortable*) versions of the world. The most valuable way to relate criminal biography to the novel, it seems to me, is not in terms of its inherent forms or concerns, but rather in terms of the "occasion" it made for the reading and writing of extended narratives about (to use Lukács's term) "problematic" lives.[2] And this "occasion," it is important to note, was defined as much by the failures and shortcomings of criminal biography as by its success.

Defoe is of course its most obvious beneficiary. Criminal biography not only provided an audience trained up to have certain tastes and expectations, it may possibly have endowed him, too, with that other grand requisite of writers, a sense of mission. Moll has dismissive words for the ordinary of Newgate, a drunk whose "Divinity run upon Confessing my Crime, as he call'd it, (tho' he knew not what I was in for) making a full Discovery, and the like, without which he told me God would never forgive me; and he said so little to the purpose, that I had no manner of Consolation from him." Moll much prefers the other minister who seeks her out in prison. Unlike the "Ordinary of the Place," she reports, "whose business it is to extort Confessions from Prisoners, for private Ends, or for the farther detecting of other Offenders . . . his business was to move me to such freedom of Discourse as might serve to disburthen my own Mind."[3] Having no official function, he has no ulterior motives. Nearly twenty years before *Moll Flanders* was published, Defoe had attacked the Newgate ordinary for offering assurances of salvation on too easy terms. By shipping "Loads of *Saints* to *Heaven*," he charged, Paul Lorrain was exalting "*Vagrants*" and "*Ungodly Knaves*" at the expense of "the *Churches Dignity*," and setting, moreover, a bad moral example. If "men of Infamy should rise, / By *Ladders* to Ascend the Skys / . . . . If Gibbets are the *Shortest Way*," he asked, "What need we Mortifie and Pray"?[4] These were not unusual criticisms of the more serious of the two myths of crime, which, nearly from its inception, was vulnerable to a variety of suspicions.

The whole enterprise of showing criminals repentant, converted, and happily sent off to heaven was impugnable on two main grounds: that it was all a pious (or not so pious) fraud, and that it encouraged too close an identification with the criminal. The danger of the latter was not so much that it might raise doubts about execution – these could be countered by making the criminal seem to wish for death, or blackening his reputation – but that it might encourage antinomianism, a disregard for moral law on the grounds that God's grace is near at hand. Thus the signatories of *A Serious Advice to the Citizens of London* thought it "necessary" to insert "a Caveat" into their account of Nathaniel Butler's near saintly demise. Afraid that his example might make others "apt to encourage themselves in sin" – they could imagine certain of their audience saying, "*Let us sin, that Grace may abound*" (a paraphrase of Romans 6:1), or even, "Let us sin, for Grace will abound" – they admonished their readers that "Man is not more prone to any thing, then to catch at eminent Acts of Grace, and to make that *Fewel* to his *Lust,* which God intended only to be *Food* to his *Faith*." Reading about penitent criminals, in the opinion of these doctors of the soul, could be dangerous to one's spiritual health. Nor did all of them think that Butler's case should be given out for public consumption, even with the warning put (so to speak) on the package. "Some of us," the pamphlet writer discloses, "were very inclinable . . . to have the story of this man suppressed [rather] then published."[5]

If other sinners were not to be encouraged to a false and perilous inference by the miraculous conversion of hardened criminals, then all such events had to seem "a rare example, hardly again to be parallel'd."[6] And yet, such miracles could seem to occur – sometimes in large

lots – every execution day, which in London was typically eight or
more times a year. For the most part the prison chaplains and others
who wrote serious criminal biography overlooked this problem, perhaps because they worried less about antinomianism than Butler's ministers or Defoe, and were more interested in disposing of their charges
case by case.[7] Nonetheless, for all the liberalness of their theology, they
tended in one respect to be remarkably discreet. Or so I interpret the
curious fact that the thief on the cross is mentioned only three times in
the scores of ordinaries' *Accounts* surviving from the period.[8] For all the
encouragement his example might have given condemned prisoners on
the verge of repentance, perhaps it seemed better to lose a few here and
there than to risk the possibility the public should misunderstand. For
all the apparent ease with which criminals were regularly reintegrated
into the social and moral order by expeditious religious conversion, the
process could not seem too easy, too expeditious, without on the one
hand losing its seeming value or on the other encouraging more of the
same.

  A far more serious problem for the myth of the criminal as sinner
turned saint, however, was the suspicion that it was all a pious fraud or,
worse, a way of shucking the public by giving it what it wanted without
regard to the actual truth. Boreman and others who ministered to Freeman Sondes, for instance, were accused of being "*Dawbers* of sin," of
"*Blanch*[ing] it with a gentle connivance." The once and future Cambridge fellow was outraged at the accusation, but there was a sense in
which his critics were not far wrong. He and others like him might
indeed be said to be part of a benign conspiracy – a conspiracy in which
minister, criminal, and the community all shared, each for his own self-
interested ends (though none was ever likely to admit to these) and all for
the help it could give them in getting through a trying time.[9] But it is in
the very nature of conspiracies that they risk exposure, and never so
much as when their main function is, if not to suppress the truth, then to
stretch it or at least to avoid examining it. So long as there was no
monopoly on writing about criminals, much of what was written would
involve contradictions, and these could call the whole business into question. Warning against "false Accounts" of "the Confession and Dying
Speeches of Malefactors at Tyburn," the Newgate ordinary in 1684 declared that "Some Criminals who have Dyed *Penitentiary's,* have several
times been Mis-represented to have been hardened in a State of Sinning,
of whose Happiness after their Death, the *Ordinary* hath had (in Charity)
a fairer Prospect. Other Dying Criminals," he went on, "have been
affirmed to be very Penitent, who have been insensible of the particular
Crimes for which they Suffer'd, and in a manner persisted in the Denial
of the Perpetuation [*sic*] of them. So that it was very difficult for any to

Judge Positively, as some Pamphleteers did, of the truth of their Repentance." Paul Lorrain published similar statements no fewer than nine times, complaining that the "several Sham-papers some Persons have lately assumed the liberty of putting out . . . are so far defective and unjust, as sometimes to mistake even the Names and Crimes of those Persons [condemned to die]." But such complaints, given frequent suspicions about the motivations and accuracy of the ordinary himself, would only further have undermined the authority of *any* writer of criminal biography.[10] The more strenuously writers assured their readers that they ought to be taken seriously – "Here is no Fiction, as is commonly used in Pamphlets of this Nature" – the more they claimed that all other accounts were "spurious," "false," "scandalous," and "fictitious," the more they have aroused suspicions about the genre as a whole.[11]

The presence of such suspicions is more than amply indicated by the measures taken to allay them. It was not uncommon, for instance, for readers to be assured they might consult the original documents on which specific accounts were based – some written in the criminal's own, now dead hand! – along with various depositions attesting to their authenticity. Such invitations might be affixed to the text itself or published as separate advertisements. "I Thomas Billings," declared one such advertisement, "being one of the unhappy Persons under Sentence of Death for the Murder of Mr. Hayes, do hereby inform the World, that what Confession or Account I shall leave of myself, and of my Conduct and Behaviour, I shall only leave to be Publish'd by Mr. John Applebee in Black Fryers, as witness my Hand this 29th Day of April, 1726." Billings's signature, it is noted, has been witnessed by Benjamin Hays, "Brother to the Deceas'd," and "the Original" is to be "seen at Mr. Applebee's."[12] Claims for authenticity could also be made on internal grounds. Thus the "abrupt breakings off" in one malefactor's dying speech, "and other expressions not so smooth as might have been," were offered as proofs that these were the "very words that the Gentleman delivered then." "I . . . have tyed my self to his own Expressions," the writer insisted, "that I may neither abuse the World, or the dying man, or my self." A novel variation on this theme occurs in the printer's advertisement to *The Life of Stanley*. That "no great Art is shown [in the] drawing up this short History," it says, indicates that "we are much more solicitous about Truth than Language." The author of the text that follows was chosen not for his literary skills but because he was "that Person" best "acquainted with . . . Mr. *Stanley*'s Life."[13]

Such assurances, even if taken as intended, could nonetheless have little effect if the criminal's dying behavior itself were suspicionable. "I have observed many dolorous complaints of Criminals against themselves to vanish away," one Newgate ordinary wrote, "upon slender

Hopes of a Reprieve." Criminals, he pointed out, could be mistaken about their true state of mind, believing that "a slight sorrow for Sin" was actually "a thorow Conversion."[14] One might credit the actual details of a dying behavior but doubt the construction a writer chose to put upon it. When Charles Drew passed through the extraordinarily large crowds that had assembled to see him hanged, for instance, he showed "Signs of the greatest Horror" – "as being ashamed," the text goes on immediately to add, "after such an Action [as murdering his father] to be seen by so many who had been his Neighbours and particular Acquaintance." But it may just have been that Drew was afraid of dying, and indeed "he expressed the utmost Reluctance at parting with Life, driving off the fatal Minute, and desiring the Officers and Executioner to defer it as long as possible."[15] Even more powerful doubts were raised when convicted criminals went to the gallows protesting their innocence.[16] Henry Harrison presented such a case, showing "great Devotion and Penitence, after his *Condemnation,*" but also making "repeated Protestations of his Innocence, to the last Moment of his Life." He thus managed "to startle and stagger as great many tender Ears; it being a little hard to conceive, that any Dying Man, especially with his professions of Piety, could look Eternity in the Face, with so many repeated Asseverations, to the Pledging of his Salvation upon the Truth of his Innocence, if really Guilty." Nonetheless, such cases have occurred, this writer points out, and goes on to cite some. Other writers, faced by similar circumstances, tried to suggest criteria by which disturbing claims like Harrison's might be judged. "The Words of dying Men are of weight, when all their Actions before have been of a piece," insisted one such writer, and he sought to explain the phenomenon of criminals denying their obvious guilt by theorizing about their state of mind. "Condemn'd Men may hope to obtain a Pardon," he pointed out, "by denying a Guilt too black to be forgiven by Men, when own'd, and after denying it so long, may be asham'd to own it at last." Though plausible, and even flattering to his audience's favored conception of human nature, this could have carried no more authority than the opinion of Harrison's biographer, who, for his part, concluded that we could not judge criminals on the basis of "humane appearance." "The heart," he insisted, "God only can judge."[17]

Doubts about the tendency, sincerity, veracity, or even mere adequacy of the more serious form of the popular literature of crime – along with the frequent efforts made to allay them – suggest that the social drama it sought to stage could sometimes seem a precarious thing. Defoe may have wanted to achieve better, solider effects in his fiction. If so, the important thing for us to note is that he would have had a fairly sophisticated audience waiting for him – one which, for a variety of reasons, would have read anything purporting to be a criminal's own life story with some degree of critical attention. The great social importance that attached to the true states of criminals' hearts would have made for readers disposed to ponder what they were reading, that is, for what we nowadays call "close" reading. One might never know for sure what went on in a crimnal's mind, if he or those about him were telling the truth, but one might guess by paying careful attention to his discourse. "The less ornament there is in a dying persons discourse," wrote Anthony Horneck, "the less it will be suspected of hypocrisy. . . . The words here are not chosen, but flow naturally." Though "we meet [very seldom] with an Accomplice in such Rogueries willing to give a true Account," another writer asserted, "in the following Sheets . . . the Reader . . . will certainly find a genuine Relation of *Facts* only: and we are the more Confident therein, because the Evidence, from whose Mouth it was taken, throughout the whole Narrative never varied, but related it with such an air of Veracity! with such Perspicuity! and in such Chronological Order, that Fiction could never support."[18] Readers accustomed to such appeals, whether moved by them or not, would have come to Defoe's novels prepared to raise a wide variety of questions, to make all sorts of inferences.

The impact of the second myth of crime on the reading public would also have benefited Defoe. With its shocking leaps and jumps, its winking claims to be factual, criminal rogue biography was more than enough all by itself to make readers wary of anything remotely resembling it. Where writers of serious criminal biography tend to be little more than conduits for the facts of any given case (or at least the purported facts), parceling them out in a highly predictable pattern, writers of criminal rogue biography are freer to improvise, and do. Though presumably they share the same point of view with their audience, yet, because their tales might take any one of several directions at any moment, they have the advantage of them. This endows the storyteller with a certain importance in his own right; he has his role, and his reader is invited to assume another. Writer and readers are not as one, he being one or more jumps ahead. As we have seen, too, the writer of criminal rogue biography often tenders options of one kind or another to his audience, proffering them viewpoints to accept or reject and bits of information to interpret as they will. Criminal rogue biography invites its readers to be critical of its discourse, then, at the same time that it makes its discourse more difficult to follow; its relations with its readers are thus far more complex and problematic than those evoked by serious criminal biography.

Though Defoe more than once scorned the putting of criminals "in such an amiable Light, that vulgar Minds are dazzled with it," this second form of the mythology of crime would seem nonetheless to have set him a useful precedent.[19] His novels, in any case, are less extensions of the mythology of crime than exploitations of the possibilities and needs it opened up. "As it is a very ordinary case for fiction to be imposed on the world for truth," the author of *Remarkable Criminals* observed, "so it sometimes happens that truth hath such extraordinary circumstances attending it, as well nigh bring it to pass for fiction." Along with this happy circumstance for novelists, the popular literature of crime produced a readership ready to agree, especially in cases of anomalous criminals, that "too much care cannot be taken to sift the truth, since appearances often deceive us and circumstances are sometimes strong where the evidence, if the whole affair were known, would be but weak."[20]

Defoe's novels play upon this alert and complex disposition by differing from actual criminal biography in ways both obvious and highly subtle. They are longer, and leave their protagonists unpunished. They allow their readers to treat them as fictions rather than pretending to be literal renderings of the truth. Their meanings (or intentions) are to a large extent mysterious, as they tend neither to the simple, clear didacticism of the one myth nor to the hectic but equally simple-minded "meaninglessness" of the other. All in all they are more teasing, provoking, and capacious than actual criminal biography, and more taking and inviting. They have the advantage, too, of seeming more authentic. Employing, rejecting, deforming, negating, and ignoring the forms and concerns supplied by the mythology of crime, they encourage their readers to "take part" in the stories they tell, to become producers, not merely consumers of meaning. Moll, Jack, Roxana, even Singleton, are no transient causes for smug or self-congratulatory rumination, no mere tubs cast off to divert Leviathan. But all this is matter for another book; if criminal biography is not as interesting as Defoe, the reason may be that that was just its point, not to be *too* interesting. One of its chief aims, after all, was to put criminals away where – as characters in old, familiar, oft-told, and at times possibly even boring stories – they would cease challenging public sensibilities.

Appendix I

Who read the popular literature of crime?

===============

"The Lives and infamous Actions of the most profligate Criminals have met with a Reception from Persons of all Ranks and Conditions," claims the author of *The Life of Waller* ([1732], p. iii), which sounds like Pope's claim that *The Beggar's Opera* "hit all tastes and degrees of men, from those of the highest Quality to the very Rabble" (*The Dunciad* [1729], 3:326 n.). Such contentions get absurdly echoed in *Anecdotes of the Most Remarkable Highwaymen* (1797): "although the utility of this Work is absolutely without limitation," its compiler declares, "the following Classes are particularly interested in the Lives and Anecdotes which we have recorded: – Magistrates, Bankers, Merchants, Tradesmen, Country Gentlemen, Company at Watering Places, Foreigners, Masters and Mistresses of Lodging-Houses, Lawyers, Publicans, Keepers of Prisons, Bailiffs, Stewards, Clerks, Shopmen, Youth of both Sexes, Female Housekeepers, Doating Old Maids, Husbands and Wives, Lovers, Peasants, &c. &c. &c." (p. vii). Certain kinds of writing about criminals nonetheless seem to have been class-specific, or so it appeared to contemporary observers. Thus the author of *The History of John Sheppard* (1724*a*) links ballads and broadsides to "the common People" and "the vulgar," apparently aiming his own, longer, more sophisticated text at "Citizens" and those of "tolerable Fashion" (pp. 148, 153, 164). The dedication of *Compleat Tryals* (1718, 1721) to the lord mayor and aldermen of London, along with the recorder and sheriffs of the city, also indicates an effort to attract a bourgeois audience, as does the dedication of *The Malefactor's Register* (1779) to Sir John Fielding. Clearly the author of *Remarkable Criminals* has the same kind of audience in mind, though his defensiveness on the subject raises interesting questions about his attitudes toward that audience and his motives in writing for them. "However contemptible" his work "may seem in the eyes of those who affect great wisdom and put on the appearance of much learning," he declares, it may nonetheless be useful "amongst the middling sort of people, who are glad to take up with books within the circle of their own comprehension" ([1735a], p. 1).

More specific references to intended audiences are rare. One writer expects that his book will be serviceable "both to the Publick, and also to private Families," even though (something he omits to mention in his preface) it contains a graphic account of a sodomy trial (*Compleat Tryals* [1718, 1721], 1:[vii], [x]; cf. 1:236–42). Another goes out of his way to direct "a Word or two to the Females," advising them that, "besides the Pleasure which they may find by perusing this Book in common with the Men" (interesting thought, that), they'll have ample opportunity to experience pleasures specific to their sex, i.e., to feel "Pity . . . in their Breasts" for "several of our celebrated Heroes" (Johnson, *Highwaymen* [1734], p. [2]). Such comments suggest that criminal biographers generally wrote neither for private families nor for women, though this apparently changed by the end of the eighteenth century. Thus *Remarkable Trials* (1765), *The Newgate Calendar* (1773), and *The Malefactor's Register* (1779) all recommend themselves to youths and their guardians, the last with a frontispiece showing "A Mother presenting [it] to her Son, and tenderly interesting him to regard the Instructions therein recorded."

Generally, however, the texts allow only limited inferences about the nature of their intended audience. Writers apparently presumed readers familiar with London and its environs, and so resident there at least part of the year; thus, for instance, the following entirely typical passage from *Remarkable Criminals:* "[they] being upon the road to St. Albans, a little on this side of it" ([1735a], p. 135). The same author possibly offers other clues to his intended audience when he speaks disparagingly of "the meaner sort of people," shows sympathy for Presbyterians, criticizes the "exterior ornaments" of the established Church, and blows hot and cold on the Quakers ([1735a], pp. 399, 117, 214). Toward the end of the eighteenth century *The Newgate Calendar* (1773) and *The Malefactor's Register* (1779) offer comparable clues to the social and political attitudes of their target audience by referring positively to Wilkes, attacking slavery, complaining about the arrogance of the aristocracy, and expressing anti-anti-Semitic sentiments as well as simple anti-Semitism (see, for example, *The Newgate Calendar*, 1:267; 5:77, 165, 221–22, 304–5; and *The Malefactor's Register*, 1:251–52, 326; 3:11, 398 n.; 4:256–57; 5:23–24).

The 1719 edition of Smith's *Highwaymen* may give us additional insight into its audience, by means of its "Table[s] of Memorable Passages." These tables, positioned at the front of each volume so as to catch the eye of browsing book buyers, may be taken to indicate Smith's (or his publisher's) view of what was eminently salable; in other words they may serve as an index to readers' tastes and biases, and so possibly to their backgrounds. Among other things, these tables list 334 separate encounters with criminals where the people involved are identified by name, class, trade, profession, or other social category. This list of persons (I'd suggest) permissibly hurt or otherwise embarrassed might be analyzed in a number of ways, and I shall give no full account of it here. Interestingly, it shows no special class bias. Thus there are some ninety-five references to victims whose chief importance is their status as gentry or nobility; ninety-four to those of the middling sort, ranging from the professions down to tradesmen and artisans; and approximately twenty-five to the lower classes (this last category excludes various social marginals such as countrymen, mountebanks, show business types, and moral, ethnic, and sexual deviants). Certain distinctive biases do appear in this "victims' list," however, in terms of trades and professions. By far the largest group of victims is clergy (twenty-seven, counting seven Roman Catholics and three dissenting clergymen but not five Quakers). Next come lawyers (twenty) and, though this is a somewhat looser group, people variously involved in the provisioning trades (also twenty, including eight victualers, two distillers, and two hostlers). Far down on the list come the next significant groups (five graziers and three farmers; five goldsmiths, a silversmith and a pewterer; five apothecaries and a physician). Such cataloguing, inasmuch as it indicates only the prejudices of Smith's audience as he saw them, says nothing about their positive values; they would seem, however, to have been fairly conventional in their biases and balanced in their feelings toward (or against) the upper and middle classes. Clergymen of course are always fair game, and lawyers too; the victualers and their like are a curious category, however, and suggest, given the relative unimportance of tailors (only two are listed), that we have less to deal with fine gentlemen here than urban bachelors (but maybe this leaves Smith's audience behind, and talks only of the hack writer himself).

Given the paucity of available information, one is tempted to make too much, too, perhaps, of the advertisements that appear both for and with the popular literature of crime. In John Applebee's advertisements for a two-volume set of *Select Trials* in 1736, for instance, we see the growing importance of the legal profession as a specific component of the audience for such publications. "These Trials," says Applebee's advertisement, "are not only very necessary for all Lawyers, Justices of the Peace, Clerks of the Indictments, and other Persons concern'd in Prosecutions, & c. but are very useful and entertaining to the Generality of Readers" (James Guthrie, Ordinary Accounts, 11 August and 2 November 1736; the same advertisement appears for *Select Trials* [1742], ibid., 7 May and 7 July 1742). Nonetheless, though lawyers had begun to play a significant role in criminal trials in the 1730s, interest in crime remained a general phenomenon, not tied to any particular trade or profession (see John Langbein, "The Criminal Trial before the Lawyers," *University of Chicago Law Review* 45 [1978]:263–316, esp. 264, 270). Other advertisements confirm, however, a definite middle-class cast to the phenomenon. Consider, for instance, the list of "Books Printed for John Back" at the end of *The Wicked Life and Penitent Death of Tho. Savage* (1688). These include Head and Kirkman's *The English Rogue* (price bound one shilling), an arithmetic text, and the following twopenny books, among others: *The School of Piety, A Guide to Devotion, The Righteous Man's Reward, The Dying Man's Good Counsel, The Danger of Despair, Rules of Civility in Good Breeding, The Gentlewomans Delight in Cookery, The New Crown Garland of Songs, The School of Holiness, The True Lovers Garland, The Art of Courtship, The Poets Jests, The History of the Valiant London Apprentice, Canterbury Tales, City and Country Recreation, A Description of Mans Life from the Cradle to the Grave, A Prospect of the Reigning Sins of the Nation,* and *The Destruction of Jerusalem* (pp. 19–20; for a similar list advertising thirty-two books sold by one of the publishers of *Compleat Tryals* [1718, 1721], see the front of vol. 3).

A somewhat different light is shed on the audience for the popular literature of crime by advertisements at the ends of sessions papers. These might, for instance, advertise remedies against deafness, scurvy, bad breath, "black or yellow Teeth," "the *French* Disease, and the *Running of the Reins,*" as well as "other *Venereal Arcana's* [*sic*]"; or lessons in Latin and French by "a very short and easie Method," or books of a definitely Whiggish tendency, or a collection of "Casuistical *Morning Exercises,* by several Ministers in and about *London*" (for all these examples see Old Bailey Sessions Paper, 26–28 February 1690; for a comparable advertisement in September 1731, see Langbein, "Criminal Trial," p. 271). One might even, perhaps, make something of the third edition of Smith's *Highwaymen* being advertised as appearing "in Pocket Volumes," just the thing, possibly, for people who traveled frequently or idled about town, wanted something to fill intervals from business, or liked to read on the sly (see Alexander Smith, *School of Venus* [1716], opposite title page). The format of the original *Remarkable Criminals* (1735) made it similarly portable, but other collections of criminal lives tend to be library size; the 1734 Johnson, with its folio format and twenty-six plates, is especially so.

The hardest evidence we have for the readership of the popular literature of crime, however, is its cost. One might cite the prices of various texts endlessly and compare these to figures for wages and income, but beyond saying there was something for nearly every purse and that some readers must have been affluent, it is hard to know what to do with such comparisons. How much of his income would a typical Londoner willingly give to be entertained? And how did the cost of the popular literature of crime compare with other diversions? The first edition of the first volume of Defoe's *History of the Pyrates* (1724), which cost four shillings, was recommended as being "not the tenth Part of the Price of a Masquerade" (*Miscellany Letters, Selected out of Mist's Weekly Journal* [1722, 1727], 4:196; for the price, see the *Monthly Catalogue*, No. 14 [May 1724], p. 3). In the absence of any adequate economic model to interpret the pricing and comparative cost of the popular literature of crime, we might possibly look for analogues in current developing nations. In Nigeria, for instance, as Emmanuel Obiechina has documented, a rich and widespread chapbook literature has developed quite comparable to that of seventeenth- and eighteenth-century England. At a time when the daily wage of a manual laborer was three shillings, these pamphlets ranged in cost from one shilling to 3/6d. Their audience, Obiechina notes, includes "grammar and elementary school boys and girls, lower-level office workers and journalists, primary school teachers, mechanics, taxi-drivers, farmers and the new literates who attend adult education classes and evening schools" (*Literature for the Masses: An Analytical Study of Popular Pamphleteering in Nigeria* [1971], pp. 17, 4, 3; see also his *An African Popular Literature* [1973], a reworking of the earlier text which includes a sampling of pamphlets). Unfortunately for these speculations, Obiechina notes no taste in Nigeria for criminal biography (and this despite a high crime rate, caused by the usual social and economic dislocations, and the occasional public execution).

Because it was necessarily restricted to the literate, based in London, and the creation of "middling" people who sought, chiefly, to speak to other "middling" people, what I've been calling the popular literature of crime may not have been quite "popular" in the sense that certain social historians would reserve for that term (thus see Preface, n. 4). But neither was it the property of an "elite" in any reasonable sense of that term. Clearly, and this may be all we can reasonably conclude about the makeup of its audience, it was widely read by a variety of people. Antony Wood's estimate that Dr. Walter Pope's *Memoires of Du Vall* (1670) sold ten thousand copies may be exaggerated (see ms. note in the copy at the Bodleian), but clearly there was big money to be made. This is the only possible explanation for the frequent publications and republications, and for the brisk market in piracies (thus, despite what I take to be its slow sale originally, there was a second edition of the 1734 Johnson's *Highwaymen* in 1742, which sold at fifteen shillings; for Paul Lorrain's complaints about false dying speeches, see Postscript, n. 10, and for similar complaints by John Applebee, see Michael Harris, "Trials and Criminal Biographies," in *Sale and Distribution of Books from 1700,* ed. Robin Myers and Michael Harris [1982], p. 20).

Appendix II

The politics of thieving

So fond was Read's *Weekly Journal* of the notion that "all the *Rogues, Whores, Pimps, Thieves, Fools,* and *Scoundrels* in the Kingdom" were Tories, and "all the Whores and Thieves . . . *High-Church*" (29 August, 18 July 1719), that it took positive exception to the following piece of news: "Four Clergymen having been to make a Visit, on Tuesday last, at Cashalton, and returning home in a Coach between Nine and Ten at Night, were set upon by two Highwaymen in a Lane half a Mile on this side Cashalton, who robb'd them of their Money, a Watch, and their Perukes, gave them ill Language, and rode off" (the *Post-Boy,* 19–21 July 1720). This seemed no innocuous or neutral report to Read's, which quotes from it, but rather – given the robbers' lack of "Respect for the Church [and its] immediate Sons" – a "witty Way" to "insinuate . . . the Highwaymen were Whigs." If so, huffs Read's, "I wou'd only have it answer'd, That they are the first Highwaymen since the Revolution that have been of that Principle" (23 July 1720).

Read's was a mouthpiece for the Whig ministry, and one would be inclined to dismiss such stuff were it not so unidirectional. Tories almost never claim that thieves are actually Whigs, though they regularly claim the reverse, that Whigs are thieves or worse than thieves (but for an account of two whores who "pretended to be mighty Whigs," then got "an ignorant young Man" drunk and robbed him, see Mist's *Weekly Journal,* 9 January 1719). Thus, celebrating the Restoration as a freeing of the country from republican tyranny, a Tory writer might ask, with high anti-Hanoverian flourish: "But . . . [s]hall we return Thanks for a Deliverance from Rogues with Swords in their Hands, when we are ruin'd by *Footmen, Pimps,* PATHICKS, *Parasites, Bawds, Whores,* nay, what is more *vexatious, old ugly Whores.* . . . 'tis barbarous to invite us to chaunt Lays of Praise, who are become a Prey to rascally peddling *Jews,* to petty *Brokers,* to the Scum, the off-scowring of *foreign* Nations, and the Dregs of our own" (Mist's, 27 May 1721). Or, as even a relatively neutral journal might declare, shortly after the first great English stock market crash, "let it be told to Posterity, that the great Cheat of Stock-Jobbing has been a Whiggish Piece of Conduct" (Applebee's *Original Weekly Journal,* 31 December 1720).

Though the South Sea Bubble heightened such rhetoric, it had long been part of the political scene. Read's claim that thieves were Tories is only a new version of the popular notion that they – at least some of the greatest of them – were Jacobites; Read's aims, with considerable shrewdness, to smear the Tories with a double brush. Certainly highwaymen declared their Jacobite sympathies frequently enough, tending, in the tradition of Hind and other Interregnum robbers, to yearn after the dethroned and absent king (Thomas Knowls, for whom see *Hinds Elder Brother* [1651], is one such figure, Richard Hannam another). Thus Whitney liked to advertise himself as a Jacobite, and the Golden Farmer likely harbored Jacobite sympathies as well (in 1691, according to Luttrell, a member of his gang refused to recognize the authority of the lord chief justice on the grounds that James was still "his lawful Sovereign" [*Brief Relation of State Affairs* (1857), 2:253]). Several other highwaymen of the 1690s salted their discourse with Jacobitical sentiments (see Luttrell, *Brief Relation,* 2:613, 630; 3:537), and the tendency persisted into the eighteenth century. A complaint was made in 1702, for instance, that condemned prisoners in Newgate and their whores regularly got drunk and "wished that God would damn King William and Parliament" (quoted by W. J. Sheehan, "Finding Solace in Eighteenth-Century Newgate," in J. S. Cockburn, ed., *Crime in England, 1550–1800* [1977], p. 244). It is in the context of such a tradition, then, that we are to understand Read's reporting the story of a onetime London haberdasher turned highwayman. Residing in Calais, he would regularly cross the channel, commit a few robberies, and then return to the safety of France; he had gone to Calais to escape his creditors and while there had become "a great Favorer of the Pretender" (Read's, 16 April 1720). In 1722 a gang of highwaymen reportedly took more definite political action. "Wishing the Court Party might miss of their Ends at the Elections," they robbed a member of Parliament in Epping Forest (Applebee's, 3 March 1722; these were to be the first elections since the passage of the Septennial Act, a Whig measure).

Obviously, the politics of thieves in actual fact was not so important as what, for various political purposes, they might be said to be. In claiming thieves were Tories, Read's aimed at disrupting the notion that Whigs themselves were crooks; far from being soft on crime, they were "ten times worse Enemies to the Art of Thieving" than their political rivals (Read's, 18 July 1719). Readers of Alexander Smith might have thought this last point reasonable, if only on the grounds that it seemed a return of compliments. The anti-Whig and (in effect the same thing) antirepublican bias of Smith's writing may in fact be quantified. Thus in forty-two of the "Memorable Passages" advertised by the 1719 edition of his *Highwaymen,* the person victimized or otherwise put at risk is sufficiently famous for his politics to be easily identified (thus, for instance, I omit from consideration three named London aldermen). In nineteen of these encounters the eminent politicos are Whigs, and in seven they are Republicans. Cromwell is robbed three times, and General and Lady Fairfax once each; the Whigs in question include Monmouth and three of the Rye-House plotters, eleven individuals with powerful connections to William (including perhaps the same Lord Wharton who wrote the words to "Lilli Bulero" and took on Addison as his protégé), five associates of Marlborough (three of his lieutenants, the wife of a fourth, and his duchess's chambermaid), and Lord Mohun (this totals twenty Whigs instead of nineteen because three individuals stand in more than one category, and two are robbed twice). Mohun was notorious enough to be singled out for nonpolitical reasons, and perhaps this was true of one or two of the other Whigs (thus Henry Howard, duke of Norfolk, and perhaps Aubrey de Vere, earl of Oxford). Of the sixteen remaining cases, half involve people notable for having no political principles but self-interest – thus, for example, General Monk, his shrewish wife (who gets robbed twice), Titus Oates, and Peter Mews (the last was a long-time Stuart loyalist and bishop of Winchester, who went over to William at the Revolution).

Only eight instances of the forty-two, then, concern Tories, Jacobites, or the like, and five of these may be immediately discounted on the grounds that the victims deserve to be robbed quite apart from their politics. Thus Judge Jeffryes of the Bloody Assizes accounts for two of these eight robberies, and another two have as their targets two incompetent Stuart commanders, George Booth, Lord Delamere, and Louis Duras, earl of Feversham. That the duke of Berwick is also robbed (he was a much more considerable soldier, in fact a hero and James II's natural son) may have something to do with his fighting for the French against the English in the War of the Spanish Succession. It would seem, then, that there are only three victims in the Tory–Jacobite group whose politics cannot be discounted, and all three were in fact notorious Jacobites (one was executed for conspiring against William, another was cashiered from his vice-admiralcy for disloyalty, and the third, by itself reason enough to be robbed, was a lawyer).

Notes

These notes are meant primarily for the curious and skeptical; trusting readers may ignore them. They bulk larger than I like because good secondary sources for my arguments were unavailable at some points and because, at others, the rich variety of recent scholarship on crime and punishment in early modern Europe demanded consideration, or at least acknowledgment.

Works of criminal biography are generally cited here and in the main text by short title and date of publication, except where longer or full titles have informational value; an *a* following the year of publication indicates a nineteenth- or twentieth-century reprint. Fuller citations appear in a separate section of the bibliography in order of date of publication. Ordinaries' *Accounts,* sessions papers, other periodicals, assize sermons, and many other sources are also cited by short title; these appear in the bibliography under the appropriate headings, in the usual alphabetical order.

PREFACE

1 Pepys, *Diary,* ed. Robert Latham and William Matthews (1970–83), 5:201; *Remarkable Criminals* (1735a), p. 438. On the "general sense of insecurity" produced by the threat of crime in Hanoverian England, see Leon Radzinowicz, *History of English Criminal Law* (1948), 1:29–31. For recent efforts to reconstruct the actual incidence of crime in seventeenth- and eighteenth-century England, see introduction to Part II, n.1, and Chapter 7, nn. 5 and 14.

2 For a general description of the popular literature of crime in England during the first half of the eighteenth century, see Michael Harris, "Trials and Criminal Biographies: A Case Study in Distribution," in *Sale and Distribution of Books from 1700,* ed. Robin Myers and Michael Harris (1982), pp. 1–36. For extended studies of the sessions papers, with a particular

view to their value as sources for legal history, see John Langbein, "The Criminal Trial before the Lawyers," *University of Chicago Law Review* 45 (1978): 263–316, and "Shaping the Eighteenth-Century Criminal Trial: A View from the Ryder Sources," ibid. 50 (1983): 1–136. Frank Wadleigh Chandler provides the widest overview of criminal biography in the period in *The Literature of Roguery*, 2 vols. (1907); though occasionally inaccurate, this remains useful for its descriptions of a number of works destroyed by bombing during World War II. Of more recent vintage, and also worth consulting, are separate chapters on the subject in Donald Stauffer, *The Art of Biography in Eighteenth Century England* (1941); John J. Richetti, *Popular Fiction Before Richardson, 1700–1739* (1968); Jerry C. Beasley, *Novels of the 1740s* (1982); Maximillian E. Novak, *Realism, Myth, and History in Defoe's Fiction* (1983); and J. A. Sharpe, *Crime in Early Modern England, 1550–1750* (1984). See also Robert R. Singleton, "English Criminal Biography, 1651–1722," *Harvard Library Bulletin* 18 (1970): 63–83, and "Defoe, Moll Flanders, and the Ordinary of Newgate," ibid. 24 (1976): 407–13; Peter Linebaugh, "The Ordinary of Newgate and His *Account*," in *Crime in England, 1550–1800*, ed. J. S. Cockburn (1977), pp. 246–69; Françoise du Sorbier, "De la Potence à la biographie, ou les avatars du criminel et de son image en angleterre (1680–1740)," *Études anglaises* 32 (1979): 257–71; J. A. Sharpe, "Domestic Homicide in Early Modern England," *The Historical Journal* 24 (1981): 29–48, and " 'Last Dying Speeches': Religion, Ideology and Public Execution in Seventeenth-Century England," *Past and Present* 107 (1985): 144–67; and two articles by the present writer, "The Myth of Captain James Hind: A Type of Primitive Fiction before Defoe," *Bulletin of the New York Public Library* 79 (1976): 139–66, and "In Contrast to Defoe: The Rev. Paul Lorrain, Historian of Crime," *Huntington Library Quarterly* 60 (1976): 59–78. For the larger context of popular literature within which criminal biography was situated, see Victor E. Neuburg, *Popular Literature, a History and Guide* (1977), chaps. 2 and 3; and Margaret Spufford, *Small Books and Pleasant Histories: Popular Fiction and Its Readership in Seventeenth-Century England* (1981).

3   No one has yet closely studied Gay's and Lillo's plays against the background of criminal biography; for such a study of Fielding's novel, however, see W. R. Irwin, *The Making of Jonathan Wild* (1941).

4   "Middling" because, strictly speaking, the popular literature of crime is not quite "popular" in the sense in which some cultural historians prefer to use that term. For the situation of "chap-book culture" midway between the "learned" culture of the "great tradition" and the "unofficial" culture of the "non-elite," even the "inarticulate," see Peter Burke, *Popular Culture in Early Modern Europe* (1978), pp. 63, [ix], 49, and chap. 2 generally; for a still stricter definition of "popular" culture, see also Robert Muchembled, *Culture populaire et culture des élites dans la France moderne (XVe–XVIIIe siècles)* (1978), esp. pp. 7–13. What evidence there is for the readership of the popular literature of crime is discussed in Appendix I.

5   Durkheim, *The Division of Labor in Society* (1933), pp. 70–110; for a develop-

ment of Durkheim's views especially relevant to the argument that follows, see also Lévi-Strauss, *Structural Anthropology* (1972), pp. 172–75. The other French sociologist is Alexandre Lacassagne (1843–1924), quoted in Harold Scott, ed., *The Concise Encyclopedia of Crime and Criminals* (1961), p. 218.

6   Foucault, *Discipline and Punish* (1977), esp. parts 1 and 2. For more on the spectacle of public execution in early modern France, see also Michel Bée, "La Societé traditionelle et la mort," *XVIIᵉ siècle* 106–7 (1975): 81–111, esp. 95–109; Muchembled, *Culture populaire,* pp. 247–55; and John Mc-Manners, *Death and the Enlightenment* (1985), pp. 368–408. For a good account of execution day ritual in London, in actual fact as well as in theory, see Peter Linebaugh, "The Tyburn Riot Against the Surgeons," in *Albion's Fatal Tree: Crime and Society in Eighteenth-Century England,* ed. Douglas Hay, Peter Linebaugh, and E. P. Thompson (1975), pp. 65–117. The public punishment of criminals in the Netherlands, which differed significantly from both French and English practice, is the subject of Pieter Spierenburg's *The Spectacle of Suffering* (1984).

PART I: INTRODUCTION

1   Malinowski, *Myth in Primitive Psychology,* in *Magic, Science and Religion, and Other Essays* (1954), p. 101; G. S. Kirk, *Myth: Its Meaning and Functions in Ancient and Other Cultures* (1970), pp. 253–54, 256, 258.

2   Malinowski, *Myth,* pp. 100–1; on Lévi-Strauss, see Kirk, *Myth,* pp. 73–75. Kirk's argument is not that Lévi-Strauss fails to take sufficiently into account the social realities of the societies whose myths he analyzes but that he fails to make allowance for the fact that what he is analyzing is only one version of a story that, told on different occasions by different narrators, may well admit of variations in detail and emphasis. That is, with the text of a myth before him, Lévi-Strauss makes the mistake of assuming that every detail in that text is equally significant and has to be taken into account to arrive at a final understanding of the myth. But that text may reflect the way that myth has been told on only one occasion, Kirk contends, or by one teller on several occasions. I shall seek to avoid a similar difficulty by trying to explain no single account of a murderer or highwayman in its entirety, but rather the elements that it and other accounts of similar criminals had in common. This same concern with typicalities means, too, that very little attention will be paid to certain of the most famous criminals of the period, e.g., Jack Sheppard, Jonathan Wild, Dick Turpin, Mary Blandy, Eugene Aram. I would like very much to quote Lévi-Strauss's definition of myth along with Cassirer's and Malinowski's, but, for all his real brilliance, he seems not to have written so succinctly (and portably) on the subject as they. See, however, Terence Hawkes, *Structuralism and Semiotics* (1977), pp. 48–49, and K. O. L. Burridge, "Lévi-Strauss and Myth," in *The Structural Study of Myth and Totemism,* ed. Edmund Leach (1967), p. 102; the latter offers the best précis I know of Lévi-Strauss's theory of myth.

3 For an overview of the most important recent scholarship, and judicious discussions of the issues it raises, see J. A. Sharpe, *Crime in Early Modern England, 1550–1750* (1984). J. M. Beattie's monumental *Crime and the Courts in England, 1660–1800* (1986), which appeared only after this book had gone to press, is also very much worth consulting for its capacious and highly useful account of "the way the English courts dealt with crime in a period in which the foundations of modern forms of judicial administration were laid" (p. 3).

4 Thus, until the appearance of James Mabbe's *The Rogue* (1622) – a very popular English version of Aleman's *Guzman de Alfarache,* with later editions in 1623, 1630, 1634 (2), and 1656 – popular writing about criminals other than the occasional murderer was (with rare exceptions) pretty much of the cony-catching variety. That is, it tended to string anecdotes of various tricks performed by various people into compendiums of crimes the reader ought to guard against, not to take the form of a single narrative about the exploits of a single criminal alleged to be an actual historical figure. The latter kind of writing tends to be rare until the mid-seventeenth century. The pamphlets on Hind are among the earliest of their kind to be found, antedated only (so far as I know) by Robert Greene's *The Blacke Bookes Messenger. Laying Open the Life and Death of Ned Browne* (1592), *The Life and Death of Gamaliell Ratsey, a Famous Theefe of England* and *Ratseis Ghost* (both 1605), and *The Life and Death of Griffin Flood Informer* (1623). Luke Hutton's *Blacke Dogge of Newgate* (1596?) and John Clavell's *Recantation of an Ill Led Life* (1628) are of the cony-catching type; they make no effort to be biographical. Similarly, the concern with the motives of the murderer and the state of his consciousness parallels the development of spiritual biography. Such concerns are notably absent, or at the most but barely apparent, in accounts of murder published early in the seventeenth century (for representative titles, see Joseph H. Marshburn, *Murder & Witchcraft in England, 1550–1640* (1971); J. A. Sharpe, "Domestic Homicide in Early Modern England," *The Historical Journal* 24 (1981): 29–48; and the bibliography at the back of this book). It is not until the Freeman Sondes case (1655; for which see Chapter 5) and that of Nathaniel Butler (1657) that we see full-blown efforts to describe the mental and spiritual state of criminals of any kind.

5 Old Bailey Sessions Paper, 21 April 1680; Johnson, *Highwaymen* (1734), p. 111.

CHAPTER 1

1 Smith, *Highwaymen* (1719a), pp. 136–40.

2 For a detailed study of the various biographies of another famous mid-seventeenth-century criminal, see Ernest Bernbaum's *Mary Carleton Narratives, 1663–1673* (1914), and also C. F. Main, "The German Princess; or, Mary Carleton in Fact and Fiction," *Harvard Library Bulletin* 10 (1956): 166–85. The longest and most considerable account of Mary Carleton is Francis Kirkman's *Counterfeit Lady Unveiled* (1673); as Bernbaum shows, in certain ways it adumbrates the techniques and interests of the developing English novel. Hind's case offers nothing so sophisticated as Kirkman's near novel, but insofar as we are interested in the consciousness of the popular audience this is no real disadvantage. Carleton, too, was best known to the eighteenth century through the medium of Smith's *Highwaymen* (2nd ed., 1714; 5th ed., 1719), but in a radical abridgment of Kirkman's text to something like one sixth of its original length. Though Smith gets most of his details from Kirkman, and many of his phrasings, he omits all the qualities Bernbaum found interesting because they anticipate the novel. Other quasi-novelistic criminal biographies in the late seventeenth century include the anonymously written *Life and Death of Mrs Mary Frith* (1662), and two works by Elkanah Settle, *The Life and Death of Major Clancie* (1680), and *The Notorious Imposter; or the Life of William Morell* (1692).

3   The *Weekly Intelligencer of the Commonwealth*, No. 45 (11–18 November 1651).

4   See *The Taking of Hind* (1651), p. 2, and G[eorge] F[idge], *The English Gusman* (1652), p. 38.

5   G. F. [George Fidge?], *Hind's Ramble, or, the Description of His Manner and Course of Life* ([27 October] 1651). The precise date of publication has been entered in hand on the title page of the copy in the British Library; most of the other pamphlets there on Hind bear similar notations, and I rely on these for my chronology.

6   Some notion of the contents of *Hind's Ramble* can be had from the title page, which mentions "the several Robberies he hath committed in England, and the Escapes he hath made upon several occasions. With his voyage into Holland and how he cheated a Dutch-man there of 200 l. And from thence went into Ireland, where he did many Robberies, and was wounded by some of his own Party. With a relation of his going to the Scotch King, where he was made Scoutmaster General, and afterwards (as 'tis generally reported) was the onely man that conveyed the Scotch King to London, who since is Shipt away for beyond Seas."

7   J. S., *An Excellent Comedy, Called, The Prince of Priggs Revels* ([11 November] 1651). A "prigg" is a thief.

8   Ibid., pp. 1, 14.

9   *Hind's Ramble* (1651), pp. 41, 42.

10 Ibid., pp. [5–6].

11 *The Taking of Hind* ([14 November] 1651), and *The Declaration of Hind* ([18 November] 1651).

12 *Declaration of Hind* (1651), p. 1.

13 *The Taking of Hind* (1651), p. 6.

14 Ibid.; *Declaration of Hind* (1651), pp. 6, 2–3.

15 *The Taking of Hind* (1651), p. 6; this passage is not reprinted in *Declaration of Hind*, though a version of it does appear in the most elaborate of the accounts of Hind, *The English Gusman* (1652).

16 G[eorge] F[idge], *The English Gusman; or the History of That Unparallel'd Thief James Hind* ([10 January] 1652).

17   *The Humble Petition of James Hind (Close Prisoner in New-Gate) to the Right Honourable the Councell of State; and Their Proceedings Thereupon* ([21 November] 1651).

18   *The Trial of Captain James Hind* ([15 December] 1651); the title page notes that it is "published for general satisfaction, by him who subscribes himself———James Hind."

19   Clavil, or rather John Clavell, was the author of *A Recantation of an Ill Led Life. Or a Discoverie of the High-Way Law* (1628), which he wrote while in prison for highway robbery. The nephew and heir of a knight banneret, he was at least scholar enough to write all his recantation (near fifty pages) in decasyllabic couplets. Charles I pardoned him.

20   F[idge], *The English Gusman* (1652), pp. 42–43, 46.

21   *Strange Newes from New-Gate* ([14 January] 1651 [/2]), t.p. and pp. 1, 4, 5.

22   *Wit for Mony. Being a Full Relation of the Life, Actions, Merry Conceits, and Pretty Pranks of Captain Iames Hind* (1652); the quotation is from the last page of an unnumbered text.

23   *No Jest like a True Jest: Being a Compendious Record of the Merry Life, and Mad Exploits of Capt. James Hind* (1674; rptd. 1817), the last page of an unnumbered text. An earlier edition of *No Jest*, apparently the first, was published in 1657; there appears to be only one copy of it in existence, at the Bodleian (I have not seen it). Still another edition was published in 1670 (?), and a fourth in 1680 (see Wing's *Short-title Catalogue*, 1st ed., F1177–F1179). The British Library also holds editions of *No Jest like a True Jest* published ca. 1750 at London and Stratford-upon-Avon; ca. 1765, 1775, and 1805 at Newcastle: and ca. 1820 at Stirling (where Hind kissed the king's hand).

24   *The Trial of James Hind*, p. 4; and "as he passed from the Bar, casting his head on one side, and looking as it were over the left shoulder," he took the opportunity to say, "These are filthy gingling Spurs; (meaning his Irons about his legs) but I hope to have them exchang'd ere long; which expressions caused much laughter" (p. 5).

25   "As he passed up the Old-bayley towards Newgate, divers people resorted to see him; who asked if he had received Sentence; which words Mr. Hind hearing, faced to the left; and smiling, said, No, no, good people, There's no hast to hang true folkes" (ibid. p. 5).

26   F[idge], *The English Gusman* (1652), pp. [iii–v].

27   *A Full and True Account of the Apprehending James Whitney, the Notorious High-Way-Man, near Bishops Gate* (1693).

28   Narcissus Luttrell, *A Brief Historical Relation of State Affairs from September 1678 to April 1714* (1857), 2:630, 644; 3:5, 10, 2.

29   Ibid., 3:16, 23–24, 26, 27.

30   Smith, *Highwaymen* (1719a), p. 50.

31   The ballad is called *The Golden Farmer's Last Farewell*, and is to be sung "*to the Tune of The Rich Merchant Man*" (1691?).

32   Samuel Smith, Ordinary Account, 22 December 1690.

33   Old Bailey Sessions Paper, 10–13 and 17 December 1690.

34   The real Golden Farmer would not of course be tried and hanged for yet another year. Cf. Smith, *Highwaymen* (1719*a*), p. 36, and Old Bailey Sessions Paper, 11–14 December 1689, which gives an account of Davis's trial.

35   We know that these adventures are fictitious not only on the grounds of internal evidence here and elsewhere in Smith's book, but also because the reports of the Golden Farmer's trial, and that of certain of his accomplices (see n. 34), include descriptions of some of his most notorious robberies. None of these – nor anything like them – appears in Smith's version of his life. Smith's version, however, is consistently more "interesting."

36   See [N.B.], *Compleat Tryals* (1718, 1721), 1:125–37. The correct information on Bennet appears to have come from the chaplain's account of his dying behavior, which *Compleat Tryals* quotes without attribution. For later accounts of the Golden Farmer, see, for instance, Capt. Charles Johnson's *Lives and Adventures of the Most Famous Highwaymen, Murderers, Street-Robbers, &c.* (1734) – hereafter referred to as the 1734 Johnson to distinguish it, and its author, from Charles Johnson's *History of the Pyrates* [1724, 1728], which is generally attributed to Defoe – and Capt. Mackdonald's *Lives and Adventures of the Most Famous Highwaymen, Murderers, Pirates, Street-Robbers, and Thief-Takers* (1758). I might add that the Golden Farmer is still identified as William Davis by the British Library Catalogue.

37   For the dying behavior of Old Mobb, whose contrition escaped Smith along with all but one or two of the real facts about him (including the actual date of his hanging), see Samuel Smith, Ordinary Account, 18 September 1691. Old Mobb's trial and conviction is reported in Old Bailey Sessions Paper, 9–12 September 1691.

38   The *Memoirs of the Right Villanous John Hall, the Late Famous and Notorious Robber* (1708; 4th ed.), purporting to be "Penn'd from his own Mouth some time before his Death," are almost certainly inauthentic. Not only are they written in an idiom that would have been entirely alien to one who "could neither Read nor Write," as Paul Lorrain described him, but they do not reveal, after all, anything particular about him or his exploits. (The title page misleadingly advertises "the *Exact* Life and character of a Thief *in general*" [my italics].) The public would have known that Hall was illiterate – thus the writer of his *Memoirs* seeks to explain away the paradox that "A man may Write without being able to Write at all" (p. 3) – and it would have known too that, though contrite, he died tight-lipped about what he had done. "He own'd in general," wrote Lorrain, "that within these 3 Years last past he had committed a great many Robberies, some of them very considerable, in and about *London;* but he would not come to Particulars, saying, he had forgot them in great measure, and it would signifie nothing to any Person to know every ill thing he had done, for he could make no other amends to the Persons he had wrong'd, than to ask their Pardon" (Paul Lorrain, Ordinary Account, 17 December 1707). The writer of Hall's *Memoirs* tried to explain Hall's diffidence away by making him comment harshly on Lorrain's exploitation of those criminals who did give him detailed confessions (see p. 16). Interestingly enough, this attack on Lorrain's character did not prevent Lorrain's *Accounts* from carrying advertisements for Hall's *Memoirs* on no fewer than seven occasions (28 January, 3 March, 28 April, 18 June, and 24 September 1708; and 23 March and 16 December 1709). Smith, as usual, cast all scruples to the wind in writing Hall's life for his *Highwaymen* (1719); here we do have the "particulars" of Hall's most interesting exploits – all of which, save for Hall's name and the year in which he was hanged, are of course utter inventions.

39 The pantomime based on Jack Sheppard's escapes from Newgate, John Thurmond's *Harlequin Sheppard. A Night Scene in Grotesque Characters* (1724), was performed seven times in late November and early December of 1724 at the Drury Lane Theatre (see *The London Stage. Part 2*, ed. Emmett L. Avery, pp. 797, 798, 801). Mist's *Weekly Journal* (5 December 1724) reports that its first performance "was dismiss'd with a universal hiss. – And, indeed, if Shepherd had been as wretched, and as silly a Rogue in the World as the ingenious and witty Managers have made him upon the stage, the lower Gentry, who attended him to Tyburn, wou'd never have pittied him when he was hang'd." For another weak effort at dramatizing Sheppard's life, see *The Prison-Breaker; or, The Adventures of John Sheppard. A Farce. As Intended to Be Acted at the Theatre Royal in Lincoln's-Inn Fields* (1725); this is interesting for its use of criminal slang and its satire on the Newgate jailors.

CHAPTER 2

1 Coke, who begins *The Third Part of the Institutes* (1644) by treating first of "the highest and most hainous crime of *High Treason*," goes on to discourse of other crimes "in order, as they are greater and more odious than others" (sig. B2r). He works his way through various kinds of treason (including petit treason, of which more later) and heresy and witchcraft, before arriving at murder.

2 The text of this unfortunately survives only at second hand, as part of "The Life, Tryal, and Behaviour, under Condemnation, and Confession of Harman Strodtman," in *Compleat Tryals* (1718, 1721), 2:193–224. On the grounds, however, that where I have been able to compare *Compleat Tryals* with the texts it plagiarizes, I have found it to give an accurate copy, I believe that Strodtman's confession as we have it here is reasonably correct. Quotations will be cited in the text.

3 Paul Lorrain, preface to *Harman Strodtman's Last Legacy to the World. Being His Divine Meditations and Prayers* (1701).

4 Ibid.

5 Ibid.

6 Robert Franklin, Thomas Vincent, Thomas Doolitel, James Janeway, Hugh Baker, *A Murderer Punished and Pardoned: Or a True Relation of the Wicked Life, and Shameful-Happy Death of Thomas Savage* (1668), p. 4; all further quotations will be cited in the text. This pamphlet reached a thir-

teenth edition by 1671; another pamphlet based on it, *A Warning to Youth: The Life and Death of Thomas Savage,* reached a twenty-second edition by 1710 and was reprinted again in 1734 and 1735. Savage's life is included in Smith's *Highwaymen* (1719), a signal honor in a book that notices only two or three others like him, as well as in *Compleat Tryals* (1718, 1721) and the 1734 Johnson's *Highwaymen.*

7 Actually, Savage did not finally leave the world so beatifically as he and his sponsors would have liked. Confessing his sins for the last time on the morning of his death – "saying, he first neglected and profaned the Sabbath, & . . . this was the beginning of all his wickedness," for starting from the "wicked Society" of Sabbath-breakers he had moved inexorably "to Alehouses, then to Brothel-houses, then to murder, then to theft, then to *Newgate* and yet at last, he hoped, to heaven" – Savage managed to die well enough the first time he was hanged (*A Murderer Punished and Pardoned* [1668], p. 35). But, taken down too soon, he revived as his friends prepared him for burial, which required that he be hanged again. This time Savage struggled violently, striking one of the bailiffs who had come to seize him in the mouth, and kicking the executioner. These last unseemly details, though published elsewhere, are discreetly omitted by Franklin et al. (See, instead, *God's Justice against Murther, or the Bloudy Apprentice Executed* [1668], p. 11.)

8 *The Trial at Large, Behaviour, and Dying Declaration, of Mary Edmondson* (1759), p. 16, and *A Genuine Narrative of the Trial and Condemnation of Mary Edmondson* (1759), p. 20, both of which offer nearly identical accounts, word for word, of Mary Edmondson's execution. Quotations from these will be cited in the text.

9 See Sessions Paper, Kingston-upon-Thames, 28–31 March and 2–3 April 1759, "Taken in Short-Hand by Isaac Harman."

10 Here for the sanguinary, or the merely curious, is the description the *Genuine Narrative* gives of the murder: " 'tis presumed, the Prisoner, having prepared all Things she thought necessary in order to murder her Aunt, on *Friday* the 23d of *February* last, between the Hours of Seven and Eight o'Clock at Night, she went into the Yard, and there, as she had done before, she began to make a terrible and hideous Noise, by Throwing down the Washing-Tubs upon the Stone Pavement. This she continued doing for some Time, when Mrs. *Walker,* then in the Parlour missing her Niece, and wondering greatly at the Noise, called her several Times, but she not answering, at length took a Resolution to go and see what was the Meaning of the Noise made by the Fall of the Tubs in the Yard. Whereupon, taking up the Candle, then standing before her on a Table, she went into the Wash-House. The Niece, perceiving her Aunt coming with a Light in her Hand, hid herself. Upon which, she looked about, and saw the Tub flung down, but saw no Person whatever. Not being able to account for what she saw, she was about to return again into the Parlour to call her Neighbours to her Assistance; when the Niece, perceiving her Aunt's Back towards her, rushed forth from her Lurking-Hole, seized her Aunt, and

with a Case-knife cut her Throat; which she did so effectually, that she died in a few Minutes.

"When the Prisoner had proceeded thus far, in Order to conceal her Guilt, she dragged the dead Body of her Aunt out of the Wash-House into the Kitchen, took her Watch and some Silver Spoons, and hid them under the Water-Tub. After this, she took off her Apron, (which was wreaking wet with the Blood of her Aunt) and taking the bloody Knife, and Handkerchief, she rolled them all up together, and threw them into the Copper.

"This done, the farther to hide her Guilt, she immediately cut her own Wrists across; and then being in a very bloody Condition, she opened the Street-Door, and alarmed the Neighbours by crying out, Murder, Thieves! Help for God's Sake; and the like [p. 6]."

11 Joseph Clarke, *A Full Refutation of the Pretended Genuine Narrative of the Trial and Condemnation of Mary Edmundson. . . . As Also That Falsely Called, The Trial at Large* (1759), p. 7; further quotations will be cited in the text.

12 *The Case of Mary Edmondson. By a Gentleman of the Law* (1759), p. 24; further quotations cited in text.

13 Richard Coleman was executed in 1749 for the rape of Sarah Green, from which she afterward died. He maintained his innocence in *The Solemn Declaration of Richard Coleman* (1749). In 1751 two men convicted of other crimes confessed that they had been responsible for the attack on Sarah Green and that Coleman was in no way involved; see *The Confession of Thomas Jones, and James Welch* (1751), and the Rev. Leonard Howard, *The Behaviour, Confession, and Dying Words of the Four Malefactors Executed at Kennington-Common* (1751).

14 Sessions Paper, Kingston-upon-Thames, 28–31 March and 2–3 April 1759.

15 Ibid.

PART II: INTRODUCTION

1 J. M. Beattie has found an overall "downward trend" in indictments for murder and manslaughter in Surrey and Sussex over the period 1660 to 1800 ("The Pattern of Crime in England, 1660–1800," *Past and Present* 62 [1974]: 61). Sussex was a rural county, but Surrey included parts of London, and the downward trend operated there as well. Beattie's figures, which suggest a homicide rate of approximately 6 to 5 per 100,000 population in Surrey in the late seventeenth century, declining to slightly above 2 in the early 1720s and to less than 1 by the 1780s and 1790s, might be compared to the homicide rate for Detroit, Michigan, in 1983 of 49.3 per 100,000 population. In 1982, at the time I write the most recent year permitting comparison, the overall homicide rate for England and Wales was 1 per 100,000 population, while in the United States it was 9.1 (figures from U.S. Bureau of the Census, *Statistical Abstract of the United States: 1985*, 105th ed. [1984], pp. 168, 186, and Central Office of Information, *Britain 1984: An Official Handbook* [1984], p. 97). For the opinion that "the true murder rate" in mid-eighteenth-century London was "remarkably

low," and even astonishing by modern standards, see John Langbein, "Shaping the Eighteenth-Century Criminal Trial," *University of Chicago Law Review* 50 (1983): 44.

2 John J. Richetti, *Popular Fiction Before Richardson* (1968), pp. 56, 31, 53.

3 Smith prints very few accounts of familiar murder, and such as he does are considerably pared down from the original pamphlets. Though in these cases Smith refrains from indulging his usual sense of humor, the grotesque and macabre qualities of which we shall soon enough confront, he generally confines himself to the most sensational parts of his sources. Richetti cites the description of Savage's murdering the servant girl as an especially effective piece of sensationalist writing, which it is, but it is not typical of such accounts because Smith omits the religious comment that follows; it may also be important that the punctuation of the original passage is changed. Smith cannot be taken to stand for all criminal biography in the eighteenth century.

4 Cf. "the Penitent Prisoner . . . is one, who although he confess himself to have been *seduc't* by evil Company, yet being under *restraint* . . . he makes a *Pulpit* of his Prison to *Preach* to him Repentance; a *Sermon* of his Shackles to teach him his *Service;* He turns his Gaole into a Shop to traffick for Heaven; and into an *Exchange* of all Devotions that may gain him Salvation" (*The Penitent Prisoner, His Character, Carriage upon His Commitment, Letany, Proper Prayers, Serious Meditations, Sighs, Occasional Ejaculations, Devotion Going to Execution, and at the Place of Execution* [1675], p. 1). Pieter Spierenberg quotes a seventeenth-century Dutch traveler to England who "noted with surprise" that, except "for the rope around his neck," the convict about to be hanged "resembled a minister in the pulpit" (*The Spectacle of Suffering* [1984], p. 63). J. A. Sharpe traces the practice of the criminal's dying speech back to the sixteenth century, seeing it as "a humble equivalent of the custom of Tudor monarchs of turning treason trials into elaborate set pieces" (*Crime in Seventeenth-Century England* [1983], p. 142; see also his article, " 'Last Dying Speeches': Religion, Ideology and Public Execution in Seventeenth-Century England," *Past and Present* 107 [1985]: 157–59). What is new in the seventeenth century, however, is the emphasis on representing as such the penitent criminal's inspired outpourings. Gilbert Dugdale's account of Elizabeth Caldwell, who accidentally poisoned a neighbor girl in trying to kill her husband, anticipates in many ways the kind of criminal biography that was later to flourish. At the point, however, where Dugdale might have detailed "her vttermost indeuors to obtaine [God's] mercie, and forgiueness," he declines describing "the perticulars thereof," for "it would not only be endlesse, and tedious, but I doubt, to the hearers and readers, it would be though[t] incredible" (*Practises of Elizabeth Caldwell* [1604], sig. [B3v]).

5 *The Life and Penitent Death of John Mawgridge* (1708), p. [2]; see also M. Misson, *Memoirs and Observations in His Travels over England* (1719), p. 311, and Thomas Brown, *Works*, 5th ed. (1720), 4:42. For Barnwell, see Theophilus

Cibber, *The Lives of the Poets of Great Britain and Ireland* (1753), 5:339, and "Some Remarks on . . . George Barnwell," the *Weekly Register*, 21 August 1731, rptd. in *Essays on the Theatre from Eighteenth Century Periodicals*, ed. John Loftis (1960). Barnwell, an apprentice who killed his uncle early in the seventeenth century, was made the subject of a ballad, some pamphlets, and an immensely popular five-act tragedy by George Lillo, *The London Merchant; or, The History of George Barnwell* (1731).

6   For more information bearing on the possible readership of criminal biography, see Appendix I. According to one historian of crime in early modern England, "the presence of a large number of household servants, for the most part young and essentially rootless, constituted a permanent problem for those trying to attain a disciplined and well-ordered society." Nor was this merely some large, abstract, ideological problem, for as seventeenth-century legal depositions reveal, "servants were very susceptible to the temptation of petty theft from their employers" (Sharpe, *Crime in Seventeenth-Century England*, p. 166).

7   John Reynolds, *The Triumphs of Gods Revenge against Murther* (1704; 1st pub. 1621–35), p. 134; James Guthrie, Ordinary Account, 17 February 1743 (see also 21 December 1739); John Dod and Robert Cleaver, *A Plain and Familiar Exposition of the Ten Commandments*, 19th ed. (1635), p. 242; *Remarkable Criminals* (1735a), p. 327 (see also p. 6); Thomas Wood, *Institute of the Laws of England*, 2nd ed. (1722), p. 346. Scottish law went further than English law, allowing for the murder of someone "under the trust, credit, assurance, and power of the Slayer" to be punished as treason (see *The Tryal of Philip Standsfield* [1688], p. 6, which refers to 51. Act Par. 11 K. Ja. 6).

8   Radzinowicz, *History of English Criminal Law*, vol. 1 (1948), p. 628; petit treason was first recognized by statute in 1350 and included, as well as those forms of homicide already mentioned, the murder by a cleric of his ecclesiastical superior. The information on the burning of women comes from a variety of sources and is probably not exhaustive; see Radzinowicz, *History*, 1:209, Applebee's *Original Weekly Journal*, 28 July 1722, 16 March and 6 April 1723, 14 March 1724, 26 April 1729, 27 March 1731; *The Newgate Calendar* (1773), 4:132; William Jackson, *The New & Complete Newgate Calendar* (1794 ff.), 4:29, 251; William Connor Sydney, *England and the English in the Eighteenth Century* (1891), 2:298–99; Arthur Griffiths, *The Chronicles of Newgate* (1884), 1:354; John Deane Potter, *The Art of Hanging* (1969), p. 129. The statute against petit treason was not repealed until 9 Geo. 4, though the burning of women at the stake had stopped some decades earlier. The last woman burned in England suffered not for the murder of her husband, interestingly enough, but for coining; this crime was considered a form of treason against the king, whose image it literally defaced. Her name was Christian Murphy, also known as Bowan, and she suffered in 1789; see Octogenarius, "Punishment of Death by Burning," *Notes and Queries* 2 (1850): 260–61.

9 Guthrie, Ordinary Account, 14 September 1741; *The Authentick Tryals of John Swan, and Elizabeth Jeffreyes: With the Tryal of Miss Mary Blandy* (1752), p. 73.

10 On this point see Coke, *The Third Part of the Institutes* (1644), p. 20. The statute book ought not, however, to be taken as a direct reflection of popular attitudes. Husbands who murdered their wives committed no special offense so far as the law was concerned, but they were as interesting to the popular literature of crime as wives who murdered their husbands. Women who killed their babies, on the other hand, despite the special legal status of their offense, got relatively little long-term attention, being rarely admitted to the big collections of criminal biography; and this is all the more remarkable given the frequency of their crime. "The 'infanticide wave,' in [seventeenth-century] England at least," writes J. A. Sharpe, "may have resulted in more executions than the more familiar witch craze"; by the end of the century, in any case, it "was being indicted roughly as often as simple homicide" (*Crime in Early Modern England, 1550–1750* [1984], pp. 61–62; for more on the subject, see R. W. Malcolmson, "Infanticide in the Eighteenth Century," in *Crime in England, 1550–1800,* ed. J. S. Cockburn [1977], pp. 187–209). Sharpe has elsewhere noted, in a study of thirty-five seventeenth-century ballads and pamphlets, that "the popular literature pays little attention to the deaths of children or apprentices," even though these were far more frequent outcomes of domestic violence than the spouse murders it generally featured ("Domestic Homicide in Early Modern England," *The Historical Journal* 24 [1981]: 41).

11 Defoe, *The Family Instructor,* vol. 2 (1718), part 1, esp. Dialogue 3; Lawrence Stone, *The Family, Sex, and Marriage in England, 1500–1800* (1977), passim. On "the relative duties" see, for instance, William Fleetwood, *The Relative Duties of Parents, Husbands, Masters, Wives, Children, Servants* (1705). It is possible, too, that interest in familiar murder was spurred by its growing prominence relative to the overall level of violence in society as a whole. "In the fourteenth century," according to Lawrence Stone, "only 8 per cent of all English homicides took place within the biological family (excluding apprentices and servants), about 15 per cent in the late sixteenth century, about 20 per cent in the seventeenth century, and about 50 per cent today." This growing proportion, he points out, is a consequence of the family homicide rate remaining fairly constant, while, since the thirteenth century, the general homicide rate has steadily declined; and this decline was "especially rapid between about 1660 and 1800" ("Interpersonal Violence in English Society, 1300–1980," *Past and Present* 101 [1983]: 27, 32; Stone relies heavily on T. R. Gurr, "Historical Trends in Violent Crime: A Critical View of the Evidence," *Crime and Justice: An Annual Review of Research* 3 [1981], 295–353).

12 In all my reading I've encountered only a few murders where explicit political issues were raised. A complete listing will show how rare the phenomenon was. In 1678 the murder of Sir Edmund Berry Godfrey touched off the hysteria of the Popish Plot, and some thought that the

murder of Thomas Thynne in 1681 (for which see Chapter 4) was similarly motivated. The discovery of parts of a corpse near the Savoy caused further suspicions of Popish skulduggery in 1688; these, however, were quickly allayed when the crime was found to be an ordinary husband-murder (see *A Hellish Murder Committed by a French Midwife* [1688] and *A Cabinet of Grief* [1688]). Otherwise, little political hay was made of murder or suspected murder. The fact that James Selby was a Tory and a notorious persecutor of Dissenters was exploited by his enemies when he murdered his mistress in 1691, and it seems that Spencer Cowper was unjustly suspected of drowning an ex-sweetheart in 1699 because his Whig activism did not suit the political prejudices of the neighborhood (see *The Unhappy Citizen. A Faithful Narrative of the Life and Death of James Selby* [1691] and, among others, *The Tryal of Spencer Cowper, John Marson, Ellis Stevens, and William Rogers for the Murther of Mrs. Sarah Stout* [1699]). In 1722 a murder was blamed on the "poisonous tenets" of the *London Journal*, a radical Whig paper, and in the same year resentments raised by the South Sea crisis figured in an unsuccessful conspiracy to murder (see Applebee's *Original Weekly Journal*, 3 February 1722, 24 March 1722; Read's *Weekly Journal*, 24 March 1722).

13 *The Bloody Murtherer, or, the Unnatural Son* (1672), p. 15.

CHAPTER 3

1   Bronislaw Malinowski, *Crime and Custom in Savage Society* (1967), pp. 87–91.

2   Howard Jones, *Crime in a Changing Society* (1967), p. 38.

3   "The Wonder in fact is," says Fielding, "that we have not a thousand more Robbers than we have; indeed, that all these Wretches are not Thieves, must give us either a very high Idea of their Honesty, or a very mean one of their Capacity and Courage" (*Late Increase of Robbers* [1751], p. 143). See also his *Proposal for Making an Effectual Provision for the Poor* (1753), where he says "the sufferings of the Poor are indeed less observed than their Misdeeds" (p. 9) but points out the two are directly connected. Fielding proposes to diminish both by forcing the poor into workhouses, an idea by no means original to him (thus see also, for example, *An Account of the Corporation for the Poor of London* [1713], pp. 17–18, and *An Account of Several Work-Houses for Employing and Maintaining the Poor*, 2nd ed. [1732], p. xii).

4   John Haslewood, Assize Sermon, 24 July 1707, p. 8. The 1734 Johnson echoes this point, saying that "a Man who has given a Loose to his Inclinations, and always placed his Happiness in the pursuit of irregular pleasures, will, when Necessity stares him in the Face, do any thing in the World, rather than quit the Chace and make Virtue the Object of his Wishes and Pains" (*Highwaymen* [1734], p. 370). The author of *Remarkable Criminals* (1735a) takes an even harder line. Noting that necessity is often "urged" by thieves because "nothing could be a greater alleviation of [their] crime," he

finds it "hard to judge the reasonableness of such an excuse" because the
meaning of the word is "so equivocal" (p. 437). Elsewhere he goes so far
as to say that "in all the loads of papers I have turned over to this purpose"
he has never found, "in strictness," a true case of necessity prompting
crime, "though as the best motive to excite compassion, and consequently
to obtain mercy, it is made very often a pretence" (p. 228). "Our Laws
[make] such provision for the poor," wrote Jeremy Collier, that it is rare
indeed that anyone should have "neither Friends nor Strength to support
him," and so be obliged to steal "to keep Life and Soul together" (*Essays
upon Several Moral Subjects. Part IV* [1709], p. 30; see also Gabriel Towerson, *An Exposition of the Catechism of the Church of England. Part II* [1681],
p. 425, and *The Explanation of the Ten Commandments* [1796?], part 3, pp.
3–4). Though Defoe would not have agreed with these last opinions, he,
too, thought little of necessity as a reason or justification for criminal
behavior. "When Men are poor, and are found guilty of little Prevarica-
tions and Infractions of Principle, Necessity and Poverty is the Plea, and
passes with some People for an Excuse; though, by the Way," he wrote,
"it is no more so, than Poverty is a Plea at the *Old baily,* for committing a
Robbery or a Burglary" (*Complete English Tradesman,* 2nd. ed. [1727], vol.
2, part. 1, p. 20). Though he believed that "Necessity will make us all
Thieves," he did not believe people became necessitous innocently: "*the
Crime,*" he insisted, "*is in the Cause of that Necessity*" (the *Review,* 3:113a [7
March 1706], ed. Arthur Wellesley Secord [1938]; see Maximillian E. Novak, *Defoe and the Nature of Man* [1963], pp. 65–88, for a thorough discussion of Defoe's views on necessity). Despite the severity of all this discourse, pleas of necessity could apparently mitigate the decisions of the
courts on degrees of guilt and punishment. Thus Douglas Hay notes that
during periods of high food prices juries tended more often to convict on
reduced and so noncapital charges than when prices were low ("War,
Dearth and Theft in the Eighteenth Century: The Record of the English
Courts," *Past and Present* 95 [1982]: 154–55). On this same subject, see also
John Langbein's anecdotal evidence on recommendations for pardon ("*Albion's* Fatal Flaws," *Past and Present* 98 [1983]: 111–12, 113) and Peter
King's interpretation of sentencing statistics as indicating "general sympathies for destitute convicts and their innocent families" ("Decision-
Makers and Decision-Making in the English Criminal Law, 1750–1800,"
The Historical Journal 27 [1984]: 41–42). Whatever people may have *said,*
they seem nonetheless to have been able to entertain, at least at some level,
the possibility that individual criminals were not entirely at fault for their
crimes. For more on the possible disparity between public talk and private
feeling, see Chapter 7. For the social and economic factors that actually
influenced eighteenth-century crime rates, often unbeknownst to contemporaries, see Hay, "War, Dearth and Theft," pp. 122–46, and J. M. Beattie, "The Pattern of Crime in England," *Past and Present* 62 (1974): 84–95.

5 Lunacy gets even shorter shrift as a motive in the popular literature of
crime, there being more than a few cases of its reporting criminals found

compos mentis despite extraordinary evidence to the contrary. One of the most lurid of these to my knowledge is the case of Edmund Audley, hanged in 1698 for the murder of Hannah Bullevant. Audley had a history of threatening people on the grounds they were conspiring against the Protestant Succession in the interests of the exiled King James. Fixing on Mrs. Bullevant, whom he saw at a meeting house, he bought pistols, stalked her through the streets, and shot her dead in the glover's shop where she had taken refuge when his first shot missed. His victim, he claimed, was Queen Mary, James's consort, and this was not the first time he had seen her in a London meeting house. He had also seen the Prince of Wales, James's son and heir, at the House of Commons. Convinced that his trial was part of the plot, he demanded to see King William to give him his information. Audley persisted in his "Whimsical Stories" even after he was found guilty, but the notion that he was "a Lunatick, or distracted Person," was utterly dismissed. The divines who gathered around him, hoping to bring him to a condign repentance, found only that he "much [depended] on his own conceited knowledge, and continued sullen and obstinate" (*Account of Audley* [1698], p. 8). Less spectacular instances of obvious insanity show the same tendency to discount madness as a source of crime. In 1712 Joseph Philips slit the throat of a six-year-old child because, he said, "he had a mind to die." "Several Witnesses endeavour'd to prove him lunatick, but by a great many others it appeared to be quite otherwise, and that he was rather sullen than mad" (*Compleat Tryals* [1718, 1721], 3:109). Philips was hanged in due course, as was the murderer of a five-year-old child in 1751, who "said, that about six Weeks before this Violence offered to the poor Infant, she had laboured under a severe Fever, which held her for three Weeks, which Nature at length got the better of, very little assisted by Physick. And she constantly affirmed, that from that Time she was always in a Hurry and Confusion of Spirits, and could have no Rest Day or Night, seldom shut her Eyes to sleep, or if she did, she was disturbed with Starts and Fears. She was continually running up and down Stairs, and could never sit down long to Business, her Spirits being continually agitated and flurried, but by what Means she could give no Account: She said, she had been several Times tempted to lay violent Hands on herself, at other Times on her own Children, of which she acquainted her husband, who only said she was whimsical or maggotty; but never took any Pains to find out the Cause of this Disorder in her Senses." "After the Warrant for Execution came down," the text adds, "she seemed much better . . . but could give no farther or better Account than as above" (*Select Trials* [1764] 2:126–27, 128). Such evidence must be treated carefully, for of course it deals only with criminals found guilty and punished. Lunacy was an allowable plea before the law in seventeenth- and eighteenth-century England, and it was not infrequently a successful defense (thus see Applebee's *Original Weekly Journal*, 25 July 1719 and 6 May 1721, for cases where criminals were judged lunatic, and also the standard history of the treatment of mental disorder in criminal law, Nigel Walker,

Crime and Insanity in England, vol. 1: *The Historical Perspective* [1968], esp.
chaps. 2 and 3). My main point, however, is that the popular literature of
crime was in no position to reopen the cases of criminals already hanged; in
fact, it wanted to keep them closed. People were "executed for Murder . . . that others may fear to offend," writes J. Brydall, "and therefore a
Man that is *non compos mentis* . . . is not . . . within the statute . . . for the
end of punishment is that others may be deterred. . . . but such punishment can be no example to mad Men" (J[ohn] B[rydall], *A Compendious
Collection of the Laws of England, Touching Matters Criminal* [1675], pp. 14,
114). We need only to consider the logic of this to see why, once they were
executed, the insanity of lunatic criminals had to be disregarded.

6 *An Account of a Bold Desperate and Notorious Robbery* (1700), and *A Full and
True Account of a Most Horrid and Barbarous Murder Committed Yesterday,
April 24th* (1711). For similar sentiments, see *A True Account of a Bloody
Murther Committed by Three Foot-Padders in Fig-Lane* (1685/6), p. 1; *An
Account of the Malefactors That Received Their Majesties Most Gracious Pardon*
(1693); and *The Life of Mr. Charles Drew* (1740), p. 3.

7 An earlier, more credulous age had been content to blame the Devil, and
the law, always conservative, retained a trace of this belief. "Not having
the fear of God before his/her eyes," bills of indictment typically ran, "but
being moved by the instigation of the Devil," the prisoner before the bar
had committed such-and-such a crime. How much this was only a figure
of speech by the late seventeenth century is difficult to know; certainly it
could not have had much explanatory power. "It is the Devil that animates
men on to murther," declared one mid-seventeenth-century writer in no
uncertain terms, but his description of the process leaves much to be desired: "when men, for want of Grace, do forsake God, God doth justly
forsake them; and then the Devil enters into them, and carrieth them forth
into all manner of wickedness." He is better when less prolix: "men kill
and slay," he rhymes, "Their dearest Friends, the Devil to obey" (*The
Devils Reign upon Earth, Being a Relation of Several Sad and Bloudy Murthers
Lately Committed* [1655], pp. 10, [14]). It is a fact that certain murderers did
lay their crimes to the Devil's power over them, even so late as the eighteenth century, and some claimed to have felt this power firsthand. "The
Devil being strong with me, persuaded me to be revenged of her," explained John Marketman in 1680 after killing his wife (*A Full and True
Account of the Penitence of John Marketman* [1680], pp. 4–50). When Paul
Lorrain asked Mary Ellenor in 1708 how she could be "so cruel and hard-
hearted" as to suffocate her infant in a jakes, pushing him down with a
broomstick when he continued to cry, she said "the Devil had too much
power over her" (Lorrain, Ordinary Account, 27 October 1708). Such
confessions were conventional enough, but sometimes the Devil could be
reported to have taken on tangible form. In 1655 Theophilus Higgons
sought to dispel a number of rumors about a murder committed in his
neighborhood, one of them being that the Devil had appeared to the
murderer "in a visible shape and that he had a conference with him"

(R[obert] Boreman, *A Mirrour of Mercy and Iudgement. Or, an Exact True Narrative of the Life and Death of Freeman Sonds Esquier* [1655], p. 20). In 1690 Edward Mangall claimed that he murdered Elizabeth Johnson because "the Devil put him upon it; appearing to him in a *Flash of Lightening*, and directing him where to find the *Club*, wherewith he committed the *Murder*" (*A Full and True Relation of the Examination and Confession of W. Barwick and E. Mangall, of Two Horrid Murders* [1690], p. 4). An even more bizarre story was told by Charity Philpot in 1681. "Being certainly Instigated by the Devil, and not having the fear of God before her eyes," she "on a sudden without cause given [had] rushed in upon her Mistress, who was in a Room with her Child . . . and told her Mistress, that she came to kill her, and then she would fire her House." Her mistress fled in fright 'but unfortunately left her child behind, and Charity slit its throat. Though she had nothing specific to say about the Devil, she did tell the people who seized her that "a Man in a High-crown'd Hat bid her to do it, and he had whetted the knife and put it into her hand, and also told her she should fire the House." How much her neighbors and friends were satisfied by such an explanation we have no way of telling, for Charity was found dead the next morning by her own hand and the case never came to trial (*Murther by a Maid Who Poysoned Her Self* [1681], pp. 1–2). Whether the Devil was accepted as a real force in human motivation or not, the mere concept of him could make for interesting stories. I particularly like the following example: "The Devil tempting a young man to one of these three sins, either to kill his Father, or else to lie with his mother, or else to be drunk; he thinking to yeeld to the lesser, namely to be drunk, that thereby he might (as he conceived) be freed from the other, which no doubt were then odious in his eyes, he yeelded to the Devil to be drunk, and then being drunk, he first killed his father, and after committed abomination with his mother" (*The Devils Reign* [1655], pp. 12–13). A version of this story appears in Defoe's *Colonel Jack* (1965; 1st pub. 1722), p. 241.

8 *Remarkable Criminals* (1735a), p. 20.

9 Ibid., pp. 136–37; see also *The Life of Mr. John Stanley* (1723), which serves as the source of the account quoted here and makes the same points at greater length and more vividly.

10 *The Suffolk Parricide, Being, the Trial, Life, Transactions, and Last Dying Words, of Charles Drew, of Long-Melford. . . . By a Gentleman of Long-Melford* (1740), pp. 3–6, 32–33. For other accounts of Drew, see *The Genuine Trial of Charles Drew. . . . By a Gentleman of Bury* (1740), and *The Life of Mr. Charles Drew* (1740). Consider also the account of Drew in *The Newgate Calendar* (1773), 3:3–9, which greatly simplifies Drew's motives, blaming the crime wholly on the instigations of his mistress, a greedy, sex-crazed widow.

11 Cf. not only Defoe's *Moll Flanders* (1722), *Colonel Jack* (1722), and *Roxana* (1724) but also plays like Edward Young's *The Revenge* (1721), Aaron Hill's *Fatal Extravagance* (1721, 1726), George Lillo's *The London Merchant* (1731), and Edward Moore's *The Gamester* (1753), each of which takes

pains to endow its leading wrongdoers with psychological case histories that, though often crude by modern standards, are more or less sufficient to explain their crimes; see, for example, Millwood's self-justifying speech in 4:2 of *The London Merchant,* which explains both her own corruption and her power over Barnwell.

12   *Remarkable Criminals* (1735a), p.324 (see also, e.g., pp. 54, 62, 114); pp. 83, 80.

13   Ibid., p. 156.

14   William Price, *The Birth, Parentage, and Education, Life and Conversation of Mr. Christopher Slaughterford* (1709), p. 2.

15   *The Suffolk Parricide* (1740), p. 7.

16   *A True and Perfect Relation of the Tryal and Condemnation, Execution and Last Speech of That Unfortunate Gentleman Mr. Robert Foulks* (1678/[9]), p. 4.

17   Johnson, *Highwaymen* (1734), pp. 316–17.

18   *Remarkable Criminals* (1735a), pp. 128, 451, 118.

19   S[amuel] Foote, *The Genuine Memoirs of the Life of Sir John Dinely Goodere, Bart. Who was Murder'd by the Contrivance of His Own Brother* (1741), pp. 7, 9, 9–10. The title page identifies Foote as "of Worcester-College, Oxford, and a Nephew to the late Sir John." For a fascinating account of the erratic (but in some ways typical) life of Sir John Dinely Goodere, and the complicated background to his murder, see Lawrence Stone, "Money, Sex and Murder in Eighteenth-Century England," in *Women and Society in the Eighteenth Century,* ed. Ian P. H. Duffy (1983), pp. 15–28.

20   [J. Penrose], *The Reverend Mr. Penrose's Account of the Behaviour, Confession, and Last Dying Words, of the Four Malefactors Executed at Bristol* (Bristol and London, 1741), pp. 11–12. Penrose prints Goodere's account of his part in Admiral Byng's expedition to Spain in 1719 and says that as a naval officer he "behaved with great gallantry and bravery." Penrose points out that he got his command by "merit and interest," and Goodere's own men had also a high opinion of him. At the trial an "abundance" of sailors appeared in his behalf, some testifying "in the most moving manner, that he was as gallant and brave a sailor as ever step [*sic*] between stem and stern of a ship, and he was so belov'd of them, that they would go to the mouth of a cannon to serve him" (pp. 6–7; *Trial of Goodere* [1741], p. 24).

21   *Remarkable Criminals* (1735a), pp. 292–93, 451, 241.

22   *Fair Warning to Murderers of Infants* (1692), p. [iii]; Edmund Kirk, *The Sufferers Legacy to Surviving Sinners: or Edmund Kirk's Dying Advice* (1684); *A Serious Advice to the Citizens of London* ([1657]; t.p. missing in Brit. Lib. copy), pp. [5–6], and also *The Unhappy Citizen* (1691), p. 9.

23   The "concept" of a separate criminal class, John J. Tobias suggests, "developed gradually after 1815" (*Crime and Industrial Society in the Nineteenth Century* [1972], pp. 59 ff.). If true, and the eighteenth century does seem to have lacked this concept, it is curious indeed that a class of professional criminals should have existed relatively unnoticed some 250 years before it was finally recognized as a social category in its own right; see also n. 26 to this chapter.

24 *Remarkable Criminals* (1735a), pp. 279, 150. "Let us labour to keep our selves from envie and hatred, and take heede of revenge," advise John Dod and Robert Cleaver, "and God will keepe us from committing murder. He that makes conscience and prayeth against the least, shall keepe himselfe safe from falling into the greatest" (*A Plain and Familiar Exposition of the Ten Commandments* [1635], p. 243). Cynthia Herrup has appropriately called such doctrine "a 'domino theory' of human character"; for its possible effect on the actual treatment of criminals within the legal process, see her article, "Law and Morality in Seventeenth-Century England," *Past and Present* 106 (1985): 102–23.

25 George Birkbeck Hill, ed., *Johnsonian Miscellanies* (1897), 2:285, and Boswell's *Life of Johnson*, ed. George Birkbeck Hill and L. F. Powell (1934), 3:271.

26 Smith includes "The Thieves' New Canting Dictionary" in the fifth edition of the *Highwaymen* (1719). Richard Head gives a word list of thieves' slang in part 1 of *The English Rogue* and claims "the first inventor of canting . . . was hanged about four-score years [ago]" (Richard Head and Francis Kirkman, *The English Rogue* [1928; 1st pub. 1665], pp. 29–34). Actually, Thomas Harman published a commentary on thieves' slang in 1566; see *A Caueat for Common Cvrsetors,* most recently rptd. by Gāmini Salgādo, ed., *Cony-Catchers and Bawdy Baskets* (1972). The existence of a criminal underworld – "these Rogues have a Society among themselves, over which they have a Principal, or President" – is indicated by *The Catterpillers of This Nation* (1659), p. 3, and also by *The Devils Cabinet Broke Open: Or a New Discovery of the High-Way Thieves* (1658), pp. 38–39; *The Life and Death of Mary Frith* (1662), p. 25; [Charles Hitchin?], *The Regulator: Or, a Discovery of the Thieves, Thief-Takers, and Locks, Alias Receivers of Stolen Goods* (1718); and of course all the accounts of Jonathan Wild stimulated by his arrest and execution in 1725.

27 Smith, *Highwaymen* (1719a), p. 304. It is typical, in fact, for thieves' lives to stress the rational calculation behind their actions. Unable to "confine himself in his Expences and Attendance, within the narrow bounds and limits of a Servant," and realizing "he must have some new way to get money," Duval is "not long unresolved what course to take, for being brought acquainted with a Knot of High-way-men, (having before observed their way of living) a little perswasion now serves his turn; he resolves to make one with Them" (*Life of Deval* [1669/70], p. 3). William Page shows even more deliberation. Before deciding to take to the highway, he "seriously consider'd the Hazards he must necessarily encounter" and his own fitness to deal with them: " 'Tis true, he was conscious that he had Courage enough. . . . But then, on the other Hand, he was equally sensible, that Courage was no Defence against the Chance Stroke of a Bullet." He is aware that highwaymen "seldom" escape hanging, but he sees "no other Way to extricate himself from [his present Distress]," and so, "being thus resolv'd, his first Care was to provide himself with a Brace of Pistols" (*Genuine Life of Page* [1758], pp. 4–5). For similar uses of the word "resolved," see, for example, Smith, *Highwaymen* (1719*a*), pp. 26, 68, 223; James Guthrie, Ordinary Accounts, 13 February 1739, 16 September 1741; *Select Trials* (1742), 1:210.

28 As it happened, two of Dr. Johnson's closest friends, Savage and Baretti, came close to proving his point. Some years before Johnson met him, Savage killed a man during the course of a fight in a tavern. Found guilty of manslaughter, he was allowed to plead benefit of clergy and so escaped hanging (see *The Life of Mr. Richard Savage, Condemned for the Murder of Mr J. Sinclair* [1727], and also *Select Trials* [1742], 3:77–89). Baretti would seem a man far less likely to get in trouble with the law, but in eighteenth-century London even an Italian musicologist could find himself involved in a brawl, kill a man, be arrested, imprisoned, and tried for his life. Walking through the Haymarket, Baretti was accosted by a prostitute who squeezed his groin. He struck her, almost by reflex, and her bully, who was standing nearby, became threatening. Baretti tried to flee but was mobbed. His glasses broken, he slashed out desperately with a knife he normally carried to peel fruit, cut a man who bled to death, and was committed to Newgate. There Johnson visited him and, typically, advised him to anticipate the worst. At his trial Baretti was acquitted on grounds of self-defense, Johnson, Goldsmith, Burke, Reynolds, and Garrick all testifying to his good character and the court deciding there was nothing suspicious in an Italian carrying a knife to peel fruit (see Old Bailey Sessions Paper, 18–21, 23 October 1769).

29 In France, for instance, such descriptions are notably absent. Thus, despite a taste for "the horrible details" in sixteenth- and seventeenth-century accounts of various accidents and catastrophes, Jean-Pierre Seguin points out, the popular literature of crime "remain[s] fairly discreet about the circumstances of murders, often recounting them in a few lines" ("L'Information en France avant le périodique: 500 canards imprimés entre 1529 et 1631," *Arts et traditions populaires* 11 [1963]: 126). In my experience the point holds true for eighteenth-century French texts as well (for sample titles, see Chapter 5, n. 17).

30 For allegations of incest in the Hayes case, see *A Narrative of the Barbarous and Unheard of Murder of Mr. John Hayes, by Catherine His Wife* (1726), pp. 24, 27, 28. In their accounts of the Hayes case, *Remarkable Criminals* (1735*a*), pp. 327–50, and *The Newgate Calendar* (1773), 2:185–211, simply assert the filial connection between Catherine and her accomplice, claiming (incorrectly) that she acknowledged it but omitting all mention of incest. In 1722 Mathias Brinsden, who had murdered his wife, was "prest so much [by the Newgate ordinary] to own . . . Incest with his Daughter" that he and the other condemned prisoners complained they were being hindered in their efforts to come to terms with God (See R. Manson, *The Case of Mathias Brinsden*, rptd. in *Select Trials* [1742], 1:254). Eugene Aram was also accused of incest with his daughter, and credited as well with atheism: "Nor is it to be wondered at . . . that he . . . shou'd make no scruple of acting contrary to, and infringing on every law both human and divine"

(*The Genuine and Authentic Account of the Murder of Daniel Clarke* [1759], pp.
11–12). In 1708 a certain R.W. was accused of having committed incest
with his mother merely because he gathered and published the letters of
another man, who was about to be hanged for matricide (see R.W., *The
Case of John Palmer and Thomas Symonds* [1708], and *The Truth of the Case.
Or, a Full and True Account of the Horrid Murders, Robberies and Burnings,
Committed [by] John Palmer, and Tho. Symonds, Gent[s]., William Hobbins,
and John Allen, Labourers* [1708], p. 3).
31 Dickens, *The Mystery of Edwin Drood* (1956; 1st. pub. 1870), p. 225.

CHAPTER 4

1 Paul Bohannon, "Theories of Homicide and Suicide," in *African Homicide
and Suicide,* ed. Paul Bohannon (1967), p. 27.
2 Increase Mather, *A Sermon Preached at Boston March 11th 1686* (1691), p. 13.
This sermon was printed in Boston the year it was given, and the same
year in London. The edition I quote is appended to *The Wonders of Free-
Grace: Or, a Compleat History of All the Remarkable Penitents Executed at
Tyburn, and Elsewhere, for These Last Thirty Years* (1690 [*sic*]). The only
earlier collection of criminals' lives I've found that might possibly be indigenous to England is *The Lives of Sundry Notorious Villains, Together with
a Novel, as It Really Happened at Roan in France* (1678). But this is most
likely a translation of a text originally French, as all the "villains" are of
that nationality.
3 William Lupton, *A Discourse of Murther* (1725), p. 17; this was long a
commonplace. For the same notion, see John Dod and Robert Cleaver, *A
Plain and Familiar Exposition of the Ten Commandments,* 19th ed. (1635), p.
241; *The Lawes and Statutes of God, concerning the Punishment to be Inflicted
upon Wilfull Murderers* (1646), p. 3; Zachary Babington, *Advice to Grand
Jurors in Cases of Blood* (1680), pp. 28–29; Paul Lorrain, Ordinary Account,
13 March 1713; *Murder Will Out* (1717), pp. 6–7; *The Murder of Mr. John
Hayes* (1726), p. 5; James Guthrie, Ordinary Account, 5 July 1736; [J.
Penrose], *Account of the Four Malefactors Executed at Bristol the 15th of April,
1741* (1741), p. 14.
4 Mather, *Sermon* (1691), pp. 9, 12, where he quotes both these verses from
the Bible. Other relevant biblical passages included Gen. 4:11–12; Num.
33:16, 35:16–18, 21, 30–31; Prov. 28:17; Jer. 48:10; Rom. 3:15, 13:4 (see
The Lawes and Statutes of God [1646], pp. 3 ff.; Lorrain, Ordinary Account,
13 March 1713; Penrose, *Account* [1741], p. 14).
5 Mather, *Sermon* (1691), p. 12; *Mistaken Justice* (1695), p. 35. For other
expressions of the view that murder was a "crying" sin, involving "national" guilt, see Dod and Cleaver, *The Ten Commandments* (1635), p. 242;
R[obert] Boreman, *Mirrour of Mercy* (1655), p. 18; *Heavens Cry against
Murder* (1657), p. 15; *The Tryal of George Borowsky* (1682), p. 55; *The Truth
of the Case* (1708), p. 32; *Murder Will Out* (1717), pp. 8, 10; *Compleat Tryals*
(1718, 1721), 1:429, 4:225; Penrose, *Account* (1741), p. 14. The notion that

unpunished murder brought guilt to the collective was long established in English law. Babington quotes from a statute of 3 Hen. 7 c. I., "If the Murtherer escape the Town shall be amerced" (*Advice* [1680], p. 89), and though this statute seems to have fallen into abeyance, the justices of the King's Bench cited it as late as 1739 (see Old Bailey Sessions Paper, 2–5 May 1739). During the religious fervor of the Interregnum the murderer's guilt could seem especially contagious, and this was probably the view of Dissenters for some time thereafter. Thus *A Serious Advice to the Citizens of London* (1657), pp. [6–7]: "We desire you to mourne over the crying sins that are to be found amongst us . . . Swearing, Drunkenness, Uncleanness, Profanation of the Lords Day, Contempt of the Gospel, and of the Ministry thereof; nay, even Blood-guiltiness. . . . And what reason have you to admire the patience of God to this *City?* Tis a wonder London is not made as Sodom, that defoliation doth not seize upon your houses, that you are not all swept away."

6   "Never more killing of men by Duels, Tavern, and Game-house Quarrels," writes Babington of the present age, "and yet never more impunity to such Man-Killers . . . especially if the Mankiller have either a fame for Honour or Valour, Mony, or Interest of Friends, to procure pity, or pardon and compassion" (*Advice* [1680], pp. 92–93). But as he insists elsewhere, citing the authority of Deut. 19:10 and 13, "*Wilful Murther cannot be pardoned without Gods high displeasure*" (pp. 36–37). For a case involving "wild Hectorian Gentlemen," who killed a man in a quarrel and were appropriately hanged, see *The Bloody Murtherers Executed* (1675); others in this genre include *Boteler's Case* (1678) and *A Barbarous Murther* (1684). Two very interesting accounts of drunken members of the upper classes killing sober members of the middle and lower classes are *Great and Bloody News. From Turnham-Green. Or a Relation of a Sharp Encounter. Between the Earl of Pembroke, and His Company, with the Constable and Watch Belonging to the Parish of Chiswick* (1680), and *A True Relation, of the Horrid and Barbarous Murther, Committed on the Body of Mr. Loggins, Gent. and the Ostler of the King's-Head in Coleshill, in the County of Warwick* (1686). The first of these pamphlets prompted some friend or flunky of the earl of Pembroke to defend him against "the tender Consciences of the People": "his Lordship is no Monster, has no Cloven-feet, no Sawcer-eyes, but is e'en just such another Man as their own Relations; onely with this difference, That he has more Gallantry and Honour, and cannot bear the insolent Affronts of the *MOBILE* without Resentment" (*An Impartial Account of the Misfortune That Lately Happened to the Right Honorable Philip Earl of Pembrooke and Montgomery* [1680], p. 4).

7   Fielding, *Examples of the Interposition of Providence in the Detection and Punishment of Murder* (1752), pp. 3–4; see also *Murder Will Out* (1717), p. 9. Essentially the same point is made by *Heavens Cry against Murder* (1657), which cites as examples of "God's severe Judgements executed against Murder" the cases of Cain, Joab, Zimri, Saul, Ahab, and Jezebel, and that of the Jews in general "for murdering the holy Prophets, and Christ him-

self" (pp. 17–32). For the author of this pamphlet the Bible is history enough, and, interestingly, almost all of it is bracketed within two murders: Abel's, showing the first full measure of human depravity, and Christ's, providing the means to redeem it.

8 Lupton, *Discourse* (1725), p. 17; Thomas Beard and Thomas Taylor, *The Theatre of Gods Judgements*, 4th ed. (1748), p. 214; this work was first published in 1597. For echoes of Beard and Taylor, see *The Murder Committed by Mr. George Strangewayes* (1659), p. 3; *The Notorious Wicked Life of Capt. Harrison* (1692), pp. 2–3; and *Most Strange and Wonderful News from a Place Call'd the Leister, in the Parish of St. Martins in the Fields* (1693?). In all these sources, it is important to note, there is a linkage between miracles in the phenomenal world and the murderer's betrayal by "his owne heart and tongue."

9 "So certainly does the Revenge of God pursue the Abominated *MUR-DERER*," writes the author of *The Examination and Confession of W. Barwick and E. Mangall* (1690), "that when Witnesses are wanting of the Fact, the very Ghost of the *Murdered-Parties* cannot rest quiet in their Graves, till they have made the Detection themselves" (p. 1). For an especially interesting account of a ghost's appearance leading to the arrest of his murderer, see *A True Relation of a Horrid Murder Committed upon the Person of Thomas Kidderminster, Gent. at the White-Horse Inn in Chelmsford in 1654. Together with a True Account of the Strange and Providential Discovery of the Same Nine Years after: For Which Moses Drague, an Hostler in the Said Inn, Was Executed in 1667, Being Thirteen Years after the Commission of the Said Murder* (1688). Belonging to an earlier era is a fifteen-page black-letter pamphlet in the Pepys Library called *Murthers' Reward; Being a True and Exact Account of a Most Cruel and Barbarous Murther Committed by One Gabriel Harding, Who Inhumanely Murthered His Own Wife, for Which Bloody & Cruel Deed He Was Justly Punished in a Severe Manner, the Devil Breaking His Neck in the Presence of Many Spectators, to the Admiration of Them All* (n.d.; listed in neither the Wing *Short-title Catalogue* nor Pollard and Redgrave's). Murderers usually underwent physical alterations somewhat less drastic. In 1675, shortly after confessing, a murderer was reported to have had a fit in which his tongue turned black and protruded from his mouth. His fit subsided only when an accomplice was arrested (*Three Inhumane Murthers, Committed by One Bloody Person, upon His Father, His Mother, and His Wife* [1675]). In 1635 Thomas Sherwood's nose gushed blood when he went to view the corpse of his victim ([Henry Goodcole?], *Heavens Speedie Hue and Cry Sent after Lust and Murther* [1635], sig. C3r), and in 1708 the same thing happened to Thomas Symonds, who rather lamely claimed at his trial that it was "the Unhappiness of [his] Constitution, to be very apt to bleed at the Nose" (*The Truth of the Case* [1708], pp. 6–7). Mather also describes the case of a murderer bleeding "at all the passages of his Body, and he died suddenly" (*Sermon* [1691], p. 10). Phenomena like these might be seen as variations on "God's usual Method of discovering Murders," i.e., by causing the corpse to bleed in the presence of its killer. The quoted phrase belongs to the

attorney who prosecuted Philip Standsfield for the murder of his father in 1688. He thought it significant that, though the elder Standsfield's corpse had been exhumed, autopsied, washed, and sewn up by the surgeons, it had nonetheless bled when Philip touched it, staining his fingers. The defense argued that "this is but a superstitious observation without any ground either in Law or Reason," but the corpse's bleeding was often mentioned in the trial, and Standsfield was convicted (*Tryal of Standsfield* [1688], pp. 4, 7, also 13, 25, 30). According to a broadside published in 1699, three people were convicted of murder in the fourth year of Charles I's reign because the corpse of their victim, when they were made to touch it, "which was before a livid and Carrion Colour . . . began to have a Dew, or gentle Sweat arise on it, which increas'd by degrees, till the Sweat ran down in drops on the Face, the Brow turn'd and chang'd to a lively and Fresh Colour, and the Dead opened one of her Eyes, and shut it again; and this opening the Eye was done three several times; she likewise thrust out the Ring or Marriage Finger 3 times" – one of the accused was her husband – "and pulled it in again, and the Finger dropped Blood from it on the Grass" (*The Case of a Murther in Hertfordshire. Found amongst the Papers of Sir John Maynard* [1699]). In 1659 the authorities made George Strangewayes touch the corpse of the man he was suspected of shooting, and when nothing happened were disappointed. But then, "to the amazing wonder of future Ages, and the farther confirmation of those continued miracles by which the All-discerning power of the eternal and everliving God pleases often to manifest it self in the discovery of black and secret murders," one of the jurors in the case, a gunsmith, recollected he had hired out a carbine to a friend of the murderer on the very day the crime was committed. With this, the case against Strangewayes fell into place, and he was hanged (*The Unhappy Marksman* [1659], pp. 13–14). The popular mind was ever alert to anomalous circumstances in cases of murder, especially if these concerned blood. Thus it seemed "very remarkable" that, on the morning of the day he murdered his wife, John Marketman, a surgeon, was called to bleed a woman but she would not bleed, though he made the incisions twice. Later, this account portentously notes, he stabbed his wife "in four several places (and not one of them Bled)" (*Penitence of Marketman* [1680?], pp. 4–5). In 1741 James Hall took great precautions against leaving any traces of his master's murder, but "some of the Blood was spilt on the Floor, which *Hall* endeavored to wipe off, but in vain; neither could the Woman, who wash'd the Chambers, ever remove it" (Guthrie, Ordinary Account, 14 September 1741). As late as 1759, though by then it seemed "a vulgar, superstitious custom," a suspected murderer could be made to touch the bones of his victim at a coroner's inquest (see *Murder of Clarke* [1759], p. 46). The rationale behind such a procedure by that date, however, was thoroughly psychological. Thus the following grisly (and unsuccessful) experiment in 1735, after an examining magistrate had ordered two surgeons to inspect the wounds of a murdered woman: "On their return they brought with them her Scalp (cut thro' in 13 Places,

and to Appearance, with a very sharp Instrument,) and 38 pieces of her
Scull, which the Justice caused to be laid before him, and holding the
Scalp, between him and the Light made [the suspect] take notice of the
different Cuts, hoping the melancholy Scene might cause a Remorse, and
work him up to a Confession, at least that it might have some effect upon
his Mind, which might make an Alteration in his Countenance, and be a
help to the Discovery; but these Views were vain, he was too harden'd to
be touched with the shocking Sight, or to be moved with any thing that
was said to him; he kept his Countenance without any visible Alteration
more then what was before observ'd . . . and persisted still in asserting his
innocence" (Philo Patriae, *Murder of Mrs. Robinson* [1735], p. 11).

10 Writes William Smythies, curate of St. Giles's, Cripplegate, and the author
of *A True Account of the Robbery and Murder of Mr. John Stockden, A Victualler in Grub-Street, and of the Discovery of the Murderers, by the several
Dreams of Elizabeth, the Wife of Thomas Greenwood, Who Was Near Neighbour
to Mr. Stockden, and Intimately Acquainted with Him* (1698): "I am sensible,
that there are many in this sceptical Age, who will ridicule and make sport
with this Relation"; it is, nonetheless, "a short, but true Account, of an
extraordinary Providence of God."

11 Fielding's stories of murders providentially discovered are gathered from
a variety of printed sources and from his own experience and that of
acquaintances. The printed sources include Plutarch's *Lives;* Richard
Knolles's *Generall Historie of the Turkes* (1st pub. 1603; 7th ed. 1701); Sir
Richard Baker's *Chronicles of the Kings of England* (1st pub. 1643; 9 eds. by
1733); Nathaniel Wanley's *Wonders of the Little World, or a General History
of Man* (1678); Richard Baxter's *The Certainty of the Worlds of Spirits*
(1691); William Turner's *Compleat History of the Most Remarkable Provi-
dences* (1697); and Andrew Moreton's (or rather Defoe's) *Secrets of the
Invisible World Disclos'd* (1729; 4th ed. 1740). Defoe provides additional
examples of the belief that providence acts in cases of murder in *Jure
Divino* (1706), part. 3, pp. 2–3, and notes; Applebee's *Original Weekly
Journal,* 3 August 1723, rptd. in William Lee, *Defoe: His Life and Recently
Discovered Writings* (1869), 3:165–68; *The Further Adventures of Robinson
Crusoe* (1905; 1st pub. 1719), p. 69; *Moll Flanders* (1971; 1st pub. 1722),
p. 325; and *Roxana* (1969; 1st pub. 1724), p. 297.

12 Fielding, *Examples of Providence* (1752), pp. 87–88, 85–87, 89. Fielding also
finds it providential that Catherine Hayes fainted in court when shown the
clothes of her murdered husband (pp. 84–85). Contemporary accounts
make a good deal less of the event (see Applebee's *Original Weekly Journal,*
23 April 1726, and *The Murder of Mr. John Hayes* [1726], p. 25). Possibly
Fielding is purposefully exaggerating for what he conceives to be a worthy
purpose; his title page gives the price of his pamphlet as one shilling per
bound copy, "or Ten Shillings a Dozen to those who give them away."

13 Fielding, *Examples of Providence* (1752), pp. 61–63. Fielding identifies his
source as Defoe's *Secrets of the Invisible World Disclosed,* p. 105 (no specific
edition is cited, and the author is given as "Moretus"), but the story also

appears in Thomas Taylor's *The Second Part of the Theatre of Gods Iudge-*
ments (1642), pp. 69–70. Other versions can be found in Smith's *Highway-*
men (1719a), pp. 415–16, and Applebee's *Original Weekly Journal*, 2 March
1723, rptd. in Lee, *Defoe* (1869), 3:110 ff. An unrelated but comparable
story is told in *Murder Will Out, or, a True and Faithful Relation of an*
Horrible Murther Committed Thirty Three Years Ago, by an Unnatural Mother,
upon the Body of Her Own Child about a Year Old, and Was Never Discovered
till This 24th of November, 1675. by Her Own Self, upon the Fears of an
Approaching Death (1675).

14 Mather, *Sermon* (1691), p. 9.

15 Babington, *Advice* (1680), p. 20; cf. Lupton, *Discourse* (1725), pp. 8–9, 15:
"God set a mark of Infamy upon bloody *Cain*, some think it was Horror of
Mind. . . . Others think, this was a continual creeping of his Flesh," and
"the First Instance of Murther in the World was followed closely by Perplexity, Oppression of Spirit, and the intolerable Gnawings of Despair it
self." See also *The Murder Committed by Mr. George Strangeways* (1659), pp.
1–2; James Guthrie, *A Sermon Preach'd in the Chapel of Newgate, upon the*
Particular Desire of Robert Hallam, under Sentence of Death, for the Murder of
His Wife Jane (1732), p. 6; Fielding, *Examples of Providence* (1752), pp. 3–4,
92–93.

16 *Heavens Cry against Murder* (1657), p. 9; Mather, *Sermon* (1691), p. 10; *The*
Tryals of John Swan, and Elizabeth Jeffryes. With the Tryal of Miss Mary
Blandy (1752), pp. i–ii. The same point is made rather more fetchingly by
Thomas Savage's "Mournful Ditty" (to be sung to the tune of "Bleeding
Heart"):

> But having done this wicked deed,
> O then my very heart did bleed,
> And Conscience terrify'd me so
> For rest I knew not where to go.
>
> Methoughts her crys did fill my Ears,
> Thus haunted with those slavish fears,
> Where e're I went, that I see,
> I thought they came to wait on me.
>
> Alas! it was in vain I fled,
> For why, that blood which I had shed,
> Did wound my Conscience, grieve my mind,
> So that I could not comfort find.
>
> Thus I my own Destruction wrought,
> Taken I was, to Justice brought,
> And likewise was to Prison sent,
> Where I in sorrow did lament.
>
> [*The Wicked Life and Penitent Death of Tho. Savage* (1688), pp. 13–14]

John Roper sings pretty much the same tune after killing his father, and the
same point is made more prosaically by Mary Hobry and Thomas Wood;

see, respectively, *The Unfortunate Family* (n.d.; but late 17th cent.), *A Cabinet of Grief* (1688), pp. 5–7, and *The Murder of Mr. John Hayes* (1726), p. 30. For more on "the hel and horror of a guiltie conscience" (*Murther of a Young Boy* [1606]), see also *A Full and the Truest Narrative of the Murder Committed by Nathaniel Butler* (1657), p. 1; Franklin et al., *A Murderer Punished and Pardoned* (1668), p. 3; *Murther of Mr. Loggins* (1686), p. 3; Guthrie, Ordinary Accounts, 5 July 1736, 29 June 1737; and Penrose, *Account* (1741), p. 15.

17 [Goodcole], *Heavens Hue and Cry* (1635), sig. B3r; *The Penitent Murderer* (1673), p. 6; Thomas Purney, *Ordinary of Newgate's Account of Mathias Brinsden* (1722); *Remarkable Criminals* (1735a), p. 101. The use of the term "infatuate" seems important; thus its appearance in *Heavens Cry against Murder* (1657), p. 9, *An Exact Narrative of the Bloody Murder of Mr. John Talbot* (1669), and *The Murder of Mrs. Robinson* (1735), p. 14. For other examples of the same phenomenon, see *Three Wicked and Bloody Murthers* (1680), pp. 3–4; *The Examination and Confession of W. Barwick and E. Mangall* (1690), p. 2; Paul Lorrain, *The Confession of John Peter Dramatti* (1703); and Guthrie, Ordinary Account, 5 October 1737.

18 Mather, *Sermon* (1691), p. 10.

19 Gilbert Burnet and Anthony Horneck, *The Confession of John Stern* (1682), p. 3.

20 Mary Hobry, in a ballad sung to the tune of "The Pious Christian's Exhortation," nicely captures the effect of such description in telling how she disposed of her husband's corpse:

> To bear him forth myself alone,
> I cut off Head, Arms, ev'ry Limb,
> Had I not a heart of Stone,
> I could not thus have Mangl'd him.
> [*Cabinet of Grief* (1688), pp. 11–12]

21 William Annand, *Elegie upon the Death of George Sands* (1655).

22 *The Bloody Murtherer, or, the Unnatural Son* (1672), p. 20. Jones was also advised "to get such Books as have been set forth of penitent malefactors, as . . . *Nathaniel Butler, Thomas Savage,* and others" (p. 17).

23 *Boteler's Case* (1678), sigs. A3v–A4r; Sir George Sondes, *His Plaine Narrative* (1655), pp. 29–30; [T.B.], *Memorials of the Family of Sir George Sondes* (1790?), p. vii.

24 *Mistaken Justice* (1695), pp. 22–23; another of Newland's friends says essentially the same thing, pp. 33–34.

25 See Keith Thomas, *Religion and the Decline of Magic* (1971), chap. 4, "Providence."

26 John Duncan, *The London Apprentice: A Narrative of the Life and Death of Nathaniel Butler* (1802), p. 6; for other claims that murderers' stories are or can be "tragical," see *Boteler's Case* (1678), sigs. A2r–v; and John Reynolds, *The Triumph of Gods Revenge against Murther,* 7th ed. (1704), sig. B2v. *Select Trials* (1764) extends the term "tragical" to "the most Part" of the cases it describes, though some are of the "tragi-comic Kind" (vol 1, sig. A2r).

27 Mather, *Sermon* (1691), pp. 9, 20; *Remarkable Criminals* (1735a), p. 468 (but also see p. 350 for a reference to "the natural tenderness of the human species").

28 This quote from *The Beggar's Opera* (3:2) has a rich history of antecedents, e.g., "man hath no greater enemy to himself then mankind[;] birds, beasts and fowls, go lovingly together in Troops and Herds not hurting each other" (*Gods Justice against Murther* [1668], p. 13). "Certainly the degenerate Nature of Man," writes the author of *Strange and Lamentable News from Dulledg-Wells* (1678), "when it abandons the Conduct of Reason, and is destitute of Grace, is more savage and brutish than the wildest Beasts that houl in the Wilderness of *Africk*. Lyons and Bears, Wolves and Tygers, are civil Companions to him . . . and then too . . . seldome, if ever, do they prey upon those of their own Kind" (pp. 2–3). Cf. Defoe's *Serious Reflections of Robinson Crusoe* (1905; 1st pub. 1720), p. 112: men "are worse than the brutes; for the brutes destroy not their own Kind, but all prey upon a different species." For more on "that generall cruelty which had taken root from the beginning in *Cain* and his posterity," and how "Inhuman Actions" like murder "evince a Barbarity in Man's Nature . . . beyond what a Considerate man could give himself leave to Imagine, or hath ever been observed in Bruits," see, respectively, Beard and Taylor's *Theatre of Gods Judgements* (1748), p. 184, and *A Most Barbarous and Inhuman Murder* (1688). Of course the existence of "considerate" men could be taken to indicate a countertendency in human nature. "No Man is so perverse, nor so much absorbed in the Desires and Concupiscence of the Flesh, who can utterly Deface, through Oblivion, the Knowledge of *Good* and *Evil*," declares Applebee's *Original Weekly Journal*, 22 June 1730. "Corrupted as our Nature is," Lupton preaches, "there is something still so shocking to us in the Sin of *Murther*, that a Man must undergo as much Struggle and Self-Denial, in Complying with This Kind of Temptation, as he usually feels in Resisting Others. The Utmost Violence must be offer'd to his own *Disposition*, before he can prevail with himself to offer Violence to his Own, or to his Neighbour's *Life*" (*Discourse* [1725], pp. 3–4). It is a short step from this to the view that murder is "an outragious Action, whereby a Man is at once divested of all Humanity, and reduced into the pestiferous nature of the most voracious and destructive Animals, whose only delight it is to tear in Pieces, and destroy their Fellow-Creatures" (Guthrie, Ordinary Account, 7 May 1740). In the early eighteenth century murder thus becomes a scandal of a very different kind from what it was to seventeenth-century writers. Guthrie calls it "a Disgrace to the Nature of Man, who is, or at least ought to be, whatever Failure may happen in particulars, a sociable, a mild, and reasonable Creature" (Ordinary Account, 18 May 1743).

29 Burnet would be raised to the see of Salisbury in 1689, as a reward for services rendered to William of Orange in the previous year. He was already well known in 1682 for his role as a religious and political moderate and, too, for his spectacular deathbed conversion of the notoriously atheistical and libertinous Lord Rochester (see Gilbert Burnet, *Some Passages of the Life and Death of the Right Honorable John Earl of Rochester* [1680]). One reason that Horneck, a Lutheran, got involved was that he spoke German (Burnet and Horneck, *Confession of Stern* [1682], p. 1; subsequent quotations are cited in the text).

30 Thynne's murder, notes Luttrell, "has made great talk, severall persons makeing different constructions of it; some, that 'twas a design against him and the duke of Monmouth (who really parted with him not a quarter of an hour before); others, that 'twas done on account of the lady Ogle" (*Brief Relation of State Affairs* [1857], 1:164). Other contemporary accounts include *The Horrid and Barbarous Murther of Thomas Thynn Esq* (1682) and *The Cruel and Bloody Murther of Thomas Thin, Esq.* (1682). See also Smith, *Highwaymen* (1719a), pp. 269–72, which engages in the usual embroideries. Vratz's enduring interest is shown by parenthetical references to him in Defoe's *Serious Reflections of Robinson Crusoe*, p. 182, and also his *Complete English Gentleman*, ed. Karl D. Bülbring (1890), pp. 30–31. The nature of these references (along with their dates, 1720 and 1730 respectively) suggest their source was Smith's *Highwaymen* rather than Defoe's own memory of the case.

31 One Newgate ordinary told two murderers "that their Offences were irrepairable, and all their Tears, all their Sorrow and Contrition, could not make any Amends for the Facts they had committed" (Guthrie, Ordinary Account, 21 December 1739). William Cannicott, a model wife-murderer, agreed: "A Man who has been guilty of the horrid Crime of Murder, which is my unhappy Case, cannot do too much for the Satisfaction of the publick, at his leaving the World" (William Cannicott, *Life and Actions* [1756], p. [3]).

32 Richard Hannam also refused to give an extensive and particular confession, "alleadging it a point of *Popery* to give an account . . . to any one but God" (*The Witty Rogue Arraigned, Condemned, & Executed* [1656], p. 47); this despite (or perhaps because of) Edward Tuke's laborious efforts to set him straight on Protestant doctrine (see Tuke, *The Soul's Turnkey* [1656]). "You may possibly . . . imagine, that if you confess your Crime to God," a clergyman wrote to Mary Blandy, "you are not obliged to confess to the World: – Generally speaking, God is the sole Confessor of Mankind; – but your Case is a particular Exception to this Rule. – You will want the Assistance of God's Ministers. – But how is it possible for you to receive any Benefit from them, if you do not represent the true State of your Soul without a Disguise? A Secret of this Nature, smothered in the Breast, is a Fire which preys upon, and consumes all Quietness and Repose. – Consider too the imminent Danger of a Lye of this Nature; consider the Justice due to your Accusers, to your Judges, and to the World." (*The Tryals of Swan and Jeffryes. With the Tryal of Blandy* [1752], p. 104). A criminal had to "come to Particulars." It was not enough for him merely to say that "he had been very wicked, and . . . had committed all manner of Sins whatsoever, and that he would confess them to God . . . and ask his Pardon." For

this meant a rejection of the "reasonable and just Methods that were proposed to him," and was a matter of his "chusing rather to have his own
wilful humour" (Lorrain, *Ordinary Account*, 12–13 September 1707).

33 Burnet's discounting of the supernatural in favor of the psychological is a
tendency to be found elsewhere. The confession of a woman who had
successfully concealed her murder of an infant for three years was attributed, by a late seventeenth-century broadside, to the fact that "Blood will
never cease Crying for Vengence." The woman's mother had known of
her crime and kept silent, "but [her] Mother Dying last Week, it tis reported that her Ghost, (*or rather her own Conscience*) so Tormented her that
she could not rest till she made a discovery Thereof." "Stings of Conscience," this writer explains, can be "like so many Gastley Ghosts to stare
the Murtherer in the Face, till it causes flames of Terror and Dispare to
break out with uncontroulable Violence" (*Concealed Murther Reveiled* [n.d.];
italics mine). The odd spelling here may be significant insofar as it shows
how far into the popular culture this psychologizing tendency had spread.
Stanley's "Terrors of Mind" were reportedly produced by a similar visita-
tion, some people affirming that "he told them he really saw, or fanceyed
he saw" the ghost of his murdered mistress come to reproach him in
Newgate. "As he was so frantick and confus'd," says his chief biographer,
"it was not improbable but such *Ideas* might appear to his Fancy and
Imagination, raised by the Horrour of his Conscience" (*Life of Stanley*
[1723], pp. 40–41). Sometimes the psychological observation anticipates
Freud. When a constable named Skinner arrested a murderer named Symonds in an alehouse, "*Symonds* deny'd the Fact, and would seem to brave
it out, calling for Ale, and drinking it as fast as he could. But, after *Skinner*
had told him, That the Murder was sworn positively upon him, he fell into
such a Confusion, and Distraction of Thought, that though he had been,
for many Years, very well acquainted with *Skinner,* yet, for an hour together, in all his Discourse, he call'd *Skinner* by the Name of *Story,* which
was the Name of the Person that then kept the County Gaol" (*Truth of the
Case* [1708], p. 9). "Few men guilty of so heinous a crime as murder can
conceal it," asserts a mid-eighteenth-century writer, "By some circumstance or other, the truth will break forth, and their own unfaithful tongues
will betray them." He goes on to tell how a suspected murderer was made
to touch part of a recently discovered skeleton and, "in his confusion,
dropt this unguarded expression, *This is no more Dan Clark's bone, than it is
mine.*" After this the coroner was sure he was guilty ([W. Bristow], *Genuine Account of Aram* [1759], p. 9).

34 "Sense" is also an important word. Three ministers who visited Henry
Jones "used their most strenuous endeavours to make him *sensible* of his
sin," which was murdering his mother, and it was noted that Charles
Drew, who killed his father, "seemed at first not to have any *Sense* of the
heinous Sin he had committed" (*The Bloody Murtherer* [1672], p. 12, and
The Trial of Charles Drew [1740], p. 33; italics mine). Lorrain found Dramatti, who killed his wife, "very stupid," but adds that "at last, I hope, he

was thoroughly made sensible of the horror of [his crime]" (*Confession of Dramatti* [1703]). For another "stupid" familiar murderer, see Lorrain's Ordinary Account, 28 April 1708. "Sense" was equivalent to "humanity and good nature," or so one writer indicates when he denies these qualities to a gang of murderers whose crime "did not seem to make the least impression on their spirits" (*Remarkable Criminals* [1735a], p. 522).

35 During the course of one of his visits, says Horneck, Vratz "was pleased to tell me, That he had far other apprehensions of God than I had, and was confident God would consider [him] a Gentleman . . . and would not take it ill if a Souldier who lived by his Sword, revenged the affront offered to him by another." Such talk made Horneck "so melancholick, that I was forced to leave him" (p. 8). Another murderer who fell short of the appropriate paradigm was Mathias Brinsden, a wife-murderer: "it was thought remarkable, and a Token of Savageness and Barbarity of Nature, that, instead of throwing himself upon the Mercy of the Court; instead of desiring death rather than Life, with Remorse of Conscience; instead of bursting out into Tears, for the Loss of the Partner of his Bed, his Joys, and Griefs; he insisted on trifling Allegations; said his Wife lov'd *Brandy* and *Geneva*, disobey'd his Commands, and would not be easy to live as he liv'd; making a Remark, that the Surgeon must swear falsely, in asserting that the Wound was 6 inches deep, when the Knife produced in Court, was not 6 inches long" (Purney, Ordinary Account, 24 September 1722). It is not my concern here to trace out sectarian differences or to follow historical trends, but what was wanted of Brinsden seems considerably less than what two ministers wanted from Savage. Telling him he was mistaken if he thought repentance alone would be enough to save him from God's judgment, these hard-nosed Calvinists (or so they would appear) "enquired whether ever he had experience of a gracious change wrought in him" (*A Murderer Punished and Pardoned* [1668]). "Wonderful change" would seem an easier, less contentious standard to apply. For more on the difference between Calvinists and Church of England latitudinarians, see Chapter 5, esp. n. 15.

36 [Goodcole], *Heavens Hue and Cry* (1635) is concerned to scotch "flying tales" (sig. B4r), and *The Bloody Murtherers Executed* (1675) is written "to prevent the further spreading of untrue Reports concerning this unhappy accident" (p. 1). When the murder of Denis Hobry "put more Freaks and Crotchets into the Heads and Minds of the Common People, than any Story of that size perhaps . . . before," the author of *A Hellish Murder Committed by a French Midwife on the Body of Her Husband* (1688) decided that "the shortest way of clearing all Difficulties [was] to Publish to the World a *Plain* and *Naked Narrative* of [the] whole Affair" (sig. A2r). One of the benefits of the ordinary's *Accounts*, argued Paul Lorrain, was that "Malefactors Confessions [bring] Things to Light which were before buried in Darkness" (Lorrain, *The Case of Paul Lorrain* [1712]). His papers show a concern with getting criminals to identify their accomplices (see 12–13 September 1707 and 18 May 1709), and on at least one occasion he advertised his willingness to help recover stolen property (24 September

1708; see also Samuel Smith, Ordinary Account, 2 March 1692; R. Wykes, Ordinary Account, 20 July 1700; John Villette, *Account of Hawke and Jones* [1774], pp. 12, 21; and also Villette's *Annals of Newgate* [1776], 2:78, 4:394–95). The confessions of criminals, says the author of *The Life of William Page* (1758), are useful both to those "who have lost their Goods, they [know] not how," and to the world at large because they expose "the various Schemes and wicked Inventions of Villains" (p. 1). More than a hundred years earlier, *Heavens Hue and Cry* (1635) gave a listing of "places, in, and about the City of *London,* [where] *Harlots* [and other bad people] watch their opportunities to surprise men" (sig. C2r).

37 See *Truth of the Case* (1708), p. 38; cf. *A Compassionate Address to Prisoners for Crimes; and More Particularly to Such of Them as Are under Sentence of Death* (1742): "The great thing therefore you are to look to is the heart and soul, whether that be renewed and changed" (p. 70).

38 In 1708 Burnet would become involved with two more murderers (see Paul Lorain [*sic*], *The Whole Life and Conversation of Mr. William Gregg. To Which Is Added, The Life of Mr. John Maugeridge and Mr. David Bayley* [1708]; this is probably a piracy and not by the actual Newgate ordinary). While visiting Bayley (or Baily), who was reportedly a relative, Burnet made the acquaintance of Mawgridge and "several Times" condescended to pray with him, and "comforted him very much, as to his State and Condition" (*The Life and Penitent Death of John Mawgridge* [1708], p. [2]). In the same year Burnet's protégé and eventual successor to the see of Salisbury, William Talbot, then bishop of Oxford and ultimately of Durham, was also involved in a murder case. When two murderers sentenced to hang intimated they might confess if given a bit more time to ponder their spiritual condition, Talbot, in his capacity as justice of the peace for Worcester (he wore more than one hat), undertook to secure them a reprieve. To do this he had to ride to Gloucester and back in wet weather. The journey took four hours one way, and Talbot wasted no time dawdling, going before the appropriate judge as soon as he changed out of his wet clothes. As it happened, all his trouble went for nothing. The murderers reneged, even though Talbot promised one of them that he would use his influence to keep his estate from forfeiture to the crown, and offered to make his son "a Queen's-Scholar . . . at the College-School . . . and contribute, if it were wanting, out of [his] own Pocket, towards his Maintenance" (*Truth of the Case* [1708], pp. 34–35, 37). In 1657 Sir Robert Tichborne, lord mayor of London, showed a similar interest in Nathaniel Butler, visiting him several times in Newgate and arranging a fortnight's reprieve "upon design to save his soul"; and in 1684 Edward Stillingfleet, then dean of St. Paul's and later bishop of Worcester, made a last-minute effort to bring John Hutchins to an "open and free" confession of murder (Randolph Yearwood, *The Penitent Murderer* [1657], pp. [iii–iv], and Samuel Smith, *The Behaviour of John Hutchins* [1684], p. 2). Generally, however, it was obscurer men who visited the condemned in prison and urged them to come to a proper sense of their crimes. These included not only the prison chaplains but other interested clergy and often even curious, well-disposed gentlemen. Not one murderer mentioned in this book escaped such attention, though it was applied of course with varying degrees of pressure.

39 *Fair Warning to Murderers of Infants* (1692), p. [i].

CHAPTER 5

1 Durkheim, *The Division of Labor in Society* (1933), p. 102; Paul Lorrain, Ordinary Account, 19 September 1712. In taking my cue from Durkheim, I may seem to be ignoring Foucault. Though a great respecter of his work, I am not one of those who believes that what he says about France translates easily or adequately to England, where the criminal's trial, repentance, and previous life, as well as his execution, were all made part of public consciousness. For a "Foucauldian" view of one aspect of the popular literature of crime in England, however, see J. A. Sharpe, " 'Last Dying Speeches': Religion, Ideology and Public Execution in Seventeenth-Century England," *Past and Present* 107 (1985): 144–67. Sharpe claims that "the state and the state church" pressured criminals to make dying speeches in order to "[legitimize] not only the punishment being suffered by the individual felon, but also the whole structure of secular and religious authority. . . . whatever their past offences, at the end they were willing to accept, and by their acceptance reinforce, a 'doctrine of absolute obedience,' or a 'polity structured in terms of unconditional obedience' " (p. 163; the quoted phrases are from L. B. Smith, "English Treason Trials and Confessions in the Sixteenth Century," *Journal of the History of Ideas* 15 [1954]: 494, and Mervyn James, *English Politics and the Concept of Honor, 1485–1642* [1978], p. 44). Sharpe goes even so far as to suggest that "it may be illuminating to compare this acceptance [of state authority] with that demanded by the all-pervasive ideologies of modern totalitarian states" ("Last Speeches," n. 66). As this chapter will show, I am far from agreeing with Sharpe; my view of criminal biography is that it had a much wider, less easily defined political function. Whatever it may have been in France, or in late Tudor and early Stuart times, the popular literature of crime in seventeenth- and eighteenth-century England was no monopoly of either the state or its church (thus see n. 15, this chapter); nor was its political value quite so narrowly confined that it served the state primarily and not some larger vision of society.

2 *Remarkable Criminals* (1735a), p. 327.

3 Thomas Horne, Assize Sermon, 12 March 1713, p. 7.

4 For cases of murder with specific political significance, see Part II: Introduction, n. 12. The larger, general issues to which murderers' conversions spoke are indicated by Cotton Mather, who from his position across the water speaks for a point of view that even his own country would eventually reject (and far more dramatically than England). There is "a Detestable Generation of men, who go under the Name of *Deists,*" he scornfully

remarks: "These Dangerous Wretches pretend unto a kind of *Moral Vertue;* Their *Moral Vertue* is this; A man expects the *Civilities* of his Neighbours; his Condition would be insupportable should his Neighbours count him unworthy of their *Civilities.* Now, that a man may not Lose the *Civilities* of others, he must then treat them with *Civilities.* These are all the *Bonds of a Good Behaviour,* that these Baptised Infidels are sensible of. This is all, that keeps the Dangerous *Monsters* from Stealing, and Lying, and Murder" (*The Curbed Sinner* [Boston, 1713], pp. 12–13).

5 Edward Tuke, *The Soul's Turnkey* (1656), p. 170; Cotton Mather, commenting on a murderer's admirable *"Desire of Death,* rather than an *Horrour* of it,"* says that "People at a distance, interpreted it as a sort of *Stupidity;* but unto them who were better acquainted with his condition, it seem'd the Effect of a better principle" (*The Curbed Sinner,* p. [xiv]). Compare Matthew Lee who, though only an armed robber, was with Methodist help able to declare: "My Flesh and Blood desire Life, but my Soul longs to be where Death shall be no more. Welcome Life; and Welcome Death: if I am reprieved, I shall bless GOD; and if I am included in the Dead Warrant, I shall still praise and magnifie his Name" (*Life of Lee* [1752], p. 14).

6 Sir George Sondes, *His Plaine Narrative* (1655), p. 29; R[obert] Boreman, *Mirrour of Mercy* (1655), pp. 30, 13.

7 Sondes, *Plaine Narrative* (1655), p. 1.

8 Ibid., pp. 12, 14, 21, and 12–21 in general.

9 Boreman, *Mirrour of Mercy* (1655), p. 35; Sondes, *Plaine Narrative* (1655), p. 21.

10 For information on Boreman (or rather Bourman), see the *Dictionary of National Biography;* Boreman, *Mirrour of Mercy* (1655), p. 7; cf. this reaction to Nathaniel Butler, by a well-wisher who visited him in prison: "I went to the Gaole and for my money had admittance with him, where instead of a bloody and unhumane wretch, I found one whose penitence, and I hope reall contrition spake much of a Saint" (*Blood Washed Away by Tears of Repentance* [1657], p. [xvi]).

11 Boreman, *Mirrour of Mercy* (1655), pp. 3, 7.

12 Ibid., p. 36.

13 Lorrain, Ordinary Accounts, 24 June 1709, 22 September 1704; [James Guthrie], *The Behaviour, Confession, and Dying Words of Thomas Homan* (1742), p. 6.

14 Sondes, *Plaine Narrative* (1655), p. 29.

15 Boreman, *Mirrour of Mercy* (1655), pp. 31–32. Boreman's special sense of triumph here may have owed something to a feeling that he had turned Calvinist rhetoric against itself. For it seems that most of the other serious criminal biographies surviving from the Interregnum are Calvinist in orientation, which suggests that the form was largely invented by Calvinists and then coopted by more moderate, mainstream Church of England

types. Thus Gilbert Dugdale's *Practises of Elizabeth Caldwell* (1604) – a protoversion of the form – is saturated with Puritan sentiment, and thus, too, sixteen of the eighteen clergymen named as signatories to *A Serious Advice to the Citizens of London* (1657) – concerning Nathaniel Butler – were ejected or otherwise lost their livings in 1662 (one of the remaining two, a staunch Presbyterian, was already dead; the other remained in the Church to become bishop of Peterborough in 1685, but resigned as a nonjuror in 1689). It should be noted as well that at least four of the five named authors of *A Murderer Punished and Pardoned* (1668) were Nonconformist divines and that Nonconformists were generally avid recruiters of criminals' souls. For eighteenth-century evidence to this effect, see, for example, Paul Lorrain's complaints about nonjurors interfering with Alexander Dalziel and James Shepperd (Ordinary Accounts, 5 December 1715 and 17 March 1718, respectively); *Life of Lee* (1752), which makes strident Methodist propaganda against the ordinary and, by extension, the empty offices of state religion; and [Humanitas], *Three Malefactors Executed near Reading* (1786), pp. 7–8. In identifying those ejected in 1662 as Nonconformists, I have used the standard references, Edmond Calamy's *Abridgement of Baxter's History*, 2nd ed. (1711), and Samuel Palmer's *Nonconformist's Memorial* (1775).

16 Boreman, *Mirrour of Mercy* (1655), pp. 31–32.

17 For the very different message given out by the popular literature of crime in New England, see the following works by Cotton Mather: *Pillars of Salt. An History of Some Criminals Executed in This Land, for Capital Crimes. With Some of Their Dying Speeches* (1699); *The Sad Effects of Sin. A True Relation of the Murder Committed by David Wallis on His Companion Benjamin Stolwood* (1713); and *The Curbed Sinner. A Discourse. . . . Occasioned by a Sentence of Death, Passed on a Poor Young Man, for the Murder of His Companion* (1713). *Magnalia Christi Americana* (1702) also includes a section on a number of famous felons. When a murderer told Cotton Mather that he thanked God "for what He has wrought in my Soul," Mather cautioned him: "But be very careful about this matter: if you build on your own good Affections instead of Jesus Christ the only Rock, if you think they shall recommend you to God, *He that made you will not have mercy on you*" (*Pillars of Salt*, pp. 78–79). More than half of *Pillars of Salt*, it is worth noting, is devoted to general moral exhortations against sinning; the remainder treats the cases of twelve criminals, not all of whom are named or even dated, and, as the title indicates, only "some" of the dying speeches are given. For Mather the main object of attention is never the criminal but the meaning of his crime. For a succinct description of the treatment of criminals in print in New England, see Richard Slotkin, "Narratives of Negro Crime in New England, 1675–1800," *American Quarterly* 25 (1973): 3–9, and also Ronald A. Bosco, "Lecturers at the Pillory: The Early American Execution Sermon," ibid., 30 (1978): 155–76. By the third quarter of the eighteenth century, criminal biographies were occasionally being published in New York as well; for a discussion of six of these, see

Douglas Greenberg, *Crime and Law Enforcement in the Colony of New York,*
1691–1776 (1974), pp. 100–7

Another counterexample to English practice is offered by France.
Though accounts of crimes and executions were regularly published there,
criminal biography comparable to that found in England or America was
relatively rare until the nineteenth century (or so I'd infer from a survey of
the holdings at the Bibliothèque nationale and the Bibliothèque municipale
de Troyes). A notable exception are the various accounts of Mandrin, the
smuggler and bandit, for which see Hans-Jürgen Lüsebrink, "Images et
représentations sociales de la criminalité au xviiie siècle: l'example de Mandrin," *Revue d'histoire moderne et contemporaine* 26 (1979):345–64; see also his
Kriminalität und Literatur im Frankreich des 18. Jahrhunderts (1983), pp. 14–
103, which repeats the substance of this article and considers popular accounts as well of Cartouche, the gangleader, Damiens, the regicide, and
Desrues, the poisoner. Almost none of the popular accounts of crimes and
criminals that survive from the two previous centuries are as particular as the
pamphlets Lüsebrink describes, or as interested in the criminal himself, and
this despite the high importance of public execution as a social and political
ritual (for the lack of interest in the motives of murderers, criminal psychology generally, or the details of trials, see Jean-Pierre Seguin, "L'Information
en France avant le périodique: 500 canards imprimés entre 1529 et 1631,"
Arts et traditions populaires 11 [1963]: 129, 134; see also Geneviève Bollème,
"Littérature populaire et littérature de colportage au 18e siècle," in *Livre et
societé dans la France du xviiie siècle,* vol. 1 [1965], pp. 61–92, where, in a
survey of popular eighteenth-century French literature, Bollème finds only a
"slow progression" toward the representation of "real" and "actual" experience [pp. 74–75] and no great number of pamphets on criminals [p. 87]).
Thus some eighteenth-century French pamphlets and broadsides can describe a murder and note that the culprits were caught and executed, without
naming them or their victims; see, for instance, *Cruel et sanglant assasinat d'un
rotisseur, et d'un de ses amis qui ont estez tuez à la petite Pologne* [Paris, 1730];
*Jugement rendu contre deux empoisonneurs, sçavoir le maistre à estre rompu vif & sa
servante à estre pendu, ensuite leurs corps jettés au feu & les cendres aux vents* [Paris,
1730]; *Cruel et sanglant Assassin commis par une jeune Fille âgee de vingt-un ans,
paroisse de sainte Marguerite de Paris, Faubourg sainte Antoine, qui a assassiné sa
mère dans son lit, pour le refus du Mariage, son enfant present* [Paris, n.d.]; and
*Relation veritable du cruel Assasin fait en la personne du Curé de Vilaine & sa
servante, près de Paris* (Paris, n.d.). Comparable publications can be found in
late seventeenth-century England, but they are very rare and, by the turn of
the eighteenth century, seem to have become nearly unthinkable. In France,
it appears, the criminal himself was not so important as what was done to
him by the state, represented by the executioner, and through him by the
church, represented by the cleric who attended him to the scaffold (on the
centrality of the criminal's confessor and what he could indicate of the
"triumph" of religion, see John McManners, *Death and the Enlightenment*

[1985], pp. 383–84). Much interesting cross-cultural work remains to be done on the very diffferent kinds of popular – and official – interest shown in crime and criminals in pre-Enlightenment Europe, and the ways in which narratives of one kind or another shaped and reflected that interest. Thus criminal biographies were also published in eighteenth-century Amsterdam (see Pieter Spierenberg, *The Spectacle of Suffering* [1984], pp. 58–59), and pictorial narratives of crime were apparently popular in sixteenth- and seventeenth-century Germany (see David Kunzle, *The Early Comic Strip* [1973], pp. 157–96, which cites some Dutch and a few French examples from the period as well, but practically none that are English).

18 Lorrain, Ordinary Accounts, 22 March 1704, 17 March 1710, and 25 September 1713.

19 When Defoe wrote a poem sharply critical of Lorrain's efforts to make criminals into "saints," he got this "answer":

> To raise Contentious Heats, and Feuds, I know
> No Instrument more useful than *D——f——*.
> No doubt but he, with a dissenting Mob,
> The Church of her deserved Fame would rob.
> 'Tis like the *zeal* of that pretended *Sect,*
> Who went from us, because they were elect
> To Righteousness, as they are wont to say,
> Tho' all know, Int'rest led them t'other way.
>   He always valu'd that Religion best
> Which breeds *Contention* and destroys all Rest.
>   [*Remarks on the Author of the Hymn to the Pillory* (1703) p. 1]

20 James Guthrie, Ordinary Account, 19 July 1738; *The Unhappy Marksman* (1659), p. 26; Lorrain, Ordinary Accounts, 24 June 1709 and 25 October 1704; Samuel Smith, Ordinary Account, 2 March 1692; *The Bloody Murtherer, or, the Unnatural Son* (1672), p. 3; Lorrain, *Walking with God* (1703), p. 8.

21 Boreman, *Mirrour of Mercy* (1655), p. 23; *Blood Washed Away by Tears of Repentance* (1657), p. [xvi], and Yearwood, *The Penitent Murderer* (1657), pp. [xviii–xix]; Burnet and Horneck, *Confession of Stern* (1682), pp. 21, 17 ff.; Kirk *Dying Advice* (1684).

22 [N.B.], *Compleat Tryals* (1718, 1721), 2:186–87; Lorrain, Ordinary Account, 5 December 1715; Guthrie, Ordinary Account, 3 March 1737; Lorrain, Ordinary Account, 17 March 1710.

23 *Penitence of Marketman* (1680), sig. A2v; [N.B.], *Compleat Tryals* (1718, 1721), 3:100; Franklin et al., *A Murderer Punished and Pardoned* (1668), p. 39; [N.B.], *Compleat Tryals*, 2:274; Burnet and Horneck, *Confession of Stern* (1682), p. 9; *Penitence of Marketman*, sig. A2v; *Mistaken Justice* (1695), p. 17; *Boteler's Case* (1678), sigs. C4v, D1r; [N.B.], *Compleat Tryals*, 3:61; *Warning for Servants. Or, the Case of Margaret Clark* (1680), p. 29; *Select Tryals* (1764), 4:172.

24 John Laughton, Assize Sermon, 28 March 1712, pp. 5–6.

25 Inevitably there were "do-it-yourselfer" criminals, who trusted "in the absolute mercy of God, without respect to a Mediator" (*Address to Prisoners* [1742], pp. 60–61). "I see not what good a Minister can doe me," said Richard Hannam, "for the matter lies upon my self" (Tuke, *The Soul's Turnkey* [1656], p. 2). The folly of such an attitude is illustrated by the case of Silvester Harlackenden, who politely but firmly refused the services of the Newgate ordinary, "and seemed to go out of the World in a stupid Insensibility, little or not at all regarding even the last Devotions perform'd at the Place of Execution; only his lips were observed to move just before the Cart drew away, but none could hear any thing he said, or knew whether he spake or no; and [he] was observed to be longer in dying than any the Ordinary had ever seen before" ([N.B.], *Compleat Tryals* [1718, 1721], 2:270). The readily inferable lesson is that big jobs of salvation are beyond the skills of amateurs; when in doubt, call in a professional soul-plumber.

26 Burnet and Horneck, *Confession of Stern* (1682), p. 9; [Goodcole], *Heavens Hue and Cry* (1635), sig. B4v; *Warning for Servants* (1680), p. 13.

27 [Goodcole], *Heavens Hue and Cry* (1635), sig.. C1r; *A True and Perfect Relation of the Tryal and Execution of Robert Foulks* (1679), p. 7; S[amuel] Foote, *The Genuine Memoirs of the Life of Sir John Dinely Goodere* (1741), pp. 34–36.

28 *A Narrative of the Murder of Mr. John Hayes* (1726), p. 25; John Hurtis, Jr., in Applebee's *Original Weekly Journal,* 7 April 1722.

29 *Boteler's Case* (1678), sigs. E2v–E3r. A similar bridging of social divisions was supposed to have occurred when Lawrence, Earl Ferrars was executed in 1760 for the unprovoked murder of his steward: "The Spectators, struck with the Novelty of seeing a Peer of *Great Britain* in such a Situation, devoted to Death for the dreadful Crime of Murder, and suffering like a common Malefactor for taking the Life of one of their Rank, beheld him with a respectful Silence, mixed with Pity, and while they commiserated his Fate, almost forgot his Crime" (*Remarkable Trials* [1765], 2:348).

30 *Mistaken Justice* (1695), p. 16; *Remarkable Criminals* (1735a), p. 209; Guthrie, Ordinary Accounts, 13 February 1739 and 21 December 1739; Lorrain, Ordinary Account, 6 June 1707.

31 Lorrain, Ordinary Account, 22 September 1704; *Boteler's Case* (1678), sig. D4v; *Mistaken Justice* (1695), p. 15.

32 Richard Newcome, Assize Sermon, 13 March 1728, p. 9; *Gentleman's Magazine* 22 (1752): 189.

33 Purney, *Account of Brinsden* (1722), p. 5; Guthrie, Ordinary Accounts, 5 July 1736 and 29 June 1737.

34 Isaac Barrow, *Theological Works* (1830) 2:142, cited by R. S. Crane, "Suggestions toward a Genealogy of the Man of Feeling," *English Literary History* 1 (1934): 227.

35 Guthrie, Ordinary Account, 19 July 1738.

36 *The Fair Parricide,* "a Tragedy of Three Acts," was published in 1752 in two editions but never acted; *Miss Mary Blandy's Own Account* (1752), pp. 46, 58; *Memoirs of the Life and Transactions of Capt. Cranston*, 2nd ed. (1753), p. 39.

37 *Blandy's Own Account* (1752), pp. [45]–46. In this connection it might be observed that the depictions of "Charles Drew shooting his Father" and of the murder of Sir John Dinely Goodere (both reproduced in this text) seem more like illustrations of scenes in plays than of actual events. Thus, note the curious perspective of the first, so suggestive of painted "flats," and the appearance of something like the edge of a stage apron cutting diagonally across the bottom of the second. Note, too, that the latter makes no effort to represent the ship's cabin where the crime actually took place.

38 *Gentleman's Magazine* 22 (1752): 115–16, also 53 (1783): 627, 802; *The Authentick Tryals of Swan and Jeffryes. With the Tryal of Blandy* (1752), pp. 94, 98.

39 The quoted phrase comes from Henry Mayhew's *London Labour and the London Poor* (1861–62) and is cited in Richard Altick's *Victorian Studies in Scarlet* (1970), p. 49; see pp. 41–66 more generally. Altick is mainly concerned with retelling the stories of famous Victorian murder cases, seeing in them "an almost unexcelled mirror of [the] epoch's mores" (p. 12). Aside from suggesting that "the Victorian masses' sustained enthusiasm for murder was in part a product of their intellectually empty and emotionally stunted lives" (p. 10), he is reluctant to explain the phenomenon (thus see pp. 287–88). His book, nonetheless, is highly interesting and may be taken as a partial sequel to this.

PART III: INTRODUCTION

1 Christopher Hibbert, *Highwaymen* (1967), p. 119. To "law" and "morality" as things the highwayman revolts against, Hibbert might have added class differential. Thus Duval becomes a highwayman because he "could not confine himself . . . within the narrow bounds and limits of a Servant," and Simms, who was sponsored at Eton by a "Noble Lord" but then apprenticed to a breeches maker at fourteen, strayed off the straight and narrow because "a Life of Servitude and Controulment ill suited my Constitution" (*Life of Deval* [1669/70], p. 3; *Life of Simms* [1747], p. 2). But having "a Spirit above being a Servant, and therefore [equipping oneself] with Pistols, &c.," was not necessarily seen in a heroic light (*Life of Page* [1758], p. 3). Page, a footman turned highwayman, "was of so proud and haughty Spirit, that he could not patiently submit to the Orders of his Superiors, nor behave himself with common Decency to those of his Equals and Fellow Servants." As a consequence – and much the same tone was taken with Duval, Simms, and a host of similarly motivated highwaymen – he became "extremely reduced in his Circumstances, without Money, without friends, and without Character," and "could think of no better Method of supplying his Wants, and freeing himself from a servile Dependency, than by turning Collecter on the Highway. This he imagin'd would not only take off that Badge of Slavery, a livery, which he had always worn with Regret, but set him on a Level with Gentlemen, a Figure he was ever ambitious of making" (*Genuine Life of Page* [1758], p. 4). For more on Page, see Chapter 8.

2 *No Jest like a True Jest* (1674a), chap. xi; *Select Trials* (1742), 1:300.

3 On the "atomizing process" at work in seventeenth-century society, see Christopher Hill, *Society and Puritanism,* 2nd ed. (1967), pp. 482–511; for the growing approval of "unlimited accumulation" as England became a "market society," see C. B. Macpherson, *The Political Theory of Possessive Individualism* (1962). Some historians, however, would argue against too sweeping an application of these views, e.g., Isaac Kramnick, in *Bolingbroke and His Circle* (1968); J. G. A. Pocock, in *The Machiavellian Moment* (1975) and "Early Modern Capitalism: The Augustan Perception," in *Feudalism, Capitalism, and Beyond,* ed. Eugene Kamenka and R. S. Neale (1975), pp. 63–83; and Alan Macfarlane, in *The Origins of English Individualism* (1978).

4 Hobbes, *Leviathan,* ed. C. B. Macpherson (1968), pp. 156–57. Despite his attack on the social order, the highwayman also remains in a sense *homo hierarchus.* For his wish is not so much to escape class distinctions as to rise within them. Thus Page, in n. 1 to this chapter, and also Jack Ovet, who "[lay] aside his mechanical employment to translate himself into a gentleman" (Smith, *Highwaymen* [1719a], p. 77). Carrick and his friends wound up as robbers, he says, because they wanted "to make a figure in the World equal to such as were born to Titles and Estates" (Carrick, *Robberies* [1722], p. 3). A counterexample is provided by Isaac Atkinson, who after being disinherited by his father could have "no Notion of turning his Mind to Business, which is generally the unhappy Case of reduced Gentlemen" (Johnson, *Highwaymen* [1734], p. 114). For more on the highwayman's complex and ambivalent relation to the social order, see Chapter 8.

5 *Life of Deval* (1669/70), p. 4. Reports an ex-shoemaker, who gave up his trade and turned to highway robbing with his journeyman: "The Sweets and benefits arising from this new Profession, my Man *Will* soon found, for he wou'd often say when we had taken any Thing of a Booty, is this not this better than Shoemaking Master?" (Henry Cook's "Account . . . of Himself, and of the several Robberies he committed," in James Guthrie, Ordinary Account, 16 September 1741).

6 Frank Osborn, a goldsmith with a taste for whores, might be taken as an emblem of the type: "His Creditors now multiplied upon him, and . . . when he found he could keep them off no longer with Honour, he took to the Highway, by which Means he made good his Payments from Time to Time, without ever being suspected of doing any Thing that was dishonest" (Johnson, *Highwaymen* [1734], p. 326; see also Smith, *Highwaymen* [1719a], p. 281). For another goldsmith, a milliner, and a mercer reputed to be highwaymen, see Luttrell's *Brief Relation of State Affairs* (1857), 3:7, 41; for a baker, two tobacconists, and an "eminent Trader" from Bristol, see Applebee's *Original Weekly Journal,* 16 March 1723 and 5 July 1729; and for three

unspecified "Tradesmen in London," see Mist's *Weekly Journal,* 17 January 1719. The phenomenon was sufficiently familiar to invite this joke, reported as if it were a news item: "Since the apprehending of several Highwaymen, and their Accomplices, abundance of Industrious Tradesmen in many parts of the Town have thought it Convenient to quit their Habitations" (Applebee's, 6 February 1720.) But others besides tradesmen were inclined to use bold and illicit means to get easy money. Lacking their usual opportunities after the South Sea crash of 1720, several stockbrokers and at least one lawyer turned highwayman (see Mist's, 2 July 1720; Applebee's, 6 February and 2 April 1720, 14, 21, and 28 October 1721; and *Life of Child* [1722], p. 24). Others arrested for highway robbery included two prisoners for debt in Wood Street Compter ("but [they] had the Liberty of going abroad"), an exciseman, a hangman, an "eminent Victualler" and "a Poulterer," and a Gentleman Rider to His Majesty's First Troop of Horse Guards (see Applebee's, 12 September 1719; Read's *Weekly Journal,* 9 December 1721; Mist's, 26 September and 17 October 1719; and *Tryal of Greenwood* [1740]). Presumably *anyone* could be a highwayman; its attraction as a way of life actually or vicariously pursued could be felt high and low. In 1720 two captured highwaymen asserted that "two Persons of great Quality" had been their accomplices, and in 1750 "gay licentious Youth of Figure and Fortune" were warned to choose their company, "lest they should happen to find their Intimates on the Road, and meet To-morrow as a highwayman the Man whom To-night they were caressing as a Friend" (see both Applebee's and Mist's, 12 November 1720; Allen, *Account of Maclaine* [1750], pp. 27–28). In 1729 there were two separate cases of otherwise respectable men pretending to be highwaymen, in the one case as a practical joke on some young ladies of their acquaintance and in the other as a way of scaring their wives for staying out too late (Applebee's, 1 November and 30 August 1729).

7   Brecht, "Notes to the Threepenny Opera," *The Threepenny Opera,* tr. Desmond Vesey and Eric Bentley (1964), p,. 101; *The Triumph of Truth* (1663/[4]), p. 31. Cf. Sir Thomas Culpeper, *The Necessity of Abating Usury Re-asserted* (1670), p. 28: "I have heard that Highway-men fancy they acquit themselves and come off with honour, by pleading, that they see no difference betwixt their courses, and some worshipful trades, but the danger, which, they suppose, much improves their title."

8   Smith, *Highwaymen* (1719), 3:266.

9   See Appendix II.

10   E. J. Hobsbawm, *Bandits* (1972), pp. 26, 43, and passim, but esp. pp. 17–29, 41–57, and also his *Primitive Rebels* (1959), pp. 13–29; Smith, *Highwaymen* (1719a), p. 452. Though Hobsbawm would not include eighteenth-century English highwaymen in the same category with Robin Hood (see *Bandits,* p. 39, and *Primitive Rebels,* p. 23), many of the highwaymen treated in the popular literature of crime conform to the list of characteristics he enumerates in *Bandits,* pp. 42–43, and *Primitive Rebels,* pp. 14–23. For further development of the concept of "social criminality," see the report of Hobsbawm's paper read before the Society for the Study of Labor

History on 20 May 1972, where he defines the phenomenon as one occurring "when there is a conflict of laws e.g. between an official and an unofficial system, or when acts of law-breaking have a distinct element of social protest in them, or when they are closely linked with the development of social and political protest" (*Bulletin of the Society for the Study of Labor History* 25 (1972): 5–6). For further considerations of "social crime," see the preface to *Albion's Fatal Tree* (1975), ed. Douglas Hay, Peter Linebaugh, and E. P. Thompson (all of whom were present at the reading of Hobsbawm's paper), and, for a balanced, careful presentation of the limitations as well as the value of the concept, see J. A. Sharpe, *Crime in Early Modern England, 1550–1750* (1984), pp. 121–42. Whether highwaymen were social criminals or not, there seems a general consensus that eighteenth-century poachers, rioters, and smugglers often had clear claims to the status; such figures, however, get little attention in the popular literature of crime.

11 The abusive descriptions of Republicans come from Hind's "Decree, to all his Royal Gang," in *Strange Newes from New-Gate* (1652), and have been quoted in Chapter 1. For the Whigs, see J. H. Plumb, *The Growth of Political Stability in England, 1675–1725* (1973), pp. 143, 142–43 and passim; see also J. P. Kenyon's *Revolution Principles* (1977), which among other things notes that the forced abdication of James II was often the actual, though generally unmentioned target of anti-Whig sermons preached to mark the anniversary of Charles I's martyrdom (see esp. pp. 69–83).

12 Garth, *The Dispensary* (1699), 1:9–10. It was proverbial that "Little thieves are hanged, but great ones escape" (first recorded in J. Clarke's *Paroemiologia Anglo-Latina* [1639]; see D. C. Browning, ed., *Everyman's Dictionary of Quotations and Proverbs* [1951], p. 482). For a sampling of quotations or paraphrases of Garth, or essentially the same idea expressed in different words, see *The Defence of Cony-Catching* (1592), by Cuthbert Cony-Catcher, in *Cony-Catchers and Bawdy Baskets,* ed. Gāmini Salgādo (1972), p. 343; Paul Godwin, intro. to *Histoire des Larrons, or The History of Theeves* (1638) sigs. A6v–A7r; Defoe, *A Hymn to Tyburn* (1703); Steele, the *Englishman,* No. 48 (23 January 1714); Smith, *Highwaymen* (1719a), pp. 212–13; [N.B.], *Compleat Tryals* (1718, 1721), 3:11; the *London Journal,* 11 March 1720 and 16 December 1721; Mist's *Weekly Journal,* 16 April 1720, 16 September 1721, 17 February 1722; Applebee's *Original Weekly Journal,* 17 February 1722; the *Post-Boy,* 20–22 March 1722; *An Epistle from Jack Sheppard to the late L——d C——ll——r of E——d* (Dublin, 1725?); *The Unparallel'd Imposter* (1731), p. 3; Johnson, *Highwaymen* (1734), pp. [1], 163, 343–44; *Life and Actions of Maclean* (1750), p. 13; Mackdonald, *Highwaymen* (1758), frontispiece; and *The Tyburn Chronicle* (1768), 1:87. The greatest subverter of the phrase "great men/man" is of course Fielding, who debases the term utterly in his *History of Jonathan Wild the Great* (1743).

13 Smith, *Highwaymen* (1719a), pp. 179–80.

14 Ibid., p. 181.

15 The *London Journal,* 6–13 August 1720; Applebee's *Original Weekly Journal,*

7 January 1721; hundreds of other examples could be adduced, throughout the period. The equation of trade with theft was no mere highwaymen's ploy. Thus commentaries on the Decalogue typically pass over the most obvious violations of the eighth commandment – "to steale by the high-way side . . . is a knowne sinne" – so they may concentrate their fire on various kinds of sharp dealing within the law (John Dod and Robert Cleaver, *A Plain and Familiar Exposition of the Ten Commandments*, 19th ed. [1635], p. 285; see also *The Whole Duty of Man, Containing a Practical Table of the Ten Commandments* [1674], single sheet; Gabriel Towerson, *An Exposition of the Catechism of the Church of England. Part II* [1681], pp. 416–20; *The Explanation of the Ten Commandments* [1796?], pp. 7–9; and the satirical but highly serious *Letter to a Member of Parliament, Containing a Proposal to Revise, Amend or Repeal the Ten Commandments* [1738], pp. 44–46, 46–48). Towerson, for instance, includes among thefts these common commercial practices: concealing defects in goods, or falsely praising them, so as to get more than they are really worth; using false weights and measures; various kinds of adulteration; wearing the seller down so he feels forced to sell; usury; engrossing; holding back wages after they are due. All this was, in its way, part of what J. G. A. Pocock calls "a basically hostile perception of early modern capitalism" (*The Machiavellian Moment* [1975], p. ix; see particularly chap. 14, "The Eighteenth-Century Debate: Virtue, Passion and Commerce," pp. 462–505). Even Defoe, for all his bourgeois boosterism, was greatly worried by the difficulty of making trade seem an honest as well as honorable pursuit. Thus, even as he celebrates the "complete" commercial man, he feels obliged to admit that "there is some difference between an *honest man* and an *honest Tradesman*," and can even say, baldly, that "Trade is almost universally founded upon Crime" (*Complete English Tradesman*, 2nd ed. [1727], 1:226, and 2, pt.2:108). For a fascinating and long overlooked debate on the morality – or immorality – of trade, and the immorality – or morality – of theft, see Jeremy Collier's dialogue, "Of Theft," in his *Essays upon Several Moral Subjects. Part IV* (1709), pp. 26 ff.

CHAPTER 6

1 Smith, *Highwaymen* (1719*a*), pp. 42–50. In plagiarizing this account, the 1734 Johnson tidies up, putting the events of Whitney's life into chronological order so that his earliest crime is described first instead of last, and omitting the mock sermon on theft that begins the narrative; see *Highwaymen* (1734), pp. 163–66.

2 The classic structuralist account of a body of a popular narrative is Vladimir Propp's *Morphology of the Folktale* (1928; tr. 1968), which finds that "all [Russian] fairy tales are of one type in regard to their structure," being composed of a finite number of "functions" arranged in an unvarying sequence (pp. 19–23 ff.). Despite my best efforts I find it impossible to make any similar claim about criminal rogue biography; it is simply too confusing, and too confused.

3   Somewhat more than 60 of the 135 names mentioned in the table of con-
    tents to Smith's *Highwaymen* (1719a) counted as highwaymen, and 56 of
    these get biographies all to themselves. Of these 56, 29 to 32 (some cases
    are arguable) are shown at their most discreditable just before their "lives"
    conclude. The 1734 Johnson notes something of this tendency – indeed ex-
    aggerates it – when he claims, "But almost all our celebrated Robbers have
    been taken in a very Silly Manner" (*Highwaymen* [1734], p. 116).

4   To some contemporary observers, thieves' lives seemed inherently disor-
    derly. Thus the 1734 Johnson narrates Phillip Stafford's life "without pro-
    posing any particular Method, which it would be impossible to follow,"
    and tells the story of Old Mobb's adventures "in the Order which we have
    received them, which is the only Method we can follow" (*Highwaymen*
    [1734], pp. 77, 150).

5   Smith, *Highwaymen* (1719a), p. 408; for a similar opinion of Robin Hood,
    see *Remarkable Criminals* (1735a), p. 306.

6   Smith, *Memoirs* (1726), pp. 139, 141, 143, 144.

7   Smith, *Highwaymen* (1719a), p. 241.

8   Smith, *Highwaymen* (1719), 2:50–53.

9   Smith, *Highwaymen* (1719a), pp. 241–43. A story that might be set alongside
    this tells how John Trippuck first met his wife. In the Bristol Newgate for
    highway robbery, Trippuck descends where Flemming rose and, slipping
    down the privy "where he was almost Smother'd in Filth," eventually
    makes his way up through the wastepipe of another privy outside the prison:
    "where groping to find the Hole, [he] feel'd a Pair of warm Buttocks, which
    happen'd to be a Gentlewoman who was newly set. The Gentlewoman
    feeling some Body Finger her Flesh behind, and not dreaming of our subter-
    ranean Passenger, shrieks out, and ran away in all haste, hardly daring to
    look behind her." Trippuck manages nonetheless to make her acquaintance,
    and she, impressed by "his very good Habit [i.e., clothing]" among other
    things, ends the evening by agreeing to marry him. Trippuck, known as
    "the Golden Tinman," was hanged in 1720 (Smith, *Memoirs* [1726], pp.
    234–35). Other outrageous stories that repay the curious reader's attention
    concern Dick Dudley and Isaac Atkinson, both robbers and murderers.
    Buying the merkin "of an old fat Hostess . . . lately hang'd for poisoning
    one of her Guests" from an anatomist in Rome, Dudley persuades the pope
    that the hairy object he has in his possession is actually the beard of St. Peter.
    The pope is so overjoyed that he "put[s] it upon his Mouth, and in a Manner
    worship[s] the Merkin . . . often kissing it." Dudley is richly rewarded, and
    the "Relique" gets pride of place "in the Repository of Rarities." Atkinson's
    brief career as a "Tow-wow-Setter" permits no brief synopsis, but perhaps
    connoisseurs of such stories will recognize its theme when I say that it
    closely resembles a joke that closes with the line, "Heigh-ho, the canary's
    next!" (Smith, *Highwaymen* [1719], 2:6–7, 173–79).

10 Smith, *Memoirs* (1726), pp. 139, 141, 142, 143–44. According to the 1734
    Johnson, the story of Sawney Beane "shews how far a brutal Temper,
    untam'd by Education and Knowledge of the World, may carry a Man in

such glaring and horrible Colours [*sic*]." Beane and his family brought up their children, he notes, "after their own Manner, without any Notions of Humanity or Civil Society" (*Highwaymen* [1734], p. 132).

11 For a more complex "grammar" of narrative, see, e.g., Tzvetan Todorov's *Grammaire du Decameron* (1969).

12 My debt to Lévi-Strauss's "culinary triangle," and through him to Jakobson's "vocalic" and "consonant" triangles, is obvious but should not be overemphasized; my diagrams operate at a simpler level than theirs. Cf. Lévi-Strauss, "The Culinary Triangle," *New Society* 22 December 1966, pp. 937–40; and Roman Jakobson and M. Halle, *Fundamentals of Language* (1956), pp. 38 ff.

13 Smith, *Memoirs* (1726), p. 213.

14 Smith, *Highwaymen* (1719a), pp. 181 (for similar statements, see also pp. 264, 315–17, 451, 491), 183.

15 Ibid., pp. 136–40, esp. 137–38.

16 When Luke Page argues that "robbing was no great sin," Smith's "Table of Memorable Passages" calls it "Scripture perverted" (*Highwaymen* [1719], vol. 2); for the incident itself, see *Highwaymen* (1719a), p. 360.

17 This episode is considerably expanded by the 1734 Johnson. The falseness of the lover illustrates "the Corruption of human Nature," and "the unfortunate young Lady," we are told, "died of Grief and Indignation." More interesting than this, however, is the way the story begins and develops, for it seems concerned to make an implicit criticism of those who would so romanticize the highwayman as to forget what is really at stake. Hind, meeting a coach "filled with gentlewomen . . . went up to them in a gentile Manner, told them, that he was a Patron of the Fair-Sex; and that it was purely to win the Favour of a hard-hearted Mistress, that he travelled the Country: *But Ladies*, added he, *I am at this Time reduced to the Necessity of asking Relief, having nothing to carry one on in my intended Prosecution of Adventures:* The young Ladies, who had most of them read a pretty many Romances, could not help conceiting they had met with some *Quixot* or *Amadis de Gaul*, who was saluting them in the Strain of Knight-Errantry: *Sir Knight*, said one of the pleasantest among them, *We heartily commiserate your Condition, and we are very much troubled that we cannot contribute to your Support; but we have nothing about us but a sacred* Depositum *which the Laws of your Order will not suffer you to violate. Hind* was pleased to think he had met with such agreeable Gentlewomen, and for the Sake of the Jest, could freely have let them pass unmolested, if his Necessities at this Time had not been very pressing." He tells the ladies who he is, which very much startles them, and (his demands are modest here), says he must have £1,000 of the £3,000 dowry they are carrying. This they give him "very thankfully," but without foreseeing the harsh and sad result (*Highwaymen* [1734], p. 88).

18 The "narrational units" of Hind's biography proceed in a sequence that suggests rather more structure than most thieves' biographies do. Thus, for what it is worth, we have his:

```
        Origins:            low
     1st robbery:           neither serious nor humorous but admirable
     2nd robbery:           humorous, serious──→satirical
     3rd robbery:           humorous?, serious?──→satirical?
     4th robbery:           neither humorous nor serious nor admirable
                              (opportunity for satire missed)
     5th robbery:           humorous, serious──→satirical
        Death:              noble
```

The arrows are meant to indicate processes within episodes, the brackets to suggest homologous relations between them.

19   Smith, *Memoirs* (1726), p. 142.

20   Smith, *Highwaymen* (1719a), p. 306.

21   Ibid., pp. 562–63; for the "nine inches," etc., see Smith, *Highwaymen* (1719), 3:298.

22   Smith, *Highwaymen* (1719a), pp. 87 ff.

23   Ibid., pp. 277, 308–10, 96. Interestingly enough, the author of *Compleat Tryals* (1718, 1721) deletes the scatology from Moll's misadventure; see 2:261.

24   Smith, *Memoirs* (1726), p. 283.

25   Smith, *Highwaymen* (1719), 2:262–63; cf. *Highwaymen* (1719a), pp. 166–67. For other such "shockers," see *Highwaymen* (1719a), pp. 24, 66, 338, and *Memoirs* (1726), pp. 132–33. One highwayman's gang goes to the gallows having committed no such atrocity but wishing they had cut the throat of the man who prosecuted them, and those "of his wife and children" (*Highwaymen* [1719a], p. 502).

26   Tinkers were outcasts in eighteenth-century England, but the cruelty of this robbery is emphasized by the illustration of it in Johnson, *Highwaymen* (1734), p. 106, which is reproduced in this book; note especially the expression on the victim's face.

27   Smith *Highwaymen* (1719a), pp. 146, 150, 46–47, 49–50.

28   Johnson, *Highwaymen* (1734), p. 89; for a prophetic indication of this last sad criminal act, look to the background of "Capt. Hind Robbing Col. Harrison in Maidenhead-Thicket," reproduced in this text. Elsewhere the 1734 Johnson tones down Smith's depiction of criminal nastiness, withholding, for instance, "a great many" of Sawney Cunningham's adventures "because they were commonly attended with Bloodshed, an Account of which only presents several melancholy Ideas to the Reader" (p. 34). In this later book the Golden Farmer does not shoot the man in Salisbury Court; it is one of Duval's men who steals the baby's bottle, and Duval returns it; and O'Bryan's rape-murder is passed over in a single sentence: "This young Lady they severally forced after one another to their brutal Pleasure, and when they had done, most inhumanly stabb'd her, because she had endeavoured to get from their Arms" (pp. 108, 91–92, 326; cf. also the stabbing described on p. 116 to the earlier account in Smith, *Highwaymen* [1719a], p. 304). The 1734 Johnson comments much more profusely on the immorality of such horrid events, *before* describing them as well as after, so that his readers encounter them forewarned, their defenses safely up.

CHAPTER 7

1   *Remarkable Criminals* (1735a), p. 28.
2   Johnson, *Highwaymen* (1734), pp. 88, 89.
3   [Henry Goodcole], *Heavens Hue and Cry* (1635), sig. Civ.
4   *Select Trials* (1764), 2:192–93; cf. Applebee's *Original Weekly Journal,* 7 January 1721: "On Thursday Night, at Eleven o'Clock, a Girl of about fifteen Years of Age, passing over Lincoln's-Inn-Fields, a Fellow, with a Leather Apron, forc'd her against her Will; the Girl crying out lamentably all the while, and none coming to her Assistance, the Rogue got away."
5   Practically everyone to be read on the subject in late seventeenth- and early eighteenth-century England claims that serious crime was greatly on the increase, and, in terms of the absolute numbers of offenses committed in certain regions of the country, they may well have been correct. The best modern opinion, however, is that the incidence of felony proportional to the population was significantly lower in the early eighteenth century than it had been in the early seventeenth, and that, with occasional fluctuations, the crime rate showed a "massive decline" (see J. A. Sharpe, *Crime in Early Modern England, 1550–1750* [1984], pp. 57–64, 71–72). Even in London, where significant differences are to be expected, no great increase in the crime rate seems to have occurred. Thus, in his study of Surrey, which included part of the London agglomeration, J. M. Beattie finds that "the three hundred per cent increase in the simple number of indictments for crimes against property . . . between the Restoration and the end of the eighteenth century in fact meant only the very slightest increase, if any at all, in the rate of such crimes." Much of this "considerable increase" in prosecuted crimes, he adds, "can be accounted for by the enlarged population," a factor contemporary writers apparently overlooked. Beattie does find in the Surrey parishes of London over the first half of the eighteenth century, however, a trend to increased violence in crime. Thus indictments for burglary and highway robbery show a significant rise and then a decline, and this decline "continued . . . after 1750." The temporary change in the character of crime, Beattie feels, may be part of the reason contemporaries believed it to be so important a social problem ("The Pattern of Crime in England, 1660–1800," *Past and Present* 62 [1974]: 74, 80, 84). Another reason, to make perhaps too obvious a point, is that news of crime would have traveled more widely in the eighteenth than in the seventeenth century, given improvements in communications and the expansion of the popular press; what otherwise would have been (at most) the stuff of indistinct and distant rumors now could get widespread, prompt, and detailed distribution.
6   *Tryal of Greenwood,* (1740), p. 10; Jonas Hanway, *The Defects of Police, the*

Cause of Immorality (1775), p. 224, cited by John J. Tobias, *Crime and Industrial Society* (1972), p. 24.

7   Quoted by A. G. L. Shaw in *Convicts and the Colonies* (1964), p. 40; cited by Tobias, *Crime and Industrial Society*, p. 38.

8   Smith, *Highwaymen* (1719a), p. 25; copied verbatim from *Second Captain Hind: Or the Notorious Life and Actions of Captain John Simpson* (1700a), n.p.

9   The *London Journal*, 6 January 1721; Applebee's *Original Weekly Journal*, 14 September 1728.

10 Pepys, *Diary*, 12 July 1664, 10 October 1667 (see also 30 January 1665); [Zacharias Conrad von Uffenbach], *London in 1710*, ed. W. H. Quarrel and M. Mare (1934), pp. 120, 156.

11 Boswell, *Life of Johnson*, ed. Hill and Powell, 3:239–40. Johnson thought it wrong to hang highwaymen merely for theft, but saw nothing wrong with shooting them in the act (on the latter see also Locke, *Second Treatise of Government*, chap. 3, para. 18). Still, Johnson wasn't so sure: "perhaps one may, a year after, hang himself from uneasiness for having shot a highwayman." The subject may have been particularly on Johnson's mind because Thrale himself had been robbed by a highwayman, who was later caught and hanged (*Life*, 2:367 n.).

12 Swift, *Journal to Stella*, Letter 38 (29 December 1711), ed. Harold Williams (1948), 2:460–61; Evelyn, *Diary*, 11 June 1652, ed. E. S. de Beer (1955), 3:69–71; Walpole, *Letters*, ed. [Helen W.] Toynbee (1903–5), 2:415–16, 3:96 (see also 8:20).

13 Applebee's *Original Weekly Journal*, 12 October 1728. To expand on the point of English thieves' insolence: in 1720 "one of the Gentleman harbingers to the King," a certain Mr. La Roch, lost £650 to a pickpocket "as he was attending his Majesty to the House of Peers" (Applebee's, 17 December 1720); in 1728 several robbers confessed to a scheme to rob the queen on one of her shopping trips into the City (James Dalton, *Life* [1730], pp. 41–42; Martin Bellamy, *Life* [1728], p. 34); in 1731 two men named Paterson and Darvan stole "his Majesty's Linnen Waistcoats, & c.," which proved a capital offense (the *Monthly Chronicle* 4 [December 1731]: 243). And, if the story can be believed, sometime during the mid-eighteenth century George II was robbed as he took the air in Kensington Gardens. A thief climbed over the wall, caught him alone, held him at gunpoint, took his watch, purse, and shoe buckles, and then, before climbing back over the wall, made him promise to keep quiet until he got safely away (Charles Cavendish Fulke Greville, *Greville Memoirs, 1814–1860*, ed. Lytton Strachey and Roger Fulford [1938], 5:147). Nothing indicates that Oliver Cromwell was ever actually robbed, despite what Smith so often claims, but his grandson did get held up as he was walking through Lincoln's-Inn-Fields (Applebee's, 5 October 1723). Victims of thieves in the latter part of the century included another prime minister, Lord North, whose postilion was shot during an attack on his coach (Walpole to Horace Mann, 6 October 1774, in *Letters*, ed. Toynbee, 9:63), and also the lord mayor of London, the Prince of Wales, the duke of York, and the lord chancellor of England. The lord mayor was

robbed in 1776, and the rest in the eighties (see George Rudé, *Hanoverian London, 1714–1808* [1971], p. 97). An earlier lord chancellor was robbed of the emblems of his office by Thomas Sadler, who was hanged for the offense in 1677 (*Sadler's Memoirs* [1677], pp. 14–16). But perhaps the best indication that thieves respected no one is the fact that the leading publisher of criminals' lives and last confessions, John Applebee himself, had his house burgled in 1727 (Applebee's, 9 September 1727).

14   Murder and manslaughter indictments in early modern London, to judge from the figures for Middlesex, dropped from 4 percent of all felony indictments between 1550 and 1625 to something less than 2 percent by the first half of the eighteenth century (Sharpe, *Crime in Early Modern England,* p. 56). Murder convictions relative to capital convictions overall are not as good an indicator of the frequency of homicide relative to other crimes, but they are nonetheless suggestive. Thus, at the London sessions (a different jurisdiction from Middlesex), there was on average less than one murder conviction per year from 1699 to 1755, i.e., 36 out of a total of 833 capital convictions in all. One might also cite figures for the Home Circuit, 1689–1718, where there were 123 convictions for murder out of a total of 1,165 capital convictions for all offenses, and 8,927 commitments (see Appendixes 4 and 6, "Report from the Select Committee on Criminal Laws" [1819], 585, *Parliamentary Papers* [Reports, 1819], vol. 8).

15   Radzinowicz, *History of English Criminal Law,* vol. 1 (1948), pp. 4–5. Historians have recently commented on the surprising ease with which these capital statutes were passed, and the infrequency with which they were used. Though notionally they seem to express a desire to "get tough" with crimes against property, their actual, practical significance, as well as their political provenance, remain problems to be worked out; for more on this matter see n. 23, this chapter.

16   Herbert Randolph, Assize Sermon, 12 March 1729; thus, according to *The Malefactor's Register* (1779), which believes that behind many a successful criminal there stands a still more criminally inclined woman, "the execution of *ten* women would do more public service than that of a *hundred* men" (1:vii).

17   For an overview of criminal prosecution and trial in early modern England, see J. H. Baker, "Criminal Courts and Procedure at Common Law, 1550–1800," in *Crime in England, 1550–1800,* ed. J. S. Cockburn (1977), pp. 15–48. See also, for their rich particulars on detection as well as prosecution, Alan Macfarlane with Sarah Harrison, *The Justice and the Mare's Ale* (1981); Cynthia Herrup, "New Shoes and Mutton Pies: Investigative Responses to Theft in Seventeenth-Century East Sussex," *The Historical Journal* 27 (1984): 811–30; John Langbein, "Shaping the Eighteenth-Century Criminal Trial: A View from the Ryder Sources," *University of Chicago Law Review* 50 (1983): 55–84; and John Styles, "Sir John Fielding and the Problem of Criminal Investigation in Eighteenth-Century England," *Transactions of the Royal Historical Society,* 5th ser. 33 (1983): 127–49. That the "essentially personal nature of law enforcement" (Sharpe, *Crime in Early Modern En-*

gland, p. 45) imposed special burdens on victims and their witnesses was recognized in 1752 and 1754, when Parliament passed legislation to pay the costs incurred by impoverished prosecutors securing felony convictions; in 1778 this subsidy was extended to all prosecutors and witnesses (see John Langbein, "*Albion's* Fatal Flaws," *Past and Present* 98 [1983]: 102, and Bruce Lenman and Geoffrey Parker, "The State, the Community, and the Criminal Law in Early Modern Europe," in *Crime and the Law: A Social History of Crime in Western Europe since 1500,* ed. V. A. C. Gatrell, Bruce Lenman, and Geoffrey Parker [1980], p. 39). Douglas Hay notes that magistrates could take an active role in the detection and capture of criminals, and that associations for the prosecution of felons arose in the latter part of the eighteenth century, but still "the vast majority of indicted crimes were prosecuted by the victim" ("War, Dearth and Theft in the Eighteenth Century: The Record of the English Courts," *Past and Present* 95 [1982]: 148–49, 151).

18 Frankland is quoted by John Deane Potter, *The Art of Hanging* (1969), pp. 156–57; see also Radzinowicz, *History,* 1:31, 512–16.

19 William Paley, *The Principles of Moral and Political Philosophy* (1785), p. 541.

20 Frankland in Potter, *Art of Hanging,* pp. 156–57. For more on this whole issue, see also James Heath, *Eighteenth Century Penal Theory* (1963), pp. 27–28, and Defoe's *Street-Robberies, Consider'd* (1728), p. 61: "I know it has been propos'd the Watch should go arm'd, but I think it a very dangerous way to cure the Evil we are treating of, unless they were better regulated. For who knows but they may take it into their Heads to do the very thing which those Arms are given to prevent, or at least make them so insolent, that they will insult Gentlemen that are coming Home at an unseasonable Hour, which, I believe, happens to every one sometimes in their Lives."

21 Douglas Hay, "Property, Authority, and the Criminal Law," in *Albion's Fatal Tree,* ed. Douglas Hay, Peter Linebaugh, and E. P. Thompson (1975), p. 21; Paley, *Principles,* p. 529.

22 Hay, "Property," pp. 43, 48–49.

23 Ibid., p. 17. Though not entirely accepted by historians of crime and the law, Hay's thesis has provoked a great deal of interest in the whole question of how and why the law was selectively applied in capital cases. See, for instance, J. A. Sharpe, *Crime in Seventeenth-Century England* (1983), pp. 144–49; Cynthia Herrup, "Law and Morality in Seventeenth-Century England," *Past and Present* 106 (1985): 102–23; Peter King, "Decision-Makers and Decision-Making in the English Criminal Law, 1750–1800," *The Historical Journal* 27 (1984): 24–58; as well as Hay's own "War, Dearth and Theft." From his perspective as a historian of the jury, Thomas Green believes that selective enforcement of the capital statutes "involved far more complex processes than solely the machination of a ruling class or classes" (*Verdict According to Conscience* [1985], p. 311, and chap. 7 generally, "Jury Trial and Its Critics in the Eighteenth Century"). Sharpe is of the same opinion, believing that "any simplistic ideas of a 'ruling class' enacting 'class legislation' should be treated with extreme caution" (*Crime* *in Early Modern England*, pp. 147 ff.), and King, in "Decision-Makers," illustrates quite substantially why these doubts are well founded. For a severe critique of Hay's thesis by an avowedly non-Marxist legal historian, see Langbein, "*Albion's* Fatal Flaws."

24 As an anonymous mid-eighteenth-century editor saw quite clearly: "The same laws which constitute a rural magistracy, to govern the known inhabitants of a country village, answer but very indifferently the purposes of great cities, where the next neighbours hardly know one another; and men live together with as little regard to what each other do, as if they inhabited an extended wilderness" (James Guthrie, Ordinary Account, 9 July 1745). Much the same observation was made by the author of *News from Newgate* (1677), who notes that, "having done their wicked Exploits," highwaymen "retire to, and lurk up and down in this great and populous City, undoubtedly the best Forest for such Beast of Prey to shelter in" (p. 4).

25 Hay, "Property," p. 48.

26 Hay gives no source for his 2:1 ratio of capital convictions to executions, but his information may come from the "Report from the Select Committee on Criminal Laws" (1819), or from Radzinowicz, *History,* vol. 1, which cites certain of its statistics. Without any means to judge the reliability of these particular statistics, or an appropriate apparatus for manipulating them, I am reluctant to draw any large inferences about their meaning. It is notable, however, that although the ratio of executions to capital convictions in London and Middlesex appears to climb as the century advances, it tends to drop in other jurisdictions (thus see Radzinowicz, *History,* 1:146 n. 26, 147–48, 149). More relevant to my concerns here, however, is the disparity between these statistics and two claims made by presumably informed contemporary sources. The first is the claim in 1718, by the author of *Compleat Tryals* (1718, 1721), that "the Numbers executed scarce amount to one Third Part of what are condemned" (1:[viii]). This may have been almost true if London were taken by itself – only 35 percent of those capitally convicted by London juries were hanged from 1710 to 1714 (Radzinowicz, *History,* 1:157) – but the larger picture seems to have been significantly different. Thus, during the twelve mayoralties from November 1700 to October 1712, 528 criminals were sentenced to death in London *and* Middlesex, of whom 217 were executed, for a figure of 40 percent overall (see Paul Lorrain, Ordinary Account, 31 October 1712). Still, *Compleat Tryals* doesn't fudge the facts as much as William Paley, who claims that "of those who receive sentence of death, scarce one in ten is executed" (*Principles*, p. 532). This was certainly not the case in London, where, over the first half of the eighteenth century, fully 10 percent of all those just *tried* on capital charges were executed (Sharpe, *Crime in Early Modern England,* p. 65; a century earlier the figure was 25 percent). In fact, in 1785, the year Paley published his claim, nearly two thirds of all those capitally convicted by the London and Middlesex courts were executed (97 out of 151, only one of whom was a murderer; see Radzinowicz, *History,* 1:147–48). The higher rate of executions in London during the latter part of the eighteenth

century might mean a number of things, but most important here is the light it casts on the peculiar clemency of the London courts around the time Alexander Smith wrote, which is to say during the halcyon days of criminal rogue biography.

27 The information that follows comes from Lorrain's Ordinary Accounts for 15 December 1710 and 31 October 1712.

28 For cases quite similar to those of Crudleigh and Price but originating in mid-seventeenth-century East Sussex, see Herrup, "Law and Morality in England," pp. 116–19.

29 Thomas Stamper, Assize Sermon, 23 March 1721, pp. 14–15.

30 Cf. Edward Tuke, *The Soul's Turnkey* (1656), pp. 71–72: "If no government, then no punishment; if no punishment, then man, whose thoughts and imaginations are only evill, would become impetuous, violent, turbulent: If no Magistracy you should see a generall ataxie and disorder in all estates. . . . In the Commonwealth such a confusion would appear as would vexe a righteous soul; the hand of *Ismael* lifted up against his neighbour; the hedges and highwayes like to the Rode between *Jerusalem & Jericho,* a harbour for the Vagabond, Thief and Robber; the open street a Stage and theater for the obscene and Adulterer: In a word the whole Republique out of order, and the whole earth groaning under the burden of the sinfull offenders." For a similar argument, and the assertion that theft is "against God" because property is a "Divine Institution," see Gabriel Towerson, *An Exposition of the Catechism of the Church of England. Part II* (1681), pp. 403 ff., esp. 425–26. The quotations in the text are from John Haslewood, Assize Sermon, 24 July 1707, pp. 14, 16, and John Conybeare, Assize Sermon, n.d. but pub. 1729, pp. 29, 14–16. See also Haslewood's Assize Sermon for 13 March 1707 or, in fact, just about any assize sermon of the period.

31 Haslewood, Assize Sermon, 24 July 1707, p. 15.

32 Babington, *Advice to Grand Jurors in Cases of Blood* (1680), p. 49; *History of Maclean* (1750), p. 2. In a commentary on the eighth commandment, Gabriel Towerson observes that capital punishment for theft "hath been a matter of controversie" (*Exposition of the Catechism. Part II* [1681], p. 426), and Haslewood refers scornfully to certain "Socinians," who would "disarm the Magistrate of his Power, and tell us that he is by no means worthy to be a Disciple of a meek and suffering Master" (Assize Sermon, 13 March 1707, p. 6). Radzinowicz traces the history of protest against capital punishment for theft from More's *Utopia* (1516) through the seventeenth and eighteenth centuries. Bacon, Bishop Jeremy Taylor, Lord Clarendon, George Fox, and Bishop Berkeley opposed it (see Radzinowicz, *History,* 1:259–67), and a number of less eminent minds. Among the latter, curiously enough, was the author of *Remarkable Criminals.* Rather diffidently – "this I propose only, and pretend not to dictate" – he suggests that thieves be put to penal servitude. In addition to doing the public some positive good, this would tend to diminish their cruelty and resolution, as they'd no longer be risking death, and it "would answer the same end as death, viz., securing the public from any of their future rapines, without sending the poor wretches to the gallows, and pushing them headlong into the other world for every little offence" (1735a, pp. 296–97). For similar thoughts by other practitioners of the popular literature of crime, see as well M.N., preface to 2nd ed. of *State-Trials* (1730), 1:viii–ix, and *The Malefactor's Register* (1779), 1:v–viii. But such sentiments are rare in their time. In 1727 even a "Person of Quality" could seem rather diffident in suggesting that "the capital Animadversion" ought to be imposed only for murder, other "Violences of an enormous Indignity," and "unnatural Impurities." Capital punishment for lesser offenses, he believed on the basis of his own experience, was "an improper Application to the Iniquity of the Age and Place," as well as "ineffectual," "mischievous in its Effect," and "an undue Treatment of the Person." "Must a whole Nation," he asked, "be bound up by a fond Superstition, to a growing Mischief, and instead of redressing the Grievance, tamely permit it to obtain?" Arguing that "Punishments are founded merely in political Convenience," he warned that "continuing the [present] Extremities" might prove "fatal not only to the Criminal, but to the Authority of the Legislators." Interesting as this is, it is even more interesting to hear this same writer refer slightingly to "the Projectors of an absurd Clemency," who would abolish *all* capital punishment, a position he rejects as contrary not only to "Moses and the Prophets" but to "Religion and common Justice" (*An Essay Concerning the Original of Society, Government, Religion and Laws, Especially Those of the Penal Kind. By a Person of Quality* [1727], pp. 60–67). These "absurd projectors" seem not to have committed their thoughts to print, but Londoners could express themselves otherwise. On numerous occasions mobs showed sympathy for thieves, even to the point of impeding their arrest or standing ready to help them escape from the gallows (see, e.g., Applebee's *Original Weekly Journal,* 23 September 1721, 14 November 1724, 19 March 1726, 1 February 1729, 13 September 1729; and also Peter Linebaugh, "The Tyburn Riot Against the Surgeons," in *Albion's Fatal Tree,* ed. Hay, Linebaugh, and Thompson [1975], pp. 65–117).

33 Guthrie, Ordinary Account, 8 June 1744; Fielding, *Voyage to Lisbon,* ed. A. R. Humphreys (1964; 1st pub. 1755), p. 195; *Remarkable Criminals* (1735a), p. 489; Tuke, *Soul's Turnkey* (1656), p. 254.

34 Babington, *Advice* (1680), pp. 52, 53; he is citing Coke's Epilogue to the *Third Institute.* John James, hanged for highway robbery in 1721, echoed the point: "If I may judge of others by myself, I believe that the execution of malefactors has but little effect upon their old companions, or others, who have inured themselves to the like vicious course of life. For I have been often present at such a time, without feeling the least concern or uneasiness, or being any ways alarmed at the sight of death" (*Tyburn Chronicle* [1768], 1:365).

35 *Hanging Not Punishment Enough* (1707; rptd. 1812), p. 9, and George Olyffe, *An Essay to Prevent Capital Crimes* (1731). See also Defoe, *Street-Robberies, Consider'd: The Reason of Their Being So Frequent, with Probable*

Means to Prevent 'em (1728), pp. 52–54; Bernard Mandeville, *An Enquiry into the Causes of the Frequent Executions at Tyburn* (1725); Fielding, *An Enquiry into the Causes of the Late Increase of Robbers* (1751); Paley, *Principles,* esp. pp. 547–48; Boswell, the *Hypochondriack,* No. 68 (May 1783).

36 Fielding, *Enquiry,* pp. 7–8, 103, 103–4, 197, 196.

37 Ibid., pp. 166, 169, 187, 199.

38 Mandeville, *Enquiry,* pp. 1, 2, 46.

39 Ibid., p. 36.

40 Ibid., p. 37. See also a letter supposedly written by Jack Sheppard to Joseph Blake, in which he advises his confederate, "well, comfort thy self, a couple of Kicks, a Shrug, a wry Neck, and a p——ss'd Pair of breeches will make thee snug and easy" (Applebee's *Original Weekly Journal,* 31 October 1724). It ought perhaps to be observed, yet again, that the sense of crisis felt by Mandeville, Fielding, and other writers on crime had, empirically speaking, no basis in actual fact. Thus, so far as modern historical research has been able to determine, "even in London, the absolute number of persons hanged declined between about 1600 and 1750, while the proportion of those accused of felony actually executed also fell appreciably" (Sharpe, *Crime in Early Modern England,* pp. 63–71).

41 Guthrie, Ordinary Account, 31 July 1741.

42 Tuke, *Soul's Turnkey* (1656), pp. 97, 104.

43 Guthrie, Ordinary Account, 13 April 1743. For a general description of the ordinary of Newgate's function, see Peter Linebaugh, "The Ordinary of Newgate and His *Account,*" in *Crime in England,* ed. J. S. Cockburn (1977), pp. 246–69. For Paul Lorrain's particular incumbency in the office (1700–19), see my article, "In Contrast to Defoe: The Rev. Paul Lorrain, Historian of Crime," *Huntington Library Quarterly* 60 (1976): 59–78.

44 Guthrie, Ordinary Account, 11 August 1736.

45 *Remarkable Criminals* (1735a), p. 164. The law was passed as a means of controlling deer poachers and others who refused to recognize the prerogatives of the crown and its assigns in the royal forests. They were called "blacks" because they sometimes blackened their faces to avoid being recognized, and they seem to have enjoyed wide popular support. For a sympathetic though fanciful view of their activities, see *Remarkable Criminals* (1735a), pp. 164–75. The background and consequences of the Black Act are the subject of E. P. Thompson's admirable *Whigs and Hunters* (1975).

46 Lorrain, Ordinary Account, 21 June 1704; see also 15 December 1710, 25 September 1713 (where he makes the point with two separate criminals), and 28 April 1708, where he preaches that "all those that hate (or do not love) their Neighbours are Murtherers." Lorrain's playing on this theme was nothing special. Tuke tried to pin the same guilt on Hannam (*Soul's Turnkey* [1656] p. 251; see also *Hannam's Last Farewell* [1656], pp. 4–5), and Guthrie also equated theft with murder (Ordinary Accounts, 27 September 1736; 18 March 1740, part. 1; and 22 November 1742). Guthrie goes so far as to argue that unpunished thieves, like unpunished murderers, threaten "divine Judgements . . . upon the Land wherein they live" (2 November 1736).

47   In the criminal-as-sinner myth there is an interesting tendency to collapse the distinction between murderers and thieves from the other end as well; thus, for instance, the emphasis on the thefts committed by Savage, Strodtman, and Edmondson, all of which were relatively inconsequential. Perhaps this was a way of diminishing the awful mystery of their crimes by giving them, in part at least, banal and recognizable motives.

48   Lorrain, Ordinary Account, 28 April 1708; *Remarkable Criminals* (1735a) p. 306; Guthrie, Ordinary Account, 2 July 1739.

49   When, for instance, Mandeville assures his audience they need feel no guilt for hanging thieves, it is on the grounds that "the Law of *England* is . . . tender of Mens Lives" (*Enquiry*, p. 2). Smith also speaks of the "merciful compassion" of British law in not putting criminals "to exquisite pains and torment." He then goes on to suggest that life imprisonment at hard labor might be an alternative to hanging them, "which perpetual labor they would count worse than hanging." Elsewhere Smith says, "it is not pity and compassion to bewail [the] misfortunes [of] these unfortunate malefactors"; "we ought not to be sorry at the hangman's meritorious act of sending [them] out of the land of the living" (*Highwaymen* [1719a], pp. 398, 269). Another notable claim for the tenderness of English justice appears on p. 6 of *A Narrative of the Barbarous and Unheard Of Murder of Mr. John Hayes, by Catherine His Wife* (1726); English law prescribed that Mrs. Hayes be burned at the stake, and she was. I may be oversensitive to the implications of fulsome self-congratulation, but behind such talk might we not detect a sneaking suspicion that the current system of criminal justice was almost as much a scandal and a disgrace as the crimes it was powerless to prevent? Consider the curious claims of the following: "The Lenity of our Laws in capital Cases; our Compassion for convicted Criminals; even the general Humanity of our Highwaymen and Robbers, compared with those of other Countries; these are concurrent Proofs, that the Spirit of Humanity is natural to our Nation" ([John Brown], *An Estimate of the Manners and Principles of the Times* [1757], p. 21). All this, "compared with . . . other Countries," may have been true. But the fact that the meaning of the passage hangs on this phrase suggests in Brown's mind the presence of a higher, unevoked standard.

50   The latter phrase is Fielding's and has already been quoted. "But it is thought horrible and grievous," wrote Babington some seventy years earlier, "that a man's life (the life of a Christian) . . . should be taken away for so small a value as thirteen pence" (*Advice* [1680], p. 53). All through the eighteenth century, Radzinowicz points out, "a simple theft of goods *above* the value of twelve-pence was considered grand larceny and was punishable by death." Certain statutes, however, specified thresholds of five and forty shillings for the crime to be capital (*History*, 1:144; also, e.g., 1:47–48).

51   *Remarkable Criminals* (1735a), p. 170; Thomas Gent, *Life* (1832), pp. 57–58; Guthrie, Ordinary Account, 18 March 1740; Leonard Howard, *A True and*

Impartial Account of the Behaviour, Confession, and Dying Words of the Four Malefactors Executed at Kennington-Common, September 6, 1751 (1751), p. 8.

52 The *Tatler*, No. 63, 3 September 1709. In 1700 John Allen was removed from his position as ordinary of Newgate for taking bribes and because, as a sideline, he had been selling funeral supplies to the families of condemned prisoners (Linebaugh, "The Ordinary of Newgate," p. 254). When the motives of Allen's successor were questioned "in a publick Place," the ensuing denial was hardly of a sort to inspire confidence. Paul Lorrain insisted he had never accepted "any Promise, or Gratuity, for his represent-ing the Case of a Malefactor, better or worse, than it really appear'd to his Judgement, nor was he ever Brib'd for obtaining or endeavouring to obtain Reprieves for any." In fact, Lorrain added, he was out of pocket for the bread and wine he gave prisoners while administering Communion (Ordi-nary Account, 4 May 1705). Note that Lorrain never says he has never taken money, only that he has never taken it with the intention of giving value. Note also, with his talk of "promises" and "gratuities," how adept he is at finding euphemisms for bribery.

53 *Remarkable Criminals* (1735a), p. 99.

54 Fielding, *Interposition of Providence in Murder* (1752), p. 93; just previous to this he has written that "it is usual" for criminals other than murderers "to find protection, and [for] the sufferer to be regarded with pity by the tender-hearted" (p. 91).

55 Lorrain, Ordinary Account, 7 February 1705. For thieves' efforts to defend themselves against the charge they are in effect murderers, see Tuke, *Soul's Turnkey* (1656), p. 48; Lorrain, Ordinary Accounts, 7 February 1705, 17 December 1707, 19 September 1712; the *London News, or the Impartial Intelligencer*, 18 February 1718; Applebee's *Original Weekly Journal*, 25 March 1721; William Hawkins, *Robberies* (1722), p. 38; Guthrie, Ordinary Account, 18 March 1740, part 2; *Memoirs of Darkin* (1761), p. 26; *Tyburn Chronicle* (1768), 1:367; Villette, *Account of Hawke and Jones* (1774), p. 5.

56 Walpole to Mann, 2 August 1750, in *Letters*, ed. Toynbee, 3:6–7.

57 Hind is of course a notable exception, as was also Major Oneby, who committed suicide in Newgate (see *Life of Oneby* [1727]). Smith's *Highway-men* includes the biography of one thief who escaped hanging and of another who died a natural death (see 1719a, pp. 477–85, 282–90), and *Remarkable Criminals* includes two who got safely away to America (see 1735a, pp. 200–4, 383–91). These lives represent notable departures in attitude and tone from standard criminal biography. "Amongst a multitude of tragical adventures," says the author of *Remarkable Criminals* at the beginning of one of these accounts, "it is with some satisfaction that I mention the life of a person who was of the number of those few which take warning in time, and having once felt the rod of affliction, fear it ever afterwards" (1735a, p. 200).

58 *Select Trials* (1742), 4:62; *Life and Death of Turner* (1663/[4]), p. 35; Johnson, *Highwaymen* (1734), p. 89. This "putting away" of the highwayman, as it might be called, is aptly epitomized by this last writer's description of the

Golden Farmer's capture and imprisonment. First he notes that "there was no Possibility to make his Escape, every one turning his Enemy now at the last Extremity; when if Love of Man had influenced them, they should have befriended him." But then the next sentence indicates that "Love of Man" is really irrelevant in the Golden Farmer's case, and no one should have any cause for regret: "and . . . during his Confinement, he behaved with the same Alacrity, as he had spent the merry Moment of his foregoing life; neither the Thought of the Place, nor the Apprehensions of Death in the least terrifying him" (p. 108). A similar impulse seems behind the comment that John Everett's narrative of his life and robberies, reprinted in *The Tyburn Chronicle* (1768), shows "an air of levity very ill becoming the circumstances and situation of the prisoner" (2:308).

59   *The Speech and Confession of Mr. Richard Hannam Immediately before His Great and Fatall Leap from off the Ladder* (1656), n.p.

60   "Harlequin Shepherd" appears to have owed much to the behavior of the man himself, or so the testimony of *Remarkable Criminals:* "far from being displeased at being made a spectacle of, he entertained all who came [to see him in prison] with the greatest gaiety that could be. He acquainted them with all his adventures, related each of his robberies in the most ludicrous manner, and endeavoured to set off every circumstance of his flagitious life as well as his capacity would give him leave, which, to say truth, was excellent at cunning, and buffoonery, and nothing else" (1735a, p. 187). Other thieves adopted, or could have attached to them, quite a different theatricality. William Backwith wrote a farewell "Soliloquy" (Guthrie, Ordinary Account, 21 December 1739), and the title page to the *Memoirs of Darkin* (1761) quotes *Othello:* "When you shall these unlucky Deeds relate, / Speak of me as I am: Nothing extenuate, / Nor set down aught in Malice."

61   Smith, *Memoirs* (1726), p. 286; see also p. 203, and in *Highwaymen* (1719a), pp. 183, 239–40, 294, 295, 304, 310.

62   Britannicus, *Letter to the House of Commons* (1750), pp. 15–16.

63   *Anecdotes, Bon Mots, Traits, Stratagems, and Biographical Sketches, of the Most Remarkable Highwaymen, Swindlers, and Other Daring Adventurers* (1797), t.p. Note also this author's hope that the "effect" of his book "on the organs of our Reader's [sic] cannot fail to produce – *astonishment!*" (p. [iii]). A significant element of the "aestheticization" of thieves' lives, I suspect, was their supposed fascination with *The Beggar's Opera.* They are often said to have attended this play, making it in effect a play within their larger play. And of course we all know that plays within plays call the "reality" of their frames into question; all life comes to seem a stage. For references to this interest in *The Beggar's Opera*, see Applebee's *Original Weekly Journal*, 21 September 1728; James Dalton, *A Genuine Narrative* (1728), pp. 24–25, 46; *Life and Actions of Joseph Powis* (1732), p. 53; *Memoirs of Isaac Darkin* (1761), p. 26; Charles Speckman, *Life* (1763), p. 41; *Life of William Cox* (1773), p. 9; and *The Newgate Calendar* (1773), 5:101.

64   Lorrain, Ordinary Account, 5 December 1715.

65 Smith, *Highwaymen* (1719*a*), p. 447.

66 A rare insight into this phenomenon is offered by *The Memoirs of Majr. Alexander Ramkins* (1719), attributed to Defoe. After Ramkins is robbed by a highwayman near London, an innkeeper entertains him by discoursing "very copiously upon the ancient and modern practise of Robbing upon the Road." Seeming "very much inclin'd to lessen the Crime," on the grounds that "now 'tis become a Gentleman-like Employment [and] is very much refin'd as to the manner," he describes how "these Gentlemen approach you decently and submissive, with their Hat in their Hand to know your Pleasure, and what you can well afford to support them in that dignity they live in." " 'Tis True," the innkeeper adds, "they often for Form sake have a Pistol in their Hand, which is part of their riding Furniture; but that is only in the Nature of a Petition, to let you know they are Orphans of Providence just fallen under your Protection." "I thought my time so well spent to hear this Landlord plead in favour of Padding," says Ramkins, "that I told my Companion I had often known the time that I wou'd willingly have parted with more Money than I was strip'd of upon the Heath, to have some Melancholy Thoughts driven away by such a merry Companion" (pp. 150–52). Ramkins's own, recent experience, it should be noted, does not at all fit the innkeeper's "merry" account.

67 Smith, *Highwaymen* (1719*a*), pp. 290–91 ff.

68 See Smith, *Memoirs* (1726), pp. 148–51; cf. Clements R. Markham, *A Life of the Great Lord Fairfax* (1870), p. 23. General Thomas Fairfax (1612–71) had one daughter, his eldest child Mary, who was born in 1638. Though he had a sister named Elizabeth, it is highly unlikely Smith had her in mind or that he had any real knowledge of the family. He gives the general the wrong first initial, "W.," apparently confusing him with his kinsman, Sir William Fairfax (1609–44), who was no general. For other attacks on the Fairfaxes, see Smith's *Highwaymen* (1719*a*), pp. 285, 323.

69 Smith, *Highwaymen* (1719*a*), p. 189; Wilmot's execution date is given as 30 April 1670.

70 Johnson, *Highwaymen* (1734), p. 322; for other slighting references to Smith's veracity, see *Life of Child* (1722), pp. 3–4, and [G. Akerby], *Spiller's Jests* (1729), pp. 6, 30.

71 Smith, *Highwaymen* (1719*a*), pp. 138, 324, 325, 365; Smith, *Memoirs* (1726), pp. 152–53.

72 "If you find a Story, or but one Sentence in all his Scribling, that is even tolerable," writes one of Smith's contemporaries, "depend upon it[,] he stole it" (*The Highland Rogue* [1723], p. vii). Sources from which Smith "stole" include the *Decameron*, *The Canterbury Tales*, both parts of *Henry IV*, Richard Head and Francis Kirkman's *The English Rogue* (1665–71), *Lives of Sundry Notorious Villains* (1678), Alex. Exquemelin's (or rather John Esquemeling's) *Bucaniers of America* (1684–85), and too many individual criminal biographies to list. (On this subject, see Frank Wadleigh Chandler, *The Literature of Roguery* [1907], 1:62, 67, 70, 163–64, 173–76.) One instance of Smith's attaching a popular and presumably well-known anecdote to a specific criminal is his having Whitney force a clergyman to preach a scholarly sermon on theft (*Highwaymen* [1719a], pp. 42–44). A similar story is told in *The Life and Death of Gamaliell Ratsey* (1605), and Frank Aydelotte quotes a manuscript sermon in praise of theft that he dates as far back as 1573; an earlier form of the same story, on Aydelotte's information, could have been extant in the fourteenth century (Aydelotte, *Elizabethan Rogues and Vagabonds* [1913], p. 102). Looking back over the course of criminal rogue biography at the end of the eighteenth century, the author of *Anecdotes of the Most Remarkable Highwaymen* (1797) observes that "by some very recent instances which have occurred at the Old Bailey, and elsewhere . . . our Modern Heroes, through the help probably of oral tradition, have revived some of the feats of their distinguished progenitors, without the smallest variation" (p. [iii]).

73 Cf. Smith, *Highwaymen* (1719a), pp. 89 ff., 464 ff., 307, 467.
74 Smith, *Memoirs* (1726), pp. 132–33; cf. Sandal's reappearance, pp. 282–83.
75 Applebee's *Original Weekly Journal*, 24 February 1722.
76 Smith, *Memoirs* (1726), pp. 275–76; for the bill of indictment, see *A True and Impartial Account of the Tryal of Col. James Turner* (1663/4), pp. 4–8; cf. *Triumph of Truth* (1663/[4]), p. 11, and *Life and Death of Turner* (1663/[4]), pp. 22–23. To give Smith his full due it ought to be noted that he (or whoever he plaqiarized) not only transcribed the information in the indictment but digested it as well. The separate values for each piece of gold and the individual jewels have been added up to get both a sum total and a total for each of the categories Smith mentions – and the addition is correct!

CHAPTER 8

1 Says Lévi-Strauss: "Les animaux du totémisme cessent d'être, seulement ou surtout, des créatures redoutées, admirées, ou convoitées: leur réalité sensible laisse transparaître des notions et des relations, conçue par la pensée speculative à partir des données de l'observation. On comprend enfin que les espèces naturelles ne sont pas choisies parce que 'bonnes à manger' mais parce que 'bonnes à penser' " (*Le Totémisme aujourd'hui* [1962], p. 128); I quote the original French because this passage does not read nearly so powerfully or well when translated into English).
2 James Guthrie, Ordinary Account, 25 April 1733; quoted subsequently by *Select Trials* (1742), 4:60.
3 *Memoirs of Mackheath* (1728), p. 8.
4 Old Mobb never robbed "in any company except sometimes with the Golden Farmer," according to Smith's *Highwaymen* (1719a), p. 36. But for evidence of his gang activity, including robberies with James Whitney, see the account of his trial in the Old Bailey Sessions Papers, 9–12 September 1691. The Golden Farmer's gang, including "a Fellow called *Old Mob*," is described in the Old Bailey Sessions Paper for 10–13 and 17 December

1690; they apparently specialized in burglaries of country houses. Luttrell mentions the Golden Farmer's gang in his *Brief Relation of State Affairs* (1857), 2:205, 253; he also speaks of Whitney's gang and the political fears raised by his outspoken Jacobitism, 2:630, 644; 3:2, 5, 10, 16, 23–24, 26, 27. For general evidence of the activities of gangs in the 1690s, see Luttrell, 2:317, 510; 4:540–41. For the same in the 1720s, see Applebee's *Original Weekly Journal*, 23 and 30 October, 4 December 1725. Though Hind's gang is mentioned in some of his earlier biographies, it is not described in action, and later accounts ignore it entirely. But Antony Wood attests to its size and efficiency in a marginalium at the back of his copy of *The English Gusman*, now at the Bodleian: "Twentie horse of Hinds company the great robber, committed 40 robberies about Barnet (not far from London) in the space of five houres – about 22. Sept. 1649."

5 *Remarkable Criminals* (1735a), pp. 306–7, 320.

6 Wild was hanged in 1725, ten years before the publication of *Remarkable Criminals*. He was arguably the first modern criminal mastermind, bringing business methods into crime and then making it into big business. He kept books, stored his stolen goods in warehouses rented for the purpose, set up factories where items could be altered beyond recognition, and even bought a ship for transporting particularly "hot" pieces abroad. For a full account of his life, see Gerald Howson, *Thief-Taker General: The Rise and Fall of Jonathan Wild* (1970). It is interesting to note that Wild seemed unprecedented to Londoners of the 1720s, though Mary Frith (d. 1659), also known as Moll Cutpurse, had also organized the London underworld with herself at the head. Or so claims *The Life and Death of Mary Frith* (1662), pp. 43, 101; Smith's *Highwaymen* (1719a), pp. 285–86, repeats the claim.

7 *Remarkable Criminals* (1735a), p. 306.

8 For the suppression of the "New Mint," see *Remarkable Criminals* (1735a), pp. 194–99. The original Mint was a haven for debtors in Southwark, where by ancient custom they were free from civil arrest. Its privileges were abolished by law in 1723, and some of its former habitués, "with unparalleled impudence," tried to set up another in its place "towards Wapping." "These people," *Remarkable Criminals* significantly notes, "made an addition to those laws which had formerly been established in such illegal sanctuaries, for they provided large books in which they entered the names of persons who entered into their association, swearing to defend one another against all bailiffs and such like," and "they very often rescued prisoners out of custody, or even entered the houses of officers for that purpose" (1735a, p. 196). Of course the authorities found this intolerable and ruthlessly suppressed them. Proroguing Parliament in 1725, after the passage of bills "disarming the Highlanders" and "to prevent Outrages and Violences in the *New Mint*," King George expressed his thanks for their taking measures to prevent "Commotions in those Parts where the publick Peace was most in Danger" (Applebee's *Original*

Weekly Journal, 5 June 1725; see also 9 January 1725, where it is asserted that the "New Minters" offer "unsufferable Violence . . . to the British Constitution").

9 *Remarkable Criminals* says almost nothing of the constitution of Burn-worth's "antisociety," and this is typical. It is not that thieves' mores and institutions were uninteresting; the various dictionaries of criminal slang, which date back to the sixteenth century, show one way in which the criminal subculture could attract attention (see [John Awdeley?], *The Frater-nitie of Vacabondes* [1565]; Thomas Harman, *A Caueat for Common Cvrsetors* [1567]; and Robert Greene, *A Notable Discouery of Coosnage* [1591] – all of which are collected in *Cony-Catchers and Bawdy Baskets*, ed. Gāmini Salgādo [1972] – and also *The Thieves' New Canting Dictionary*, at the back of vol. 1. of the 1719 edition of Smith's *Highwaymen*, and *The Thieves' Exercise*, at the back of vol. 3). Few writers, however, let their imaginations rove over the political arrangements thieves would necessarily have had to work out for themselves, for even. antisocieties must have governments. Among these few are Richard Head, who offers a rare description of a ritual induc-tion into a gang of highwaymen (*The English Rogue* [1928; 1st pub. 1665], pp. 142–43); Smith, who sets forth a ludicrous code of behavior suppos-edly followed by the original Blackguards (*Highwaymen* [1719a], pp. 362–63); and the author of *Remarkable Criminals*, who provides a curious and probably fanciful account of a gathering of the so-called Waltham Blacks, a fraternity of deer poachers led by a certain "Prince Oroonoko, King of the Blacks" (1735a, pp. 171–74). Generally, however, it is only in narratives of pirate life, and particularly in Defoe's narratives of such life, that social and political arrangements become objects of regular interest. Here of course to some extent the aim is verisimilitude. The very nature of their business requires pirates to work in groups; ships are more capital-intensive than horses and more labor-intensive as well. But it is possible to see more than merely a concern for plausibility in the political issues that interlard Defoe's *History of the Pyrates* (1724, 1728). In plugging this book, Defoe claimed it showed "how a Parcel of Out-Laws, who were Enemies to all Men, and all Men so to them, whom no Land would receive, could subsist upon an Element which does not furnish the Necessaries of Life to Man." No previous writer on pirates, he says, "had ever taken Notice how they were governed amongst themselves," i.e., how it was they "did not cut one anothers Throats, upon the least Division." There was something to be learned from their political system, especially "considering what the Per-sons were who fram'd it," which might be relevant to "other Common-wealths" concerned with limiting the exercise of "arbitrary Power" (*Letters out of Mist's Weekly Journal* [1722–27], 4:196–97). For more on Defoe's interest in pirates, see Maximillian Novak's introduction to *Of Captain Mission* (1961; an Augustan Reprint Society selection from *The History of the Pyrates*), pp. i–iii; Joel H. Baer, " 'The Complicated Plot of Piracy': Aspects of English Criminal Law and the Image of the Pirate in Defoe,"

The Eighteenth Century: Theory and Interpretation 23 (1982): 3–26; and Christopher Hill, "Radical Pirates?" in *The Origins of Anglo-American Radicalism,* ed. Margaret Jacob and James Jacob (1984), pp. 17–32. The new twist that pirates provided on the old ship-of-state metaphor might just as easily have been applied to "land pirates," as highwaymen were often called. I find it suggestive that it was not, nor to any other organized gangs of thieves.

10 Thus Mist's *Weekly Journal,* 22 July 1721: "Last Tuesday Morning a Gentleman coming from Highgate, was attacked at the Bottom of the hill by two Foot Pads, who robbed him of about twenty Guineas and a Gold Watch, and afterwards beat him very barbarously. 'Tis hop'd, by the Help of this Booty, they may be able to mount on Horseback for the next Adventure." When in 1722 a footpad was reproached for leaving his victim bound naked in a cold field, he defended himself on the grounds that "any man would endeavour to secure himself from danger, as well as I have done; I know no odds between one way of robbing and another; and as (for want of horses) we could go no faster then our legs would carry us, we thought it the wisest way to slacken the pace of those we robbed, for fear they should overtake us" (John Villette, *Annals of Newgate* [1776], 1:86). In this context, Johnson's *Highwaymen* (1734) shows Defoe's Colonel Jack and his companion treating Mrs. Smith and her friend with extreme diffidence. Though there is real pain on Jack's victims' faces, note, in the illustration reproduced in this text, the all too typical barbarity of the event taking place down the road.

11 Guthrie, Ordinary Account, 3 March 1736/7.

12 Luttrell, *Brief Relation of State Affairs,* 3:497; Applebee's *Original Weekly Journal,* 5 May 1722 and 3 January 1730. Many more such incidents might be related.

13 Even when real-life highwaymen tried to live up to the highest heroic standards, there was always the possibility of things going wrong. To the story of Walpole's "accident" might be added that of a gentleman and his lady robbed on Hounslow Heath. The two highwaymen who stopped them "seem'd dispos'd to have treated them very civilly, and to have took their Money with a great deal of good Manners," but when a servant attempted to escape "and alarm the Country," they not only "beat him very severely, and wounded him," but cut short their complaisance with the lady and gentleman. Forcing them out of their carriage, they "rifled them of every thing of Value they had about them" (Applebee's *Original Weekly Journal,* 5 December 1719).

14 For these phrases used in context, see Johnson, *Highwaymen* (1734), p. 339; *Select Trials* (1742), 1:114, 300 (and also 175); *Genuine Life of Page* (1758), p. 4.

15 *Triumph of Truth* (1663/[4]), p. 3.

16 J.M., *The Traveller's Guide; and the Country's Safety. Being a Declaration of the Laws of England against High-Way-Men, or Robbers upon the Road* (1683), pp. [iii–iv]. Cf. John Clavell:

> You have got by this vile course of sinning
> A kinde of state, nere known to your beginning;
> And from attending others, are become
> The principall, and best men in the roome;
> Where (like the Asse in trappings) you do awe
> The silly beasts, that Beere and Claret draw;
> For they you Captaines, and Lieutenants call,
> And tremble when a frowne you doe let fall,
> for *Peerelesse* now your selves are masters grown;
> That in mans memorie were Foot-boyes Known.
>   [Clavell, *Recantation* (1628; 3rd ed. 1634), pp. 7–8]

17 John Taylor, Ordinary Account, 3 October 1750, pp. 84–85; *Life and Actions of Maclean* (1750), p. 10.

18 *Life and Transactions of Parsons* (1751), p. 8. Parsons, however, had a more legitimate claim to the rank of gentleman than most highwaymen, as he was the son of Sir William Parsons, Bart., "a very worthy Gentleman" though much impoverished by his Jacobitism (p. 3); *Memoirs of Parsons* (1751) claims that he was a nephew of the late duchess of Northumberland (p. 2). But, we may well ask, what would the Newgate ordinary and anonymous hack writers have known of true gentility? Who were they to say a man was not a gentleman? Maclean in fact was supported and encouraged by a number of people of quality (and there were rumors that a good many noblewomen had succumbed to his charms). The point nonetheless, in his case as well as Parsons's, is that one is hardly a gentleman if one's status can be called into question – especially by someone himself of doubtful status.

19 Note the rich and wounding irony of the following: "From frequent Conversation with Mr. *Darkin,* it was easy to collect his Maxims. He had a proper Abhorrence to the most dreadful Crime of Murder; hence, in all his Attacks, though he was by no means sparing in his Threats, yet he never put them in Execution. He had a high notion of *Honour;* which he thus defined: The being grateful for Favors received, the fulfilling of his Engagements; and the not appearing *mean.* As a Delicacy in Conversation, (if it turned upon his own Employment,) he never mentioned a *Robbery, Robber,* or *Highwayman:* he spoke of Persons who had been *injured;* and of the injured *Parties.*" It is hard to know how much of this irony is intended and how much emerges from the situation; the writer is not unsympathetic – "his Conversation was rather agreeable . . . and his Discourse . . . not affectedly larded with *flash Terms*" – but neither is he entranced (*Memoirs of Isaac Darkin* [1761], p. 21). I shall have more to say about the complex attitudes a highwayman like this could call forth toward the end of this chapter.

20 *Genuine Life of Page* (1758), p. 44; Guthrie, Ordinary Account, 3 March 1736/7; Smith, *Highwaymen* (1719a), p. 179.

21 "False Notions of true Greatness are the chief Causes of the Degeneracy of the present Times," says a writer who signs himself Britannicus. "The bad Conduct of those who should be Examples of Virtue and Piety . . . is a great Encouragement to the Sons of Vice" (*Letter to the House of Commons* [1750], pp. 22, 24). For similar views see Allen, *Account of Maclaine* (1750), p. 27; and Walpole to Horace Mann, 8 September 1782, in *Letters*, ed. Toynbee, 12:330. Consider also the thrust of this comment by "a worthy Divine" concerned at Darkin's behavior in prison: "He was afraid Mr. *Darkin* studied more to appear like a Gentleman than a Christian" (*Memoirs of Darkin* [1761], p. 27).

22 Steele, the *Spectator*, No. 151, 23 August 1711.

23 *Select Trials* (1742), 1:221.

24 The quoted phrases are borrowed from *Memoirs of Darkin* (1761), p. 4.

25 *Select Trials* (1742), 4:63. More than a hundred years before Gordon was hanged, John Clavell whiled away his time in prison by writing a poem to the king; eventually it procured him a pardon. At one point he addresses his fellow robbers in language that almost seems designed for Gordon's case:

> You beleeve you have deserv'd to bee
> Admir'd not scorn'd, for your past villany,
> And that the actions, you have done are such
> As pace with honour, can endure the touch
> Of cruel'st censure, whilst you fondly deeme
> That men you brave, and valiant doe esteeme,
> And so are bound with your ills to connive,
> And in despite of Law keepe you alive.
>
> [Clavell, *Recantation* (1628; 3rd ed. 1634), p. 16]

Early in the nineteenth century, the pathos of Gordon's suicide attempt would be further undercut by the claim that he and the surgeons were engaged in a plot to save his life, the throat cutting being part of an experiment to enable him to survive hanging (see Andrew Knapp and William Baldwin, *The New Newgate Calendar*, vol. 1 [1811], p. 481).

26 The on-again–off-again nature of the highwayman's status as "gentleman," along with its potential for comedy, is nicely illustrated by Mrs. Peachum in act 1, scene 4, of *The Beggar's Opera* (1728). "There is not a finer gentleman upon the road," she says approvingly of Macheath. But then, informed that he wastes his money in chocolate houses, she asks: "What business hath he to keep company with lords and gentlemen?"

27 Read's *Weekly Journal*, 29 August 1719; see also 23 July 1720.

28 See Appendix II.

29 [Christopher Bullock], *Woman's Revenge: Or, a Match in Newgate*, 2nd ed. (1728), pp. 2, 3, 4–6; this play, first performed and published in 1715, was apparently revived in 1728 to cash in on the vogue of *The Beggar's Opera*.

30 Consider what happens to James Shaw's claim to be a "social" criminal.

Before being hanged in 1722 for robbery and murder, he tried "to convince the chaplain of Newgate that he was not so great a reprobate as some might imagine," saying "it was his firm opinion, that it was a much greater sin to rob a poor man, or the church of God, than those who would have spent the money he took from them in gaiety and luxury, or those who perhaps had unjustly acquired it by gaming." This gets the following contemptuous dismissal: "What a conscientious foot-pad and murderer was this! how great his compassion for the poor and distressed! how extraordinary his justice in punishing evil-doers, and his care in preventing the rich from making an ill use of their money! and, above all, what a pious regard does he shew for the church of God! and yet it does not appear, that in any of his robberies he gave himself the trouble of enquiring into these particulars" (Villette, *Annals of Newgate* [1776], 1:69). For similar responses to "conscientious" thieves, see Guthrie, Ordinary Account, 5 October 1737, and *Select Trials* (1764), 3:15, where a highwayman's version of "brave and generous Sentiments, which only heroic spirits are inspired with," is dismissed as "fallacious Arguments, which those of that Profession commonly use to quiet their Consciences."

31 Smith, *Highwaymen* (1719a), p. 211. "In a Word," says the 1734 Johnson of one highwayman who "pretended to dispute the Lawfulness of Robbing," "the Behaviour of this Fellow was such, that there was no judging whether he was really stupid, or whether he had a Mind to argue himself into a Love of his own vices" (*Highwaymen* [1734], p. 347).

32 *The Devils Cabinet Broke Open: Or a New Discovery of the High-Way Thieves* (1658), p. 17.

33 *Genuine Life of Page* (1758), pp. 41, 40–41; the ellipses in the newspaper paragraph are mine.

34 This complexity of attitude is of course to be found in other accounts of dying highwaymen, but rarely is it so clearly and compactly expressed. Applebee's *Original Weekly Journal*, 21 July 1722, reports that James Carrick "died in a kind of antick Bravery, between Jest and Earnest, but without discovering any Remorse at his Crimes." More than twenty years later he is remembered for his "foppish Airs," his "Levity and Unconcern" (*Select Trials* [1742], 1:212). *Remarkable Criminals* dismisses "that silly contempt of death, which with the vulgar passes for resolution" (1735a, p. 323), and Isaac Darkin is ridiculed for wanting to "die like a hero" and believing that "he had at different Times been almost as much the Subject of Conversation as the King of Prussia" (*Memoirs of Darkin* [1761], p. 27). But in the same year that Carrick died, Applebee's describes two other doomed highwaymen in more positive terms, saying "they are Persons of a genteel and extraordinary Behaviour, of good Countenance and Address, which render them Objects of much Pity and Concern" (5 May 1722). Elsewhere, however, Applebee's debunks "a very Romantick Account" of a highwayman who refused to plead before the court, and so was sentenced to be pressed. Rumor had it that "when they brought some Cords to tye him, he broke them asunder several Times like Twine, and said, that if they

brought Cables, he would serve them in the same Manner; as if another Sampson had again appear'd on the Stage." No such thing happened, says Applebee's, most emphatically. But then it offers as the truth a not unaffecting account of his making "no manner of opposition," of his undressing, lying down, and extending his arms and legs so that a great board could be laid across his chest, "and eight half hundred Weights were lay'd upon it; which he endured for the Space of an Hour, wanting seven Minutes." The highwayman hoped to die in this manner, so that his property would pass to his wife and child and not be seized by the crown. (This was the case with all convicted felons; if the suspect refused to plead, however, he could not be convicted.) "But at last, thro' the Torture of the Press, and the Entreaties of a Friend of his, that kept crying over him, he alter'd his Mind, and was thereupon taken out" (21 January 1721).

35 "The highway seems as tempting to [juvenile tempers]," says *Remarkable Criminals,* "as Chivalry did to Don Quixote" (1735*a,* p. 28). For an account of Don Quixote in eighteenth-century England, see Edward L. Niehus, "The Nature and Development of the Quixote Figure in the Eighteenth-Century English Novel" (Ph.D. diss., University of Minnesota, 1971; *Dissertation Abstracts International* 32 [December 1971]: 3319A–3320A).

36 *Genuine Life of Page* (1758), pp. 4, 41.

37 The Old Bailey sessions papers, which began to be published in an expanded format with the number for 3–6 December 1729, show an increasing interest in the dramatic and colorful. Thus they take pains to represent dialect, and make a habit of covering cases where whores have robbed their customers, even though these usually result in acquittal. Their preference for the "dramatic" heavily influences the *Select Trials* collections of 1734–35, 1742, and 1764, and may be seen operating as well in *Remarkable Trials* (1765), which emphasizes the visual spectacle of the criminal's situation, thus: "Here [the reader] may behold (at least in Imagination) the Felon holding up his trembling Hand at the Bar; by and by he sees him struck with Horror and Confusion at the dreadful Sentence of Death pronounced against him; after this he finds him in his gloomy Cell, perhaps wringing his Hands, beating his Breast, and cursing his Folly. . . . Anon he is led forth, manacled, to the fatal Tree. See his ghastly Looks, his Joints trembling, his Knees knocking! Hear his piteous Cries," etc. (1:viii–ix). The last major collection of criminal lives *not* to be influenced by the expanded trial coverage of the sessions papers is *Remarkable Criminals* (1735), which tends to remain resolutely biographical and to give roughly equal attention to all the criminals it notices, whatever their crimes. By the latter part of the century the wealth of material offered by the sessions papers appears to have raised such basic narratological problems for criminal biographers that, on occasion, they abandoned the usual requirements of the form. Thus *The Tyburn Chronicle* (1768) notes that "in some instances . . . the narrative stile could not be adopted, for in the depositions of the witnesses in some trials . . . there is something so singular, and . . . so *ridiculously*

diverting that it would have been depriving our readers of great pleasure to have given these accounts in any other Words." In at least one other instance, it notes, "throw[ing a case] into the narrative form" would have meant "rendering it less intelligible than it is in its present form," there being "so many questions asked, and so many replies given, in the course of the . . . trial" (1:viii, 2:34; see also 2:359).

38   For the ordinary of Newgate's account of John Rann, see Villette, *Annals of Newgate* (1776), 4:378–88; see also *Account of Rann* (1774), and *Life of Rann* (1774*a*). The dismissive description can be found in Andrew Knapp and William Baldwin, *The New Newgate Calendar,* vol. 3 (1819?), pp. 351, 353, which closely follows *The Malefactor's Register* (1779), 5:138–46. Rann might be taken as proof of "a common observation" in the late eighteenth century, itself evidence of a shift in feeling, "that thieves are bad oeconomists" (*The Newgate Calendar* [1773], 1:25).

39   The 1734 Johnson was published by J. Janeway as a serial, in seventy-three fascicules priced at two pence each (see R. M. Wiles, *Serial Publication in England before 1750* [1957], p. 293). Apparently sales were slow, or demand overestimated, for the same fascicules were bound together with a new title page and reissued in 1736 by Olive Payne (Wiles seems not to have been aware of this reissue). Perhaps it is a sign of the original publisher's desperation that, in midpublication, his writer or writers abruptly switched from plagiarizing Alexander Smith and started instead on the original Capt. Charles Johnson's (i.e., Defoe's) *History of the Pyrates* (1724, 1728). The severity of tone that becomes noticeable in the 1734 Johnson has, by the 1770s, advanced to the point that *The Newgate Calendar* (1773) and *The Malefactor's Register* (1779) are thoroughly humorless and practically without irony – qualities amply enough indicated by their stodgily fulsome title pages.

40   For a sampling of accounts of crimes closely paralleling the sort of stuff to be found in Alexander Smith, see, e.g., Applebee's *Original Weekly Journal,* 2 July 1720, 23 August 1721, 29 December 1722, 8 August 1724, 6 June and 21 November 1730. In Applebee's, which I take to be typical of the weekly press in general, crime coverage increases significantly around the beginning of 1722, perhaps not accidentally. The South Sea Bubble had faded away, and the Atterbury Plot had not yet surfaced, leaving a dearth of "Intelligence, to satisfy the greedy Stomachs of Mankind with News." Under such circumstances, Mist's *Weekly Journal* pointed out, "we are forced to stuff our Accounts with [among other things] Horsemen and Footpads that take the Air on the Roads" (16 December 1721); for similar comments, see Applebee's, 21 and 28 August 1725.

41   Walpole to Horace Mann, 20 September 1750, in *Letters,* ed. Toynbee, 3:18. It may be relevant to note that a parallel fatigue may sometimes have been aroused by serious criminal biography. "The Town has been so cloy'd with such Variety of this Species of Production," one writer observes at midcentury, "that it is no wonder that the Publick Taste should take a different Turn, and look upon all further Attempts in that Way in a

despicable Light" (*Memoirs of Cranstoun* [1753], p. 1). Doubtless *The Cruel Son* (1707) was responding to much the same feeling when it declared, before getting down to its story of matricide, "Too many are the Instances of Unnatural and Barbarous Murthers in this degenerate Age; but there is none so immediately *new* as the following Relation makes mention of" (p. 2; italics mine).

42 Knapp and Baldwin, *New Newgate Calendar*, vol. 1 (1811), p. 417.

43 "Forgers are seldom among the low and abandoned part of mankind," observes *The Malefactor's Register* (1779), "Forgery is very often the last dreadful refuge to which the distressed tradesman flies" (1:vii). Lady Lyttleton would doubtless have agreed; thus, appearing as a character witness for Robert Perreau and "being asked, if she thought him capable of such a crime, [she] 'supposed she could have done it as soon herself' " (Villette, *Annals of Newgate* [1776], 4:409).

44 For accounts of Dodd, see, e.g., John Villette's *Genuine Account of William Dodd* (1777) and his *Relation of Dr. Dodd's Behaviour in Newgate* (1777), as well as *The Malefactor's Register* (1779), 5:207–27. For the Perreau brothers and Mrs. Rudd, see, among others, Villette's *Genuine Account of Daniel Perreau and Robert Perreau* (1776), also his *Annals of Newgate* (1776), 4:399–421, and *The Malefactor's Register* (1779), 5:161–85. The hardening of the laws against forgery is described by Radzinowicz, *History of English Criminal Law*, vol. 1 (1948), pp. 642–50; according to J. A. Sharpe this appears to have been caused by changing social attitudes and not by any "rising tide of forgers" (*Crime in Early Modern England, 1550–1750* [1984], 177–78). By the turn of the century, in any case, forgery could seem the third great crime against society, murder being the first and treason the second (thus see Knapp and Baldwin, *New Newgate Calendar*, vol. 1 [1811], pp. iii–iv; cf. Coke's rather different ranking of crimes by seriousness in *The Third Part of the Institutes* [1644], mentioned in Chapter 2, n. 1).

45 Consider, as an instance of such class consciousness, the absolutely counterfactual claim by *The Newgate Calendar* (1773) that, although "many [highwaymen] have lived in very reputable circumstances," "most [footpads] are such as have been originally brought up among the rascally off-scourings of the people." This supposed difference in social background is taken to explain why highwaymen "seldom treat any person with cruelty," while footpads commit "crimes of so horrid a nature, that makes it absolutely necessary for them to be cut off that people may live in safety" (2:346). For its part, *The Malefactor's Register* (1779) finds "few . . . violators of the law, who are not the offspring of the poorer classes of the people," and blames this in part on their child-rearing practices: "It is but too common with women of the lower ranks of life to ruin their children by an extravagant tenderness" (5:295, 1:325).

46 *The History of John Sheppard* (1724a), pp. 148, 153, 149, 150, 155, respectively.

47 Villette, *Annals of Newgate* (1776), 4:417.

POSTSCRIPT

1 Aleman, *The Rogue* (1655), sig. [B6r]; this edition is an abridgment of James Mabbe's translation of *Guzman de Alfarache*, first published as *The Rogue* in 1622 and frequently reissued. Cf. John Smith, who compares the Scriptures to "a pleasure Garden bedecked with flowers, or a fruitful field of precious treasures," discoverable only to the reader who knows how to read (*The Mysterie of Rhetorick Unveil'd* [1657], quoted by Perry Miller, *The New England Mind: The Seventeenth Century* [1961], pp. 310–11). Cf. also Defoe's preface to *Colonel Jack* (1965; 1st pub. 1722), p. 2: "The various Turns of his Fortunes in the World, make a delightful Field for the Reader to wander in; a Garden where he may gather wholesome and medicinal Plants, none noxious or poisonous."

2 See Lukács, *The Theory of the Novel* (1920; tr. 1971), passim. Says Lucien Goldmann, following Lukács's lead, "the novel [has] always been the literary form of the problematic search and the absence of positive values" (*Towards a Sociology of the Novel* [1964; tr. 1975], p. 13, and chap. 1 generally).

3 Defoe, *Moll Flanders* (1971; 1st pub. 1722), pp. 277, 288. For a real-life analogue to Moll's situation, with Alexander Cruden the Bible indexer playing the role of the other, disinterested minister, see Charles Speckman, *Life* (1763), pp. 49–50.

4 Defoe, *A Hymn to the Funeral Sermon* (1703), n.p.

5 *A Serious Advice to the Citizens of London* (1657), p. [8]. As Edward Tuke told Richard Hannam, "it were a brave world, if a man might run all his dayes in a course of violence and sinne, and for two or three words at last come to heaven, receive so great wages for so little work" (*The Soul's Turnkey* [1656], p. 56).

6 Franklin et al., *A Murderer Punished and Pardoned* (1668), p. 40.

7 Butler's ministers, writing in the midst of the Interregnum, felt they lived in an age when the "Spirit of Presumption" had never been greater (ibid.); they did not want his case to give religious deviants straws to grasp at.

8 See Samuel Smith, Ordinary Account, 20 December 1693; Paul Lorrain, Ordinary Account, 22 March 1704; and James Guthrie, Ordinary Account, 12 June 1741. In all else that I have read pertaining to the dying behavior of criminals in the period, I have found only nine other references to the thief on the cross, viz., *Account of Behavior of Weller* [*et al.*] *in Newgate* (n.d.); Sir George Sondes, *His Plaine Narrative* (1655), p. 30 (which is quoted by R[obert] Boreman, *A Mirrour of Mercy* [1655], pp. [1]–2); Tuke, *Soul's Turnkey* (1656), pp. 97–104; *Remarks on the Author of the Hymn to the Pillory. With an Answer to the Hymn to the Funeral Sermon* (1703); the account of Harmon Strodtman in *Compleat Tryals* (1718, 1721), 2:221; John Bellers, *To the Criminals in Prison* (1725?); Dr. Allen, *An Account of Maclaine* (1750); Philo-Patria, *A Letter to Henry Fielding, Esq. Occasioned by His Enquiry into the Causes of the Late Increase of Robbers* (1751?), pp. 13–14; and *An Address*

to All Who Frequent Our Numerous Executions (1762), p. 11. In raising the example of the thief on the cross, Smith, Tuke, and Philo-Patria warn against its dangerousness, the latter two insisting that really it has no application. "When other Robbers hear and read" that "their Case was exactly parallel to the Case of the Thief on the Cross," writes Philo-Patria, "it greatly encourages them to continue their wicked Course of Life; and there can be no doubt, they say within themselves; – 'It is but to dye Penitent at last, and we shall be saved in the next Life.' "

9 Boreman, *Mirrour of Mercy* (1655), p. 37. "By some (we know before hand)," wrote the author of *The Unhappy Citizen* (1691), "we shall be slighted, and censured as being too busie, and may be, too Credulous; but our aim being Publick Good, and the Discharge of our Conscience, we are not Discouraged" (p. 7).

10 Smith, Ordinary Account, 23 May 1684; Lorrain, Ordinary Account, 13–14 October 1703, and also 21 June, 22 September, and 25 October 1704, 4 May 1705, 2 May 1707, 27 October and 17 December 1708, 24 June 1709. For countercomplaints about the accuracy, authority, and interpretations of the ordinaries' *Accounts,* see *History of the Press-Yard* (1717), pp. 30–32, 45–47, 52–53; *Remarkable Criminals* (1735a), pp. 348, 480, 542; *Select Trials* (1742), 1:95, 244–46, 255, 324–26, 3:180–81, 4:41; *Life of Matthew Lee* (1752), pp. 12–13; Speckman, *Life* (1763), p. 53; and (even!) Smith's *Highwaymen* (1719a), pp. 1–2, and his *Memoirs of Wild* (1726), p. 98. The mere fact that one Newgate ordinary "set" his name to an account of a criminal's life, declared one inmate of the prison, was "sufficient reasons for the World to suspect the Truth of it" (Charles Newy, *Newy's Case* [1700], p. 14). "Whatever the Ordinary may take upon him to set forth after my Death," wrote another, could not possibly be the whole truth: "Notwithstanding all his Importunities to be apprized of my most intimate Secrets," he declared, "I always industriously avoided entring upon Particulars . . . so that I must request of his Readers not to give credit to what he shall publish concerning me, if it shall be in contradiction to what I have here related" (Carrick, *Robberies* [1722], pp. 1–24). Scorn for the Newgate ordinary was so endemic that one correspondent to Mist's *Weekly Journal* wrote in to ask, "For God's Sake, . . . wherein lies the Infamy of assisting some of the unhappiest Men in the World in their Passage to Eternity, and endeavouring to save their Souls?" (14 November 1719).

11 *Life of Waller* (1732), p. [3]; the string of adjectives is taken from announcements in Applebee's *Original Weekly Journal,* 13 May and 22 July 1721. *Remarkable Criminals* (1735a) marks this situation and exploits it as a means of establishing its own impartiality and objectivity. "There are several facts which have happened in the world," it informs its readers, "the circumstances attending which, if we compare them as they are related by one or other, we can hardly fix in our own mind any certainty of belief concerning them, such equality is there in the weight of evidence on one side and of the other" (p. 211). See also *Select Trials* (1742), which offers "extracts" from two mutually contradictory accounts of a particular criminal's life, so

that "the Reader may the better compare them, and judge which deserves the most Credit" (1:244). The self-credentialing process here is interesting, especially for what it suggests about the audience to whom these remarks were directed. They would not have shared the great failing of the German Princess, who, according to Alexander Smith, "believ[ed] all she read to be true" (*Highwaymen* [1719a], p. 153).

12 Applebee's *Original Weekly Journal*, 7 May 1726. The same printer was also about to publish *The Life of Catherine Hayes,* "the whole taken from the Mouths of the several Criminals themselves, and confirmed by their Friends and Relations, and by the Kindred of the deceas'd Mr. Hayes; and the most Authentick Accounts of the whole Matter taken upon Oath before the Coroner and divers of his Majesty's Justices of the Peace" (ibid.; I've not been able to find a surviving copy of this publication). Were space to allow, I might quote another thirty such declarations ranging from 1674 up through the middle of the eighteenth century. Of particular interest for what it suggests of the overall context in which such claims for authenticity were read, however, is the following: "As to the Declaration of me *Dean Bryant,* in the *Daily Advertiser* of *Sept.* 20, it is possible I might set my Hand to a Paper, not knowing the Contents thereof, I being at that time in a *high Fever,* and consequently might be *light-headed.* Those Persons, in my opinion, were not my Friends, who urged me to sign it. . . . that Paper, (of *Sept.* 20) . . . is an Imposition on the Publick" (Guthrie, Ordinary Account, 20 and 22 December 1738). We might note here as well that the claim made for authenticity by Carrick's *Robberies* (1722) – see n. 10, this chapter – was itself discredited by *Select Trials* (1742), which found it "fictitious" except for "a few Hints borrowed from the Sessions-Paper and" – delicious irony! – "the *Ordinary's* Account" (1:215).

13 John Hinde, *Sir Henry Hide's Speech on the Scaffold* (1650), p. 3; *Life of Stanley* (1723), p. v. Claims for inauthenticity could also be made on the basis of internal evidence. William Talbot, bishop of Oxford, judged that a letter he got from two murderers retracting their confessions was not written by them and concluded, once he saw "their pretended Dying-Speeches," that "they were all made by the same Person" (*The Truth of the Case of Palmer* [1708], p. 39; these same speeches are closely examined by another reader convinced some third person wrote them, pp. 50–52). Coherence, or its lack, could be read either way. "I have not had time to digest [my confession] into Method, because Time is precious with me now," wrote Henry Harrison, and he begged "the Reader to make no Nice Construction of my words, but to take the real honest meaning" (Harrison, *Last Words* [1692], p. 1). The author of *The Genuine Trial of Charles Drew* (1740), on the other hand, compares his "authentick" account to the "several Fictitious Trials, or rather incoherent Accounts" that others had published (p. 3). For similar uses of the word "incoherent," see James Guthrie, *Sermon Preach'd upon the Desire of Hallam* (1732), p. [i], and S[amuel] Foote, *Life of Goodere* (1741), p. 5.

14 Smith, Ordinary Account, 28 February 1694; for essentially the same senti-

ment, see also Guthrie, Ordinary Accounts, 27 September 1736, 7 April 1742. "Insincerity and Prevarication," Guthrie warned, "is too constantly discover'd in these unhappy Wretches" (Ordinary Account, 5 October 1737).

15 Trial of Drew (1740), pp. 3, 40. A similarly "happy" construction was placed on the dying gesture of George Strangewayes, hanged nearly a century earlier for the murder of his brother-in-law. Strangewayes went to his death "cloathed all in white; wastcoat, stockings, drawers, and cap, over which was cast a long mourning Cloak." The source of this information would have us believe that this was "a dress that handsomely emblem'd the condition he was then in, who though his soul wore a sable roab of mourning for her former sins, it was now become her upper garment, and in some few minutes being cast off, would discover the immaculatte dress of mercy which was under it" (Unhappy Marksman [1659], p. 27). There was no other evidence to show that Strangewayes, even at his death, had been especially pious, and certainly he never seemed particularly sorry for his crime. His extravagant dress could just as easily have seemed a vain and egoistic gesture, the act of a man who had already done more than enough to indicate his derangement. For yet another instance of someone supposedly dying piously, though "without such outward Demonstrations of it as some have done," see Fair Warning to Murderers of Infants (1692), p. 3.

16 See, e.g., Mistaken Justice (1695), p. 4; Tryal of Capt. Green (1705); The Truth of the Case of Palmer (1708), p. 41; Johnson, Highwaymen (1734), p. 304; Guthrie, Ordinary Account, 31 July 1741; Select Trials (1742), 1:37, 80–81; 4:301–2; and esp. the brief accounts of Mary Edmondson in The Newgate Calendar (1773), 5:35–38, and The Malefactor's Register (1779), 4:128–31.

17 The first writer is Robert Rowe, author of Harrison the Murtherer (1692), see pp. [i–ii]; the second is the author of The Truth of the Case of Palmer (1708), see pp. 51–52. Remarkable Criminals (1735a) agrees with Rowe, saying that "in cases like these, He only can judge who is acquainted with the secrets of all hearts and who, as He is not to be deceived, so His penetration is utterly unknown to us, who are confined to appearances and the exterior marks of things" (pp. 33–34). On the other hand, the 1734 Johnson suggests, "tho' we cannot impartially Guess at other Men's Thoughts, yet their Actions frequently discover their Intentions and Imaginations" (Highwaymen [1734], p. 193). People on both sides of the question would likely have agreed with the author of The Life and Death of Turner (1663/[4]), who, concerning his particular problematic criminal, had this to say: "There are questionless some Concealments and Depths, which will never be fathomed here by any Life or Research, unless Providence by its All-seeing Eye shall unfold the Mystery" (p. [iii]). The impossibility of knowing for sure what went on in criminals' minds was no bar, however, to eager writers; quite the opposite. The author of the History of Maclean (1750) was moved to write his version of the highwayman's life, he said,

on the grounds "that Accounts publish'd by such People themselves, or their profess'd Friends, are either partial in the Relations of Facts, or defective in that Part of the Narrative, in which the Publick is chiefly interested, *viz.* the secret Springs and Motives of Actions" (p. 4).

18 Burnet and Horneck, *Confession of Stern* (1682), p. 12; Guthrie, Ordinary Account, 5 October 1744. "Now, let the Reader judge," writes William Talbot, bishop of Oxford, about some repudiated confessions, "whether there could have been more direct and plain confessions of their Guilt made, than these which follow, and are transcribed, *verbatim,* from the Originals" (*Truth of the Case of Palmer* [1708], p. 34; see also pp. 3, 12). Having given an account of his robberies that looked "something Romantick," John Simpson was reproved by the ordinary of Newgate, who "told him he suspected his Relation, and that it was hardly possible it should all be true, and he thought he only told these things to be talked of" (*Compleat Tryals* [1718, 1721], 2:30–31; for the original source, see R. Wykes, Ordinary Account, 20 July 1700). The paper Mary Hanson left behind her, "though . . . very agreeable to the nature of her case" according to *Remarkable Criminals* (1735a), was "penned in [a] manner not likely to come from the hands of a poor ignorant woman" (p. 220). Nor was plausibility necessarily indicated by mere circumstantiality, as Applebee's *Original Weekly Journal* shows by saying that James Dalton "could scarce remember the tenth Part of the Villainies he had committed," there being so many (16 May 1730). The close examination of criminals' confessions was no more certain a path to sure knowledge than the close examination of their actions. Thus, after giving a highly circumstantial account of a sailor's recruitment into a pirate crew, taken from his own pocket journal, the 1734 Johnson warns that "it is very probable this Journal might be a Contrivance, to confront the Evidence against him if ever he should be taken" (*Highwaymen* [1734], p. 303).

19 Defoe, *Street-Robberies, Consider'd* (1728), pp. 48–49; for the same opinion in nearly the same phrasing, see also his *Augusta Triumphans* (1728), pp. 47–48.

20 *Remarkable Criminals* (1735a), pp. 525, 374.

Select bibliography

This bibliography is limited to a listing of works specifically cited in the main text or the notes, with the exception of certain additional criminal biographies, etc., included for purposes of information. Unless otherwise noted, all places of publication are London.

    I. Criminal biographies, or other accounts of criminals, their crimes, trials, and executions
    II. Seventeenth- and eighteenth-century periodicals
       A. Ordinaries' *Accounts* and sessions papers
       B. Journals
    III. Other contemporary secondary sources
    IV. Post-eighteenth-century sources

I. CRIMINAL BIOGRAPHIES, ETC., BY DATE OF PUBLICATION

The year is assumed to begin in January. Where title pages are dated Old Style, this is noted at the end of the entry. Within years, entries appear in alphabetical order by last name of author or, where anonymous, by the first noun in the title. Capitalization has been normalized, but the original punctuation and spellings have been maintained. Works published in several volumes over several years are listed under the date of the first volume.

N.d.

An Account of the Behaviour of Henry Weller, John Ralph, Clement Snell, Joseph Rumney, Matthew Smith, Ralph Cook, in Newgate. Since Their Condemnation. With Seasonable Advice to All Condemned Prisoners; Published by Their Earnest Request and Desire.

The Unfortunate Family: In Four Parts. Part I. How One John Roper, through Want of Grace, Broke the Heart of His Mother, and Strangled His Father, Taking

What Money Was in the House, and Fled to a Wood. Part II. How the Spirit of His Mother Appeared to Him in a Wood, in an Angry Manner; and How Conscience Drove Him into the Hands of Justice. Part III. His Lamentation in Dorchester Gaol. Part IV. His Last Dying Speech, Desiring All Young Men to Take Warning by Him.

Concealed Murther Reveiled. Being a Strange Discovery of a Most Horrid and Barbarous Murther . . . by Mary Anderson, Alias Farrel, on the Body of Hannah Jones an Infant of 8 Weeks Old, the Child of Mr. Jones, an Eminent Joyner at the Globe in Hounds-Ditch. As Also How It Was Conceal'd 3 Years . . . . With Her Examination before Justice Webber . . . and Her Commitment to Newgate.

Murthers' Reward; Being a True and Exact Account of a Most Cruel and Barbarous Murther Committed by One Gabriel Harding, of Tredenton in the County of Westmoreland, Who Inhumanely Murthered His Own Wife, for Which Bloody & Cruel Deed He Was Justly Punished in a Severe Manner, the Devil Breaking His Neck in the Presence of Many Spectators, to the Admiration of Them All.

1592

The Araignment, Examination Confession and Iudgement of Arnold Cosbye: Who Wilfvully Murdered the Lord Burke, neere the Town of Wansworth, on the 14. Day of This Present Month of Ianuary and Was Executed the 17. of the Same Moneth. 1591[/2].

"Cuthbert Cunny-Catcher." *The Defence of Conny Catching. Or a Confvtation of Those Two Iniurious Pamphlets Published by R.G. against the Practitioners of Many Nimble-Witted and Mysticall Sciences.*

R[obert] G[reene]. *The Blacke Bookes Messenger. Laying Open the Life and Death of Ned Browne One of the Most Notable Cutpurses, Crosbiters, and Conny-Catchers, That Ever Lived in England.*

The Manner of the Death and Execution of Arnold Cosbie, for Murthering the Lord Boorke, Who Was Executed at Wanswoorth Townes End on the 27. of Ianurie. With Certain Verses Written by the Said Cosby in the Time of His Imprisonment, Containing Matter of Great Effect, as Well Touching His Life as Also His Penitencie before His Death. 1591[/2].

W.R. *The Most Horrible and Tragicall Murther of the Right Honorable, the Vertuous and Valerous Gentleman, Iohn Lord Bourgh, Baron of Castell Connell. Committed by Arnold Cosby, the Fourteenth of Ianuarie. Together with the Sorrowful Sighes of a Sadde Soule, vppon His Funerall: Written by W.R. a Servaunt of the Said Lord Bourgh.* 1591[/2].

1596

[Luke Hutton]. *The Blacke Dogge of Newgate: Both Pithie and Profitable for All Readers.* [N.d.; Pollard and Redgrave *STC* tentative attrib.]

1598

L.B.   *The Examination, Confession, and Condemnation of Henry Robison Fisherman*
         of Rye, Who Poysoned His Wife in the Strangest Maner That Ever Hitherto
         Hath Been Heard Of.
Luke Hutton.   *Luke Huttons Lamentation: Which He Wrote the Day before His*
         Death, Being Condemned to Be Hanged at Yorke This Last Assises for His
         Robberies and Trespasses Committed. To the Tune of Wandering and Wauering.

1604

Gilbert Dugdale.   *A True Discourse of the Practises of Elizabeth Caldwell, Ma:*
         Ieffrey Bownd, Isabell Hall Widdow, and George Fernely, on the Parson of Ma:
         Thomas Caldwell, in the County of Chester, to Have Murdered and Poysoned
         Him, with Divers Others. Together with Her Manner of Godly Life during Her
         Imprisonment, Her Arrainement and Execution . . . the 18. of Iune. 1603.

1605

The Life and Death of Gamaliell Ratsey, a Famous Theefe of England, Executed at
         Bedford the 26. of March Last Past, 1605.
Two Most Unnatural and Bloodie Murthers: The One by Maister Cauerley, a York-
         shire Gentleman, Practised upon His Wife, and Committed uppon His Two
         Children, the Three and Twentie of April 1605. The Other, by Mistris Browne,
         and Her Servant Peter, upon Her Husband, Who Were Executed in Lent Last
         Past at Bury in Suffolke.
Ratseis Ghost. Or the Second Part of His Madde Prankes and Robberies.

1606

The Most Crvell and Bloody Mvrther Committed by an Inkeepers Wife, Called Annis
         Dell, and Her Sonne George Dell, Foure Yeeres Since. On the Bodie of a
         Childe, Called Anthony Iames in Bishops Hatfield in the Countie of Hartford,
         and Now Most Miraculously Reuealed by the Sister of the Said Anthony, Who
         at the Time of the Murther Had Her Tongue Cut Out, and Foure Yeeres
         Remayned Dumme and Speechlesse, and Now Perfectly Speaketh, Reuealing the
         Murther, Hauing No Tongue to Be Seen. With the Seuerall Witch-crafts, and
         Most Damnable Practices of One Iohane Harrison and Her Daughter vpon
         Seuerall Persons, Men and Women at Royston, Who Were All Executed at
         Hartford the 4 of August Last Past. 1606.
The Horrible Murther of a Young Boy of Three Yeares of Age, Whose Sister Had Her
         Tongue Cut Out: and How It Pleased God to Reueale the Offendors, by Giving
         Speech to the Tongueles Childe. Which Offendors Were Executed at Hartford the
         4. of August. 1606.

1613

Three Bloodie Murders: The First, Committed by Francis Cartwright upon William Storre, Mr. of Art, Minister and Preacher at Market Raisin in the Countie of Lincolne. The Second, Committed by Elizabeth Iames, on the Body of her Mayde, in the Parish of Egham in Surrie: Who Was Condemned for the Same Fact at Saint Margarets Hill in Southwark, the 2. of Iuly 1613. and Lieth in the White Lion till Her Deliuerie: Discouered by a Dombe Mayde, and a Dogge. The Third, Committed vpon a Stranger, Very Lately neare High-Gate Foure Miles from London: Very Strangely Found Out by a Dogge Also, the 2. of Iuly. 1613.

1616

A Pitilesse Mother. That Most Unnaturally at One Time, Murthered Two of Her Owne Children at Acton within Six Miles from London uppon Holy Thursday Last 1616. the Ninth of May. Beeing a Gentlewoman Named Margret Vincent, Wife of Mr. Jarvis Vincent, of the Same Towne. With Her Examination, Confession and True Discovery of All the Proceedings in the Said Bloody Accident. Whereunto Is Added Andersons Repentance, Who Was Executed at Tiburne the 18. of May Being Whitson-Eve. 1616. Written in the Time of His Prisonment in Newgate. [N.d.; Brit. Lib. attrib.]

1618

Henry Goodcole. A True Declaration of the Happy Conuersion, Contrition, and Christian Preparation of Francis Robinson, Gentleman, Who for Counterfeiting the Great Seale of England, Was Drawen, Hang'd, and Quartered at Charing-Cross, on . . . the Thirteenth Day of Nouember, 1618.

1620

[Henry Goodcole.] Londons Cry Ascended to God, and Entred into the Hearts and Eares of Men for Reuenge of Bloodshedders, Burglaiers, and Vagabonds. Manifested the Last Sessions, Holden at Iustice Hall in the Old Baily the 9. 10. 11. 12. of December, Anno Dom. 1619. Likewise Heerein Is Related, the Courts Legall Proceedings, against the Malefactors That Were Executed at Tiburne and about London, and the Chiefest Offenders, There Offences and Confessions at Large Expressed.

1623

The Life and Death of Griffin Flood Informer. Whose Cunning Courses, Churlish Manners, and Troublesome Informations, Molested a Number of Plaine Dealing People in This City of London. Wherein Is Also Declared the Murther of Iohn Chipperford Vintner, for Which Fact the Said Griffin Flood Was Pressed to Death the 18. Day of Ianuary Last Past.

1628

Iohn Clavell. *A Recantation of an Ill Led Life. Or a Discoverie of the High-Way Law. With Vehement Dissuasions to All (in That Kind) Offenders. As Also Many Cautelous Admonitions and Full Instructions, How to Know, Shun, and Apprehend a Theefe. Most Necessarie for All Honest Travellers to Peruse, Observe and Practise.* ["Approved by the *KINGS* most excellent Majestie, and published by his expresse Command. *The Third Edition, with Addition."*] 1634.

1633

A True Relation of a Barbarous and Most Cruell Murther Committed by One Enoch ap Evan, Who Cut Off His Own Naturall Mothers Head, and His Brothers. The Cause Wherefore He Did This Most Execrable Act; Most Remar[?able for] the Warning of Others; with His Condemnation and Execution. With Certaine Pregnant Inducements, Both Diuine and Morall, [?to Deterre] *Men from the Horrible Practice of Murther and Manslaughter.*

1635

H.G. [Henry Goodcole?]. *Heavens Speedie Hue and Cry Sent after Lust and Murther. Manifested upon the Suddaine Apprehending of Thomas Shearwood, and Elizabeth Evans, Whose Manner of Lives, Death, and Free Confessions, Are Heere Expressed . . . . Who Were Executed the One upon the 14. and the Other on the 17. of This Moneth of April 1635.*

1637

[Henry Goodcole?]. *Natures Cruell Step-Dames: Or, Matchless Monsters of the Female Sex; Elizabeth Barnes, and Anne Willis. Who Were Executed the 26. Day of April, 1637, for the Unnaturall Murthering of Their Owne Children. Also, Herein Is Contained Their Severall Confessions, and the Courts Just Proceedings against Other Notorious Malefactors, with Their Severall Offences This Sessions. Further, a Relation of the Wicked Life and Impenitent Death of Iohn Flood, Who Raped His Owne Childe.*

1638

Paul Godwin, tr. and ed. *Histoire Des Larrons, or the History of Theeves. Written in French, and Translated out of the Originall.*

1641

The Apprentices Warning-Piece. Being a Confession of Peter Moore, Formerly Servant to Mr. Bidgood, Apothecary in Exeter, Executed There the Last Assises, for Poysoning His Said Master. Wherein Is Observed Such Lamentable Expressions

*Proceeding from Him, as May Produce a Trembling to All Who Reade or Heare
Thereof, and Be a Warning to Such Leud Servants Who Walk the Same Steps,
Lest They Receive the Same Punishment.*

1643

*The Arraignment, Tryall, Conviction, and Confession of Francis Deane a Salter, and
of John Faulkner a Strong-Water Man, (Both Annabaptists, and Lately Received
into That Sect) for the Murther of One Mr. Daniel a Soliciter . . . and for
Which Fact Were Executed at Tyburne on Munday Last . . . the 17. of April.
1643.*

1646

*An Exact Relation of the Bloody and Barbarous Murder, Committed by Miles Lewis,
and His Wife, a Pinmaker upon Their Prentice . . . in Southwark. Wherein Is
Declared, the Manner of His Cruell Tortures, Shewing How He Were Whipt
with Rods of Wire, and Put to Death with Red-Hot Irons; the Like Never Heard
Of Before in Any Age.*

1650

John Hinde. *A True Copy of Sir Henry Hide's Speech on the Scaffold, Immediately
before His Execution . . . on the 4th of March, 1650. Taken in Short-Hand from
His Mouth.*

1651

*The Declaration of Captain James Hind (Close Prisoner in New-Gate) and His
Acknowledgment, Protestation, and Full Confession at His Examination before
the Councel of State, on the 10. of This Instant Novemb. 1651. Together with a
Perfect Narrative, (Written by His Advice) of All His Strange Proceedings and
Travels; Setting Forth the Great Difficulties and Dangers He Escaped in Sever-
all Countreyes, upon His Adventuring to the King of Scots at Sterling. With His
Letter to the Said King; and His Resolution to Suffer Any Kind of Death,
Rather Then to Impeach or Betray Any Man.*
*A Second Discovery of Hind's Exploits: Or a Fuller Relation of His Ramble, Robber-
ies, and Cheats in England, Ireland, Scotland, with His Voyage to Holland.
Wherein Is Set Forth the Notorious Villanies of Theeves and High-Way-Men.
Full of Delight, and May Serve as a Guide to Gentlemen and Travellers, to
Avoid Their Treacheries.* [T.p. dated 1652 for 1651.]
G.F. [George Fidge?]. *Hind's Ramble, or, the Description of His Manner and
Course of Life. Wherein Is Related the Several Robberies He Hath Committed
in England, and the Escapes He Hath Made upon Several Occasions. With His
Voyage into Holland, and How He Cheated a Dutch-Man There of 200. 1. And
from Thence Went into Ireland, Where He Did Many Robberies, and Was
Wounded by Some of His Own Party. With a Relation of His Going to the*

Scotch King, Where He Was Made Scoutmaster General, and Afterwards (as
'Tis Generally Reported) Was the Onely Man That Conveyed the Scotch King
to London, Who Since Is Shipt Away For beyond Seas.

Hinds Elder Brother, or the Master Thief Discovered, Being a Relation of the Life of
Major Thomas Knowls, His Many Exploits, Escapes and Witty Robberies.

The Humble Petition of James Hind (Close Prisoner in New-Gate) to the Right
Honourable the Councell of State; and Their Proceedings Thereupon. Together
with the Speech and Confession of the Bishop of Clonwel at the Place of Execution at Limmerick in Ireland, on the 9 of This Instand November, 1651.

The True and Perfect Relation of the Taking of Captain James Hind: on Sabbath-Day
Last in the Evening at a Barbers House in the Strand neer Clements Church.
With the Manner How He Was Discovered and Apprehended: His Examination
before the Council of State; and His Confession Touching the King of Scots.
Also, an Order from the Council of State Concerning the Said Captain Hind;
the Bringing of Him down to Newgate (Yesterday) in a Coach; and His Declaration and Speech Delivered in Prison.

J.S.   An Excellent Comedy, Called, The Prince of Priggs Revels: Or, the Practices of
That Grand Thief Captain James Hind, Relating Divers of His Pranks and
Exploits, Never Heretofore Published by Any. Repleat with Various Conceits,
and Tarltonian Mirth, Suitable to the Subject.

The Trial of Captain James Hind on Friday Last before the Honourable Court at the
Sessions in the Old-Bayley. With His Examination and Confession; His Speech
Touching the King of Scots; His Merry Conceits and Witty Pranks Presented to
the Judges; the Manner of His Gallant Deportment; an Order for His Further
Trial at Oxford; the Reasons Demonstrated; and a Charge of High-Treason
Exhibited against Him. With His Narrative and Declaration Touching All His
Pranks and Proceeding.

The Last Will and Testament of James Hynd, High-Way Lawyer. Now Sick to
Death, in His Chamber in Newgate. Full of Various Conceits, beyond Expectation.

1652

G[eorge] F[idge].   The English Gusman; or the History of That Unparallel'd Thief
James Hind. Wherein Is Related I. His Education and Manner of Life; Also a
Full Relation of All the Severall Robberies, Madd Pranks, and Handsom Jests
Done by Him. II. How at Hatfield He Was Enchanted by a Witch for Three
Years Space; and How She Switch'd His Horse with a White Rod, and Gave
Him a Thing like a Sun-Dial, the Point of Which Should Direct Him Which
Way to Take When Persued. And III. His Apprehension, Examination at the
Councel of State, Commitment to the Gatehouse, and from Thence to Newgate;
His Arraignment at the Old Baily; and the Discourse betwixt His Father, His
Wife and Himself in Newgate.

A Pill to Purge Melancholy: Or, Merry Newes from Newgate: Wherein Is Set Forth,
the Pleasant Jests, Witty Conceits, and Excellent Couzenages, of Captain James
Hind, and His Associates. . . . With Variety of . . . Delightful Passages, Never
Heretofore Published by Any Pen.

We Have Brought Our Hogs to a Fair Market: Or, Strange Newes from New-Gate; Being a Most Pleasant and Historical Narrative, of Captain James Hind, Never Before Published, of His Merry Pranks, Witty Jests, Unparallel'd Attempts, and Strange Designs. With His Orders, Instructions, and a Decree, to All His Royal Gang, and Fraternity; the Appearing of a Strange Vision on Munday Morning Last, with a Crown upon His Head; the Speech and Command That Were Then Given to Cap. Hind; and the Manner How It Vanished Away. As Also How He Was Enchanted by a Witch at Hatfield, for the Space of Three Years; and How She Switch'd His Horse with a White Rod, and Gave Him a Thing like a Sun-Diall, the Point of Which Should Direct Him Which Way to Take When Persued. With His Speech; the Old-Hags Charm; and the Raising of the Devil in the Likeness of a Lyon; to the Great Admiration and Wonder of All That Shall Read the Same. 1651/[2].

Wit for Mony. Being a Full Relation of the Life, Actions, Merry Conceits, and Pretty Pranks of Captain Iames Hind the Famous Robber, Both in England, Holland, and Ireland. With His New Progresse through Berkshire, Oxfordshire, and the Adjacent Counties, Begun on Monday the First of March, 1651. with the Judges of the Assize for That Circuit.

1655

William Annand.   *A Funeral Elegie upon the Death of George Sonds, Esq; & c. Who Was Killed by His Brother, Mr. Freeman Sonds, August the 7th. Anno Dom. 1655.*

R[obert] Boreman.   *A Mirrour of Mercy and Iudgement. Or, an Exact True Narrative of the Life and Death of Freeman Sonds Esquier, Sonne to Sir George Sonds of Lees Court in Shelwich in Kent. Who Being about the Age of 19. for Murthering His Elder Brother . . . the 7th of August, Was Arraigned and Condemned at Maidstone, Executed There . . . the 21. of the Same Moneth.*

The Devils Reign upon Earth, Being a Relation of Several Sad and Bloudy Murthers Lately Committed, Especially That of Sir Geo. Sands His Son, upon His Own Brother.

Sir George Sondes.   *Sir George Sondes His Plaine Narrative to the World of All Passages upon the Death of His Two Sonnes.*

1656

Hannam's Last Farewell to the World; Being a Full and True Relation of the Notorious Life and Shamfull Death of Mr. Richard Hannam, the Great Robber of England; with the Manner of His Apprehension, Examination, Confession and Speech Made to the Sheriffs a Little before His Execution . . . the 17. of June, 1656.

The Speech and Confession of Mr. Richard Hannam on Tuesday Last in the Rounds of Smithfield, (Being the 17. of This Instant June) Immediately before His Great and Fatall Leap from off the Ladder. Together with a True and Perfect Description of His Life and Death; His Several Rambles, Figaries, Exploits, and Designs, Performed in Most Parts of Europe; Especially upon the King of Scots, the Queen of Sweden, the Kings of France, Spain, and Denmark, the High and Mighty States of Holland, the Great Turk, and the Pope of Rome.

The Witty Rogue Arraigned, Condemned, & Executed. Or, the History of That Incomparable Thief Richard Hannam. Relating the Several Robberies, Mad Pranks, and Handsome Jests by Him Performed, as It Was Taken from His Own Mouth, Not Long before His Death. Likewise the Manner of Robbing the King of Denmark, the King of France, the Duke of Normandy, the Merchant at Rotterdam, cum Multis Alliis. Also, with His Confession, Concerning His Robbing of the King of Scots. Together with His Speech at the Place of Execution.

Edward Tuke. The Soul's Turnkey, or, a Spiritual File for Any Prisoner Lockt Up in the Dungeon and Chains of Sinne and Satan. . . . Prepared for the Hand of Master Hannam Prisoner in Newgate, the Night and Morning before He Suffered. But Now Tended and Commended to the Use of Every Man and Woman under the Bondage of Ignorance, Iniquity, and Affliction.

The English Villain: Or the Grand Thief. Being a Full Relation of the Desperate Life, and Deserved Death of That Most Notable Thief, and Notorious Robber, Richard Hannam: Who for His Arch Villanies, and Notorious Robberies Committed Both in England, Scotland, France, and Ireland, Denmark, Sweden, Yea Rome It Self; Far Exceeds That Arch Villain the Spanish Gusman, and the Late Famous Robber of England Captain Iames Hind; Yea, and All the Notorious Thieves That Ever Yet Were Heard Of: the Like to Whom Hath Not Been Known. With the Manner of the Execution, and His Speech at His Last Farewell to the World.

1657

A Serious Advice to the Citizens of London, by Some Ministers of the Gospel in the Said City: Upon Occasion of the Horrid Murder and Dreadful Death of Nathaniel Butler, an High Malefactor. [T.p. missing in Brit. Lib. copy; signed by the following clergymen, in this order: Edmund Calamy, Arthur Jackson, James Nalton, Tho. Jacomb, John Fuller, Robert Hutchison, Thomas White, Thomas Parson, Thomas Doelittle, Simon Ashe, Thomas Case, Will Taylor, Roger Drake, Will. Jenkyn, Geo. Griffith, Matthew Poole, Dan. Batcheler, Ralph Venning.]

Blood Washed Away by Tears of Repentance: Being an Exact Relation of the Cause and Manner of That Horrid Murther Committed on the Person of John Knight an Apprentice to Mr. Arthur Worth in Milk-Street, by Nathaniel Butler: With His Unfained Repentance for the Same. Together with His Apprehension, Examination and Conviction: the Several Conferences Had between Him and the Right Honourable the Lord Mayor, and Most of the Pious Ministers about This City. Likewise an Exact Relation of His Life, from His Cradle to His Death. A Discovery of Such of His Confederates as Have Deceived Their Masters. Written with His Own Hand.

Heavens Cry against Murder. Or, a True Relation of the Bloudy and Unparallel'd Murder of John Knight . . . on . . . Aug. 6. 1657. by One Nath: Butler.

A Full and the Truest Narrative of the Most Horrid, Barbarous and Unparalleled

Murder, Committed on the Person of John Knight. . . . Which Most Wicked and Cruell Murder was Committed by the Desperate and Bloody Hand of Nathaniel Butler, His Most Intimate and Bosome Friend, as They Lay in Bed Together, on Thursday, Morning August 6, 1657. Together with the Manner of His Being Apprehended and Examined; and the Confession from the Mouth of the Said Butler, Word for Word: And His Earnest Repentance for His Desperate Fact. Also, an Account of the Tryall, Condemnation and Sentence Pronounced against Him, Which Was Executed upon Him on Monday, August 31. 1657. And His Last Speech upon the Ladder Immediately before His Death, Which He Desired Might Be Printed after His Death; and to That End Gave It At Large in Writing from off the Ladder, to Mr. Yearwood Chaplain to the Right Honourable Sir Robert Titchbourn Lord Mayor of London. With Observations and Reflections upon the Whole. Published after Many Lying and False Relations Both before and since His Death, with a Detection of Many Lyes and Absurdities; and That the Truth May Be Known.

Randolph Yearwood, compiler. *The Penitent Murderer. Being an Exact Narrative of the Life and Death of Nathaniel Butler; Who (through Grace) Became a Convert, after He Had Most Cruelly Murdered John Knight.*

1658

The Devils Cabinet Broke Open: Or a New Discovery of the High-Way Thieves. Being a Seasonable Advice of a Gentleman Lately Converted from Them, to Gentlemen and Travellers to Avoyd Their Villanies. Together with a Relation of the Laws, Customes, and Subtilties, of House-Breakers, Pick-Pockets, and Other Mecanick Caterpillars of This Nation. As Also, the Apprehension and Imprisonment of the Hang-Man of the City of London.

1659

The Catterpillers of This Nation Anatomized, in a Brief Yet Notable Discovery of House-Breakers, Pick-Pockets, &c. Together with the Life of a Penitent High-Way-Man, Discovering the Mystery of That Infernal Society. To Which Is Added, the Manner of Hectoring and Trepanning, as It Is Acted in and about the City of London.

The Unhappy Marksman. Or, a Perfect and Impartial Discovery of That Late Barbarous and Unparallel'd Murther Committed by Mr. George Strangwayes, Formerly a Major in the Kings Army, on His Brother-in-Law Mr. John Fussel an Attorney . . . the Eleventh of February. Together with a Full Discovery of the Fatal Cause of Those Unhappy Differences Which First Occasioned the Suits in Law betwixt Them. Also the Behavior of Mr. Strangwayes at His Tryal. The Dreadful Sentence Pronounced against Him. His Letter to His Brother-in-Law, a Member of Parliament; and His Stout, but Christian-like Manner of Dying. Published by a Faithful Hand.

A True Relation of the Most Horrid Murder Committed by Mr. George Strangewayes on the Person of His Brother in Law Mr. George [or rather John] Fussill.

1662

The Life and Death of Mrs. Mary Frith. Commonly Called Mal Cutpurse. Exactly Collected and Now Published for the Delight and Recreation of All Merry Disposed Persons.

1663

A True Account of the Tryal of Mrs. Mary Carlton, at the Sessions in the Old-Bayly . . . the 4th of June, 1663. She Being Indicted by the Name of Mary Mauders alias Stedman. Published for Her Vindication, at Her Own Request.

The Arraignment, Tryal and Examination of Mary Moders, Otherwise Stedman, Now Carleton, (Stiled, The German Princess) . . . for Having Two Husbands; viz. Tho. Stedman of Canterbury Shooemaker, and John Carleton of London, Gent. Who upon a Full Hearing Was Acquitted . . . June 4, 1663.

F.B.   *Vercingetorixa: Or, the Germane Princess Reduc'd to an English Habit.*

Carleton, John.   *The Ultimum Vale of John Carleton, of the Middle Temple London, Gent. Being a True Description of the Passages of That Grand Imposter, Late a Pretended Germane-Lady.*

[Mary Carleton?].   *An Historicall Narrative of the German Princess, Containing All Material Passages, from Her First Arrivall at Graves-End, the 30th of March Last Past, untill She Was Discharged from Her Imprisonment, June the Sixth Instant. Wherein Also Is Mentioned, Sundry Private Matters, between Mr. John Carlton, and Others, and the Said Princess; Not Yet Published. Together with a Brief and Notable Story, of Billing the Brick-Layer, One of Her Pretended Husbands, Coming to New-Gate, and Demanding of the Keeper Her Deliverance, on Monday the Eighth Instant. Written by Her Self, for the Satisfaction of the World, at the Request of Divers Persons of Honour.*

The Lawyer's Clarke Trappan'd by the Crafty Whore of Canterbury. Or, a True Relation of the Whole Life of Mary Mauders, the Daughter of Thomas Mauders, a Fidler in Canterbury. With Her Strange and Unparallel'd Pranks, Witty Exploits, and Unheard Of Strategems, Touching Her Being a Wife for a Week, and a Lady of Pleasure.

Some Luck Some Wit, Being a Sonnet upon the Merry Life and Untimely Death of Mistress Mary Carleton, Commonly Called the German Princess. To a New Tune, Called the German Princess Adieu. [N.d.; Brit. Lib. attrib.]

T[homas] P[orter].   *A Witty Combat: Or the Female Victor. A Trage-Comedy.* [A play based on Mary Carleton's 1663 trial.]

The Great Tryall and Arraignment of the Late Distressed Lady, Otherwise Called the Late Germain Princess. . . . The Tenure of Her Indictment, of Having Two Husbands, and Her Answer to the Same. Also the Several Witnesses Which Came In against Her, with Her Absolute Confutation upon Each of Their Evidences by Her Acute Wit and Impregnable Reasons Whereby She Was Acquitted by Publique Proclamation.

1664

A True and Impartial Account of the Arraignment, Tryal, Examination, Confession and Condemnation of Col. James Turner for Breaking Open the House of Frances Tryon Merchant in Limestreet London. With the Several Tryals and Examinations of John Turner, William Turner, Mary Turner, and Ely Turner, Confederates. At Justice-Hall in the Old-Bailey, Lond. the 15. 16. and 19. of January 1663. 1663[/4].

The Life and Death of James Commonly Called Collonel Turner. Executed at Lime-Street End Ianuary the 21. 1663. For a Burgulary and Fellony Committed in the House of Mr. Francis Tryon of Limestreet, Merchant. 1663[/4].

The Triumph of Truth: in an Exact and Impartial Relation of the Life and Conversation of Col. Iames Turner. Which He Imparted to an Intimate Friend a Little before His Execution. To Which Is Added, His Deportment and Discourses in Prison: The Manner of His Execution and Burial. With Other Occurrences Never Yet Made Publique, and Now Published as a Seasonable Warning for Others to Avoid Such Strange Miscarriages. 1663[/4].

1668

Robert Franklin, Thomas Vincent, Thomas Doolitel, James Janeway, Hugh Baker. A Murderer Punished and Pardoned: Or a True Relation of the Wicked Life, and Shameful-Happy Death of Thomas Savage, Imprisoned, Justly Condemned, and Twice Executed at Ratcliff, for His Bloody Fact in Killing His Fellow-Servant. By Us Who Were Often with Him in the Time of His Imprisonment in Newgate, and at His Execution.

God's Justice against Murther, or the Bloudy Apprentice Executed. Being an Exact and True Relation of a Bloudy Murther Committed by One Thomas Savage an Apprentice to a Vintner at the Ship Tavern in Ratliffe upon the Maid of the House His Fellow Servant, Being Deluded Thereunto by the Instigations of a Whore. How and in What Sort He Performed the Same, How He Robbed His Master, and Was Persued and Taken by Hue and Cry at Coome Farm betwixt Greenwich and Woolwich. Sent to Newgate, Afterwards Arrained and Cast at Justice Hall in the Old Bayly, Condemned to Be Hanged over against the Place Where He Committed the Fact, and Being Once Hanged and Cut Down Afterwards Reviving Again, Was the Second Time Hanged till He Was Dead . . . October 28. 1668.

1669

An Exact Narrative of the Bloody Murder, and Robbery Committed. By Stephen Eaton, Sarah Swift, George Rhodes, and Henry Prichard, upon the Person of Mr. John Talbot, Minister. With the Manner of Their Apprehension, Arraignment and Condemnation. Also, a List of All the Other Persons That Are Condemned, with the Several Offences for Which They Were Executed.

A True Relation of a Cruel Robbery and Bloody Murther, Committed on the Body of Mr. John Talbot Late Curate of Lainesdone in Essex, in a Garden by Anna St.

Clare near Shoreditch) [sic] . . . the 2. of July 1669. As He Was Going from
Grays-Inn to His Lodging in Bishops-Gate-Street. And the Manner of the
Apprehension of Geo. Roads, Steven Eaton, Hen. Pritchard, & Sarah Swift, the
Wicked Actors of the Same. As Also an Account of Their Arraignment, Convic-
tion, and Execution.

1670

The Life of Deval. Showing How He Came to Be a Highway-Man; and How He
Committed Several Robberies Afterwards. Together with His Arraignment and
Condemnation. As Also His Speech and Confession, at the Place of Execution.
1669[/70].
[Dr. Walter Pope].   The Memoires of Monsieur Du Vall: Containing the History of
His Life and Death. Whereunto Are Annexed His Last Speech and Epitaph.

1672

The Bloody Murtherer, or, the Unnatural Son His Just Condemnation. At the Assizes
Held at Monmouth, March 8. 1671/2. With the Suffering of His Sister and
Servant, for the Murther of His Mother, Mrs. Grace Jones. For Which the Said
Son Was Prest to Death, His Sister Burnt, and His Boy Hang'd. With a True
Accompt of Their Trials, Penitent Behaviour, Prayers, Speeches, and Circum-
stances Thereunto Relating; With Letters of Several Worthy Divines.

1673

An Elegie on the Famous and Renowned Lady, for Eloquence and Wit, Madam Mary
Carlton, Otherwise Styled, the German Princess.
[J.G.].   The Memoires of Mary Carleton: Commonly Stiled, the German Princess.
Being a Narrative of Her Life and Death. Interwoven with Many Strange and
Pleasant Passages, from the Time of Her Birth to Her Execution at Tyburn,
being the 22th. [sic] of January 1672/3. With Her Behaviour in Prison, Her Last
Speech, Burial & Epitaph.
F[rancis] K[irkman].   The Counterfeit Lady Unveiled. Being a Full Account of the
Birth, Life, Most Remarkable Actions, and Untimely Death of Mary Carleton,
Known by the Name of the German Princess.
The Penitent Murderer: Or, an Exact and True Relation Taken from the Mouth of
Mr. William Ivy (Lately Executed) Concerning the Murder by Him Committed
upon the Body of William Pew, Servant to Sir Robert Long in Westmin-
ster . . . the 28th of April 1673: With the Reasons Inducing Him to That Horrid
Crime, His Resolution Likewise to Have Killed the Maid; His Taking Away
Seven Hundred-Pound Bags, and His Manner of Disposing Them. As Also, His
Tryal, Conviction, and Condemnation; with His Confession of the Whole Fact,
and His Contrition for the Same; as It Was Delivered from His Own Mouth to a
Particular Friend, and by Him Published, to Prevent All False Reports.

1674

The Confession of the Four High-Way-Men; as It Was Written by One of Them, and Allowed by the Rest the 14th. of This Instant April (Being the Day before Their Appointed Execution). Viz. John Williams, alias Tho. Matchet. Francis Jackson, alias Dixie. John White, alias Fowler. Walter Parkhurst. This Being Desired to Be Made Publick by the Persons Themselves, to Prevent False Reports of Them When They Are Dead.

[Richard Head]. *Jackson's Recantation, or, the Life & Death of the Notorious High-Way-Man, Now Hanging in Chains at Hampstead. Delivered to a Friend, a Little before Execution; Wherein Is Truly Discovered the Whole Mystery of That Wicked and Fatal Profession of Padding on the Road.*

No Jest like a True Jest: Being a Compendious Record of the Merry Life, and Mad Exploits of Capt. James Hind, the Great Rober of England. Together with the Close of All at Worcester, Where He Was Drawn, Hanged and Quartered, for High Treason against the Common Wealth, September 24, 1652. [Rptd. G. Smeeton, 1817.]

1675

Murther Will Out, or, a True and Faithful Relation of an Horrible Murther Committed Thirty Three Years Ago, by an Unnatural Mother, upon the Body of Her Own Child about a Year Old, and Was Never Discovered till This 24th of November, 1675. by Her Own Self, upon the Fears of an Approaching Death: for Which Crime She Was Taken from Her Bed, and Carried in a Coach to Prison, Where She Remains Very Penitent. With an Account from Her Own Mouth How She Was Tempted to Commit This Murther by the Devil: As Also How She Finished It.

The Bloody Murtherers Executed; or, News from Fleet-Street. Being the Last Speech and Confessions of the Two Persons Executed There . . . the 22 of October, 1675. With an Exact Account of All the Circumstances of Their Muthering the Knight, Sir R.S. in White-Fryers. The Manner of Their Being Apprehended, and Their Deportment in Newgate.

Three Inhumane Murthers, Committed by One Bloudy Person, upon His Father, His Mother, and His Wife, at Cank in Staffordshire. And the Manner How He Acted This Bloudy Tragedy. Together with His Examination, Confession, Condemnation, and Execution. At the General Assises Held at Stafford the 13th Day of March . . . 1674/5. Also His Deportment and Behaviour Both at His Tryal, and Place of Execution.

1677

News from Newgate: Or, a True Relation of the Manner of Taking Seven Persons, Very Notorious for Highway-Men, in the Strand; upon Munday the 13 of This Instant November, 1677. And of Another Apprehended on Friday the 16th: All Now Prisoners in Newgate. With an Account of Several Grand Robberies Com-

*mitted Lately in Divers Places: And Particularly, How Fifteen Countrymen,
Returning from a Fair, Were Set Upon by Seven Highwaymen, Who Took from
Them Several Hundreds of Pounds. As Likewise the Robbing of a Stage-Coach;
and Strange Discovery of Some of the Thieves Now in Custody, by Means of
Two of the Passengers, Supposed to Be Confederates with Them.*

Sadler's Memoir's: Or, the History of the Life and Death of That Famous Thief
Thomas Sadler. *Giving a True Account of His Being Fifteen Times in the Goal
of Newgate, and a Relation of His Most Notorious Pranks in City and Coun-
trey. With a Particular Description of the Manner of His Robbing the Lord High
Chancellour of England; for Which He Was Condemned to Dye, and Executed
at Tyburn on Fryday the Sixteenth of March, 1677.*

1678

Boteler's Case. *Being an Impartial Narrative of the Tryal, & Penitent Behaviour of,
Master William Botler. Executed, September 10th. at Chelmsford, about the
Murther of Capt. Wade.* [N.d.; Brit. Lib. attrib.]

The Lives of Sundry Notorious Villains. *Memorable for Their Base and Abominable
Actions. Together with a Novel, as It Really Happened at Roan in France.*

Strange and Lamentable News from Dulledg-Wells; or, the Cruel and Barbarous
Father. *A True Relation How a Person Which Used to Cry Dulledg Water
about the Streets of London, Kill'd His Own Son . . . the Second of This
Instant July, in a Most Inhumane Manner, for Which He . . . Now Remains a
Prisoner, in Order to a Tryal. Together with an Account of Another Sad
Accident That Lately Happened at Bromly by Bow, where a Person Being Much
in Debt, and Severely Haunted by His Creditors, Hang'd Himself in a
Mulberry-Tree, &c.*

1679

An Alarme for Sinners: *Containing the Confession, Prayers, Letters, and Last Words
of Robert Foulkes, Late Minister of Stanton-Lacy in the County of Salop;
Who Was Tryed, Convicted, and Sentenced, at the Sessions in the Old Bayly,
London, January 16th 1678/9, and Executed the 31st Following. With an
Account of His Life. Published from the Original, Written with His Own
Hand, during His Reprieve, and Sent by Him at His Death to Doctor Loyd,
Dean of Bangor.*

The Execution of the 11 Prisoners that Suffer'd at Tyburn, and One in Little-
Britain . . . the 22th [sic] of . . . January, 1679. *With the Manner of Their
Behaviour in Newgate before Execution. . . . With the Description of Every
Mans Fact for Which He Dyed.*

A True and Perfect Relation of the Tryal and Condemnation, Execution and Last
Speech of That Unfortunate Gentleman Mr. Robert Foulks Late Minister of a
Parish near Ludlow in Shropshire, *Who Received Sentence of Death in London,
for Murder and Adultery, and Accordingly Was Carried Privately in a Coach to
the Place of Execution . . . the last of January 1678[/9]. Also His Behaviour in
Prison, Both before and after Sentence, with His Speech to the People at the*

Place of Execution, and the Words of His Text. Published for to Satisfy All People That Are Incensed with Base and Foolish Reports on This Unhappy Man. Likewise the Tryal, Condemnation and Execution of Two Grand Traytors, Will. Ireland and John Grove Both Jesuits, Being the Persons That Was Hired to Kill His Majesty.

1680

An Impartial Account of the Misfortune That Lately Happened to the Right Honorable Philip Earl of Pembrooke and Montgomery.

A Full and True Account of the Penitence of John Marketman, during His Imprisonment in Chelmsford Gaol for Murthering His Wife. With His Letter to Mr. Bonah, That Kept Her Company; Also His Confession, and Admonitions, at the Place of Execution. To Which Is Prefixed a Sermon Preached before Him at West-Ham in the County of Essex, on Saturday, April 17. 1680. Immediately before His Execution. By Richard Hollingworth, M.A. Vicar of West-Ham.

The True Confession of Margret Clark, Who Consented to the Burning of Her Masters Mr. Peter Delanoy's House in Southwark. Delivered in Prison to Many Witnesses a Little before Her Death. And Confirmed by Her Self at the Place of Execution, by Answering All the Questions Then Put to Her by the Reverend and Worthy Divine, Dr. Martin, Now Minister at St. Saviours Southwark.

The True Narrative of the Execution of John Marketman, Chyrugian, of Westham in Essex, for Committing a Horrible and Bloody Murther upon the Body of His Wife, That Was Big with Child When He Stabbed Her.

A True Narrative of Three Wicked and Bloody Murthers Committed in Three Several Months: The First Was at Oxford, Committed by Thomas Hovell, a Taylor; upon the Body of John White, a Schollar of Bealy-Colledge [i.e., Balliol] through Covetousness for His Money. The Second in London, Done by a Young Lady upon Her Lover, by Reason He Had Promis'd Her Marriage, and Got Her with Child, She Went to Pistol Him, but Failing in That, She Stabb'd Him with a Pen-Knife. The Third Was Done by a Victualler on Bednal-Green, within Two Miles of London; Who Comming Home Late, Run His Wife Through with a Rapier, She Being Bigg of Her First Child. The Reasons of These Murthers, and How They Was Acted, the Book Within Does More Largely Make Mention.

Great and Bloody News. From Turnham-Green. Or a Relation of a Sharp Encounter. Between the Earl of Pembroke, and His Company, with the Constable and Watch Belonging to the Parish of Chiswick on the 18 Instant. In Which Conflict One Mr. Smeethe a Gentleman, and One Mr. Halfpenny a Constable of the Said Parish Were Mortally Wounded, of Which Wounds the Former within a Short Time After Died and the Latters Recovry Despaired Of, as Also of His Lordships Being Knocked Down, and Taken Prisoner by Mr. Smeeth Aforesaid, after He Had Received His Deaths Wound; with Several Other Remarkable Circumstances That Happened in and after the Dispute.

[Elkanah Settle]. *The Life and Death of Major Clancie, the Grandest Cheat of This Age. Wherein Is Set Forth Many of His Villanous Projects (Real Matter of*

Fact) Both in England, Ireland, France, Spain and Italy; at Last Was Executed at Tyburn, the Reading of Which Will Give the Reader Great Satisfaction.

Warning for Servants: And a Caution to Protestants. Or, the Case of Margret Clark, Lately Executed for Firing Her Masters House in Southwark. Faithfully Relating the Manner (as She Affirmed to the Last Moment of Her Life) How She Was Drawn In to That Wicked Act; Set Forth under Her Own Hand after Condemnation. Her Penitent Behaviour in Prison. Her Christian Advice to Visiters, Discourses with Several Ministers, and Last Words at Execution. Impartially Published, with the Attestations of Persons of Worth, and Many Substantial Eye and Ear Witnesses, Whose Names Are Inserted in This Narrative.

1681

A True and Wonderful Relation of a Murther Committed in the Parish of Newington, the 12th . . . of . . . January. By a Maid Who Poysoned Her Self, and Cut the Throat of a Child.

1682

An Account of the Confession and Execution of Captain Vratz, Geo. Boraski, and John Sterne, Who Were This Present Friday, Being the Tenth of March, Executed at Pell-Mall, for the Barbarous Murther of Thomas Thynne Esquire. Together with a Particular Relation of Their Behaviour in Newgate since Their Condemnation, and Manner of Their Passing to the Place of Execution.

A True Account of the Horrid and Barbarous Murther of Thomas Thynn Esq; on . . . the Twelfth of . . . February, in the Pall-Mall about Eight of the Clock in the Evening. With the Manner of Taking the Bloody and Inhumane Murtherers.

A True and Impartial Account of the Cruel and Bloody Murther, Committed upon the Body of Thomas Thin, Esq; Well Known in the West of Engl. for an Estate of near 12000 l. a Year. On Sunday the 12th of February, 1682. between the Hours of Seaven and Eight at Night, Who Was Barbarously and Inhumanely Butcher'd in His Own Coach, in the Open Street, by Three Out-Landish Villains, Named, Frederick Fratz, a German Captain; and George Boroskie, a Polander; and John Stern, a German. Giving You an Exact Account of How They Were Severally Examined before the Councill; Who after Their Examinations Were All Three Committed to Newgate. . . . Letting You Understand the Cause of This Assassination; Which They Alledge Was in the Vindication of Count Charles John Conningsmarke. . . .

Gilbert Burnet and Anthony Horneck.   *The Last Confession, Prayers and Meditations of Lieuten. John Stern, Delivered by Him on the Cart Immediately before His Execution, to Dr. Burnet. Together with the Last Confession of George Borosky, Signed by Him in the Prison, and Sealed Up in the Lieutenants Pacquet. With Which an Account Is Given of Their Deportment Both in the Prison and at the Place of Their Execution . . . in the Pall-Mall, on the Tenth of March.*

The Tryal and Condemnation of George Borowsky alias Boratzi, Christopher Vratz, and John Stern; for the Barbarous Murder of Thomas Thynn, Esq.; Together with the Tryal of Charles Count Coningsmark, as Accessory before the Fact to the Same Murder. Who Was Acquitted of the Said Offence. At the Sessions in the Old Bailey, Tuesday February 28. 1681.

1683

Groans from New-Gate or an Elegy on the Suspension of the Famous Thief Thomas Sadler, Fifteen Times Student in That Renowned Colledge, Who to the Great Regret of All His Assotiates [sic], Was Translated to Tyburn, March, 16th. 1677.

1684

A Full Relation of a Barbarous Murther, Committed upon the Body of Esq; Beddingfield, on . . . the 20th. . . . of July, 1684. by Mr. Barney: As Also the Further Account of the Tryal and Conviction of the Said Mr. Barney, Who Is to Be Executed for the Same, at the Market-Cross in Norwich, on . . . the . . . First . . . of August, 1684.

An Exact and True Relation of the Behaviour of Edmund Kirk, John Bennet, Morgan Reading, and Andrew Hill during Their Imprisonment, and at the Place of Execution . . . the 11th of This Instant July. With the Last Dying Words and Speeches at Tyburn.

Edmund Kirk. The Sufferers Legacy to Surviving Sinners: Or Edmund Kirk's Dying Advice to Young Men, Wrote by His Own Hand in Newgate, and Delivered to His Friend with a Desire the Same Might Be Published, on . . . the 11th. of June, 1684 . . . the Day on Which He Was Executed at Tyburn, for Murthering His Wife.

Samuel Smith. The Behavior of John Hutchins, in Newgate. Together with His Dying Words as He Was Going to Be Executed in Fleet-Street, on . . . the 17th. of December, 1684. For Murdering of John Sparks a Waterman, near Serjeants-Inn London, on . . . the 3d. of December.

1686

A True Account of a Bloody Murther Committed by Three Foot-Padders in Fig-Lane, near St. Pancrass-Church, on the Wife of Phillip Stanton, as She Was Comeing with Her Husband out of the Country . . . the 2d of March Instant. 1685/6.

A True Relation, of the Horrid and Barbarous Murther, Committed on the Body of Mr. Loggins, Gent. and the Ostler of the King's-Head in Coleshill, in the County of Warwick, by Four Persons; Whereof Three Were Apprehended, and Committed to the County-Goal.

1688

A Cabinet of Grief: Or, the French Midwife's Miserable Moan for the Barbarous Murther Committed upon the Body of Her Husband. With the Manner of Her

Conveying Away His Limbs, and of Her Execution: She Being Burnt to Ashes on the 2d of March in Leicester-Fields.

The Wicked Life and Penitent Death of Tho. *Savage, Who Was Twice Executed at Ratcliff, for Murthering His Fellow-Servant. With a Full Account of the Manner of His Fact. Together with His Flight, and How He Was Taken and Committed Close Prisoner to Newgate; Where He Remained Very Penitent and Truly Sorrowful for His Mis-Spent Life, and the Many Sins He Had Committed, Especially the Horrid Sin of Murther.* [N.d.; Bodleian Cat. attrib.]

A Hellish Murder Committed by a French Midwife on the Body of Her Husband, *Jan. 27. 1687/8. for Which She Was Arraigned at the Old-Baily, Feb. 22. 1687/8. and Pleaded Guilty. And the Day Following Received Sentence to Be Burnt.*

The Murtherer Turned True Penitent; *or, an Account of the Wicked and Notorious Life of Thomas Savage, a Young Man about Sixteen Years of Age; Who, at the Instigation of One Hannah Blay, a Leud Strumpet, Killed His Fellow-Servant by Beating Out Her Brains with a Hammer and Robbed His Master. For Which Being Apprehended, He Became Wonderfull Penitent before and after His Condemnation; and More Especially at the Place of Execution: Where Being Once Cut Down Alive, He Was Hanged Up the Second Time.* [N.d.; Bodleian Cat. attrib.]

A True Relation of a Horrid Murder Committed upon the Person of Thomas Kidderminster *of Tupsley in the County of Hereford, Gent. at the White-Horse Inn in Chelmsford in the County of Essex, in the Month of April, 1654. Together with a True Account of the Strange and Providential Discovery of the Same Nine Years After: For Which Moses Drague, an Hostler in the Said Inn, Was Executed at Brentwood in the Same County, in the Year 1667, Being Thirteen Years after the Commission of the Said Murder. Whose Arraignment, Conviction, and Attainder Appears by the Records of the Circuit of That Year.*

A True and Full Relation of a Most Barbarous and Inhuman Murder, *Committed upon the Body of a Man Found in Parkers-Lane, near Little-Queen-Street, on the 30th of January, between the Hours of Nine and Ten at Night. Giving an Account of How the Salvage Murderers Had Most Cruelly Mangled the Said Corps, and How Several Parts Thereof Were Dropt in the Thames, at the Savoy, and Carried Thence to the Coach and Horses, Where the Body Itself Was Laid at Its Taking Up.*

The Tryal of Philip Standsfield, *Son to Sir James Standsfield, of New-Milus, for the Murther of His Father, and Other Crimes Libell'd against Him, Feb. 7. 1688. For Which He Had Judgment, That on the 15th, betwixt the Hours of Two and Four in the Afternoon, to Be Carried to the Mercat-Cross of Edinburgh, and Hang'd on a Gibbet, until He Be Dead; His Tongue to Be Cut Out and Burnt on a Scaffold; and His Right-Hand to Be Cut Off, and Affixt on the East Gate of Hedington. And His Body to Be Hung in Chains. Which Doom and Sentence Was Accordingly Put to Due Execution upon the Said Philip Standsfield.* Edinburgh and London.

1690

A Full and True Relation of the Examination and Confession of W. Barwick and E. Mangall, of Two Horrid Murders, One Committed by William Barwick upon His Wife Being with Child, near Cawood in Yorkshire, upon the 14th. of April Last: As Likewise a Full Account How It Came to Be Discovered by an Apparition of the Person Murderer'd [sic]. *The Second Was Committed by Edward Mangall, upon Elizabeth Johnson alias Ringrose, and Her Bastard Child, on the 4th of September Last, Who Said He Was Tempted Thereto by the Devil. Also Their Trials and Convictions* . . . *at the Assizes Holden at York, on the 16th. of September, 1690.*

The Wonders of Free-Grace: Or, a Compleat History of All the Remarkable Penitents That Have Been Executed at Tyburn, and Elsewhere, for These Last Thirty Years. To Which Is Added, a Sermon Preached in the Hearing of a Condemn'd Malefactor Immediately before His Execution. [The sermon, by Increase Mather, was delivered at Boston in 1686; it has a separate t.p. indicating pub. at London, 1691.]

1691

The Golden Farmer's Last Farewell. Who Was Arraigned and Found Guilty of Wilfull Murther, and Likewise Many Notorious Robberies, for Which He Received a Due Sentence of Death, and Was Accordingly Executed on the 22d. of December, 1690 in Fleetstreet. To the Tune of The Rich Merchant Man. [N.d.; Brit. Lib. attrib.]

The Unhappy Citizen. A Faithful Narrative of the Life and Death of James Selby, Late Distiller in London. Who Was Convicted for the Murder of One Mrs. Bartlet; and Executed in Goodman's-Fields, by Lemon Street, Saturday, May 2d. 1691. Giving a Particular Account of His Former Conversation, and Behaviour; of His Being One of the Chief of the Grand Tory-Club, in the Reign of King Charles II. His Burning the Effigies of the Late Duke of Monmouth, Shaftesbury and Argyle, Lord Russel, Collonel Sidney, Doctor Oats, and a Non-Conformist Minister. His Wicked Design to Burn the Bible. His Being Suspected to Be the Person That Fired and Robbed the House of Mrs. Johnsons in Spittle-Fields; and That Murthered the Three Women Lately in Well-Close. With a Prayer: and His Last Dying Words, at the Place of Execution.

1692

The Arraignment, Tryal, Conviction and Condemnation of Henry Harrison, Gent. For the Barbarous Murther of Andrew Clenche . . . *Doctor of Physick.*

God's Revenge against Murther: Containing the Confessions, Prayers, Discourses, and Last Dying Sayings, of Mr. Edward [sic] *Harrison, Who Was Try'd, Convicted, and Deservedly Sentenced the Sixth and Ninth of* . . . *April, 1692. for the* . . . *Murther of Dr. Clench; and Accordingly Executed in Holbourn* . . . *the Fifteenth Following.*

Henry Harrison. *The Last Words of A Dying Penitent: Being an Exact Account of the Passages, Proceedings, and Reasons on Which Was Grounded the First Suspicion of His Being Concerned in the Bloody Inhumane Murder of Dr. Clinch, on the 4th of January 1691. . . . for Which He Was Executed on the 15th of April 1692. the Which He Leaves to the World to Judg. Trusting as to His Innocency in This, and Relying on God Almighties Pardon. . . . Written with His Own Hand after Condemnation.*

Fair Warning to Murderers of Infants: Being an Account of the Tryal, Co[n]demnation and Execution of Mary Goodenough at the Assizes Held in Oxon, in February, 1691/2. Together with the Advice Sent by Her to Her Children, in a Letter Sign'd by Her Own Hand the Night before She Was Executed; with Some Reflections Added upon the Whole.

Murder Will Out: An Impartial Narrative of the Notorious Wicked Life of Capt. Harrison, Who Was Arraign'd, Try'd, and Convicted, at the Sessions-House in the Old-Baily, on Wednesday Last, the Sixth Instant, for the Late Barbarous, Cruel, and Unheard Of Murder of Doctor Clench. Giving a Particular Account of His Birth, Parentage, and Education . . . and . . . of the Motives and Reasons That Induced Him to Commit the Said Barbarous and Unheard Of Murder . . . with the Manner of It, and the True Causes of Its Discovery.

Robert Rowe. *Mr. Harrison Proved the Murtherer: Or, His Late Villany Unmask'd. With a Justification of the King's Evidence. In Answer to the Several Pamphlets, Which Were Written by Hen. Harrison, after His Condemnation, and Publisht since His Execution, for the Horrible Murther of Dr. Andrew Clench.*

[Elkanah Settle]. *The Notorious Imposter; or the History of the Life of William Morrell, Alias Bowyer, Sometime of Banbury, Chirugeon. Who Lately Personated Humphrey Wickham of Swackly, in the Country of Oxon, Esquire, at a Bakers House in the Strand, Where He Died the Third of Jan. 1691/2.*

1693

A Full and True Account of the Apprehending James Whitney, the Notorious High-Way-Man; near Bishops Gate. With His Examination and Confession before Sir Thomas Cook, Sheriff, and the Recorder of the City of London.

An Account of the Malefactors That Received the Benefit of Their Majesties Most Gracious Pardon, at Justice-Hall in the Old-Baily . . . the . . . 11th . . . of December . . . 1693.

The Life of Captain James Whitney. Containing, His Most Remarkable Robberies and Other Adventures, &c. Continued to His Execution near Smithfield Bars the First of February 1692/3.

Most Strange and Wonderful News from a Place Call'd the Leister, by Castle-Street, in the Parish of St. Martins in the Fields: of a Most Dreadful Discovery of a Murther of an Man and a Child, Made on Sonday Morning Being the 11th Instant, on a Dunghill There; of the Finding the Skin, and Nails of a Mans Hands, with his Privy-Members, Heart, Liver, Breast, and Great Quantities of the Flesh of His Buttocks, &c. as Also the Hart, Liver, Hand &c. of a Child, with the Strange Manner of the Discovery by a Butcher, and One John Williams a Labouring Man.

The Jacobite Robber. An Account of the Famous Life, and Memorable Actions of Capt. Jam. Whitney, the Notorious Highway-Man, Who Was Apprehended, and Committed to Newgate, on Saturday the 31. of December, 1692/3. The Most Remarkable of Whose Robberies Were as Followeth: on a Fat Parson of His Money, Canonick, &c. and Bestowing it on a Non-Jurant. Madam Palmer at Grays in Essex. Esq; Bird near Ware. The Lady Butler in Essex. Sir J. Read. Sir T. Draper. Reading and Bristol Coaches. Finchley, Highgate, Hamstead. Three Brother Highway-Men. A Quack Doctor. Sir. R. Buckley. Madam Boulds in Essex. Wickham Fair. From Uxbridge to Hide Park. Farnum Butchers. Chessum Butchers. An Old Usurer. Manchester Carrier, & Smith Laceman.

1694

The Notorious Robbers Lamentation, or, Whitneys Sorrowful Ditty in the Gaol of Newgate: Together with an Account of His Dream That Morning before He Was Taken. [N.d.; Brit. Lib. tentative attrib.]

1695

Mistaken Justice: Or, Innocence Condemn'd, in the Person of Francis Newland, Lately Executed at Tyburn, for the Barbarous Murther of Mr. Francis Thomas. Being a True Account of the Evidence against Him, of the Truth of His Case, and of His Behaviour, from the Time of His Sentence, till His Execution, Attested by Divers Credible Persons.

[Samuel Smith]. *A True Account of the Behaviour of Mr. Francis Newland, Who Was Executed at Tyburn . . . the 19th of April, 1695. for the Murther of Francis Thomas, Esq; Together with a Paper Delivered to the Ordinary, Attested with His Own Hand, Desiring That He Would Publish It, for the Benefit of His Friends and Acquaintance.*

1698

A True and Impartial Account of the Birth, Parentage, Education, Life and Conversation of Edmund Audley, Who Was Executed at Tyburn . . . the 22d of June, 1698 for the Barbarous Murther of Mrs. Hannah Bullevant in St. Martins le Grand, near Aldersgate. As Also, an Account of His Marriage with a Ministers Daughter at Exeter; the Occasion of His Leaving Her, and His Coming to London; with Other Strange Passages of His Life from His Birth, to the Time of His Shameful Death. To Which Is Added, the Particulars of His Tryal and Condemnation; as Also His Disputes with Several Divines in Newgate, Together with His Speech and Confession at the Place of Execution.

William Smythies. *A True Account of the Robbery and Murder of John Stockden, a Victualler in Grub-Street, in the Parish of St. Giles's Cripplegate, and of the Discovery of the Murderers, by the Several Dreams of Elizabeth, the Wife of Thomas Greenwood, Who Was Near Neighbour to Mr. Stockden, and Intimately Acquainted with Him.*

1699

Cotton Mather.   *Pillars of Salt. An History of Some Criminals Executed in This
    Land, for Capital Crimes. With Some of Their Dying Speeches. Collected and
    Published, for the Warning of Such as Live in Destructive Courses of Ungodli-
    ness.* Boston.
Sir John Maynard.   *The Case of a Murther in Hertfordshire. Found amongst the
    Papers of That Eminent Lawyer, Sir John Maynard, Late One of the Lords
    Commissioners of the Great Seal of England.*
*The Tryal of Spencer Cowper, Esq; John Marson, Ellis Stevens, and William Rogers,
    Gent. . . . for the Murther of Mrs. Sarah Stout, a Quaker . . . at Hertford
    Assizes, July 18, 1699. of Which They Were Acquitted.*

1700

*An Account of a Bold Desperate and Notorious Robbery, Committed on Monday
    Morning Last, in His Majesties Exchequer at Westminster. Particularly How
    Several Strong Doors, Locks, Chests, and Desks Were Forced Open; with an
    Account of the Quantity of Money That the Thieves Carry'd Off, and How
    Strang[e]ly They Made Their Escape, with Other Remarkable Circumstances.*
*The Life and Conversation of the Pretended Captain Charles Newey: Together with
    Some Remarks upon a Scurrilous and Scandalous Pamphlet, Called Newey's
    Case.*
Charles Newey.   *Captain Charles Newy's Case Impartially Laid Open; or, a True
    and Full Narrative of the Clandestine Proceedings aginst Him, as It Was
    Hatched, Contrived, and Maliciously Carried On by Mrs. Margaret Newey,
    Widdow.* ["Printed for the author."]
*Second Captain Hind: Or the Notorious Life and Actions of That Infamous Highway-
    man and Housebreaker, Captain John Simpson, Alias Holiday, Who Was Exe-
    cuted at Tiburn . . . the 20th of July, for Fellony and Burglary.* [Rptd. G.
    Smeeton, 1817.]

1701

Paul Lorrain.   *Harman Strodtman's Last Legacy to the World. Being His Divine
    Meditations and Prayers, Written in High-Dutch, during His Confinement in
    Newgate, for the Murther of His Fellow-Prentice, Peter Wolter. Together with
    His Last Speech and Prayers at the Place of Execution, June 18. 1701.*

1703

Paul Lorrain.   *The Confession of John Peter Dramatti, a Frenchman, Executed at
    Tyburn, on Wednesday the 21th [sic] of July, 1703, for the Barbarous Murther of
    Frances His Wife, about Bloody Bridge near Chelsea.*

1705

Observations on the Tryal of Capt. Green, and the Speech at His Death.

1707

The Cruel Son; or, the Unhappy Mother. Being a Dismal Relation of One Mr. Palmer and Three Ruffians, Who Barbarously Murder'd His Own Mother and Her Maid, at Upton Snagsbury, in the Parish of Grafton, in the County of Worcestor, November the 7th, 1707. by Cutting Their Throats from Ear to Ear, in a Cruel and Unnatural Manner; and Afterwards Setting the House on Fire.

1708

An Account of the Life and Conversation, Birth, Parentage, and Education of William Greg; Who Was Drawn Hang'd and Quartered for High Treason; and John Maugridge Kettle-Drummer, for the Murther of Captain Cope. As Also David Baily, for the Murther of His Own Brother. Together with Their Behaviors in Newgate, Their Confessions, and Last Dying Speeches at the Place of Execution.

The Life and Penitent Death of John Mawgridge, Gent. Who Was Executed for the Murder of Captain Cope. Penn'd from His Own Account of Himself, and Approv'd Of by Him, before His Death. Wherein Is Contain'd a True State of the Case of the Murder for Which He Dy'd; with an Account of the Tryal, and the Judges Opinions upon the Special Verdict; with His Own Sentiments of That Matter. His Escape out of the Queen's-Bench: How He Liv'd in Flanders, and Was Brought Over; with His Farther Usage to His Execution. His Manner of Behaviour during His Last Imprisonment. With Reflexions on the Whole.

Paul Lorain [sic]. *The Whole Life and Conversation, Birth, Parentage and Education of Mr. William Gregg, Who Was Executed . . . the 28th . . . of April, 1708 for High Treason: With His Several Examinations and Confessions before the Committees of Lords. And Also His Behaviour Whilst under Condemnation in Newgate: And His Last Dying Speech and Confession at the Place of Execution. To Which Is Added, The Life of Mr. John Maugeridge the Kettle-Drumer, and Mr. David Bayley, the First to the Murder of Captain Cope at the Town; and the Latter for the Murder of His Own Brother in Leicester-Fields; Who Were Executed at Tyburn on . . . the 28th of April. With Their Tryals, Examinations, and Condemnation at the Sessions-House in the Old-Baily. Their Behaviour and Confessions, and Last Dying Speeches at the Place of Execution.*

Memoirs of the Right Villanous John Hall, the Late Famous and Notorious Robber, Penn'd from His Own Mouth Some Time before His Death. Containing the Exact Life and Character of a Thief in General. As Also a Lively Representation of Newgate, and Its Inhabitants, with the Manners and Customs Observed There. The Nature and Means by Which They Commit Their Several Thefts and Robberies, and the Distinctions Observed in Their Respective Functions. To Which Is Added, the Cant Generally Us'd by Those Sort of People to Conceal Their Villanies; and Rules to Avoid Being Robb'd or Cheated by Them. 4th. ed.

The Truth of the Case. Or, a Full and True Account of the Horrid Murders, Robberies and Burnings, Committed at Bradforton and Upton Snodsbury, in the County of Worcester, and of the Apprehension, Examination, Tryal, and Conviction, of John Palmer, and Tho. Symonds, Gent[s]., William Hobbins, and John Allen, Labourers, for the Said Crimes. To Which Is Added, an Account of the Bp. of

Oxford's Going to the Prisoners after Their Condemnation, and of His Lordship's Whole Transaction with Them; Written by the Said Bishop. Likewise, an Account of What Pass'd between the Ordinary and the Prisoners. And Remarks on Their Dying Speeches. ["Publish'd on Occasion of a Late Imperfect, False, and Scandalous Libel, Entituled, The Case of John Palmer and Thomas Symonds, Gent. Who Were Executed, &c. By R. W———."]

R.W.   *The Case of John Palmer and Thomas Symonds, Gentlemen. Executed near Worcester on the 7th of May 1708, upon the Evidence of Gyles Hunt, Who Having Obtain'd His Own Pardon, Charg'd Them to Have Been Concern'd with Himself in the Murther of Mrs. Alice Palmer, Mother to the Said Mr. John Palmer, and Her Maid. With the Letter of the Said Two Gentlemen to the Lord Bishop of Oxon, Asserting Their Innocence, and Giving an Account How They Were Prevail'd on to Confess Themselves Guilty, by Some Who Put Them in Hopes of a Pardon on That Condition. His Lordship's Answer, with a Form of Prayer He Compos'd and Sent Them. Mr. Palmer's Letter to a Noble Lord in London on the Day of His Death, Denying the Fact. And Mr. Palmer and Mr. Symond's Dying Speeches, Wherein They Deny It upon Their Salvation.*

1709

The Guilford Ghost. Being an Account of the Strange and Amazing Apparition or Ghost of Mr. Christopher Slaughterford; with the Manner of His Wonderful Appearance to Joseph Lee, His Man, and One Roger Voller, at Guilford in Surrey, on Sunday and Monday Night Last, in a Sad and Astonishing Manner, in Several Dreadful and Frightful Shapes, with a Rope about His Neck, a Flaming Torch in One Hand, and a Club in the Other, Crying, Vengeance, Vengeance. With Other Amazing Particulars. [N.d.; Brit. Lib. attrib.]

William Price.   *The Birth, Parentage, and Education, Life and Conversation of Mr. Christopher Slaughterford, Who Was Executed at Guilford in Surry . . . the 9th of July, 1709. for the Barbarous Murther of Jane Young His Sweetheart. With an Account of His Courtship, and Manner of the Said Murther, with the Strange Discovery Thereof. His Apprehension and Commitment: His Tryal at Kingstone Assizes, and Acquitment: His Being Try'd a Second Time upon an Appeal at the Queens-Bench-Bar, Westminster: His Condemnation and Sentence There: His Behaviour in Prison: His Confession and True Last Dying Speech at the Place of Execution. As Also, a True Copy of a Paper That He Gave to the Sheriff at the Place of Execution.*

1710

A Warning to Youth: The Life and Death of Thomas Savage: Who Was Imprison'd in Newgate, Condemn'd, and Twice Executed at Ratcliff, for the Murther of His Master's Maid-Servant, on October 2. 1668. . . . To Which Is Added, a Sermon Preach'd at His Funeral. With an Account of the Vicious Life, and Ignominious Death of Hannah Blay, Who Was Condemn'd and Executed, for Being Guilty of the Said Murther. [N.d.; Brit. Lib. attrib.]

1711

A Full and True Account of a Most Horrid and Barbarous Murder Committed Yesterday, April 24th, in St. James's-House, by Eliz. Smith, upon the Body of Her Own Male Child, by Running of a Penknife into Its Heart, and Thrusting It into a Hole of the Cieling [sic] *in a Garret. With Her Examination and Confession . . . at Whitehall, and Commitment to Newgate.*

1713

Cotton Mather. *The Curbed Sinner. A Discourse upon the Gracious and Wondrous Restraints Laid by the Providence of the Glorious God, on the Sinful Children of Men, to Withold Them from Sinning against Him. Occasioned by a Sentence of Death, Passed on a Poor Young Man, for the Murder of His Companion. With Some Historical Passages Referring to That Unhappy Spectacle.* Boston.

[Cotton Mather]. *The Sad Effects of Sin. A True Relation of the Murder Committed by David Wallis on His Companion Benjamin Stolwood . . . the First of August, 1713. With His Carriage after Condemnation; His Confession and Dying Speech at the Place of Execution, &c. To Which Are Added, the Sermons Preached at the Lecture in Boston, in His Hearing, after His Condemnation; and on the Day of His Execution . . . Sept. 24. 1713.* Boston.

1718

[N.B.]. *A Compleat Collection of Remarkable Tryals of the Most Notorious Malefactors, at the Sessions-House in the Old Baily, for near Fifty Years Past. . . . Together with a Particular Account of Their Behaviour under Sentence of Death, and Dying Speeches. Faithfully Collected from the Books of Tryals, and Papers of Mr. Smith, Mr. Allen, Mr. Wikes, and Mr. Lorrain, Ordinaries of Newgate, from the First Printing of Them, down to This Present Time: and from Other Authentic Narratives.* 4 vols. [Vols. 3 and 4 pub. 1721, with slightly different t.p.]

1719

Captain Alexander Smith. *A Compleat History of the Lives and Robberies of the Most Notorious Highway-Men, Footpads, Shop-Lifts, and Cheats of Both Sexes, in and about London, Westminster, and All Parts of Great Britain, for above an Hundred Years Past, Continu'd to the Present Time.* 5th ed. 3 vols. [1st ed. pub. 1713–14, and a 2nd and 3rd ed. by 1714, but only vols. 1 and 2 of the 2nd ed. survive in the Brit. Lib.]

Captain Alexander Smith. *A Complete History of the Lives and Robberies of the Most Notorious Highwaymen, Footpads, Shoplifts, & Cheats of Both Sexes.* Edited (and slightly bowdlerized) by Arthur L. Hayward. 3 vols. in 1. 1933.

1722

James Carrick. *A Compleat and True Account of All the Robberies Committed by James Carrick, John Malhoni, and Their Accomplices, in Dublin, Cork, Limerick,*

Waterford, and Other Places in Ireland. As Also on the Highway in England, and in the Streets of London and Westminster, and Places Adjacent. To Which Is Added, a True Copy of His Dying Words, Which He Gave to a Friend the Day before His Execution. Together with the Particulars of Their Unhappy Birth and Education. Written by James Carrick. With Several Original Letters.

William Hawkins.   *A Full, True and Impartial Account of All the Robberies Committed in City, Town, and Country, for Several Years Past by William Hawkins, in Company with Wilson, Wright, Butler Fox, and Others Not Yet Taken. Wherein He Had Discover'd the Most Unparallel'd and Surprizing Adventures Ever Done upon the High-Way. Likewise a Detection of Wilson's False Account of Robberies, and a Full Relation of What Robberies the Said Wilson Was Actually Assisting In, and How Cowardly He Behav'd Himself in Such Dangerous Enterprizes. Also the Names of the Persons Whom We Robb'd, the Time When and Place Where They Were Attack'd, and Where and How We Dispos'd of the Things Taken from Them. Written by William Hawkins, Brother of John Hawkins, Lately Executed at Tiburn, for Robbing the Bristol Mail.*

The Whole Life and History of Benjamin Child, Lately Executed for Robbing the Bristol Mail. Containing His Being Clerk in an Office, and Dismission Thence; His Setting Up a School in the Country, and the Tricks He Play'd There, with His Flying from Thence, and Falling into the Company of Sharpers; of Robbing the Mails, and Putting of Sham-Bills Off; with an Account of His Cheating Two Mercers on Ludgate-Hill, a Peruke-Maker in Covent-Garden, and a Banker in Lombard-Street, &c. As Also His Intended Legacies, His Charities in His Way to Execution, and His Behaviour at the Gallows. With the True and Genuine Speech He Deliver'd to a Friend before He Was Executed.

Thomas Purney.   *The Ordinary of Newgate's Account of the Behaviour, Confession, and Last Dying Speech of Matthias Brinsden, Who Was Executed at Tyburn . . . the 24th of September, 1722. for the Murther of His Wife Hannah Brinsden, on the 16th . . . of July . . . in the Parish of St. Anne, Black-Fryars.* ["Omitted in the Common Account of the Dying Speech, for want of Room, and the largeness of this Account."]

Ralph Wilson.   *A Full and Impartial Account of All the Robberies Committed by John Hawkins, George Sympson, (Lately Executed for Robbing the Bristol Mails) and Their Companions. Particularly the Robbing of General Evans on Putney-Common, Where His Man Was Killed; the Robbing the Bristol, Worcester, Oxford, Bath, Gloucester, Ipswich, Bury, &c. Stage-Coaches; as Also, the Earl of Burlington and Lord Bruce: With the Case of Butler Fox, Who Was Executed for Robbing Colonel Archibald Hamilton; and the Robberies of the Earl of Westmoreland, and Others, in the Streets in and about London; and Remarks on the Tryal of the Above Persons. With an Account of Hawkins's Defacing Several Pictures in the Bodleian Library at Oxford: With a Proposed Project of Robbing the Harwich Mail. Written by Ralph Wilson, Late One of Their Confederates.*

1723

The Highland Rogue: Or, the Memorable Actions of the Celebrated Robert Mac-Gregor, Commonly Called Rob-Roy. Containing a Genuine Account of His

Education, Grandeur, and Sudden Misfortune; His Commencing Robber, and Being Elected Captain of a Formidable Gang; His Exploits on the Highway, Breaking Open Houses, Taking Prisoners, Commencing Judge, and Levying Taxes; His Defence of His Manner of Living; His Dispute with a Scotch Parson upon Predestination; His Joining with the Earl of Marr in the Rebellion; His Being Decoy'd and Imprison'd by the Duke of ——, with the Manner of His Escape, &c. Introduc'd with a Relation of the Unequal'd Villanies of the Clan of the Mac-Gregors for Several Years Past. The Whole Impartially Digested from the Memorandums of an Authentick Scotch Ms.

The Life of Mr. John Stanley, of His Parents: How Serv'd by Officers in His Education. How Harden'd When a Boy in Spain. Gets to Be an Ensign in Ireland. How Used by Mrs. Old——d. Triumphs over Three of Mrs. Needham's Virgins in Clerkenwell Bridewell. Attack'd and Admir'd by Thieves. With Captain Faulconer before He Was Kill'd, but Escapes Mr. Winchurch's Sword. Why Forced to Turn Knight Errant. Preaches to Strumpets. How He Miss'd the Murder of the Watchman in the Strand. Of His Going on the Highway. Sent by the African Company to Cape-Coast Castle, but Runs from Capt. Massey at Portsmouth. Goes to Flanders &c. Of His Children by Mrs. Maycock; The Exact Account of Stabbing Her; Her Dying Expressions, His Behaviour and Expressions Then, and in Newgate. His Fancied Sights. His Defence, &c. at His Trial. His Own Reasons to a Friend for the Murder. His Behaviour in the Condemn'd Hole to His Death. And Other Particulars.

1724

[Daniel Defoe, as "Captain Charles Johnson"]. *A General History of the Robberies and Murders of the Most Notorious Pyrates, and Also Their Policies, Discipline and Government, from Their First Rise and Settlement in the Island of Providence, in 1717, to the Present Year 1724. With the Remarkable Actions and Adventures of the Two Female Pyrates, Mary Read and Anne Bonney. To Which Is Prefix'd an Account of the Famous Captain Avery and His Companions; with the Manner of His Death in England.* 2 vols [Vol. 2 pub. 1728, with different t.p.]

The History of the Remarkable Life of John Sheppard. Containing a Particular Account of His Many Robberies and Escapes. . . . The Whole Taken from the Most Authentick Accounts . . . and from the Confession of Sheppard Made to the Rev. Mr. Wagstaff, Who Officiated for the Ordinary of Newgate. [Rptd. in Horace Bleackley with S. M. Ellis, *Jack Sheppard* (1933).]

Authentic Memoirs of the Life and Surprising Adventures of John Sheppard: Who Was Executed at Tyburn, November the 16th, 1724. By Way of Familiar Letters from a Gentleman in Town, to His Friend and Correspondent in the Country. [Rptd. in Bleackley, *Jack Sheppard* (1933).]

A Narrative of All the Robberies, Escapes, &c. of John Sheppard: Giving an Exact Description of the Manner of His Wonderful Escape from the Castle at Newgate, and of the Methods He Took Afterward for His Security. Written by Himself during His Confinement in the Middle Stone Room, after His Being

Retaken in Drury Lane. 6th ed. [Rptd in Bleackley, *Jack Sheppard* (1933).]

John Thurmond.   *Harlequin Sheppard. A Night Scene in Grotesque Characters: As It Is Perform'd at the Theatre-Royal in Drury-Lane. . . . With New Scenes Painted from the Real Places of Action. To Which Is Prefix'd an Introduction, Giving an Account of Sheppard's Life.*

1725

H.D.   *The Life of Jonathan Wild, from His Birth to His Death. Containing His Rise and Progress in Roguery; His First Acquaintance with Thieves; by What Arts He Made Himself Their Head, or Governor; His Discipline over Them; His Policy and Great Cunning in Governing Them; and the Several Classes of Thieves under His Command. In Which All His Intrigues, Plots and Artifices Are Accounted For, and Laid Open.*

[Daniel Defoe].   *A True & Genuine Account of the Life and Actions of the Late Jonathan Wild, Not Made Up of Fiction and Fable, but Taken from His Own Mouth, and Collected from Papers of His Own Writing.*

An Epistle from Jack Sheppard to the Late L——d C——ll——r of E——d, Who when Sheppard Was Try'd, Sent for Him to the Chancery Bar. Dublin. [N.d.; Brit. Lib. tentative attrib.]

An Authentick History of the Parentage, Birth, Education, Marriages, Issue, and Practices of the Famous Jonathan Wild, (Citizen and Thief-Taker of London) Together with the Crimes He Now Stands Charg'd With in Custody of the Keeper of Newgate. 2nd. ed. Stamford. ["Printed . . . from the London Copy."]

The History of the Lives and Actions of Jonathan Wild, Thief-Taker. Joseph Blake Alias Bleuskin [sic], *Foot-Pad. And John Sheppard, Housebreaker. Giving a Full and Exact Account of Jonathan's Being Crown'd King of the Gypsies; the Ways and Means He Made Use Of to Reduce Young People into Robberies, and Afterwards Hang Them for Their Desarts, and of the Reasons That Induced Blueskin to Cut Jonathan Wild's Throat. As Also a True Relation of the Pranks Jack Sheppard Played, and of His Being Retaken. Taken from Several Papers Found since Jonathan's Death, with Letters and Private Confessions to Friends, Never Yet Publish'd*. 3rd ed. [Likely pub. 1725 or 1726, according to G. Howson, *Thief-Taker General* (1970).]

News from the Dead: Or, a Dialogue between Blueskin, Shepperd, and Jonathan Wild. [N.d.; Brit. Lib. attrib.]

N.P.   *Weighley, Alias Wild. A Poem, in Imitation of Hudibras. To Which Is Annex'd a More Genuine and Particular Account in Prose, than Any Yet Publish'd, of the Most Remarkable Events, and Transactions, of His Life, from the Time of His Birth to His Execution. Also Jonathan's Last Farewel and Epitaph, with a Song, Never Before Printed.*

The Prison-Breaker; or, the Adventures of John Sheppard. A Farce. As Intended to Be Acted at the Theatre Royal in Lincoln's-Inn Fields.

1726

A Narrative of the Barbarous and Unheard Of Murder of Mr. John Hayes, by Catherine His Wife, Thomas Billings, and Thomas Wood, on the 1st of March at Night. Wherein Every Minute Circumstance Attending That Horrid Affair, and the Wonderful Providence of God in the Discovery of the Actors Therein, Are Faithfully and Impartially Related. Together with the Examinations and Confessions of the Said Thomas Billings and Thomas Wood before Several of His Majesty's Justices of the Peace. . . . With Some Account of the Wicked Life and Conversation of the Said Catherine, and Likewise of Those of Thomas Billings and Thomas Wood. . . . Published with the Approbation of the Relations and Friends of the Said Mr. John Hayes. 2nd ed.

Captain Alexander Smith. *Memoirs of the Life and Times of the Famous Jonathan Wild, Together with the History and Lives, of Modern Rogues, Several of 'Em His Acquaintance, That Have Been Executed before and since His Death, for the High-Way, Pad, Shop-Lifting, House-Breaking, Picking of Pockets, and Impudent Robbing in the Streets, and at Court.* [Facsim. rpt., with intro. by Malcolm J. Bosse (New York, 1973).]

1727

[Charles Beckingham]. *The Life of Mr. Richard Savage. Who Was Condemn'd with Mr. James Gregory, the Last Sessions at the Old Baily, for the Murder of Mr. James Sinclair, at Robinson's Coffee-House at Charing-Cross. With Some Very Remarkable Circumstances, Relating to the Birth and Education, of that Gentleman, Which Were Never Yet Made Publick.*

A True and Faithful Narrative of the Life and Actions of John Oneby, Esq; Commonly Called Major Oneby; Who Was to Have Been Executed Last Monday at Tyburn, for the Murder of William Gower, Esq; Giving an Account of His Birth, Parentage and Education . . . and the Murder of Himself in Newgate.

1728

Martin Bellamy. *The Life of Martin Bellamy; with an Account of All the Several Street Robberies, Burglaries, Forgeries, and Other Crimes by Him Committed. Also the Method Practised by Himself, and His Companions, in the Perpetration Thereof. Necessary to be Perus'd by All Persons, in Order to Prevent Their Being Robb'd for the Future. Dictated by Himself in Newgate, and Publish'd at His Request, for the Benefit of the Publick.*

James Dalton. *A Genuine Narrative of All the Street Robberies Committed since October Last, by James Dalton, and His Accomplices, Who Are Now in Newgate, to Be Try'd Next Sessions, and against Whom, Dalton (Call'd Their Captain) Is Admitted an Evidence. Shewing I. The Manner of Their Snatching Off Womens Pockets; with Directions for the Sex in General How to Wear Them, So That They Cannot Be Taken by Any Robber Whatsoever. II. The Method They Took to Rob the Coaches, and the Many Diverting Scenes They*

Met With While They Follow'd Those Dangerous Enterprizes. III. Some Merry Stories of Dalton's Biting the Women of the Town, His Detecting and Exposing the Mollies, and a Song Which Is Sung at the Molly-Clubs: With Other Very Pleasant and Remarkable Adventures. To Which Is Added, a Key to the Canting Language, Occasionally Made Use Of in This Narrative. Taken from the Mouth of James Dalton. ["Mollies" were homosexuals, and "Molly-Clubs" early eighteenth-century London's version of gay bars.]
Memoirs Concerning the Life and Manners of Captain Mackheath.

1730

James Dalton. *The Life and Actions of James Dalton, (the Noted Street-Robber.) Containing All the Robberies and Other Villanies Committed by Him, Both Alone and in Company, from His Infancy down to His Assault on Dr. Mead. With a Particular Account of His Running Away with the Ship When He Was First Transported; and Likewise of the Tricks He Play'd in the West-Indies. As Taken from His Own Mouth in His Cell in Newgate.*

[M.N.]. *A Complete Collection of State-Trials, and Proceedings for High-Treason, and Other Crimes and Misdemeanours; from the Reign of King Richard II. to the End of the Reign of King George I.* 2nd ed. 6 vols.

1731

The Unparallel'd Imposter: Or, the Whole Life, Artifices and Forgeries of Japhet Crook, Alias Sir Peter Stranger, Bart. With All the Proceedings against Him.

1732

Joseph Powis. *A Compleat and Genuine Account of the Life and Actions of Joseph Powis, Convicted at the Sessions-House in the Old-Bailey, for Burglary, September, the Sixth, 1732. Executed at Tyburn . . . the Ninth of October. Likewise, Some Letters, by Way of Address, Which He Sent to the Mistress of His Affections. Faithfully Collected and Written by Himself.*

The Life and Infamous Actions of That Perjur'd Villain John Waller, Who Made His Exit in the Pillory, at the Seven-Dials . . . the 13th . . . of . . . June. Containing All the Villainies, Tricks, and Devices, Which He Practised in Defrauding and Cheating People, and in Swearing Robberies against Innocent Persons, to Take Away Their Lives, for the Sake of the Rewards Granted by Act of Parliament.

1734

Capt. Charles Johnson [but not Defoe, d. 1730]. *A General History of the Lives and Adventures of the Most Famous Highwaymen, Murderers, Street-Robbers, &c. To Which Is Added, a Genuine Account of the Voyages and Plunders of the Most Notorious Pyrates.*

Select Trials for Murders, Robberies, Rapes, Sodomy, Coining, Frauds, and Other Offences: At the Sessions-House in the Old-Bailey. To Which Are Added, Genuine Accounts of the Lives, Behaviour, Confessions and Dying-Speeches of the Most Eminent Convicts. 2 vols. [Vol. 2 pub. 1735.]

1735

Lives of the Most Remarkable Criminals Who Have Been Condemned and Executed for Murder, the Highway, Housebreaking, Street Robberies, Coining or Other Offences. Edited by Arthur L. Hayward. 3 vols. in 1. New York, 1927.

Philo Patriae. *A Full and Genuine Account of the Murder of Mrs. Robinson, by Elton Lewis, on Monday Night, April 21, 1735.*

1739

The Trial of the Notorious Highwayman Richard Turpin, at York Assizes, on the 22d Day of March, 1739. . . . Taken Down in Court by Mr. Thomas Kyll, Professor of Short-Hand. To Which Is Prefix'd, an Exact Account of the Said Turpin, from His First Coming into Yorkshire, to the Time of His Being Committed Prisoner to York Castle; Communicated by Mr. Appleton of Beverly, Clerk of the Peace for the East-Riding of the Said County. . . . To Which Is Added, His Behaviour at the Place of Execution . . . the 7th of April, 1739. Together with the Whole Confession He Made to the Hangman at the Gallows. . . . To Which Is Prefix'd, a Large and Genuine History of the Life of Turpin, from His Birth to His Execution. . . . The Whole Grounded on Well-Attested Facts, and Communicated by Mr. Richard Bayes, at the Green Man on Epping-Forest, and Other Persons of the County of Essex. 4th ed. York.

The Genuine History of the Life of Richard Turpin, the Noted Highwayman, Who Was Executed at York for Horse-Stealing . . . Ap. 7, 1739 . . .

1740

An Authentick Account of the Life of Mr. Charles Drew. Late of Long-Melford in the County of Suffolk. Who Was Tried and Convicted at Bury Assizes, for the Murder of His Father, Mr. Charles John Drew, Late an Attorney at Law. . . . With a Particular Relation of the Discovery of the Fact; and the Conduct of the Malefactors, Both before and after the Fact. To Which Is Added, a Faithful Account of the Trial of the Said Charles Drew, and the Depositions of Several Witnesses against Him. With Several Original Papers, Informations, Examinations, &c.

Gilbert Langley. *The Life and Adventures of Gilbert Langley, Formerly of Serle-Street near Lincoln's-Inn, Goldsmith. . . . Written by Himself, in Maidstone-Goal, when under Condemnation, for a Robbery Committed on the Highway.*

The Faithful Narrative; or an Impartial Account of the Tryal of Bartholomew Greenwood, Gent. Rider to His Majesty's First Troop of Horse-Guards, on a Suspicion of Robbing Roger Wheatly Esq, of Camberwell, on the Highway . . . at the

Assizes at Kingston . . . the Second . . . of August, 1740. With the Pleadings of
the Counsel, at Large. . . . Taken in Short Hand, by a Gentleman in Court.
The Suffolk Parricide, Being, the Trial, Life, Transactions, and Last Dying Words, of
Charles Drew, of Long-Melford, in the County of Suffolk; Who Was Executed
at St. Edmund's-Bury . . . the 9th of April, for the Inhuman Murder of His
Father, Charles John Drew, Esq; Attorney at Law, by Shooting Him thro' the
Body, at His Own House . . . the 31st of January 1739–40. By a Gentleman of
Long-Melford.
The Genuine Trial of Charles Drew, for the Murder of His Own Father, at the
Assizes Held at Bury St. Edmond's: on . . . March 27. 1740. . . . To Which Is
Added, an Account of His Behaviour, Whilst under Sentence of Death; Extract
of the Sermon Preach'd to Him the Morning before His Execution; His Last
Dying Speech and Confession Deliver'd by Him to the High Sheriff of the
County; His Letter to His Sisters; Authentic Letters between Him and Mrs.
Boyer; and His Behaviour at the Place of Execution. By a Gentleman of Bury,
Well Acquainted with the Family of the Drews, Who in Court Took the Trial
Down in Short-Hand. 2nd ed.

1741

S[amuel] Foote.   The Genuine Memoirs of the Life of Sir John Dinely Goodere,
Bart. Who Was Murder'd by the Contrivance of His Own Brother, on Board the
Ruby Man of War, in King-Road near Bristol, Jan. 19. 1740. Together with the
Life, History, Tryal, and Last Dying Words, of His Brother Capt. Samuel
Goodere, Who Was Executed at Bristol . . . the 15th . . . of April, 1741.
[J. Penrose].   The Reverend Mr. Penrose's Account of the Behaviour, Confession,
and Last Dying Words, of the Four Malefactors Who Were Executed . . . at
Bristol . . . the 15th of April, 1741, viz. Samuel Goodere, Esq; Commander of
the Ruby Man of War. Matthew Mahony, and, Charles White. All Three for
the Murder of Sir John Dinely Goodere, Bart. a Worcester-Shire Gentleman of
4000 l. a Year. And Jane Williams, for the Murder of Her Bastard Child. With a
Copy of the Papers that Captain Goodere Deliver'd to the Rev. Divine Who
Attended Him at the Place of Execution. Bristol and London.
The Genuine Trial of Samuel Goodere, Esq; (Late Commander of the Ruby Man of
War) Matthew Mahony, and Charles White, at the General Sessions of Oyer
and Terminer for the City of Bristol . . . the 26th Day of March, 1741 . . . for
the Murder of Sir John Dinely Goodere, Bt. ["Taken in Short-Hand by
Order and Direction of S. Foot, of Worcester-College, Oxford, Esq; and
Nephew to the late Sir John Dinely Goodere, Bart."]

1742

[James Guthrie].   The Behaviour, Confession, and Dying Words of Thomas Homan, Who Was Executed . . . the 18th of This Instant November, at the End of
Fetter-Lane in Holborn, for the Barbarous Murder of Mrs. Dix; Together with a
Particular Account of the Said Murder, after What Manner He Committed It,
and Likewise a Very Remarkable Account of His Life, from His Birth to His

Fatal Exit: to Which Are [Added] *Some Letters Sent to Him While under Condemnation by Some Methodists.*

Select Trials, for Murders, Robberies, Rapes, Sodomy, Coining, Frauds, and Other Offences. At the Sessions-House in the Old-Bailey. To Which Are Added, Genuine Accounts of the Lives, Behaviour, Confessions, and Dying-Speeches, of the Most Eminent Convicts. 2nd ed. [1st ed. pub. same year.] 4 vols.

1747

Henry Simms. *The Life of Henry Simms, Alias Young Gentleman Harry. From His Birth to His Death at Tyburn . . . June 17, 1747. Containing a Full and Plain Narrative of the Vast Number of Remarkable Robberies He Has Committed. And the Particulars of His Extraordinary Adventures Both at Home and Abroad. All Wrote by Himself While under Sentence of Death in Newgate.*

1749

The Solemn Declaration of Richard Coleman, Who Was Executed at Kennington-Common . . . April 12, 1749, for the Murder of Sarah Green.

1750

Dr. ———— Allen. *An Account of the Behaviour of Mr. James Maclaine, from the Time of His Condemnation to the Day of His Execution, October 3. 1750. By the Reverend Dr. Allen, Who Attended Him All That Time, to Assist Him in His Preparations for Eternity. Drawn Up and Published at the Earnest Desire of Mr. Maclaine Himself.*

A Genuine Account of the Life and Actions of James Maclean, Highwayman, to the Time of His Trial and Receiving Sentence at the Old-Bailey. Containing, His Robberies, Gallantry at Publick Places, with Other Remarkable Transactions. Together with Some Account of Plunket His Companion.

A Complete History of James Maclean, the Gentleman Highwayman, Who Was Executed at Tyburn . . . October 3, 1750, for a Robbery on the Highway. Containing the Particulars of His Life, from His Birth to His Death. In Which Is Included, an Account of the Robberies He Committed with His Companion Plunkett. And a Series of Letters, That Pass'd between Him and Plunket; As Well during the Time He Was in Holland, as in England; in Which Are Open'd Some Extraordinary Scenes. Also, the Particulars of Their Fortune-Hunting Schemes; in Which Maclean Generally Pass'd for a Gentleman of Worth, and Plunket Personated His Footman. Likewise a Number of Original Letters Sent to Maclean by Different Ladies, Some of Which Contain Narratives of Facts So Exceeding Tender, as Must Raise Pity and Compassion in the Breast of Every Reader.

1751

The True and Genuine Account of the Confession . . . of Thomas Jones, and James Welch, for the Barbarous Rape and Murder of Sarah Green. . . . Together with a Genuine Account of the Remarkable Robberies Committed by Mathias Keys and Henry Bryan.

A Genuine and Authentick Account of the Life and Transactions of William Parsons, Esq; Who Was Executed at Tyburn . . . Feb. 11, 1750–1. Containing a Full Account of the Many Frauds, Forgeries and Robberies He Has Been Guilty of, from His Infancy, to the Time of His Being Transported for Life, with Those He Committed during His Short Stay in America; Together with the Particulars of His Escape from Thence. Likewise an Account of His Arrival at Whitehaven, with the Remarkable Forgery He Committed on a Merchant There. Also of the Five Robberies He Committed since His Return from Transportation, Which Was But Seven Weeks before He Was Apprehended and Committed to Newgate.

Leonard Howard.   *A True and Impartial Account of the Behaviour, Confession, and Dying Words of the Four Malefactors, Who Were Executed at Kennington-Common . . . September 6, 1751. Publish'd with the Approbation and Consent of the Reverend Leonard Howard, D.D. Rector of St. George the Martyr, in Southwark, Who Attended Them Whilst under Sentence of Death, and in Their Last Moments.*

William Parsons.   *Memoirs of the Life and Adventures of William Parsons, Esq; from the Time of His Entering into Life, to His Death. Being a True and Faithful Narrative of Every Memorable Occurrence That Attended Him; Interspers'd with Several Interesting Scenes. Written by Himself, and Corrected (with Additions) at His Own Request by a Gentleman.*

1752

Some Account of the Life and Death of Matthew Lee, Executed at Tyburn, October 11, 1752, in the 20th Year of His Age. 2nd ed.

A Candid Appeal to the Publick, Concerning the Case of the Late Miss Mary Blandy: Wherein, All the Ridiculous and False Assertions Contained in a Pamphlet, Entitled, Miss Mary Blandy's Own Account of the Affair between Her and Mr. Cranstoun, &c. Are Exploded, and the Whole of That Mysterious Affair Set in a True Light. By a Gentleman of Oxford.

Miss Mary Blandy's Own Account of the Affair between Her and Mr. Cranstoun, from the Commencement of Their Acquaintance, in the Year, 1746. To the Death of Her Father, in August 1751. With All the Circumstances Leading to That Unhappy Event. To Which Is Added, an Appendix. Containing Copies of Some Original Letters Now in Possession of the Editor. Together with an Exact Relation of Her Behaviour, Whilst under Sentence; and a Copy of the Declaration Signed by Herself, in the Presence of Two Clergymen, Two Days before Her Execution. Published at Her Dying Request. [Rptd. in *The Trial of Mary Blandy*, ed. William Roughead (1914).]

The Case of Miss Blandy: Consider'd as a Daughter, as a Gentlewoman, and as a Christian. With a Particular Reference to Her Own Narrative. By an Impartial Hand. Oxford.

The Fair Parricide. A Tragedy of Three Acts. Founded on a Late Melancholy Event. [i.e., the Blandy case.]

*The Secret History of Miss Blandy, from Her First Appearance at Bath, to Her
Execution at Oxford, April 6, 1752. Containing an Account of Her Several
Lovers before Her Fatal Engagements with Cranstoun, of Her Behaviour during
His Intercourse with Her, and of the Imprudent Conduct of Her Parents in That
Affair. Communicated to a Gentleman at Henley by Some of Her Domestics,
and Confirm'd by Herself in Prison after Her Sentence.*

*Original Letters to and from Miss Blandy and C—— C——. In Which Is Contained
the Artful Evasions He Used to Prevent His Clearing His Character to Her
Father, and the Whole History of That Parricide.*

*Memoirs of the Life of William-Henry Cranstoun, Esq, in Which His Education and
Genius Are Consider'd. A Great Variety of Incidents in the Junior Part of His
Life, to the Time of His Marriage with Miss Murray in Scotland. . . . His
Amours in London, before His .Acquaintance with Miss Blandy. The Whole
Affair of Miss Blandy Considered; with Some Remarks on Her Trial; in Which
(Supposing All the Facts Sworn against Her to Be True) Her Innocence is
Rationally Accounted For.*

*The ★★★★ Packet Broke-Open; or, a Letter from Miss Blandy, in the Shades Below,
to Capt. Cranstoun, in His Exile Above. . . . Proving, That She Was Guilty
of the Most Heinous Crime for Which She Justly Suffered, from Miss Blandy's
Own Account of the Whole Affair between Her and Mr. Cranstoun. . . .*

*The Authentick Tryals of John Swan, and Elizabeth Jeffryes, for the Murder of Mr.
Joseph Jeffryes of Walthamstow in Essex: With the Tryal of Miss Mary Blandy,
for the Murder of Her Own Father.*

1753

Capt. —— Mackelcan. *A General History of the Lives and Adventures of the
Most Famous Highwaymen, Murderers, Street-Robbers, and Pyrates.*

*Memoirs of the Life and Most Memorable Transactions of Capt. William Henry
Cranstoun.* 2nd ed.

1756

William Cannicott. *A Genuine Account of the Life and Actions of William Canni-
cott, Who Was Executed at Tyburn . . . September 20, 1756, for the Murder of
His Wife . . . the 20th of July, 1756. Written by Himself, While Confined in
Newgate.*

1758

*Life and Surprising Robberies and Adventures of William Page the Noted Highway-
man; Who Was Tried at Rochester for Robbing Capt. Farrington, near Black
Heath, Found Guilty, and Executed on Pennenden Heath near Maidstone in
Kent, April 6, 1758. With an Account of His Several Robberies Committed on
the Highway during the Course of Twelve Years, by an Accomplice. With a*

Consolatory Letter Sent to His Wife the Morning of His Execution, and Another to His Mother at Hampton. To Which is Added, a Short Account of John Birt, the Soldier Who Was Executed with Page for Breaking into the Dwelling-House of Mr. Bacon in Rochester. [A 1d. plagiary of a 1s. original; see next entry but one.]

Capt. ———— Mackdonald. *A General History of the Lives and Adventures of the Most Famous Highwaymen, Murderers, Pirates, Street-Robbers, and Thief-Takers.*

A Genuine Narrative of the Life and Surprising Robberies and Adventures of William Page. Who Was Executed on Pennenden-Heath, near Maidstone in Kent . . . the 6th of April, 1758. For Robbing Capt. Farrington, near Black Heath, with an Account of His Several Robberies by His Accomplice, Viz. of His Desperate Engagement with Capt. Jasper, Whom He Robb'd on Hounslow-Heath. Of His Robbing the Hon. Taylor White, a Welch Judge, on the Circuit. His Unsuccessful Attempt on Lord Downe, in Which He Was Dangerously Wounded. His Famous Robbery of the East-India Company's Supercargo, on Shooter's-Hill, with Many Other Robberies He Committed on the Highway, during the Course of Twelve Years. Together, with His Several Trials at the Old Bailey, Hertford, and Rochester. With a Consolatory Letter to His Wife, Sent the Morning of His Execution, and Another to His Mother at Hampton. Also, a Short Account of John Birt the Soldier, Who Was Executed with Page, for Breaking into the Dwelling-House of Mr. Bacon in Rochester.

1759

The Genuine and Authentic Account of the Murder of Daniel Clarke, Shoemaker, on the 8th of February, 1744–5. Also the Material Part of the Arraignment and Tryal of Richard Houseman, Henry Terry, and Eugene Aram, for the Said Murder, at the Assizes Held at York Castle, July 28, 1759. . . . To Which Is Added, a Succinct Account of the Behaviour of Eugene Aram, from the Time of His Receiving Sentence to That of His Execution; the Particulars He Confess'd, and the Reasons He Left in Writing for the Horrid Attempt He Made on His Own Life. Containing in the Whole, Every Circumstance and Transaction Relating to the Said Murder, before, at, and after the Perpetration Thereof. York.

[W. Bristow]. *The Genuine Account of the Life and Trial of Eugene Aram, for the Murder of Daniel Clark. . . . To Which, after a Short Narration of the Fact, Is Prefixed, An Account of the Remarkable Discovery of the Human Skeleton at Thistle-Hill: A Detail of All the Judicial Proceedings from the Time of the Bones Being Found, to the Commitment of Richard Houseman, Eugene Aram, and Henry Terry to York Castle: The Deposition of Anna Aram, Philip Coates, John Yates, &c.[:] The Examination and Confession of Richard Houseman: The Apprehending of Eugene Aram, at Lynn, in Norfolk: With His Examination and Commitment. To Which Are Added, The Remarkable Defence He Made on His Trial: His Own Account of Himself, Written after His Condemnation: With the Apology, Which He Left in His Cell, for the Attempt He Made on His Own Life; and His Plan for a Lexicon, Some Pieces of Poetry, &c.*

All Taken Immediately from the Original Depositions, Papers, and the Manu-scripts of E. Aram. [Authorship attrib. Brit. Lib.]

The Case of Mary Edmondson. By a Gentleman of the Law.

Joseph Clarke.   *A Full Refutation of the Pretended Genuine Narrative of the Trial and Condemnation of Mary Edmundson.* . . . *As Also That Falsly Called, The Trial at Large, Said to be Taken by a Person Who Attended Her in the New Goal, and at the Stockhouse Prison at Kingston. Compared with That Inserted in the Genuine Proceedings, Taken in Short Hand by Mr. Isaac Herman, with Permission of the High Sheriff.* . . . *With Some Observations on the Two Spurious Accounts Above-Mentioned, and Their Absurdities and Inconsistencies Pointed Out.*

A Genuine Narrative of the Trial and Condemnation of Mary Edmondson, for the Murder of Mrs. Susannah Walker, Her Aunt. At the Assizes Held at Kingston upon Thames . . . March 31, 1759. . . . *With an Account of Her General Behaviour, Last Dying Words, and Execution . . . April 2, 1759. With Animadversions on the Whole Proceedings.* 2nd ed.

The Trial at Large, Behaviour, and Dying Declaration, of Mary Edmondson, Who Was Try'd and Convicted at the Assizes Held at Kingston upon Thames, in Surry, on Saturday, the Thirty-First Day of March, 1759. for the Murder of Mrs. Susanna Walker, Widow, Her Aunt, at Rotherhith, on the 23d . . . of February. . . . *With an Authentic and Genuine Narrative of That Unfortunate Young Woman, from Her Commitment to the New Gaol in Southwark, to Her Execution at Kennington-Common, on Monday the Second Day of April, 1759. And Copies of Some Papers That She Delivered at the Stockhouse Prison at Kingston Just Before She Set Out to the Place of Execution.*

1761

The Authentic Trial, and Memoirs of Isaac Darkin, Alias Dumas, Capitally Convicted for a Highway-Robbery, near Nettlebed . . . at the Lent Assizes at Oxford . . . the Sixth, and Executed for the Same . . . the 23d of March, 1761. Wherein Are Given, a Faithful History of His Life; Several Original Letters, among Which Are Those That Were the Occasion of His Being Apprehended; His Capital Conviction at Chelmsford; His Conditional Pardon, and Return from Antigua; the Robbery of Lord Percival, and His Acquittal at Salisbury; Together with His Behaviour after His Sentence at Oxford, and at the Place of Execution. Oxford.

1763

Charles Speckman.   *The Life, Travels, Exploits, Frauds and Robberies of Charles Speckman, Alias Brown, Who Was Executed at Tyburn . . . the 23d of November, 1763. By Far the Most Dextrous of His Profession in This or Any Other Country. Containing a Genuine Recital of More than Five Hundred Thefts, Frauds, and Felonies, Committed by Him in England, Scotland, Ireland, North America, and the West Indies, during the Course of Fifteen Years. With Several Maxims, Hints, and Remarks, by Way of Caution to the Public, to Prevent or*

Detect the Designs of Sharpers and Thieves. . . . The Whole Narrative Being Wonderful and Surprizing, and Yet in All Respects Strictly True. Written by Himself, Whilst under Sentence of Death in Newgate.

1764

Select Trials for Murder, Robbery, Burglary, Rapes, Sodomy, Coining, Forgery, Pyracy, and Other Offences and Misdemeanours, at the Sessions-House in the Old-Bailey, to Which Are Added Genuine Accounts of the Lives, Exploits, Behaviour, Confessions, and Dying-Speeches, of the Most Notorious Convicts, from the Year 1741 to the Present Year, 1764, Inclusive; Which Completes the Trials from the Year 1720. 4 vols.

1765

Remarkable Trials and Interesting Memoirs, of the Most Noted Criminals, Who Have Been Convicted at the Assizes, the King's Bench Bar, Guildhall, &c. For High-Treason, Murder, Conspiracy, Rape, Highway, Felony, Burglary, Imposition, and Other Atrocious Crimes, Villainies, and Misdemeanours. From the Year 1740, to 1764. With an Account of Their Most Memorable Exploits, Adventures, Confessions, and Dying-Behaviour. 2 vols.

1768

The Tyburn Chronicle: Or, Villainy Display'd in All Its Branches. Containing an Authentic Account of the Lives, Adventures, Tryals, Executions, and Last Dying Speeches of the Most Notorious Malefactors of All Denominations, Who Have Suffered for Bigamy, Forgeries, Highway-Robberies, House-Breaking, Murders, Perjury, Piracy, Rapes, Riots, Sodomy, Starving, Treason, and Other the Most Enormous Crimes. The Whole Being the Most Faithful Narrative Ever Yet Published of the Various Executions, and Other Punishments, in England, Scotland, and Ireland, from the Year 1700, to the Present Time. 4 vols.

1773

The Genuine Life of William Cox, Who Is Now under Sentence of Death, in Newgate, for Robbing Mr. John Kendrick of Bank-Notes and Cash to the Amount of More than Four Hundred Pounds; Containing a Recital of the Particulars of a Very Great Number of the Most Artful Felonies Ever Committed in This Kingdom; Faithfully Penned from Authentic Accounts, Received from the Indubitable Authority of Cox's Intimate Acquaintance.

The Newgate Calendar; or, Malefactors Bloody Register. Containing Genuine and Circumstantial Narratives of the Lives and Transactions, Various Exploits and Dying Speeches of the Most Notorious Criminals of Both Sexes, Who Suffered Death, and Other Punishments, in Great Britain and Ireland, from the Year 1700, to the Present Time; for High Treason, Petty Treason, Murder, Sodomy, Piracy, Felony, Highway Robberies, Forgery, Rapes, Bigamy, Burglaries, Riots, &c. and Various Other Crimes and Misdemeanors, on a Plan Entirely New, Wherein Will Be Fully Displayed the Regular Progress from Virtue to Vice, Interspersed with Striking Reflexions on the Conduct of Thos[e] Unhappy Wretches Who Have Fallen a Sacrifice to the Injured Laws of Their Country. The Whole Tending to Guard Young Minds from the Allurements of Vice, and the Paths That Lead to Destruction. 5 vols.

1774

An Account of John Rann, Commonly Called Sixteen String Jack. Being a Circumstantial Narrative of His Principal Transactions, and His Amours to the Celebrated Miss La Roache.

The Life of John Rann, Otherwise Sixteen Strings Jack, Who Was Sentenced to Death for Robbing Dr. William Bell, Chaplain to Her Royal Highness the Princess Amelia, of His Watch and Money, on the Highway. Containing a Great Number of Interesting Particulars, Which Highly Concern the Public. Together with Anecdotes of Miss Roche, and Several Other Persons Connected with Rann. [Rpt. Frederick Wheeler, 1884.]

John Villette. A Genuine Account of the Behaviour, Confession, and Dying-Words of William Hawke and William Jones, Who Were Executed at Tyburn on the 1st of July, 1774.

1776

John Villette. A Genuine Account of the Behaviour and Dying Words of Daniel Perreau and Robert Perreau, Who Were Executed at Tyburn . . . the 17th of January, 1776 for Forgery.

John Villette, "and others." The Annals of Newgate; or, Malefactor's Register. Containing a Particular and Circumstantial Account of the Lives, Transactions, and Trials of the Most Notorious Malefactors, Who Have Suffered an Ignominious Death for Their Offences, Viz. for Parricide, Murder, Treason, Robbery, Burglary, Piracy, Coining, Forgery, and Rapes; from the Commitment of the Celebrated John Sheppard, to the Acquittal of the Equally Celebrated Margaret Caroline Rudd. Including a Period of Fifty Years and Upwards, Both in Town and Country. Calculated to Expose the Deformity of Vice, the Infamy and Punishments Naturally Attending Those Who Deviate from the Paths of Virtue; and Intended as a Beacon to Warn the Rising Generation against the Temptations, the Allurements, and the Dangers of Bad Company. The Former Part Extracted from Authentic Records; and the Histories and Transactions of the Modern Convicts, Communicated by the Unhappy Sufferers Themselves, Since the Author Has Been Appointed to His Present Office. 4 vols.

1777

John Villette. A Genuine Account of the Behaviour and Dying Words of William Dodd, LLD. Who Was Executed at Tyburn for Forgery . . . the 27th of June 1777. [4 eds. pub. in 1777.]

John Villette. *A Relation of Dr. Dodd's Behaviour in Newgate According to the Rev. Mr. Villette the Ordinary's Account, with Reflexions Thereon; and the Doctor's Last Solemn Declaration.*

1779

The Malefactor's Register; or, the Newgate and Tyburn Calendar. Containing the Authentic Lives, Trials, Accounts of Executions, and Dying Speeches, of the Most Notorious Violators of the Laws of Their Country; Who Have Suffered Death, and Other Exemplary Punishments, in England, Scotland and Ireland, from the Year 1700 to Lady-Day 1779. Together with Numerous Trials in Extraordinary Cases, Where the Parties Have Been Acquitted. This Work Comprehends All the Most Material Passages in the Sessions-Papers for a Long Series of Years, and Complete Narratives of All the Capital Trials for Bigamy, Burglary, Felony, Forgery, Highway-Robbery, High-Treason, Murder, Petit-Treason, Piracy, Rapes, Riots, Street-Robbery, Unnatural Crimes, and Various Other Offences. To Which Is Added, a Correct List of All the Capital Convictions at the Old Bailey, &c. since the Commencement of the Present Century; Which Will Be of the Highest Use to Refer To on Many Occasions. The Whole Tending, by a General Display of the Progress and Consequence of Vice, to Impress on the Mind Proper Ideas of the Happiness Resulting from a Life of Strict Honor and Integrity: and to Convince Individuals of the Superior Excellence of Those Laws Framed for the Protection of Their Lives and Properties. 5 vols. [A "Supplement" carrying forward to 1781, and a "Continuation of the Supplement" to 1791, are bound into vol. 5 of the Brit. Lib. copy.]

1786

[Humanitas]. *An Account of the Behaviour of the Three Malefactors, Who Were Executed near Reading, in Berkshire, on the 25th of March, 1786.*

1790

[T.B.]. *Authentic Memorials of Remarkable Occurrences and Affecting Calamities in the Family of Sir George Sondes, Bart. In Two Parts. The First Being His Own Narrative. The Second the Narrative of Persons Attendant upon His Son Freeman Sondes, Esq. during His Imprisonment, and at His Execution.* [N.d.; Brit. Lib. tentative attrib.; see listings for 1655.]

1794

William Jackson. *The New & Complete Newgate Calendar; or Villany Displayed in All It's [sic] Branches. Containing Accounts of the Most Notorious Malefactors from the Year 1700 to the Present Time.* 7 vols. [N.d.; vols. 2–6, with different t.pp., pub. by 1795; vol. 7, also with different t.p., as a "Supplement" by 1803, or later.]

1797

Anecdotes, Bons Mots, Traits, Stratagems, and Biographical Sketches, of the Most Remarkable Highwaymen, Swindlers, and Other Daring Adventurers, Who Have Flourished, from a Very Early Period, to the Present Time. To Which Is Added, a Great Number of Apposite Curiosities. Collected and Comprised, so as to Render the Whole Both Cautionary and Entertaining; and as Much an Object of Wonder as of Pity!

1802

Rev. John Duncan, LLD. *The London Apprentice: A Narrative of the Life and Death of Nathaniel Butler, Who Was Executed in Cheapside, Sept. 1657. For the Murder of John Knight, His Fellow Apprentice.* [The substance of the 1657 pamphlets is here "re-published."]

1811

Andrew Knapp and William Baldwin. *Criminal Chronology; or, the New Newgate Calendar; Being Interesting Memoirs of Notorious Characters, Who Have Been Convicted of Outrages on the Laws of England, during the Seventeenth Century, and Brought Down to the Present Time, and Chronologically Arranged. . . . With Occasional Essays on Crimes and Punishments, Original Anecdotes, and Observations of Particular Cases; Explanations of the Criminal Laws; the Speeches, Confessions, and Last Exclamations of Sufferers.* 5 vols. [Vol. 1 is dated 1811; vols. 2–5 omit "Criminal Chronology" from title and show n.d.; a 4-vol. set, available at Yale and the Brit. Lib., is dated 1809–10, and a 5-vol. set at Columbia Univ. Lib. shows 1819 on the bindings.]

II. SEVENTEENTH- AND EIGHTEENTH-CENTURY PERIODICALS

A. Ordinaries' Accounts *and sessions papers*

Ordinaries' *Accounts* published under the name of Samuel Smith date back at least to 1679. Until 1700 their titles generally read, "A [or The] True Account of the Behaviour, Confession, and Last Dying Speeches of the [*number*] Prisoners [or Criminals] That Were Executed at Tyburn, on [*day of week*] the [*day of month*] of [*month, year*]." With the assumption of the office by Paul Lorrain in 1700, the typical title changes to "The Ordinary of Newgate His Account of the Behaviour, Confessions, and Last [*or* Dying] Speeches of the Malefactors Who [*or* That] Were Executed at Tyburn, on [*day of week*], [*month, day, year*]."

Old Bailey sessions papers are to be found as early as the 1670s, but do not begin to offer a detailed, unbroken series of trial reports until 1730, when

they appear as pamphlets typically bearing this title: "The [Whole] Proceedings at the Sessions of the Peace, and Oyer and Terminer, for the
City of London, and County of Middlesex; on [days of week and month], in
the [number] Year of His Majesty's Reign. Being the [number] Sessions in
the Mayoralty of the Right Honourable [name] Lord Mayor of the City of
London, in the Year [number]." The titles of earlier issues vary; for examples, see Brit. Lib. Cat., "London. II. Civic and Municipal Institutions. Sessions."

B. Journals

Specific citations of dates and numbers appear only in those cases where no
more than a few references have been made to any particular journal.

[Applebee's] *Original Weekly Journal, with Fresh Advices, Foreign and Domestic.*
The *Covent Garden Journal* [by Henry Fielding]. No. 20 (10 March 1752). Edited
   by Gerald Edward Jensen. 2 vols. New Haven, 1915.
The *Englishman* [by Sir Richard Steele]. No. 48 (23 January 1714). Edited by
   Rae Blanchard. Oxford, 1955.
The *Gentleman's Magazine; and Historical Chronicle.* Vols. 22 (1752), and 53
   (1783).
The *Hypochrondriack* [by James Boswell]. No. 68 (May 1783). Edited by Mar-
   gery Bailey, as *Boswell's Column, Being His Seventy Contributions to The
   London Magazine . . .* 1951.
The *London Gazette.* 23–27 December 1669.
The *London Journal.*
The *London News, or the Impartial Intelligencer.* 18 February 1718.
[Mist's] *Weekly Journal; or Saturday's-Post.*
The *Monthly Catalogue: Being an Exact Account of All Books and Pamphlets Pub-
   lished . . .* No. 14 (May 1724).
The *Monthly Chronicle.* Vol. 4 (December 1731).
The *Post-Boy. With Foreign and Domestic News.* 19–21 July 1720.
[Read's] *Weekly Journal; or, British Gazetteer.*
The *Review* [by Daniel Defoe]. Edited by Arthur Wellesley Secord, as *Defoe's
   Review.* 22 vols. New York, 1938.
The *Spectator.* No. 151 (23 August 1711) [by Sir Richard Steele]. Edited by
   Donald F. Bond. 5 vols. Oxford, 1965.
The *Tatler.* No. 63 (3 September 1709).
The *Weekly Intelligencer of the Commonwealth, Faithfully Communicating All Af-
   fairs Both Martiall and Civill.* No. 45 (11–18 November 1651).

III. OTHER CONTEMPORARY SECONDARY SOURCES

[Akerby, G.]. *Spiller's Jests: Or the Life and Pleasant Adventures of the Late
   Celebrated Comedian James Spiller; Containing His Merry Jests, Diverting
   Songs, and Entertaining Tales.* 1729.
Aleman, Mateo. *The Rogue, or the Life of Guzman de Alfarache.* Written in

Spanish by Mateo Aleman and Done into English by James Mabbe, Anno 1623. Introduction by James Fitzmaurice-Kelly. 4 vols. 1924.

Anonymous. *An Account of Several Work-Houses for Employing and Maintaining the Poor*. 2nd ed. 1732.

An Account of the Corporation for the Poor of London. 1713.

An Address to All Who Frequent Our Numerous Executions, or Were Ever Present at Any of Those Sad Spectacles; Especially All Those Who Were Present at the Execution of John Placket . . . July 28. . . . 1762.

A Compassionate Address to Prisoners for Crimes; and More Particularly to Such of Them as Are under Sentence of Death. With Prayers Suited to the Condition of Both. 1742.

An Essay Concerning the Original of Society, Government, Religion and Laws. Especially Those of the Penal Kind. By a Person of Quality. 1727.

The Explanation of the Ten Commandments. [1796?]

Hanging Not Punishment Enough. 1701. Edited by Basil Montagu. 1812.

The History of the Press-Yard: Or, a Brief Account of the Customs and Occurrences That Are Put in Practice, and to Be Met With in That Antient Repository of Living Bodies, Called, His Majesty's Goal of Newgate in London. 1717.

The Lawes and Statutes of God, Concerning the Punishment to be Inflicted upon Wilfull Murderers. 1646.

A Letter to a Member of Parliament, Containing a Proposal for Bringing in a Bill to Revise, Amend or Repeal Certain Obsolete Statutes, Commonly Called The Ten Commandments. 1738.

Murder Will Out; or, the Heinous Guilt of Murder and Assasination Laid Open, in a Sermon upon the 5th of November 1717. Edinburgh, 1717.

The Penitent Prisoner, His Character, Carriage upon His Commitment, Letany, Proper Prayers, Serious Meditations, Sighs, Occasional Ejaculations, Devotion Going to Execution, and at the Place of Execution. By a Friend to the Souls in Prison. 1675.

Remarks on the Author of the Hymn to the Pillory. With an Answer to the Hymn to the Funeral Sermon. [1703.]

"Some Remarks on . . . *George Barnwell*." Originally published in the *Weekly Register* (21 August 1731), and reprinted in *Essays on the Theatre from Eighteenth Century Periodicals*, edited by John Loftis. Los Angeles, 1960.

The Whole Duty of Man, Containing a Practical Table of the Ten Commandments; wherein the Sins Forbidden, and the Duties Commanded, or Implied, Are Clearly Discovered. 1674.

[Awdeley, John?]. *The Fraternitie of Vacabondes*. 1565.

Babington, Zachary. *Advice to Grand Jurors in Cases of Blood. Asserting from Law and Reason That in All Cases (Where a Person by Law Is to Be Indicted for Killing Another Person) the Indictment Ought to Be for Murther, Where the Evidence is That the Party Intended to Be Indicted, Had His Hands in Blood, and Did Kill the Other Person*. 1680.

Beard, Thomas, and Thomas Taylor. *The Theatre of Gods Judgements; Wherein Is Represented the Admirable Justice of God against All Notorious Sinners, Great and Small, Specially against the Most Eminent Persons in the World,*

Whose Exorbitant Power Had Broke through the Barres of Divine and Humane Law. 4th ed. 1748.

Bellers, John.   *To the Criminals in Prison.* [1725?]

Boswell, James.   *Life of Johnson. Together with Boswell's Journal of a Tour to the Hebrides and Johnson's Diary of a Journal into North Wales.* Edited by George Birkbeck Hill and L. F. Powell. 6 vols. Oxford, 1934.

Britannicus, Esq.   *A Letter to the Honourable House of Commons, Relating to the Present Situation of Affairs. To Which Is Added, an Address to All Generous and Humane Minds, Occasioned by the Execution of Mr. James Maclaine, &c.* 1750.

[Brown, John].   *An Estimate of the Manners and Principles of the Times.* 2nd ed. 1757.

B[rydall], J[ohn].   *A Compendious Collection of the Laws of England, Touching Matters Criminal. Faithfully Collected and Methodically Digested, Not Only for the Use of Sheriffs, Justices of the Peace, Coroners, Clerks of the Peace and All Others within That Verge; but of All the People in General.* 1675.

[Bullock, Christopher].   *Woman's Revenge: Or, a Match in Newgate. A Comedy.* 2nd ed. 1728.

Burnet, Gilbert.   *Some Passages of the Life and Death of the Right Honorable John Earl of Rochester.* 1680.

Calamy, Edmund, D.D.   *An Abridgement of Mr. Baxter's History of His Life and Times. With an Account of the Ministers, &c. Who Were Ejected after the Restauration, of King Charles II . . . and the Continuation of Their History, to the Passing of the Bill against Occasional Conformity, in 1711.* 2nd ed. 2 vols. 1713.

Cibber, Theophilus.   *The Lives of the Poets of Great Britain and Ireland.* 5 vols. 1753.

Coke, Sir Edward.   *The Third Part of the Institutes of the Laws of England: Concerning High Treason, and Other Pleas of the Crown, and Criminall Causes.* [1644.]

Collier, Jeremy.   *Essays upon Several Moral Subjects. Part IV.* 1709.

Conybeare, John.   *The Penal Sanctions of Laws Consider'd. A Sermon Preach'd at St. Mary's in Oxford at the Assizes, before the Honourable Mr. Justice Reynolds; and before the University.* Oxford and London, 1727.

Culpepper, Sir Thomas.   *The Necessity of Abating Usury Re-Asserted; in a Reply to the Discourse of Mr. Thomas Manly Entituled, Usuray at Six Per Cent Examined, &c.* 1670.

Defoe, Daniel.   *Augusta Triumphans: Or, the Way to Make London the Most Flourishing City in the Universe.* 1728.

   Of Captain Mission. Introduction by Maximillian E. Novak. Augustan Society Reprint. Los Angeles, 1961.

   A Collection of Miscellany Letters Selected out of Mist's Weekly Journal. 4 vols. 1722–27.

   The Complete English Gentleman. Edited by Karl D. Bülbring. 1890.

   The Complete English Tradesman in Familiar Letters Directing Him in All the Several Parts and Progressions of Trade. 2nd ed. 2 vols. 1727.

The Family Instructor. Vols. 15 and 16 in *The Novels and Miscellaneous Works of Daniel Defoe.* Oxford and London, 1841.

The Fortunes and Misfortunes of the Famous Moll Flanders. Edited by G. A. Starr. 1971.

The Further Adventures of Robinson Crusoe. Vol. 2 of *The Works of Daniel Defoe.* Edited by G. H. Maynardier. New York, 1905.

The History and Remarkable Life of the Truly Honourable Col. Jacque, Commonly Call'd Col. Jack. Edited by Samuel Holt Monk. Oxford, 1965.

A Hymn to Tyburn. Being a Sequel of the Hymn to the Pillory. 1703.

Jure Divino: A Satyr. In Twelve Books. By the Author of the True-Born-Englishman. 1706.

[?] *The Memoirs of Majr. Alexander Ramkins, a Highland-Officer, Now in Prison at Avignon.* 1719.

Roxana the Fortunate Mistress: Or, a History of the Life and Vast Variety of Fortunes of Mademoiselle de Beleau, afterwards Called the Countess of Wintelsheim in Germany. Edited by Jane Jack. Oxford, 1969.

Serious Reflections of Robinson Crusoe. Vol. 3 of *The Works of Daniel Defoe.* Edited by G. H. Maynardier. New York, 1905.

Street-Robberies, Consider'd: The Reason of Their Being So Frequent, with Probable Means to Prevent 'em. . . . Written by a Converted Thief. 1728.

Dod, John, and Robert Cleaver. *A Plain and Familiar Exposition of the Ten Commandments.* 19th ed. 1635.

Evelyn, John. *Diary.* Edited by E. S. de Beer. 6 vols. Oxford, 1955.

Fielding, Henry. *An Enquiry into the Causes of the Late Increase of Robbers, &c. With Some Proposals for Remedying This Growing Evil. In Which the Present Reigning Vices Are Impartially Exposed; and the Laws That Relate to the Provision for the Poor, and to the Punishment of Felons Are Largely and Freely Examined.* 2nd ed. 1751.

Examples of the Interposition of Providence in the Detection and Punishment of Murder. Containing, above Thirty Cases, in Which This Dreadful Crime Has Been Brought to Light, in the Most Extraordinary and Miraculous Manner; Collected from Various Authors, Antient and Modern. 1752.

Jonathan Wild. [And] *The Journal of a Voyage to Lisbon.* Edited by A. R. Humphreys. 1964.

A Proposal for Making an Effectual Provision for the Poor, for Amending Their Morals, and for Rendering Them Useful Members of the Society. 1753.

Fleetwood, William. *The Relative Duties of Parents, Husbands, Masters, Wives, Children, Servants, Consider'd in Sixteen Sermons.* 1705.

Garth, Samuel. *The Dispensary. A Poem.* 1699.

Gay, John. *The Beggar's Opera.* 1728.

Gent, Thomas. *The Life of Mr. Thomas Gent, Printer, of York; Written by Himself.* 1832.

Greene, Robert. *A Notable Discouery of Coosnage. Now Daily Practised by Sundry Lewd Persons, Called Connie-Catchers and Crosse-Biters.* 1591.

Grew, Obadiah. *Meditations upon Our Savior's Parable of the Prodigal Son. Being Several Sermons on the Fifteenth Chapter of St. Luke's Gospel.* 1678.

Guthrie, James. *A Sermon Preach'd in the Chapel of Newgate, upon the Particular Desire of Robert Hallam, under Sentence of Death, for the Murder of His Wife Jane, Then Being Big with Child, upon Sunday, the 6th of February, 1732.* [1732.]

Hanway, Jonas. *The Defects of Police, the Cause of Immorality, and the Continual Robberies Committed, Particularly in and about the Metropolis.* 1775.

Harmon, Thomas. *A Caueat of Warening, for Common Cvrsetors Vvlgarely Called Vagabones.* 1567.

Haslewood, John. *A Sermon Preach'd at the Assizes Held at Kingston upon Thames, July the Twenty Fourth, 1707. Before the Right Honorable Lord Chief Justice Holt.* 1707.

   A Sermon Preach'd at the Assizes Held at Kingston upon Thames, on Thursday the Thirteenth of March, 1706/7. 1707.

[Head, Richard]. *The English Rogue Described in the Life of Meriton Latroon, a Witty Extravagant. Being a Compleat History of the Most Eminent Cheats of Both Sexes.* [Part I.] 1665.

Head, Richard, and Francis Kirkman. *The English Rogue Described in the Life of Meriton Latroon.* Originally published in four parts, 1665–71. New York, 1928.

[Hitchin, Charles?]. *The Regulator: Or, a Discovery of the Thieves, Thief-Takers, and Locks, Alias Receivers of Stolen Goods in and about the City of London. With the Thief-Takers Proclamation. Also an Account of All the Flash Words Now in Vogue amongst the Thieves, with an Explanation of Each Word. By a Prisoner in Newgate.* 1718.

Hobbes, Thomas. *Leviathan, or the Matter, Forme, & Power of a Common-Wealth Ecclesiasticall and Civill.* Edited by C. B. Macpherson. Harmondsworth, Middlesex, 1968.

Horne, Thomas. *A Sermon Preach'd at the Assizes Held at Kingston upon Thames . . . March 12. 1712/13.* 1713.

Huet, Pierre Daniel. "Monsieur Huet's Letter to Monsieur de Segrais . . . upon the Original of Romances." In *A Select Collection of Novels,* ed. S[amuel] C[roxall], 1:i–lii. 1722.

Le Blanc, [Jean Bernard]. *Letters on the English and French Nations; Containing Curious and Useful Observations on Their Constitutions Natural and Political.* 2 vols. 1747.

Lillo, George. *The London Merchant; or, The History of George Barnwell.* 1731.

Locke, John. *The Second Treatise of Government (An Essay Concerning the True Original, Extent and End of Civil Government).* Edited by J. W. Gough. 3rd ed. 1966.

Lorrain, Paul. *The Case of Paul Lorrain, Ordinary of Newgate, Most Humbly Offer'd to the Honourable House of Commons.* [1712.]

   Walking with God: Shewn in a Sermon Preach'd at the Funeral of Mr. Thomas Cook . . . Aug. 13th, 1703. 1703.

Lupton, William. *A Discourse of Murther, Preach'd in the Chapel at Lincoln's-Inn, and Publish'd at the Request of the Worshipful the Masters of the Bench.* 1725.

Luttrell, Narcissus. *A Brief Historical Relation of State Affairs from September 1678 to April 1714.* 6 vols. Oxford, 1857.

M. J. *The Traveller's Guide; and the Country's Safety. Being a Declaration of the Laws of England against High-Way-Men, or Robbers upon the Road; What Is Necessary and Requisite to Be Done by Such Persons as Are Robbed in Order to the Recovering Their Damages; against Whom They Are to Bring Their Action, and the Manner How It Ought to Be Brought. Illustrated with Variety of Law Cases, Historical Remarks, Customs, Usages, Antiquities, and Authentick Authorities.* 1683.

Mandeville, Bernard. *An Enquiry into the Causes of the Frequent Executions at Tyburn; and a Proposal for Some Regulations Concerning Felons in Prison, and the Good Effects to Be Expected from Them.* 1725.

Mather, Cotton. *Magnalia Christi Americana; or the Ecclesiastical History of New-England, from Its First Planting in the Year 1620 unto the Year . . . 1698.* 1702.

Mather, Increase. *A Sermon Occasioned by the Execution of a Man Found Guilty of Murder: Preached at Boston in New-England, March 11th 1686.* 1691.

Misson, M. *Memoirs and Observations in His Travels over England. With Some Account of Scotland and Ireland. Dispos'd in Alphabetical Order. Written Originally in French, and Translated by Mr. Ozell.* 1719.

Newcome, Richard. *A Sermon Preach'd in the Cathedral Church of Winchester . . . at the Assizes Held There . . . March 13, 1727/28.* 1728.

Olyffe, George. *An Essay Humbly Offer'd, for an Act of Parliament to Prevent Capital Crimes, and the Loss of Many Lives; and to Promote a Desirable Improvement and Blessing in the Nation.* 1731.

Paley, William. *The Principles of Moral and Political Philosophy.* 1785.

Palmer, Samuel. *The Nonconformist's Memorial: Being an Account of the Ministers, Who Were Ejected or Silenced after the Restoration, Particularly by the Act of Uniformity.* 2 vols. 1775.

Pepys, Samuel. *The Diary of Samuel Pepys.* Edited by Robert Latham and William Matthews. 11 vols. 1970–83.

Philo-Patria. *A Letter to Henry Fielding, Esq. Occasioned by His Enquiry into the Causes of the Late Increase of Robbers, &c.* [1751?]

Pope, Alexander. "A Discourse on Pastoral Poetry." In *Poetry and Prose of Alexander Pope,* ed. Aubrey Williams, pp. 3–7. Boston, 1969.

The Dunciad, Variorum. With the Prolegomena of Scriblerus. 1729.

Randolph, Herbert. *Legal Punishment Consider'd. A Sermon Preached at the Assizes Held at Rochester . . . March the 12th 1728/9.* 1729.

Reynolds, John. *The Triumphs of Gods Revenge against the Crying and Execrable Sin of Wilful and Premeditated Murther with His Miraculous Discoveries, and Severe Punishments Thereof, in Thirty Several Tragical Histories.* 7th ed. 1704.

Smith, Capt. Alexander. *The School of Venus, or, Cupid Restor'd to Sight; Being a History of Cuckolds and Cuckold-Makers, Contain'd in an Account of the Secret Amours and Pleasant Intrigues of Our British Kings, Noblemen, and*

Others; with the Most Incomparable Beauties, and Famous Jilts, from Henry the Second, to This Present Reign. 1716.

Stamper, Thomas. *The Great Necessity, and Proper Methods, of National Justice. A Sermon Preach'd at Kingston on Thames, March 23d, 1721. At the Assizes Held There . . .* 1721.

Swift, Jonathan. *The Correspondence of Jonathan Swift, D.D.* Edited by F. Elrington Ball. 6 vols. 1910–14.

Journal to Stella. Edited by Harold Williams. 2 vols. Oxford, 1948.

Taylor, Thomas. *The Second Part of the Theatre of Gods Iudgments.* 1642.

Towerson, Gabriel. *An Exposition of the Catechism of the Church of England. Part II. Containing an Explication of the Decalogue or Ten Commandments.* 1681.

[von Uffenbach, Zacharias Conrad]. *London in 1710, from the Travels of Zacharias Conrad von Uffenbach.* Edited by W. H. Quarrel and M. Mare. 1934.

Walpole, Horace. *The Letters of Horace Walpole, Fourth Earl of Orford; Chronologically Arranged.* Edited by Mrs. Paget [i.e. Helen W.] Toynbee. 16 vols. Oxford, 1903–5.

Wood, Thomas. *An Institute of the Laws of England; or, the Laws of England in Their Natural Order, According to Common Use. Published for the Direction of Young Beginners, or Students in the Law; and of Others That Desire to Have a General Knowledge in Our Common and Statute Laws.* 2nd ed. 1722.

IV. POST-EIGHTEENTH-CENTURY SOURCES

Where more than one place of publication is listed on the title page, only the first is given.

Altick, Richard. *Victorian Studies in Scarlet.* New York, 1970.

Aydelotte, Frank. *Elizabethan Rogues and Vagabonds.* Oxford, 1913.

Baer, Joel H. " 'The Complicated Plot of Piracy': Aspects of English Criminal Law and the Image of the Pirate in Defoe." *The Eighteenth Century: Theory and Interpretation* 23 (1982) : 3–26.

Baker, J. H. "Criminal Courts and Procedure at Common Law, 1550–1800." In *Crime in England,* ed. Cockburn, pp. 15–48.

Bakhtin, M. M. "Discourse in the Novel." In *The Dialogic Imagination: Four Essays by M. M. Bakhtin,* ed. Michael Holquist, tr. Caryl Emerson and Michael Holquist, pp. 259–422. Austin, 1981.

Beasley, Jerry C. *Novels of the 1740s.* Athens, Ga., 1982.

Beattie, J. M. *Crime and the Courts in England, 1660–1800.* Princeton, 1986.

"The Pattern of Crime in England, 1660–1800." *Past and Present* 62 (1974): 47–95.

Bée, Michel. "La Societé traditionelle et la mort." *XVIIe siècle* 106–7 (1975): 81–111.

Bernbaum, Ernest. *The Mary Carleton Narratives, 1663–1673: A Missing Chapter in the History of the English Novel.* Cambridge, Mass., 1914.

Bleackley, Horace, and S. M. Ellis. *Jack Sheppard.* Edinburgh, 1933.

Bohannon, Paul. "Theories of Homicide and Suicide." In *African Homicide and Suicide,* ed. Paul Bohannon, pp. 3–29. New York, 1967.

Bollème, Geneviève. "Littérature populaire et littérature de colportage au 18ᵉ siècle." In *Livre et societé dans la France du xviiiᵉ siècle,* vol. 1, pp. 61–92. Paris, 1965.

Bosco, Ronald A. "Lecturers at the Pillory: The Early American Execution Sermon." *American Quarterly* 30 (1978): 156–76.

Brecht, Bertolt. *The Threepenny Opera.* Translated by Desmond Vesey and Eric Bentley. New York, 1964.

Browning, D. C., ed. *Everyman's Dictionary of Quotations and Proverbs.* 1951.

Burke, Peter. *Popular Culture in Early Modern Europe.* 1978.

Burridge, K. O. L. "Lévi-Strauss and Myth." In *The Structural Study of Myth and Totemism,* ed. Edmund Leach, pp. 91–115. London, 1967.

Cassirer, Ernst. *The Myth of the State.* New Haven, 1947.

Central Office of Information. *Britain 1984: An Official Handbook.* 1984.

Chandler, Frank Wadleigh. *The Literature of Roguery.* 2 vols. Boston, 1907.

Cockburn, J. S., ed. *Crime in England, 1550–1800.* Princeton, 1977.

Crane, R. S. "Suggestions toward a Genealogy of the Man of Feeling." *English Literary History* 1 (1934): 205–30.

De Quincey, Thomas. "On Murder Considered as One of the Fine Arts." In *De Quincey's Collected Writings,* ed. David Masson, 13:9–69. Edinburgh, 1889–90.

Dickens, Charles. *The Mystery of Edwin Drood.* Oxford, 1956.

Durkheim, Emile. *The Division of Labor in Society.* Translated by George Simpson. New York, 1933.

du Sorbier, Françoise. "De la Potence à la biographie, ou les avatars du criminel et de son image en Angleterre (1680–1740)." *Etudes anglaises* 32 (1979): 257–71.

Faller, Lincoln B. "In Contrast to Defoe: The Rev. Paul Lorrain, Historian of Crime." *Huntington Library Quarterly* 60 (1976): 59–78.

"The Myth of Captain James Hind: A Type of Primitive Fiction before Defoe." *Bulletin of the New York Public Library* 79 (1976): 139–66.

Foucault, Michel. *Discipline and Punish: The Birth of the Prison.* Translated by Alan Sheridan. New York, 1977.

Goldmann, Lucien. *Towards a Sociology of the Novel.* Translated by Alan Sheridan. 1975.

Green, Thomas. *Verdict According to Conscience: Perspectives of the English Criminal Trial Jury, 1200–1800.* Chicago, 1985.

Greenberg, Douglas. *Crime and Law Enforcement in the Colony of New York, 1691–1776.* Ithaca, N.Y., 1974.

Greville, Charles Cavendish Fulke. *Greville Memoirs, 1814–1860,* ed. Lytton Strachey and Roger Fulford. 8 vols. 1938.

Griffiths, Arthur. *The Chronicles of Newgate.* 2 vols. 1884.

Gurr, T. R. "Historical Trends in Violent Crime: A Critical View of the Evidence." *Crime and Justice: An Annual Review of Research* 3 (1981): 295–353.

Harris, Michael. "Trials and Criminal Biographies: A Case Study in Distribu-

tion." In *Sale and Distribution of Books from 1700,* ed. Robin Myers and
Michael Harris, pp. 1–36. Oxford, 1982.

Hawkes, Terence. *Structuralism and Semiotics.* Berkeley, 1977.

Hay, Douglas. "Property, Authority, and the Criminal Law." In *Albion's
Fatal Tree,* ed. Hay, Linebaugh, and Thompson, pp. 17–63.

"War, Dearth and Theft in the Eighteenth Century: The Record of the
English Courts." *Past and Present* 95 (1982): 117–60.

Hay, Douglas, Peter Linebaugh, and E. P. Thompson, eds. *Albion's Fatal
Tree: Crime and Society in Eighteenth-Century England.* 1975.

Heath, James. *Eighteenth Century Penal Theory.* 1963.

Herrup, Cynthia. "Law and Morality in Seventeenth-Century England." *Past
and Present* 106 (1985) : 102–23.

"New Shoes and Mutton Pies: Investigative Responses to Theft in Seventeenth-Century East Sussex." *The Historical Journal* 27 (1984): 811–30.

Hibbert, Christopher. *Highwaymen.* 1967.

Hill, Christopher. "Radical Pirates?" In *The Origins of Anglo-American Radicalism,* ed. Margaret Jacob and James Jacob, pp. 17–32. 1984.

Society and Puritanism in Pre-Revolutionary England. 2nd ed. New York, 1967.

Hill, George Birkbeck, ed. *Johnsonian Miscellanies.* 2 vols. Oxford, 1897.

Hobsbawm, E. J. *Bandits.* Harmondsworth, Middlesex, 1972.

"Distinctions between Socio-Political and Other Forms of Crime: Social
Criminality." *Bulletin of the Society for the Study of Labor History* 25 (1972):
5–6.

*Primitive Rebels: Studies in Archaic Forms of Social Movement in the 19th and 20th
Centuries.* Manchester, 1959.

House of Commons. *Report from the Select Committee on Criminal Laws.* 585,
Parliamentary Papers (Reports, 1819). Vol. 8. 1819.

Howson, Gerald. *Thief-Taker General: The Rise and Fall of Jonathan Wild.*
1970.

Irwin, W. R. *The Making of Jonathan Wild.* New York, 1941.

Jakobson, Roman, and M. Halle. *Fundamentals of Language.* The Hague, 1956.

Jones, Howard. *Crime in a Changing Society.* Harmondsworth, Middlesex,
1967.

Kenyon, J. P. *Revolution Principles: The Politics of Party, 1689–1720.* Cambridge, 1977.

King, Peter. "Decision-Makers and Decision-Making in the English Criminal
Law, 1750–1800." *The Historical Journal* 27 (1984): 25–58.

Kirk, G. S. *Myth: Its Meaning and Functions in Ancient and Other Cultures.*
Cambridge, 1970.

Kramnick, Isaac. *Bolingbroke and His Circle: The Politics of Nostalgia in the Age
of Walpole.* Cambridge, Mass, 1968.

Kunzle, David. *The Early Comic Strip: Narrative Strips and Picture Stories in the
European Broadsheet from c. 1450 to 1825.* Berkeley, 1973.

Langbein, John. "*Albion's* Fatal Flaws." *Past and Present* 98 (1983): 96–120.

"The Criminal Trial before the Lawyers." *University of Chicago Law Review*
45 (1978) : 263–316.

"Shaping the Eighteenth-Century Criminal Trial: A View from the Ryder Sources." *University of Chicago Law Review* 50 (1983): 1–136.

Lee, William. *Defoe: His Life and Recently Discovered Writings*. 3 vols. 1869.

Lenman, Bruce, and Geoffrey Parker. "The State, the Community, and the Criminal Law in Early Modern Europe." In *Crime and the Law: A Social History of Crime in Western Europe since 1500*, ed. V. A. C. Gatrell, Bruce Lenman, and Geoffrey Parker, pp. 11–48. 1980.

Lévi-Strauss, Claude. "The Culinary Triangle." *New Society*, 22 December 1966, pp. 937–40.

———. *Structural Anthropology*. Translated by Claire Jacobson and Brooke Grundfest Schoepf. Harmondsworth, Middlesex, 1972.

———. *Le Totémisme aujourd'hui*. Paris, 1962.

Linebaugh, Peter. "The Ordinary of Newgate and His *Account*." In *Crime In England*, ed. Cockburn, pp. 246–69.

———. "The Tyburn Riot against the Surgeons." In *Albion's Fatal Tree*, ed. Hay, Linebaugh, and Thompson, pp. 65–117.

The London Stage, 1660–1800. Part 2: 1700–1729, ed. Emmett L. Avery. Carbondale, Ill., 1960.

Lukács, Georg. *The Theory of the Novel: A Historico-Philosophical Essay on the Forms of Great Epic Literature*. Translated by Anna Bostock. 1971.

Lüsebrink, Hans-Jürgen. "Images et représentations sociales de la criminalité au xviiiᵉ siècle: l'exemple de Mandrin." *Revue d'histoire moderne et contemporaine* 26 (1979): 345–64.

———. *Kriminalität und Literatur im Frankreich des 18. Jahrhunderts: Literarische Formen, soziale Funktionen und Wissenkonstituenten im Zeitalter der Aufklärung*. Munich, 1983.

Macfarlane, Alan. *The Origins of English Individualism: The Family, Property and Social Transition*. Oxford, 1978.

Macfarlane, Alan, with Sarah Harrison. *The Justice and the Mare's Ale: Law and Disorder in Seventeenth-Century England*. Oxford, 1981.

Macpherson, C. B. *The Political Theory of Possessive Individualism: Hobbes to Locke*. Oxford, 1962.

Main, C. F. "The German Princess; or, Mary Carleton in Fact and Fiction." *Harvard Library Bulletin* 10 (1956): 166–85.

Malcolmson, R. W. "Infanticide in the Eighteenth Century." In *Crime in England*, ed. Cockburn, pp. 187–209.

Malinowski, Bronislaw. *Crime and Custom in Savage Society*. Totowa, N.J., 1967.

———. *Myth in Primitive Psychology*. In *Magic, Science and Religion, and Other Essays*, pp. 93–148. Garden City, N.J., 1954.

Markham, Clements R. *A Life of the Great Lord Fairfax, Commander-in-Chief of the Army of the Parliament of England*. 1870.

Marshburn, Joseph H. *Murder & Witchcraft in England, 1550–1640*. Norman, Okla., 1971.

McManners, John. *Death and the Enlightenment: Changing Attitudes to Death among Christians and Unbelievers in Eighteenth-Century France*. Oxford, 1985.

Miller, Perry. *The New England Mind: The Seventeenth Century.* Boston, 1961.

Muchembled, Robert. *Culture populaire et culture des élites dans la France moderne (XVe–XVIIIe siècles): essai.* Paris, 1978.

Neuburg, Victor E. *Popular Literature, A History and Guide: From the Beginning of Printing to the Year 1897.* Harmondsworth, Middlesex, 1977.

Niehus, Edward L. "The Nature and Development of the Quixote Figure in the Eighteenth-Century English Novel." Ph.D. dissertation, University of Minnesota, 1971. Abstract in *Dissertation Abstracts International* 32 (December 1971): 3319A–3320A.

Novak, Maximillian E. *Defoe and the Nature of Man.* Oxford, 1963.

———. *Realism, Myth, and History in Defoe's Fiction.* Omaha, 1983.

Obiechina, Emmanuel. *An African Popular Literature: A Study of Onitsha Market Pamphlets.* Cambridge, 1973.

———. *Literature for the Masses: An Analytical Study of Popular Pamphleteering in Nigeria.* Enugu, Nigeria, 1971.

Octogenarius. "Punishment of Death by Burning." *Notes and Queries* 2 (1850): 260–61.

Plumb, J. H. *The Growth of Political Stability in England, 1675–1725.* Harmondsworth, Middlesex, 1973.

Pocock, J. G. A. "Early Modern Capitalism: The Augustan Perception." In *Feudalism, Capitalism, and Beyond,* ed. Eugene Kamenka and R. S. Neale, pp. 62–83. 1975.

———. *The Machiavellian Moment: Florentine Political Thought and the Atlantic Republican Tradition.* Princeton, 1975.

Potter, John Deane. *The Art of Hanging.* New York, 1969.

Propp, Vladimir. *Morphology of the Folktale.* 2nd ed. Translated by Laurence Scott. Revised and edited by Louis A. Wagner. Introductions by Svatava Pirkova-Jakobson and Alan Dundes. Austin, 1968.

Radzinowicz, Leon. *A History of English Criminal Law and Its Administration from 1750.* Vol 1: *The Movement for Reform, 1750–1833.* 1948.

Richetti, John J. *Popular Fiction Before Richardson, 1700–1739.* Oxford, 1968.

Roughead, William, ed. *Trial of Mary Blandy.* Edinburgh, 1914.

Rudé, George. *Hanoverian London, 1714–1808.* Berkeley, 1971.

Salgādo, Gāmini, ed. *Cony-Catchers and Bawdy Baskets: An Anthology of Elizabethan Low Life.* Harmondsworth, Middlesex, 1972.

Scott, Sir Harold Richard, ed. *The Concise Encyclopedia of Crime and Criminals.* New York, 1961.

Seguin, Jean-Pierre. "L'Information en France avant le périodique: 500 canards imprimés entre 1529 et 1631." *Arts et traditions populaires* 11 (1963): 20–32, 119–45, 203–80.

Sharpe, J. A. *Crime in Early Modern England, 1550–1750.* 1984.

———. *Crime in Seventeenth-Century England: A Country Study.* Cambridge, 1983.

———. "Domestic Homicide in Early Modern England." *The Historical Journal* 24 (1981): 29–48.

———. " 'Last Dying Speeches': Religion, Ideology and Public Execution in Seventeenth-Century England." *Past and Present* 107 (1985): 144–67.

Singleton, Robert R.   "Defoe, Moll Flanders, and the Ordinary of Newgate."
     Harvard Library Bulletin 24 (1976): 407–13.
"English Criminal Biography, 1651–1722." *Harvard Library Bulletin* 18
     (1970): 63–83.
Slotkin, Richard.   "Narratives of Negro Crime in New England, 1675–1800."
     American Quarterly 25 (1973): 3–31.
Spierenburg, Peter.   *The Spectacle of Suffering: Executions and the Evolution of
     Repression, from a Preindustrial Metropolis to the European Experience.* Cam-
     bridge, 1984.
Spufford, Margaret.   *Small Books and Pleasant Histories: Popular Fiction and Its
     Readership in Seventeenth-Century England.* 1981.
Stauffer, Donald.   *The Art of Biography in Eighteenth Century England.* Prince-
     ton, 1941.
Stone, Lawrence.   *The Family, Sex, and Marriage in England, 1500–1800.* New
     York, 1977.
"Interpersonal Violence in English Society, 1300–1980." *Past and Present* 101
     (1983): 22–33.
"Money, Sex and Murder in Eighteenth-Century England." In *Women and
     Society in the Eighteenth Century,* ed. Ian P. H. Duffy, pp. 15–28. Bethle-
     hem, Pa., 1983.
Styles, John.   "Sir John Fielding and the Problem of Criminal Investigation in
     Eighteenth-Century England." *Transactions of the Royal Historical Society,*
     5th ser. 33 (1983): 127–49.
Sydney, William Connor.   *England and the English in the Eighteenth Century:
     Chapters in the Social History of the Times.* 2 vols. 1891.
Thomas, Keith.   *Religion and the Decline of Magic.* New York, 1971.
Thompson, E. P.   *Whigs and Hunters: The Origin of the Black Act.* 1975.
Tobias, John J.   *Crime and Industrial Society in the Nineteenth Century.* Har-
     mondsworth, Middlesex, 1972.
Todorov, Tzvetan.   *Grammaire du Decameron.* The Hague, 1969.
U.S. Bureau of the Census.   *Statistical Abstract of the United States: 1985.* 105th
     ed. Washington, D.C., 1984.
Walker, Nigel.   *Crime and Insanity in England.* Vol. 1: The Historical Perspec-
     tive. Edinburgh, 1968.
Wiles, R. M.   *Serial Publication in England before 1750.* Cambridge, 1957.

Index